# Chinese vs. Western Perspectives

# Chinese vs. Western Perspectives

## *Understanding Contemporary China*

### Jinghao Zhou

LEXINGTON BOOKS
Lanham • Boulder • New York • Toronto • Plymouth, UK

Published by Lexington Books
A wholly owned subsidiary of Rowman & Littlefield
4501 Forbes Boulevard, Suite 200, Lanham, Maryland 20706
www.rowman.com

10 Thornbury Road, Plymouth PL6 7PP, United Kingdom

British Library Cataloguing in Publication Information Available

**Library of Congress Cataloging-in-Publication Data**
Zhou, Jinghao, 1955–
Chinese vs. western perspectives : understanding contemporary China / Jinghao Zhou.
pages cm
Includes bibliographical references and index.
ISBN 978-0-7391-8045-7 (cloth) -- ISBN 978-0-7391-8046-4 (electronic)
1. China--Politics and government--2002- 2. China--Economic conditions--2000- 3. China--Social conditions--2000- 4. China--Foreign relations--United States. 5. United States--Foreign relations--China. I. Title.
DS779.46.Z577 2014
951.06--dc23
2013029804

ISBN 978-1-4985-2091-1 (pbk)

 TM

To the loving memory of my father

To my mother

# Contents

# Preface

China is back onto the world stage. China's rise is a fascinating phenomenon, which greatly generates Westerners' enthusiasm to learn about China. However, China is a country of complexity with a long history. She has gone through various social systems in the past 3,000 years, including the slavery society, feudal society, semi-colony and semi-feudal society, and the communist political system. The term "Contemporary China" in this book refers to the People's Republic of China (PRC), founded on October 1, 1949, as the result of the Chinese communist revolution led by Mao Zedong, the head of the Communist Party of China (CPC). Mao ruled China until he died in 1976. The current president of the PRC is Xi Jinping.

China is the world's largest country in terms of its population of 1.34 billion people. There are 56 ethnic groups in China; the Han is the largest group, making up about 92 percent of China's total population. The official Chinese language is *Putonghua*, or Mandarin, which is one of six official languages of the United Nations (Arabic, Chinese, English, French, Russian, and Spanish). Geographically, China is the fourth largest country, covering 3,691,502 square miles and bordered by 13 countries, including Russia and North Korea to the East, Russia and Mongolia to the North, Kazakhstan, Kyrgyzstan, Tajikistan, Afghanistan, Pakistan, and India to the West, and Nepal, India, Bhutan, Myanmar, Laos, and Vietnam to the South. China is massive in size and is rich in natural resources and human capital, so it has a great potential to develop.

China has carried out the socialist market system in the framework of the communist political system in the post-Mao era. The centralized Chinese administration system is divided into five levels: the central government, provincial government, city government, county government, and town government. China has twenty-three provinces, five autonomous regions, four municipalities, and two special administrative regions. The twenty-two provinces include Anhui, Fujian, Gansu, Guangdong, Guizhou, Hainan, Hebei, Heilongjiang, Henan, Hubei, Hunan, Jiangsu, Jiangxi, Jilin, Liaoning, Qinghai, Shaanxi, Shandong, Shanxi, Sichuan, Yunnan, Zhejiang. The five autonomous regions are Guangxi, Inner Mongol, Ningxia, Xinjiang, and Tibet. The four Municipalities are Beijing, Chongqing, Shanghai, and Tianjin. The two special administrative regions are Hong Kong and Macau. Hong Kong was ceded to Great Britain after the first Opium War in 1839 and returned to China in 1997. Macau was a Portuguese colony and returned to China in 1999. Taiwan is part of China, but it has not returned to mainland China yet.

The Chinese government has made significant efforts to reform its economic system and achieved incredible success since 1978. The Chinese economy surpassed the Japanese economy in 2010 and has become the second largest economy in the word in terms of its GDP. China's economy today is more than ten times larger than it was in 1978. China's rise has created opportunities for global development, but, at the same time, it has unavoidably changed the landscape of global powers and imposed challenges to other countries in many regards. China's roles in the global governance have been increasingly growing. It is almost impossible to solve any important global issues without China's participation. Thus, it is necessary for Western countries to learn how to live with China.

China used to be the most glorious country in the world, yet, it was isolated in the first twenty-seven years of the communist regime between 1950 and 1977. China was a mystery to many people around the world during that period of time. Although China reopened its door to the rest of the world in 1978, it is not easy for Westerners to understand contemporary China due to the complexity of Chinese history and culture. There are many misconceptions about China, such as: Premodern China was a backward country; the "one child policy" is a violation of human rights; Chinese women are tiger women; the Chinese economy will collapse sometime soon; Confucianism represents the future of Chinese culture; Marxism is still alive in China; China remains a Lenin-state; Mao's policy is the only solution for China to establish an equal and harmonious society; the Chinese people are not a religious people; the Chinese developmental model is universal; Christianity will play a critical role in China's democratization; modern democracy does not fit in China; China's rise threatens the United States; China will become a world superpower in 15 years; and China and the U.S. cannot coexist peacefully. All these misconceptions mislead people's understanding of contemporary China, and, ultimately, negatively affect U.S.-China relations. It is important for Western societies to further understand China in order to avoid unnecessary mistakes in making foreign policy toward China.

This book is only one of many voices in ongoing debates on understanding contemporary China, which not only challenges the misconceptions, but also to seek to synthesize Western and Chinese scholarship in order to spur mutual understanding between China and other countries, especially the United States. The original intention of this book is to provide an integrated picture of contemporary China through systematically examining the major aspects of contemporary Chinese society and culture, providing the most recent data collected by the author from his fieldwork and existing databases, summarizing the basic issues that China faces today, and developing major arguments to bridge the gap between Chinese and Western perspectives. This book attempts to be an interdisciplinary and comprehensive guide to China for a general audience through the author's extensive research and thoughtful examination of many controversial issues related to contemporary China with a balance of Chinese and Western scholarship.

The terms "Chinese Perspective" and "Western Perspective" are general terms, which are difficult to define, because there is no unified perspective in China and Western societies. Both perspectives could refer to the governments' perspective, the mainstream of public opinions in a society, or perspectives from different schools of thoughts. This means that Chinese perspective is not necessarily in opposition to Western perspective. They could be either inclusive or exclusive, so the differences between Chinese and Western perspectives are not judged by "black" and "white."

It should be noted that it is almost impossible for anyone to be absolutely "objective" in balancing the two perspectives. To be sure, the author does not intend to demonstrate "a PRC tilt" or to have an overly PRC position. Different viewpoints should be welcome by academia. Every country needs to have different voices because only diverse viewpoints are helpful for scholarly debates, public education, healthy society, and policy-making process. An anonymous reader has made comments after reading the first draft of this manuscript: "This book is one of the few that are authored by scholars who originate from China and have their professional career in the United States, [but] it is distinctive from the rest of studies on this subject in that the author is committed to examining today's China from Chinese as well as Western perspectives." Another reader says that "university instructors in English-speaking universities are, by and large, keen to include Chinese voices on their reading lists. There are not many books available in English, so a readable and concise Chinese view of China would indeed be valuable."

This book includes eighteen chapters in addition to the bibliography, which cover the major aspects of contemporary Chinese society and embrace main hot topics discussed in Western societies. Chapter 1 will discuss the roots of contemporary China from a historical perspective. Chapters 2 and 3 will discuss the basic elements of Chinese society—Chinese family and population. Chapters 4 and 5 will discuss "Half the Sky" of China from gender and sociological perspectives by presenting two topics: "The status of Chinese women" and "globalization and Chinese women." Then, this book will move to the next phase to discuss the major support systems of Chinese society. Chapters 6 and 7 will examine the Chinese economy and the by-product of Chinese economic development—environmental degradation. Chapters 8 and 9 will examine the Chinese political system and the by-product of the current political system—China's corruption. Chapters 10 and 11 will discuss the sub-political system—Chinese belief system, including two topics: traditional Chinese religion and the roles of Christianity in China. Due to the fact that China is an ideological country and Chinese ideology is inseparable part of the Chinese politics, Chapters 12, 13, and 14 will discuss Chinese ideology: Confucianism—Chinese official ideology in premodern China; Marxism and Maoism—Chinese official ideology in communist China; and media in China, and Internet and Chinese cinema. After that, Chapters 15, 16, and 17 will explore contemporary China in a global context focusing on U.S.-China relations. Chapter 15 will generally discuss U.S.-China relations in the twenty-first century; Chapter 16 will clarify the misconception that China's rise threatens the United States; and Chapter 17 will analyze causes of conflicts between the two countries in order to find common ground between the two countries. Finally, Chapter 18 will analyze the model of China's development and reach a conclusion that non-democratic China can't rule the world.

This is a concise, but a scholarly book, which can be used as a textbook for a semester long course related to China, including but not limited to "contemporary China," "modern China," "international relations," "comparative politics," "comparative economics," "Chinese society and culture," "Chinese women," "Chinese cinema," and "Chinese religions." Hopefully, this book will assist teachers and professors in teaching about China, help students in preparing their international journey, and contribute to politicians in making foreign policy toward China.

Jinghao Zhou
Geneva, NY, USA

# Acknowledgments

I am grateful to Hobart and William Smith Colleges for their financial support, which has enabled me to complete this project. I would like to thank Praeger Publishers, The Edwin Mellen Press, and Lexington Books for their permissions to allow me to revise paragraphs from the three published books: *Remaking China's Public Philosophy for the Twenty-first Century* (Praeger Publishers, 2003); *Remaking China's Public Philosophy and Chinese Women's Liberation*: *The Volatile Mixing of Confucianism, Marxism, and Feminism* (Mellen Press, 2006); *China's Peaceful Rise in a Global Context: A Domestic Aspect of China's Road Map to Democratization* (Lexington Books, 2010).

I would like to thank *International Journal of China Studies* and *American Journal of Chinese Studies* for allowing me to revise the articles and include them in this book: They are "American Perspective versus Chinese Expectation on China's Rise," *International Journal of China Studies* 2. No. 3 (2011); "China's Rise and Environmental Degradation," *International Journal of China Studies* 4, No. 1 (April 2013); and "Legitimacy without Democracy: Way of Transition toward Superpower?" *American Journal of Chinese Studies* 19, no. 2 (2012).

My thanks are also extended to Kristyna Bronner, Samantha Dighton, and Amanda Reusch, my student research assistants at Hobart and William Smith Colleges. Kristyna and Samantha read nine chapters of the first draft of the manuscript, and Amanda read the second draft of the manuscript. They made corrections and offered fresh comments. I have benefited from their contributions. I very much appreciate anonymous reviewers' selfless efforts in reading the second draft of the manuscript. Their critiques and suggestions inspired me to rethink my perspectives and revise it for the third draft of the manuscript.

Finally, I want to give my heartfelt thanks to Yi-Tung Wu, who helped me go through a very difficult time in my life. Her caring encouraged me to keep working on the manuscript until the completion of it. This scholarly work embodies her invaluable contributions.

*Chapter One*

# Roots of Contemporary China

Today's China is the continuation of its past and the beginning of its future. History is a mirror that reflects contemporary society, and so studying historical China will help one to understand contemporary China and China's future. As Pye noted, "No serious analysis of ideology can go far without an examination of historical traditions."[1] Contemporary China was a long time in the making. At the very least, China is one of the cradles of world civilization. Based on written records, China developed its own political system, culture, ideology, religion, and educational program over a period of 3,000 years. China today is "the only giant of the ancient world to survive into the twentieth century."[2] While the mainstream public opinion in China is that the country has both rich material civilization and cultural heritage, some Western viewpoints suggest that China has lagged behind in modern times, not because it lacked the necessary materials, but because it lacked advanced cultural and political systems. According to Lucien W. Pye, "No culture in the world matches China's in durability. More, it is a culture long under siege. For two hundred years it has staved off a challenge from the West."[3] Thus, some questions are raised: How do we understand China's history? Specifically, what is the legacy of Chinese history? Does the legacy of Chinese history help China's modernization and democratization? Or, is the legacy of Chinese history a burden as China works to develop a modern society? This chapter will respond to these questions through discussing Chinese civilization and the main characteristics of Chinese history in order to find out where contemporary China comes from and discover the similarities and differences between historical China and contemporary China.

# APPROACHES TO CHINESE HISTORY

The term history refers to "inquiry, knowledge acquired by investigation," which is the study of the human past. Scholars who write about history are called historians. Since historians are observers and participants, the work they produce is written from the perspective of their own experience. In this sense, all history is not absolutely objective, but subjective. History does not go beyond time and space, so it is always specific. In a perspective of time, history can be divided into ancient history, medieval history, modern history, and contemporary history. In a perspective of space, history can be categorized as American history, German history, Japanese history, or Chinese history, etc. In terms of aspects of a society, history can refer to history of politics, economics, education, religion, philosophy, and technology, etc. To be sure, there are close relationships among different aspects of history.

According to Immanuel C. Y. Hsü, "The key to an understanding of any period of Chinese history is the government's policies and institutions which to a large extent determined the ebb and flow of the country's fortune."[4] Government policy can be generally defined as a system of laws or regulatory measures which the government intends to influence society and individuals. Government policy is a gauge of a society and reflects the needs of individuals. In turn, individuals and societies try to shape government policy through education, advocacy, and mobilization. To understand Chinese history, it is required to understand the relationship between society, culture and the state.

A society is the totality of social relationships among human beings. A group, an association, a community, a region or a country can be called a society; and all nations of the world can be called the international society. A society consists of human relations. Everyone in any society unavoidably is involved in human relations and functions as part of the society. No one is able to escape from human relations and society. The relationship among human beings is culture—the way of people's life, transmitted from one generation to the next through learning and practice.[5] Culture basically includes two components: The material component is essential for physical survival; and the ideological component sets human relations in a normative frame of social order. Material culture is the foundation of a society; ideological culture functions as cultural DNA, which carries civilization from one generation to another. Material goods cannot determine the nature of a society, because material goods, such as a computer, TV, car, radio, or air conditioner, can be used by different societies at different stages of human history. All goods are only vehicles that carry civilization to continue developing. Thus, it is ideological culture that makes distinctions among different societies at different stages.

Traditional Chinese society is a Confucian society. Culture is diverse during globalization. Many types of cultures co-exist and work together in the same country, and they are the primary sources of conflict in the contemporary world. According to Samuel Huntington, there are currently seven or eight chief civilizations: Western, Confucian, Japanese, Islamic, Hindu, Orthodox Slav, Latin American, and "possibly" African. The conflict between different nations in the twenty-first century is essentially cultural.[6] Although there is great potential for conflicts between Chinese culture and Western cultures, the Chinese people and Chinese culture are becoming more and more Westernized. In turn, Westerners and their cultures are also influenced by Chinese culture.

The state involves the process of governing, especially the control and administration of public policy in a political unit. There are several theories that explain where the state comes from: The evolution theory argues that government springs from the spontaneous development of nature. The class struggle theory suggests that the state is the product of class struggle. The social contract theory believes that there is a contract between authority and society. The create-theory denies all these theories and argues that government originates in the right of the father to govern his child; it derives its right from the immediate and express appointment of God from God through the people and the natural law. All these theories suggest that the goal of the state is to avoid moral degeneration and social chaos in order to maintain its power and social order through implementing laws and regulations, propagandizing ideology, organizing economic programs, and promoting a social welfare system.

The state/government in Chinese, *guo-jia*, means "nation-family." In traditional China, the father is the head of family. Logically, as a big family—a nation—the emperor is the father of the nation. In contemporary China, the state refers to the Chinese legislative, judicial, administrative, and military institutions. More specifically, the state in China refers to the National People's Congress (NPC) and provincial people congresses and their functional committees. There are 2,987 members of the Eleventh National People's Congress (2008-2013) and, theoretically, all of them are elected by the people and, thus, they should represent the people. However, all members of NPC are not elected by the people, but by the government. Thus, they do not have to be responsible for the people.

Chinese history can be divided into different periods of time. Periodization studies of Chinese history are plentiful. The two-period theory is among many theoretical models for dividing Chinese history. According to this theory, the first cycle of Chinese history is from the beginning to A.D. 383 and is characterized as Classical China. The second cycle is from A.D. 383 until today, and is characterized as Tartar-Buddhist China.

A second model is the three-period theory. This theory sees an ancient period lasting from the Xia dynasty (2100-1700 B.C.) to the end of the Warring States period (475-221 B.C.) and might be characterized as the aristocratic political structure and self-development of the Chinese people. Then, the medieval period follows from the Qin dynasty (221-206 B.C.) to the middle of the Qing dynasty (A.D. 1795), and was characterized by autocratic government. Finally, the modern period extends from the middle of the Qing dynasty (1795) to contemporary time (1912), an era marked by transformation and modern government. [7]

A third model is the four-period theory: the ancient period from the Xia dynasty to the end of the Warring States period, the medieval period from the Qin dynasty to the end of the Tang dynasty (A.D. 618-907), the early modern period from the Five dynasties (907-960) to the Ming dynasty (1368-1644), and the modern period from the Qing dynasty until contemporary time. Miyazaki Ichisada has divided Chinese history into four stages: the establishment of an ancient empire, an aristocratic society, a period of autocratic government, and a period of modernizing progress. [8]

A fourth model is the five-period theory. According to John Meskill, Karl Marx divided history into five main types of relations of production: "primitive communal period, the slave society, the feudal society, the capitalist society, and the socialist society." [9] When Marx's theory is applied to Chinese history, the five periods are as follows: the period of primitive communism from the Xia dynasty to the Shang dynasty (1700 -1100 B.C.), the slave society from the Western Zhou dynasty (1100-771 B.C.) to the Spring and Autumn period (770-476 B.C.), the feudal society from the Warring States period (475-221 B.C.) to the first Opium War (A.D. 1840), the semicolonial and semi-capitalist society from the first Opium War to the end of the Nationalist Government (1912-1949), and the socialist society from the founding of the People's Republic of China to the present time. According to Marxism, modern China began with the Opium War of 1839, while traditional Chinese scholars suggest that the starting point of modern China is the arrival of European missionaries during the fourteenth century. [10]

The majority of Chinese scholars agree that the origin of Chinese civilization began in the Yellow River basin, northwest China, the cradle of early Chinese civilization and the heartland of an imperial China, and, first expanded eastward and later southward toward the Yangtze River valley, and then to other parts of China. The Han Chinese are the origin and majority of the Chinese nation (*Zhonghua minzu*). Chinese people refer to themselves as "Descendants of the Dragon." Many other Chinese also call themselves Descendants of the Yan Di (Yan Emperor) and Huang Di (Yellow Emperor).

Almost every dynasty in Chinese history falls into a dynastic cycle. The early part of a new dynasty often brought exciting growth and innovation, and the latter parts often brought decline and stagnation. According to

Rhoads Murphey, usually, the first period of time of a new dynasty would be one of vigor, expansion, and efficiency. The second would build on or consolidate what the first had achieved. Third, vigor and efficiency would wane, corruption would mount, banditry and rebellion would multiply, and the dynasty would ultimately fall.[11] This theory is especially true in Chinese history. The longest dynasties in Chinese history, the Zhou, Han, Tang, Song, and Ming dynasties, clearly reflect the theory of dynastic cycle.

Although the connection between the West and China has a long history, Western people had only little knowledge about China before 1978. China had come a long way from a sneering rejection of the West in the early nineteenth century to the worship of it by 1920. The convergence of Chinese and Western societies ended China's seclusion and resulted in its increasing involvement in world affairs. In the post-Mao era, China has opened its door to the rest of the world and is at the center of the global stage. However, the major currents of the two civilizations moved them farther apart, rather than toward each other from many perspectives.[12] It is an important task for both China and Western societies to bring the two civilizations together for the future of the world.

## A BRIEF HISTORY OF CHINA

China has a long history, more than 4,000 years according to written records and archaeological discoveries. The Xia dynasty (2205-1766 B.C.) is the earliest Chinese civilization. Although some scholars still suggest that the Xia dynasty is mythical, palace-like buildings and tombs along with the earliest known bronze vessels have been excavated, which have proven that the Xia dynasty is the first Chinese civilization.

Tan Wang led the revolution to overthrow the Xia dynasty and established the Shang dynasty which marked the beginning of authentic Chinese history.[13] The Shang Dynasty (1766-1122 B.C) is the second dynasty in Chinese history. Much of the information available on the Shang society comes from inscriptions made on shells of turtles, known as the oracle bones. Over 150,000 fragments of oracle bones have now been identified. According to the oracle inscriptions, production in the Shang dynasty reached the Bronze Age and moved into the stage of agriculture.

Many Chinese scholars agree that the Zhou Dynasty (1122-221 B.C) is the first Chinese federal society in which China developed iron tools, money and written laws. The Zhou dynasty is divided into two periods, Western Zhou (1027-771 B.C.) and Eastern Zhou (770-221 B.C.). The Western Zhou dynasty was a prosperous agricultural society.[14] Politically, the Western Zhou dynasty began forming the primary political structure, and the state was a well-organized hierarchy. Because of its centralized government, the Zhou dynasty was the longest dynasty in Chinese history, extending from about 1100 to 221 B.C. In the Zhou dynasty, the king of China, the symbol of the Son of Heaven, was at the top of the pyramid political structure. Under the king, officials were divided into five ranks: duke, marquis, earl, viscount, and baron. During this period, "local government officials were appointed by the court to serve limited terms in a succession of different places as opposed to the system of hereditary posts."[15] This political system was "closely connected with the patriarchal system."[16]

After China entered into the Eastern Zhou in 770 B.C., the central Chinese government gradually lost its control, and the power of the central government shifted to different local warlords. Six states survived through many crucial battles and fought each other, trying to seize the central power. Through several hundred years' bloody wars, the King of the Qin, one of the six kingdoms during the Warring States Period, finally unified six kingdoms and established the first unified feudal empire in Chinese history, proclaiming himself Shi Huang Di, or the First Emperor of the Qin Dynasty. He believed that his family would rule China forever and wanted his successors to be titled Emperor of China I, II, and III.

The first emperor made remarkable contributions to Chinese civilizations. He established the provincial and county system, which was adopted and improved upon later by every feudal dynasty and became a permanent institution in the Chinese body politic.[17] He introduced standard weights and measures, the length of cart axels, the calendar, currency, national laws, and a unitary script. He also widened and paved roads all over China, established local prefecture administration, and began building the Great Wall of China and construction of the first canal (Lingqu) in Guangxi Province.

However, the Qin dynasty carried out a highly centralized political system by ruthless means and military forces. The Qin dynasty was the first absolute monarchical government. To keep absolute power, the first emperor campaigned against Confucian scholars and other Chinese intellectuals, burned hundreds of thousands of books, and buried more than 400 Confucian scholars alive. To justify his crucial persecution of intellectuals, he promoted and practiced Legalism. Based on Legalism, the tool to check human selfishness and depravity was law. Thus, severe punishment was the basic way for the Qin dynasty to govern Chinese society.

The Qin dynasty was replaced by the Han dynasty in 206 B.C. There are various reasons to explain why the Qin Dynasty fell only 15 years after it was established. One reason is that there was no previous experience for the Qin dynasty to follow in governing a big country. The government also made many mistakes, imposing high taxes, implementing rigid laws and severe punishments, which produced great hatred and dissatisfaction among Chinese people and society. Endless labor in the later years of his dynasty also contributed to the peasants' rebellions, including the link-up of the Great Wall of China and the widening and paving of countless roads all over China.

The first emperor of the Han dynasty learned from the Qin dynasty and carried out more flexible policies in regard to Chinese peasants. The reform policy during the Han dynasty significantly contributed to the prosperity of its economy and improved the living standard of the Chinese people. Accordingly, art, literature, philosophy, music and statecraft flourished in the Han. Paper was first made in 105 A.D. Confucius' teachings became a dominant cornerstone of Chinese culture. Buddhism from India was introduced to China in the early Han dynasty and began to merge with Chinese belief systems. The Han Dynasty is the first golden age in Chinese history.

There was a short period of disunity in Chinese history (220-589 A.D.) between the Han dynasty and the second golden age, the Tang dynasty. Various kingdoms and dynasties fought each other for domination during this period. Thirty-seven years after the Sui dynasty reunited China (581-618 A.D.), China entered into the Tang dynasty (618-907 A.D.). The centralized Chinese empire reached its most glorious height in the Tang dynasty. The Tang dynasty perfected the civil service examination system, and its political system was the "most elaborate and complete in the long monarchical age."[18] As China's territory expanded and population grew, the Chinese political system became more and more centralized. The government enhanced its military power and continued to expand its territory. The capital Chang An was a cosmopolitan city of wealth and splendor unparalleled in the world. The Tang Dynasty is the second golden age in Chinese history.

The Qing dynasty (1644-1911) is the last dynasty of feudal society in Chinese history. The Manchu invaded inland China in the beginning of the seventeenth century and finally took over the capital of the Ming dynasty, Beijing, and established the Qing dynasty. The Qing dynasty was full of energy at its inception, but gradually became a stagnant and corrupt government. In the beginning of the Qing, national comprehensive power was strong, the political system was transparent, and the national living standard increased. There were several factors which contributed to the failure of the Qing: In the second half of the Qing dynasty, the government became very corrupt and triggered many internal rebellions, such as the Taiping Rebellion and the Boxer Uprising, which resulted in domestic chaos. Because of corruption and the lack of advanced technology, China lost military capability in fighting against foreign invasion. China lost a war with Japan and the two Opium Wars in the first half of the twentieth century. As a result, China ceded its land, Hong Kong and Macau, to Western powers, and signed many unequal treaties with Western countries, such as the Treaty of Nanking, the Sino-Portuguese Treaty, and the Boxer Protocol. China and its people were humiliated by the West for a century. Rhoads Murphey points out that China's decline into poverty was primarily the result of its own internal prob-

lems, such as corruption, poverty, weak military force, unequal treaties, fa-
mine, and rebellions. [19]

Finally, the revolution broke out in Wuchang in October 10, 1911, which
was the national day during the republican era. The first president of the
Republic of China, Sun Yat-sen, was neither a great strategist nor a profound
ideologist, [20] but he was the first man in Chinese history to systematically
advocate democratic principles, arguing that the revolution could not win
without a democracy. [21] The CPC rapidly developed during the war between
Japan and China and, finally, defeated Nationalist troops. As a result, the
nationalist government withdrew from the mainland to Taiwan in 1949. The
People's Republic of China was founded on October 1, 1949, signifying that
a new chapter of China officially began.

## ONE OF THE ORIGINS OF WORLD CIVILIZATION

China, before the seventeenth century, was the most advanced country in the
world in agriculture, education, science, and technology, and its resources
were rich and plentiful. China developed the earliest irrigation system in the
world. The oldest known hydraulic engineers of China were Sunshu Ao in
the Spring and Autumn Period and Ximen Bao in the Warring States period,
both of whom worked on large irrigation projects. In the Sichuang region,
belonging to the State of Qin, the Du Jiang Yan irrigation system was built in
256 BCE to irrigate an enormous area of farmland that today still supplies
water.

China established the earliest educational system in the world. Confucius
was the first great teacher in Chinese history and he had more than 3,000
students during his time 2,500 years ago. The Chinese government began
adopting the civil service examination system as early as the Han dynasty to
recruit elite Chinese officials. Whoever wanted to become a Chinese official
was required to pass the exams. In this sense, the Chinese government used
to be the most advanced bureaucratic system in the world.

China is the home of ancient inventions in the world, and many ancient
inventions come from China, including the four great inventions of ancient
China: paper, the compass, gunpowder, and movable type. The technology of
producing noodles, rice, salt, silk, and pottery appliances also comes from
China. The Chinese also made great contributions to astronomical observato-
ry, the astronomical clock, meteorology, mathematics, geography, acupunc-
ture, medicine, art, musical instruments, and craft. Chinese traditional culture
is also well-known in the world, such as medicine, food, folk arts, painting,
calligraphy, architecture, furniture, chop engraving, clothing, tea, Peking Opera, jade, written language, music, pottery and porcelain, Chinese dance,
martial arts, philosophy, Chinese macramé, embroidery, paper cutting, and

wine. However, most modern technologies were invented by Western people.

The Chinese civilization was witnessed not only by the Chinese people but also by Westerners. Marco Polo (1254-1324), an Italian, is probably the most famous Westerner who traveled on the Silk Road. He began his journey from Europe through Asia in 1271, lasting 24 years. In 1265, he arrived in Kaifeng, the capital of ancient China. He witnessed the glorious civilization and was amazed with China's enormous power, great wealth, complex social structure and internal economy. He reported that iron manufacturing was around 125,000 tons a year and salt production was on a prodigious scale, 30,000 tons a year in one province alone. A canal-based transportation system linked China's huge cities and markets in a vast internal communication network in which paper money and credit facilities were highly developed. The citizens could purchase paperback books with paper money, eat rice from fine porcelain bowls, wear silk garments, and live in a prosperous city that no European city could match. [22]

Another Westerner also personally witnessed Chinese civilization. Matteo Ricci (1552-1610) was born in Italy, but died in Beijing on May 11, 1610. Ricci began his sea trip in 1577, arrived in Macau in 1582, and later settled in Guangdong Province for over ten years. He went to Nanjing in 1599 and was well received. Finally, he made his trip to Beijing and died there in 1610. While staying in China, he dressed in Chinese robes, learned Chinese, and wrote in Chinese. He wrote *The Secure Treatise on God* (1603), *The Twenty-five Words* (1605), *The First Six Books of Euclid* (1607), and *The Ten Paradoxes* (1608). Through Ricci's eyes, China was a prosperous country with superior virtue. The Chinese people enjoyed perfect social harmony, and were held together by Confucian moral orthodoxy and governed by meritorious scholar-officials. Thus, China was a model of peace and civilization in the world. [23]

## THE LEGACY OF CHINESE HISTORY

The term legacy means something transmitted by or received from an ancestor or predecessor or from the past. To understand the relationship between historical China and contemporary China, it is necessary to find the basic characteristics of Chinese legacy that affect Chinese social and political systems and that have shaped the way of Chinese people's life for more than 2,000 years. In short, the patriarchal system is the main legacy of Chinese history.

The Chinese patriarchal system is based on its agricultural economy. China's economy was agricultural before its doors opened to Western countries in the nineteenth century. [24] China became an agricultural society 4,000 years ago. By the thirteenth century, China was the most sophisticated agricultural country in the world.[25] Jacques Gernet classified Chinese culture as agricultural culture. The Chinese people lived "with a highly developed agriculture which forms their predominant activity."[26] Chinese civilization was closely tied to "a highly developed agriculture which confined itself almost exclusively to the plains and valleys."[27] The peasants needed reasonable living conditions in order to survive. If peasants lost their essential needs, it would lead to rebellion—either to overthrowing the government or forcing the government to reform its economic policy. This explains why Confucius persuaded China's rulers to establish a benevolent government in order to keep the government functioning and lasting longer. Some rulers in China long ago realized the truth that "common people are like water in the river, and the emperor is like a boat. The water could carry the boat and it could overturn the boat as well." Good governments encouraged officials to treat the common people as their own children. Accordingly, good officials were honorably called "parent officials." Thus, Chinese officials in traditional China naturally felt superior to common Chinese citizens so they easily abused their power instead of using it for the people.

The Chinese political system is highly centralized with a pyramidal political system. Some scholars try to argue that it was necessary to develop a highly centralized government in ancient China. When the Chinese government organized massive projects such as a water-control system, water channels, and a national road system, it became necessary, in some respects, to establish a centralized government in order to make connections among families, villages, and counties and to efficiently control the entire country from top to bottom. Chao-ting Chi put it in this way, "The premodern Chinese empire was an agricultural one in which the decisive factor of political control was based on control over the key economic areas."[28]

However, there is no unified opinion on the characteristics of the Chinese political system. Five models can be described as exhibiting the characteristics of the Chinese political system: aristocratic government, autocratic government, monarchical government, absolute monarchical government, and the authoritarian imperial system. Aristocratic government refers to rule by a hereditary ruling class. Autocratic government refers to government by a member of a ruling family: this type of government is despotism. Monarchical government takes at least two forms: constitutional monarchical government and absolute government. Constitutional monarchical government refers to government power exercised by a single person, by his power checked by the constitution and other branches of the government. In contrast, absolute monarchical government refers to a monarch who is ultimately the sole ruler of the country and is accountable only to God. The absolute monarchical right to rule is generally hereditary and lifelong. Authoritarian government is characterized by the people's obedience to an authority. The term centralized government describes only a form of government, not the nature of the government. An aristocratic government, an autocratic government, an absolute monarchical government, and an authoritarian government could all be highly centralized, but centralization does not describe the essential distinctions among these four types of government. Thus, it is necessary to further explore the question of which model of Chinese political system ruled in premoden China.

The Western Zhou dynasty had begun implementing a centralized governmental system. Then, the Qin dynasty formed the first absolute monarchical government, and the first emperor of the Qin concentrated all power in his own hands and proceeded to establish a huge bureaucracy by using military power and coercive forces. Although the Han dynasty's political structure continued its predecessor's centralized system with an absolute monarchical government, it improved upon and stabilized the system. The brief Sui dynasty (A.D. 581-618) continued the political model of the Qin dynasty and the Tang's political system even became more centralized. The Qing dynasty (1644-1911) was the last absolute monarchical system and its government structure was largely inherited from the system of the Ming, "but was more highly centralized."[29]

The modern nation-state emerged in Europe in the eighteenth century, and it was "several centuries ahead of the same development in China."[30] China did not accept and practice the theory of the modern nation-state until the beginning of the twentieth century. The modern reform movement in China began in 1898, led by Kang Youwei, Liang Qichao, Tan Sitong, and Yan Fu, and was supported by the Emperor Guang Xu. During the reform movement, the Chinese government reformed the civil service examination system, established Westernized schools, opened modern banks, developed mines, railways, and other industrial enterprises, and sent students abroad. However, the reform movement still was not tolerated by the Chinese government, even though all reform measures were implemented within the old political framework. The reform movement only lasted 100 days. Some reformers were killed, and the others fled China for Japan. The causes of the failure of the reform movement obviously were not "the inexperience of the reformers" and "ill-considered strategy."[31] Rather, the reform movement failed because it was limited to a small group of Confucian scholars and politicians, and did not touch the core of the political system.

The failure of the reform movement of 1898 led reformers to organize a violent revolution of 1911, which overthrew the last absolute monarchical emperor and established the first modern government, the Republic of China. According to F. W. Mote, the modern nation-state possesses at least four characteristics: "political power is established through national self-determination"; "there is recognition of the coexistence of other nations and the maintenance of reciprocal diplomatic relations"; "law is respected and political institutions are stressed"; and there is "wider popular participation in political power."[32] Based on this criterion, the Republic of China theoretically started the history of the modern nation-state in China.

In premodern China, a patriarchal social system supports a highly centralized political system. The basic patriarchal principle places the father at the center of family and society. The government is an enlarged family; the emperor was the father of the nation and the high priest of religion. The emperor/father held both secular and divine power to rule the entire society. The main characteristic of the patriarchal system is that government power combines with clan power, divine power, and the authority of the husband. It also extended to public life and political relations. The ruler-subject relationship was exactly the same as the relationship between fathers and sons. As Cho-yun Hsu says, "The familial network embraced all of China with the feudal structure as the political counterpart of the family structure."[33] Thus, some scholars view Chinese culture as family spirit.

According to the patriarchal ideology, the human being is an integral part of nature under heaven. Everything on earth, including people and their property, belonged to the emperor.[34] In an old Chinese saying, "under the wide heaven all is the king's land; within the sea-boundaries of the land, all are the king's servants."[35] The emperor was the sole source of power, final authority, and all laws. There were no distinctions among law, policy, and the leader's speech. Common people were expected to unconditionally respect the emperor's power in order to follow the law and nature. No one was permitted to violate the emperor's teachings of the deceased and the "forefathers' discipline. In periods ruled by wise and open-minded emperors, philosophers might rebuke rulers with impunity, "but in the unified empire one might be put to death."[36] When authoritarianism was taken to an extreme, family ethics, social organization, the political system, economic activity, and daily life were controlled by the emperor's power. Therefore, centralized power, autocracy, and dictatorship became a historical heritage; arbitrary rule became the political style in premodern China.

The patriarchal system supported a rigid hierarchical system to fit its political structure. Under this system, the Chinese people were divided into different ranks: farmer, soldier, merchant, artist, politician, official, and Confucian. This tradition discouraged people from going into business because the rank of the merchant in the social structure was of a very low status, below that of a peasant. Even a successful merchant was not highly regarded, but was merely a "small man." Officialdom was divided into more than twenty ranks in the Qin dynasty and reduced to less than twenty ranks in later dynasties. Under the emperor, the order of ranks was as follows: "chief minister, great officer, upper scholar, middle scholar, and lower scholar."[37] Different ranks of officials received different salaries, wore different types of clothes, possessed different carriages, and enjoyed different privileges. The hierarchical system was pyramidal. Everyone had to follow the social ethical code of "letting the King be a king, the minister a minister, the father a father, and the son a son."

The patriarchal culture contributed to China's adoption of a closed-door policy. Chinese peasants usually concentrated on farm work, but neglected commerce; concentrated on reality but ignored imaginations; concentrated on the present situation, but neglected the future; and concentrated on human relationships, but neglected metaphysics and spiritual life. Chinese peasants did not communicate with one another, though the crowing of their cocks and the barking of their dogs were within hearing of each other. Much of China was inland, and the Chinese people knew little of the outside world. The imperial government regarded its territory as the principal body of the world and the center of the world. The term China in Chinese, *Zhong-Guo*, literally refers to the center of the world, the so-called Middle Kingdom. Based on this fantasy, Chinese emperors required every official visitor from abroad to pay tributes and to obey Chinese tradition by cowtowing (kneel down) before the emperor. Even when Lord Macartney, an English ambassador, came to China in 1793, "he was forced to kneel in obeisance."[38]

In the sixteenth century, the Renaissance reached a peak and brought Europe into a new era of philosophy, art, literature, and natural science. The Renaissance was followed by the Industrial Revolution and the bourgeois revolution. Europe accumulated a huge industrial power in the middle of the eighteenth century, colonized other regions in the nineteenth century, and brought China into a semi-colonial period. Some Western scholars call this period the ruin of Asia. The Manchu (Qing dynasty) aristocrats were not prejudiced against Western science and technology at the beginning of the Qing dynasty. The emperor Kangxi sent a delegation to France to hire scientists for China and often called missionaries to his palace to lecture on the sciences, including geometry, physics, optics, and astronomy, However, at the end of the eighteenth century, the ruling class became very corrupt and lost its appetite for learning about foreign cultures and science. Gradually, China completely cut off any cultural and commercial exchange with Western countries and blindly enjoyed its parochial arrogance.

## CONCLUSION

Characteristics of Chinese history are twofold: China possesses great cultural wealth, but it also has a heavy historic burden that suffocates its democratic development. China's highly centralized political system inherited a strong patriarchal tradition from its predecessors. While Western societies rose rapidly and stepped into democratic systems in the eighteenth century, China slept under the traditional concept of the "Middle Kingdom," and gradually became a weak country partially colonized by Western interests. Under these circumstances, it was impossible for China to fully develop into a capitalist society. Modern China was congenitally deficient in a modern political and economic sense. The distinguishing characteristics of premodern China were an agricultural economy with a primitive mode of production, a highly centralized political system ruled by a single person without the regulation of law for more than 2,000 years. An agricultural economy provides the best soil for the centralized political system. The two are twins. At this point, economic modernization is very important to political reform. One hundred years after the last Chinese emperor was overthrown, China is growing rapidly towards economic modernization, the first step for Chinese democratization. However, patriarchal political and ideological cultures are still very much present in contemporary China. This implies that even if the economy reaches a high level, Chinese political power still possibly resists political changes unless it fundamentally changes its cultural and political tradition.

## NOTES

1. Lucian W. Pye, *The Mandarin and the Cadre: China's Political Cultures* (Ann Arbor: The University of Michigan, 1988), 21.

2. H. Stephen Gardner, *Comparative Economic Systems* (New York: Dryden Press, 1998), 654.

3. Pye, *The Mandarin and the Cadre*, ix.

4. Immanuel C. Y. Hsü, *The Rise of Modern China* (Oxford: Oxford University Press, 2000), 7.

5. Timothy Brook and Hy V. Luong, eds. *Culture and Economy: The Shaping of Capitalism in Eastern Asia* (Ann Arbor, Mich.: University of Michigan Press, 1999), 23.

6. Samuel Huntington, *Clash of Civilizations and the Remaking of World Order* (New York: Simon & Schuster, 1996), 8.

7. Chun-shu Chang, ed. *The Making of China: Main Themes in Premodern Chinese History* (Englewood Cliffs, N.J.: Prentice-Hall, Inc., 1975), 4.

8. Miyazaki Ichisada, "The Four Ages of Chinese History," in John Meskill, ed. *The Pattern of Chinese History: Cycles, Development, or Stagnation?* (Westport, Conn.: Greenwood Press, 1965), 53.

9. Quoted in Meskill, *The Pattern of Chinese History*, x.

10. Immanuel C. Y. Hsü, *The Rise of Modern China* (Oxford: Oxford University Press, 2000), 4.

11. Rhoads Murphey, "The Historical Context," in *Understanding Contemporary China*, ed. Robert E. Gamer (Boulder, Colo.: Lynne Rienner Publishers, 2008), 49.

12. Immanuel C. Y. Hsü, *The Rise of Modern China* (Oxford: Oxford University Press, 2000), 11.

13. Mousheng Lin, *Men and Ideas: An Informal History of Chinese Political Thought* (New York: Hohn Day, 1942), 18.

14. Jian Bozan, Shao Xunzheng, and Hu Hua, *A Concise History of China* (Beijing: Foreign Languages Press, 1981), 12.

15. Bai Shouyi, ed. *An Outline History of China* (Beijing: Foreign Languages Press, 1976), 19.

16. Bozan Jian, Shao Xunzheng, and Hu Hua, *A Concise History of China* (Beijing: Foreign Languages Press, 1981), 13.

17. Mousheng Lin, *Men and Ideas: An Informal History of Chinese Political Thought* (New York: Hohn Day, 1942), 124.

18. Ibid., 128.

19. Rhoads Murphey, "The Historical Context," in *Understanding Contemporary China,* Robert E. Gamer, ed. (Boulder, Colo.: Lynne Rienner Publishers, 2008), 56.

20. Harold Z. Shiffrin, *Sun Yat-sen, Reluctant Revolutionary* (Boston: Little, Brown and Company, 1980), 4.

21. A. James Gregor, *Marxism, China & Development: Reflections on Theory and Reality* (New Brunswick, N.J.: Transaction Publishers, 1995), 233.

22. John Larner, *Marco Polo and the discovery of the world* (New Haven: Yale University Press, 2001).

23. Jonathan Spence, *The Memory Palace of Matteo Ricci* (New York: Penguin Books, 1985).

24. Tse-tsung Chow, *The May Fourth Movement: Intellectual Revolution in Modern China* (Stanford, Calif.: Stanford University Press, 1967), 8.

25. Mark Elvin, *The Pattern of the Chinese Past* (Stanford, Calif.: Stanford University Press, 1973), 129.

26. Jacques Gernet, *A History of Chinese Civilization* (New York: Cambridge University Press, 1982), 14.

27. Ibid., 26.

28. Chao-ting Chi, "Key Economic Areas in Chinese History: From the Huangho Basin to the Yangtze Valley," in *The Making of China: Main Themes in Premodern Chinese History,* ed. Chun-shu Chang (Englewood Cliffs, N.J.: Prentice-Hall, Inc., 1975), 230.

29. Bozan Jian, Shao Xunzheng, and Hu Hua, *A Concise History of China* (Beijing: Foreign Languages Press, 1981), 81.

30. F. W. Mote, *A History of Chinese Political Thought* (Princeton, N.J.: Princeton University Press, 1979), 25.

31. Immanuel C. Y. Hsü, *The Rise of Modern China* (New York: Oxford University Press, 1995), 380.

32. Mote, *A History of Chinese Political Thought*, 25.

33. Cho-yun Hsu, "The Transition of Ancient Chinese Society," in *The Making of China: Main Themes in Premodern Chinese History*, ed. Chun-shu Chang (Englewood Cliffs, N.J.: Prentice-Hall, Inc., 1975), 64.

34. Gilbert Rozman, ed. *China's Modernization* (Jiangsu Province, China: People's Publishing House, 1998), 63.

35. Mote, *A History of Chinese Political Thought,* 23.

36. H. G. Greel, "The Eclectics of Han Thought," in *The Making of China: Main Themes in Premodern Chinese History*, ed. Chun-shu Chang (Englewood Cliffs: N.J.: Prentice-Hall, Inc., 1975), 141.

37. Lin, *Men and Ideas,* 19.

38. Mote, *A History of Chinese Political Thought,* 24.

*Chapter Two*

# Chinese Family

The family is the basic unit of society, and plays a critical role in carrying a society to move forward and maintaining social order. The development of family values reflects social transformation. In this sense, examining family relations is the door to understanding China. Premodern China was an enlarged family; Chinese social relations were exactly the same as hierarchical family relations, i.e. every member of the family must have obeyed the head of the family, the father. Thus, family relations are the foundation of the social and political system.

In the *Analects*, Confucius says, "Cultivate individual moral character, run the family in unison, manage the nation in order, and peace will prevail throughout the universe." Although the nation-state replaced the family-based state in China a century ago, traditional family values remain pervasive in contemporary China and continue to influence social order and politics. However, a great transformation in China is under way in the post-Mao era. Accordingly, the Chinese people have begun to challenge the traditional family values and accept Western family values. Do several Chinese generations still live under the same roof? Is the arrange marriage still prevalent in China? Are the Chinese people still prohibited to have sex before marriage? Are children morally and legally obliged to support elderly parents in China? How do the Chinese people view divorce? Is same sex marriage legal in China? In order to understand how transformation of Chinese family shapes social order of China and the characteristics of Chinese society, this chapter will examine the changes in the people's daily life through examining the structure of the Chinese family, family relations, family values, sexual relations, housework, marriage, and divorce.

# FAMILY

Family in traditional societies is an economic unit composed of persons who are related by blood, marriage, or adoption, and who partake in a common property and a common purpose. This means that family is a work unit of economy, a procreation unit, and a basic unit of hereditary relationships. In premodern China, the father was at the center of family and society; and the government was actually seen as an extension of the family unit. The emperor acted as the father of the nation. The ruler-subject relationship was the same as the relationship between fathers and sons. According to Chinese tradition, an ideal social order is comprised of a harmonious relationship between the individual, family, and the country. Thus, the family was the basic unit in private life, public life and in political relations as well. Cho-yun Hsu states that "the familial network embraced all of China with the feudal structure as the political counterpart of the family structure."[1]

The vast majority of families were farmers and they were subject to heavy physical labor, an isolated lifestyle in the agricultural society. They were virtually caged in the farm and home. As a common Chinese saying puts it, they were "born there, grew up there, and died there." Laborers were very important to a peasant's family, so Chinese parents preferred to have male offspring over girls. The size of the Chinese family usually was big in traditional China. The Chinese emphasize blood ties, so the family circle is extended much farther than the nuclear family model of the West.[2] Chinese parents preferred to produce as many children as they could as long as their financial situation permitted. The main purpose for parents to produce children is to keep their family going and prepare for their future when they become old. Children were legally and morally required to provide financial support for their parents when they became old. Family members of several generations used to live under the same roof. In a Chinese saying, those whose parents are still alive are not supposed to travel to distant lands, because children have the responsibility to take care of their elders. In ancient China, it was "extremely difficult, if not impossible, to move out of the family home without parental consent."[3] When a family had daughters, the parents "were held responsible for the moral qualities of unmarried daughters, [so] they commonly exercised stringent control over their daughters' lives. Thus, living away from home before marriage was far less acceptable for daughters than for sons."[4] However, after marriage, daughters were seen as outsiders, since their new loyalty was to their husband's family.

Since China implemented the one-child policy in 1979, the size of the Chinese family has gradually decreased. China went from having an average of six children per family in the early 1970s to a fertility rate about 1.22 in 2000. However, many scholars believe that the population was underreported and the fertility rate was really around 1.5 or 1.6.[5] One of the consequences of the one-child policy is the change in Chinese family dynamics. Parents who were born between 1949 and the late 1970s were accustomed to having four or five siblings.[6] Within a large family, children were more independent since they could not receive all of their parents' attention. Once the one-child policy was implemented, family relations changed dramatically. Esther Ngan-ling Chow and S. Michael Zhao have observed several major attributes of a single-child family: the child is the only carrier of the family name and lineage, so the parents have extraordinarily high expectations for the child's accomplishments, and the parents spend more money on one child than they would if they had two children. The family with only one child promotes the spoiling of the child. Although the child receives all of the parents' attention, they have no peers within their family. The pressure for the child to do well is also much greater than when there are siblings. The parents put all of their hope into one child, which leaves little room for the only child to fail. This consequence of the one-child policy has created a generation of lonely children under extreme pressure. In recent years some Chinese provinces have made new laws which strongly reemphasize traditional Chinese family values and encourage adult children to make regular visits to their parents' homes to take care of their elderly parents.[7] In 2013, the Chinese government passed a new law, which enforces young people to look after their elderly parents and empowers elderly parents' rights to sue their ungrateful offspring.

The Chinese imperial state provided strong ideological support to the maintenance of family unity. The ideological foundation of the subordination of children to their parents was filiality, and the idea that the younger generation was ethically bound to support, and be obedient to their seniors. In comparison with the West, Chinese parents may live with one or more married children.[8] Martin King Whyte finds that the Maoist era overall had a greater and more durable impact on the Chinese "family" than the recasting of China's economy following Mao Zedong's death.[9] With the increasing modernization in China in recent years, the dominant form of relationship within a family has gradually changed from the traditional vertical one between father and son to the relationship between husband and wife. Most young people are no longer recognizing the norm of large extended families and they move out of their parents' home after marriage.[10] Nuclear families are increasing. About 60 percent of Chinese families are nuclear families and they are expected to go higher. Families with married sons living at home were at more of a risk for separating from the family. The division from the family was also more likely if a married son had multiple brothers. All the factors contributing to family division are most probable within five years of the marriage.[11]

## MARRIAGE

From ancient China to the present, marriage has been a family social institution between a man and woman. Marriage refers to the state of being united to a person of the opposite sex as husband or wife in a consensual and contractual relationship recognized by law. Unlike Western societies, same sex marriage is illegal in China, and the majority of the Chinese people reject the notion of same sex marriage. Chinese law does not recognize same sex marriage. The majority of the Chinese people believe that human society could not continue without marriage and producing children.

The term "marriage" in Chinese is *hun-yin*, implying that marriage was a relationship between families. The title of husband, *fu*, means head of a family. In English it can be said, "he married her," "she married him," or "they were married by the justice of the peace."[12] In China, different verbs are used to refer to the actions of different parties. According to Patricia Buckley Ebrey, the man's family took a daughter-in-law, and the man himself could be said to take a wife. From the bride's side, her parents could be said to give her to someone, to get her a home (*jia*), or to confer her as a bride on someone (*qi*), which was the common legal term for a wife.[13]

In premodern China, marriage was largely arranged by parents. After an unmarried boy's parents identified a girl as their future daughter-in-law, they would find a matchmaker who would formally present his or her client's proposal to the identified girl's parents. If the potential bride's parents accepted the proposal, the bridegroom's family would then arrange the matchmaker to present betrothal gifts along with the betrothal letter, to the bride's family. After the betrothal letter and betrothal gifts were accepted, the bridegroom's family would formally send wedding gifts to the bride's family. On the selected day the bridegroom would depart with a troop of escorts and musicians, playing happy music all the way to the bride's home. Before the bride departed to her bridegroom's home, she would put on new clothes and wear a pair of red shoes, signifying good luck. At that moment, the bride would have to cry to show that she did not want to leave her parents. Meanwhile, the bridegroom set out to receive his bride. Usually he would be crowded among his friends as escorts and musicians who would play music all the way to the bride home. After the bride arrived in the bridegroom's home, the wedding ceremony began, and by that time, the bride and bridegroom were led to the family altar, where the couple would play *kotows* (a traditional Chinese custom of touching the forehead on ground signifying respect or submission) to Heaven and Earth, the family ancestors and parents. Finally, they would bow to each other and be led to the bridal chamber.

In addition to arranged marriage, there were other types of marriage in premodern China, such as exchange marriage and *tong yan xi*. The term "exchange marriage" refers to the situation where girls were treated as commodities. In such a marriage, contractual negotiation would have been more complex partly because a bride's running away after marriage might be viewed as a breach of contract. *Tong yang xi* means a daughter-in-law raised from her childhood. That being said, when a girl is born, she is often given away or sold when only a few weeks or months old, or one or two years old, to be the future wife of a son in the family, which has a little son not betrothed in marriage. Such practice is recorded as early as the Song Dynasty (960-1279) and *tong-yang-xi* constituted roughly 20 percent of marriages in premodern China.

The CPC has made specific efforts to reform the old way of marriage. As early as 1931, the Chinese Soviet Republic proclaimed the first marriage law. After the CPC settled in Yanan, the Chinese Soviet Republic further developed this law and ensured the freedom of marriage, so women in the liberated area had the right to step out of the home to join the revolution. After they were married, women supported their husbands' enlistment in the Red Army to participate in the guerilla war. Inspired by the communist ideas, some urban intellectual women escaped from their homes to the liberated area. The first law of the new China was the Marriage Law, which was promulgated in 1950, challenging the feudal marriage system and promoting freedom of marriage. The freedom of marriage was essentially a contradiction with the patriarchal system and traditional family. In order to gain support from male peasants, the party always attempted a balance between women's and men's interests. Some Western scholars believe that socialist China is a patriarchal system.[14] Kay Ann Johnson points out that the road of socialist China "has restored, preserved and utilized traditional rural communities and traditional family orientations and obligations."[15]

By contrast, the mainstream of public opinion in China believes that the marital relationship between men and women is moving toward equality. Both sides enjoy a certain amount of autonomy and have the right to make decisions about their own bodies and minds. Most Chinese men and women in urban and rural areas have achieved the right of autonomy to decide on a first marriage. The notion that "a woman must remain faithful to one man until the end of her life" has been challenged. Generally speaking, in urban and rural areas, husbands and wives manage the family's income together.[16] Husbands also share the responsibilities of housework with their wives. According to surveys, about 44 percent of urban women have access to opportunities for self-improvement, and 92 percent of these women can decided on their own whether to pursue further training without permission from someone else.

Marriage was a civil bureaucratic procedure in communist China. In the post-Mao era, the marriage law of 1980 has simplified the marriage process. Marriage licenses are issued by the Ministry of Civil Affairs PRC. To get the marriage license, the married couples are only required to present to following documents to the officials: residence booklet, and ID card and marital status certificate, issued by the county-level unit or above-county-level unit, where he or she is working sub-district office or town people's government where he or she is living. According to the marriage law of 1980, the minimum age of marriage is 20 and 22 years old for women and men, respectively, but Chinese minorities are exceptional. The legal marriage age for Chinese minorities is 20 years old for males and 18 years old for females. The marriage law prohibited marriage between immediate blood relatives and between collateral relatives within three generations, as well as marriage in which one partner suffered from leprosy or any other disease that was deemed by medical science to render the person unsuitable for marriage.

Marriage is one of the most important aspects of women's lives. In premodern China, Chinese women spent their most of time in the home—the domestic sphere. After marriage, Chinese women were obligated to be with their husbands under any circumstances, and morally they were not allowed to remarry after their husband died. One of the most sacred duties of a daughter/daughter-in-law was to provide descendants for her ancestors. To do so, she must marry. Unmarried women were almost unknown, unless the betrothed man was dead before the marriage and the girl chose to become a virgin widow. The husband's home was the destination of the majority of married women because housewives had no public career. Family was the whole world of Chinese women and the central institution of women's oppression. However, in China today, more and more women enter into marriage later in life, and some married women choose not to have children for years after marriage. Many Chinese women no longer view marriage as a necessary step in a woman's life so they choose to remain celibate or cohabitate with their boyfriends without being married. This lifestyle has been gradually accepted by urban youth in China. In Guangzhou Province, there are 1.5 million unmarried white-collar professional single women. Most of these single women hold a relatively high standard for the selection of a husband and prefer starvation or death to marrying a bad husband. They want personal freedom instead of being controlled by a man.

The home is still the basic institution in which women produce children, take care of husbands, parents and children, and take responsibility for housework, including raising children, cooking, cleaning, and washing. Chinese women have less free time to enjoy their daily life and develop their potentials. The quantity and quality of free time is one of the standards used to evaluate the quality of a women's life. Housework is unpaid, including giving birth, shopping, cooking, washing, childcare, eldercare, and patient care, etc. Generally speaking, men devote more time to public work and women spend more time with housework. According to an investigation conducted by the International Labor Organization, men work on average 40 hours per week and women work 80 hours per week. Women even work more than 80 hours in developing countries. For instance, Chilean women spend about 100 hours working, and Bolivian women spend about 107 hours.[17] Although technology for housework services has greatly increased in the past two decades in China, Chinese women have spent much more time than Chinese men doing housework, especially shopping, cleaning the house, laundering, cooking and washing dishes.[18] According to David J. Maume and Marcia L. Bellas's survey, between 35 percent and 47 percent of women report that they and their husbands are "both responsible" for housework, but Chinese husbands only do 24 percent of the cooking on average, 34 percent of the dish washing, 26 percent of the laundry, and 20 percent of the shopping. Although there is no accurate data to show what percentage of housework Chinese men do on average, the current literature indicates that the Chinese tradition of women bearing the main responsibility of housework is very much present in contemporary China.[19]

Marriage is a turning point of human life, so both Chinese men and women take the ceremony of marriage and birth very seriously, reflecting their religious beliefs and cultural tradition. In contemporary China, unlike Western societies, most marriage ceremonies are held not in religious temples, but in secular places, such as restaurants and hotels, and only a small percentage of marriage ceremonies are held in churches or temples. The Chinese people are becoming rich, and married couples are willing to spend a great deal of money on their weddings. A survey conducted in 2006-2007 showed that about 560,000 *yuan* (90,000 USD) on average is spent for an apartment, furniture, household appliances and a vehicle, and the rest of money was spent on the wedding, such as the ceremony, photography, wedding dress, jewels and feast. According to new statistics, the current average cost for a young couple's wedding in Shanghai is 650,000 *yuan*, excluding the cost of an apartment. This sum of money, which usually comes from their own savings and their parents and loans from relatives, is generally used for doing interior home decoration, buying household appliances, jewelry and new clothes, as well as paying for wedding feasts and honeymoon trips. The relevant studies indicate that most brides and bridegrooms are ready to spend more than 80 percent of their total savings on their weddings. Most newlyweds choose some domestic resorts, although some prefer spending their honeymoon on domestic or international trips.

## DIVORCE

After marriage, there are at least two possibilities: a happy family or an unhappy family. If it is an unhappy family, the married couples have only two options: tolerance or divorce. Every unhappy marriage is different, but happy marriages share something in common. First, "greater freedom of mate choice will be associated with higher marriage quality."[20] Second, receiving approval from one's parents is positively related to marriage quality. Third, being able to have both the husband and wife's equal input on decision-making allows for married Chinese couples to feel closer and experience a better marriage. Happy marriage reduces the risk of divorce; and unhappy marriage greatly increases the risk of divorce.

The right to divorce in ancient China was only the Chinese men's privilege. Chinese tradition laid down seven reasons for a man to "put away," divorce, his wife. These grounds were a part of the legal code of the empire until the fall of the Qing dynasty and the final revision of the code.[21] The seven grounds on which the husband could divorce his wife were: she is rebellious or unfilial toward her parents-in-law; she has failed to produce a son; she has been unfaithful to her husband; she has shown jealousy toward her husband's other women; she has a repulsive and incurable disease (such as leprosy); she speaks hurtfully or talks too much; and she is a thief. Chinese women could stop the divorce process if they had legitimate reasons. There were three grounds on which a wife could prevent her husband from divorcing her: she has mourned three years for her husbands' parents; she has no family to which to return; and she married her husband when he was poor, and now he is rich.[22]

Divorce cases were rare in traditional China, because Chinese women were basically not allowed to divorce their husbands. In addition, common Chinese male citizens, especially peasants, could not afford to divorce their wives. If a wife was very unhappy, she might separate from her husband and go home to her own parents, but there was strong social pressure for her to return. By contrast, there was no need for Chinese men from the gentry class to divorce their wives, because they could have more than one wife if they wanted. Concubinage was a unique historical phenomenon in China. There are many reasons that explain why Chinese wives tolerated their husbands' concubines. Financially, Chinese wives were dependent on their husbands. They could not survive if they left their husbands. Morally, Chinese wives were bound to the Confucian ethics code—the principle of the three obediences. Socially, if a husband had concubines, it usually symbolized that the family was rich and at a higher level of social status. Sometimes the first wife of the husband wanted to get concubines for her husband, because of some practical reasons. For example, if her family was rich and big, she needed to get some help from concubines to manage the family business. The first wife may have needed her husband to have a concubine to produce son in order to maintain her status in the home, because according to Chinese tradition, the greatest sin for a Chinese woman in ancient China was to fail at producing a son.

The liberation of divorce began to make substantial progress in the Republican era. The family law of the National Government of 1931 provided for divorce by mutual consent and unilateral divorce. According to Kathryn Bernhard and Philip C. Huang, "The new civil code radically revised the legal grounds for divorce, making them equally available to men and women. The eleven grounds as listed in Article 1052 of the code are: bigamy, adultery, spousal ill-treatment of a degree that makes living together intolerable, the wife's ill-treatment of her husband's lineal ascendants, their ill-treatment of her to a degree that makes living together intolerable, ongoing malicious desertion, the attempted murder of one spouse by the other, an incurable loathsome physical disease, a serious and incurable mental illness, disappearance over three years, and imprisonment of more than three years' duration or for the commission of an infamous crime.[23] Legally speaking, the Republican government granted Chinese women equal rights to access to divorce, but the divorce rights for women were mainly limited to those married women who were wealthy and educated in Republican era.

The marriage law of 1950 makes it possible for common Chinese women to divorce their husbands. The Marriage Law is also sometimes referred to as the Divorce Law. According to *Xinhua* reports, there were only 167 divorce cases in China in 1950, but after the Marriage Law came into effect in 1950, the number of divorce cases suddenly rose. There were about 409,500 divorce cases in 1951 and 398,243 in the first half of 1952. The Marriage Law soon met with resistance in rural China, because the husband and his family objected to losing their "investment." Thus, instead of improving women's status within the family, divorce actually destroyed the family. Due to the loss of their investment, narrow minded husbands began to resist the Marriage Law. As violent incidents and murders occurred, the CPC immediately revoked the Marriage Law.

The number of divorce cases dropped during the period of the Cultural Revolution from 1966 to 1976, because the whole legal system was seriously undermined. The Chinese government adopted the new Marriage Law in 1980, which consisted of 37 articles in five chapters, of which ten articles concern divorce. In theory, the new Marriage Law makes divorce easier in cases where only one party seeks divorce. While the old law stipulated that it "may" be granted if mediation fails, the new law states that in such a situation it "should" be granted. The law contributed the second peak of divorce rates during the communist regime. Erika Platate suggests that there are three major reasons that explain why divorce rates suddenly soared after the Marriage Law of 1980. Firstly, divorces were granted in cases that had been long overdue; secondly, verdicts included appeals that had been unsuccessful in the past; thirdly, the new law was misunderstood and abused by some people.[24]

There are several forms of divorce. Divorce by mutual agreement is handled by the civil affairs departments. Another form of divorce is by court mediation which has two possible outcomes. If the mediation effort is successful, the divorce request is withdrawn. Otherwise, the court issues a mediated divorce certificate, which carries the legal weight of a verdict. Finally, when one party seeks divorce without the other party's agreement, he/she may appeal directly to the people's court. According to statistics, about 31 percent of petitions were canceled after mediation when officials of the marriage registration office convinced people to settle their differences and remain married. About 57 percent of the marriage certificates were withdrawn and a divorce certificate issued.[25]

The reasons for divorce are historical. In the 1950s, women appealed to the court for divorce mainly in order to free themselves from arranged marriages imposed on them by their parents. In the 1960s and 1970s, most divorce cases involved politics. The guilty party was usually accused of deviating from social/ideological norms. In recent years, the reasons for the high percentage of divorce petitioners have become more complex, but similar to the divorce cases in Western societies, such as imprisonment of one of the spouses, conflicting interests and personalities, economic family disputes, lack of love for each other, trouble with a mother-in-law, hasty marriages, medical conditions, sexual incompatibility, in-law problems, and an inferiority complex of one of the spouses. However, the main reason cited is hasty marriages. Some people marry simply to achieve certain selfish aims. In a recent survey of young married couples, it was found that 60 percent of those questioned lacked real and spontaneous love for their partners.

According to Zeng Yi and Wu Deqing, three main factors contribute to the increase of divorce rates. First, the new Marriage Law of 1980 relaxed the restriction on divorce. Article 24 of the marriage law reads, "The Marriage registration office, after clearly establishing that divorce is desired by both parties and that appropriate measures have been taken for the care of any children and property, should issue the divorce certificate without delay."[26] Second, since China reopened its door to the West, Chinese people's attitudes towards divorce have changed. Western values in China have removed some of the negative stigmatization of women, which typically results from divorce. A divorced woman now is less likely to be regarded negatively. Third, the reform movement creates more opportunities, which help women become more economically independent. This independence may allow women to further seek divorce if they are unhappy.[27] This change implies that married couples face more risks for divorce in modernized cities, but the divorce rate differs across the different provinces in China with no obvious pattern. Actually, provinces with the lowest divorce rate include both the less developed provinces, such as Jiangxi and Anhui, and the more developed provinces, such as Zhejiang, Haina, Guangdong, and Shandong provinces.[28]

Interestingly, Xinjiang, a less developed area in China, has the highest divorce rate, in which about 17 people out of every 1,000 people are divorced. The divorce rates of Xinjiang are so high because a large portion of its population is of Islamic decent, while only a small portion of the population is of Han decent. Under Islamic tradition divorce is much more acceptable. More than half of the population belongs to the Uygur ethnic group, which are Muslims and followers of Islam who believe in having multiple wives and easy divorce rules. By contrast, the Han culture does not favor divorce. Islamic culture does not regard divorce as disgraceful, and women can easily find economic support after divorce. In addition, low education levels, early and arranged marriages, and large age differences between husbands and wives also contribute to the high divorce rate.[29] Thus, "there is not linear relationship between levels of socioeconomic development and divorce rates in contemporary China."[30]

It is worth noting that some divorce cases involve a "third party," which usually means that one party has had or is having an affair. This is probably the most common reason, which is similar to Western societies, for marriage breakups, and has increased quickly in recent years. It is believed to reflect a person's moral degeneration. Some local regulation can be applied to punish third parties. According to a survey, about 90 percent of corrupt Chinese officials have second or third wives (in Chinese *er nai*) or even more. In order to protect legal marriage and women's rights, China's top court recently reinterpreted China's Marriage Law. Under the new interpretation of Marriage Law, mistresses are not allowed to sue their married lovers for reneging on promises of money, property or goods. Nor would wayward husbands be allowed to seek the courts help in retrieving money or goods that they bestowed upon mistresses, but legal wives could sue to recover money or property that ended up in the hands of a "little third," the colloquial term for a mistress.[31]

The present divorce rate in China is lower than most countries of the industrialized West. The divorce rate is about 3.9 percent in China, 15 percent Japan, 19.7 percent in West Germany, 24.7 percent in Sweden, 27.5 percent in Canada, 28.3 percent in Australia, 29.5 percent in England, 29.7 percent in East Germany, 34.7 percent in Russia, and 48.8 percent in the United States. As in many other Asian societies, the persistence of deeply rooted traditions in the area of family behavior has played a role as well and will continue to do so, particularly in rural China. In addition, divorced parents and children may be more likely to experience a higher level of distress than typically experienced by families from Western societies where divorce is more commonly accepted.[32] Thus, Chinese parents are careful about the negative impact of divorced parents tending to neglect their children.

## CONCLUSION

Chinese family is the miniature model of Chinese society. The nation of China is an enlarged family. The relationship between family members is the same as the relationship between the government, society and individuals, especially in the premodern China. The changes in the Chinese family structure and relations reflect the changes of social structure and social norms, and the political system as well. Although the last emperor was overthrown a century ago, the father-centered family structure and relations are still very much present in Chinese families and will continue to influence Chinese society and the political system. However, during the process of modernization and globalization, family life and marriage are unavoidably experiencing a great transformation. New family values and family relations are emerging. The young generation of China has enjoyed freedom of marriage and equality between wives and husbands. Having sex experience before marriage is no longer strange to the people in China. The number of single adults is growing. The nuclear family has become the dominant family form. The divorce rate in China, as a social phenomenon during globalization, will continue to climb.[33] All these changes of family life profoundly affect the quality and style of people's lives and reshape Chinese society and culture. However, it is still a slow process in comparison with the rapid growth of China's urbanization and industrialization.

## NOTES

1. Cho-yun Hsu, "The Transition of Ancient Chinese Society," in *The Making of China: Main Themes in Premodern Chinese History*, ed. Chun-shu Chang (Englewood Cliffs: N.J.: Prentice-Hall, Inc., 1975), 64.

2. Kwok-fai Ting and Stephen W. K. Chiu, "Leaving the Parental Home: Chinese Culture in an Urban Context," *Journal of Marriage and Family* 64, No. 3 (August, 2002): 625.

3. Ibid., 615.

4. Ibid.

5. Robert D. Retherford, Minja Kim Choe, Jiajian Chen, Li Xiru, and Cui Hongyan, "How Far Has Fertility in China Really Declined?" *Population and Development Review* 31, No. 1 (March, 2005): 58.

6. Esther Chow Ngan-ling and S Michael Zhao, "The One-Child Policy and Parent-Child Relationships: A Comparison of One-Child with Multiple-Child Families in China." *The International Journal of Sociology and Social Policy* 16, no. 12 (1996): 55.

7. Yu Ran, "New law to protect elderly parents," *China Daily*, 22 January 2011.

8. Martin King Whyte, "Continuity and Change in Urban Chinese Family Life," *The China Journal* 53 (January, 2005): 9.

9. Ibid. 10.

10. Shuzhuo Li, Marcus W. Feldman, and Xiaoyi Jin, "Marriage Form and Family Division in Three Villages in Rural China," *Population Studies* 57, No. 1 (March, 2003): 105.

11. Ibid., 8.

12. Patricia Buckley Ebrey, *The Inner Quarters: Marriage and the Lives of Chinese Women in the Sung Period* (Berkeley: University of California Press, 1993), 46.

13. Ibid.

14. Judith Stacey, *Patriarchy and Socialist Revolution in China* (Berkeley: University of California Press, 1983), 20.

15. Kay Ann Johnson, *Women, the Family and Peasant Revolution in China* (Chicago: The University of Chicago Press, 1983), 218-19.

16. Xiong Yu, "The Status of Chinese Women in Marriage and the Family," in *Holding Up Half the Sky*, eds. Tao Jie, Zheng Bijun, and Shirley L. Mow (New York: The Feminist Press, 2004), 175.

17. Tian Cuiqin, "Nong chun fu nü fa zhang yu xian xia shi jian de xing bie bu ping deng yang jiu,"*Fu Nü Yan Jiu Lun Cong* (*Journal of Women's Studie*s) 5 (2004)25.

18. Li Yinhe, "Fu nü, jia ting yu sheng yu," (*Women and Family*) *Jiangsu She Hui Ke Xue* 4 (*Social Science of Jiangsu*) (2004): 171.

19. David J. Maume and Marcia L. Bellas, "Chinese Husbands' Participation in Household Labor," *Journal of Comparative Family Studies* 31 no. 2 (Spring 2000): 192.

20. Ellen Efron Pimentel, "Just How Do I Love Thee?: Marital Relations in Urban China," *Journal of Marriage and Family* 62, No. 1 (February 2000): 34.

21. Susan Hill Gross & Marjorie Wall Bingham, *Women in Traditional China: Ancient Times to Modern Reform* (Hudson, Wisconsin: G.E. McCuen Publications, 1973), 102.

22. Ibid.

23. Kathryn Bernhard and Philip C. Huang, *Civil Law in Qing and Republican China* (Stanford: Stanford University Press, 1999).

24. Erika Platate, "Divorce Trends and Patterns in China: Past and Present." *Pacific Affairs* 61, No. 3 (Autumn 1988): 428.

25. Ibid., 435.

26. Zeng Yi and Wu Deqing, "Regional Analysis of Divorce in China since 1980," *Demography* 37, No. 2 (May 2000): 215.

27. Ibid.

28. Ibid.

29. Ibid., 217.

30. Ibid., 218.

31. Sharon LaFraniere, "Court Considers Revising China's Marriage Law," *New York Times*, 16 February 2011.

32. Qi Dong, Yanping Wang, Thomas H Ollendick, "Consequences of Divorce on the adjustment of Children in China" *Journal of Clinical Child and Adolescent Psychology* 31, No. 1 (2002): 109.

33. Erika Platate, "Divorce Trends and Patterns in China: Past and Present," *Pacific Affairs* 61, No. 3 (Autumn 1988): 445.

*Chapter Three*

# Population and Development

The development of population is closely related to family values and family relations and also affects national comprehensive power. China's population stood at 583 million in 1949, but it reached 1.34 billion people in 2011. China is vast in territory and rich in resources, yet China's arable land is scarce and the people are many,[1] so it is difficult for the Chinese government to provide a sufficient food supply to feed its own people. Although the Chinese government began to implement the one-child policy in 1979, China's population has continued and will continue to grow to reach 1.53 billion by 2030.

This development trend of population growth has become one of the key factors affecting China's pace of modernization.[2] Western societies have seriously criticized the one-child policy, viewing it as a violation of human rights and insisting that the one-child policy is brutal and coercively excessive.[3] The fundamental questions as to China's population issue are whether China needs to control its population growth and how to manage the population issues derived from the one-child policy. This chapter will examine the development of China's population, the government's population policy, and the necessity of amending the current population policy in order to develop a well-balanced society.

## IMPLICATION OF THE GAP BETWEEN CITY AND COUNTRYSIDE

China's prosperity hinges on three balancing acts between city and country, between population and food, and between regions of hardship and regions of prosperity.[4] The Chinese people developed their cities much earlier than European countries. Xi An (Chang An in the old Chinese pronunciation), capital of the Han dynasty, was the largest cosmopolitan metropolis during the Han dynasty. During the Tang dynasty, a large number of foreign residents including official ambassadors lived in Chang An.[5] In order to defend the city, a high and solid wall was built around it, which is called the city wall. Canals were built around every city wall to protect the city wall too. The city wall and canal river separated the urban residents from the countryside. Residential and commercial areas in Chinese cities are mixed together. Chinese cities were the place for Chinese people to seek a better life due to the fact that Chinese cities were the center of politics, economy, culture and commerce.

Chinese peasants were not free to move from the countryside to the city without official permission because of the registration system. The registration system changed from time to time, but the nature of the system is the same from ancient times to present-day China—to prohibit rural people from freely moving from the countryside to city, control the growth of urban population, and manage the social order of the urban areas. This explains why 90 percent of Chinese people resided in the countryside before the reform movement in 1978 and why the economic and cultural gaps are so wide between the city and countryside. In the post-Mao era, Chinese peasants are allowed to relocate to urban areas, but they are obligated to maintain their rural registration in Chinese *hukou*. In recent years, some cities in China have implemented a new policy, which issues temporary residential permits for Chinese peasant workers or offers them permanent resident status if they meet government requirements. However, the foundation of traditional registration system remains and continues to negatively affect the quality of peasant life.

The reform movement has directly produced two important trends, urbanization and migration. The two trends are closely interrelated. Chinese cities demand more laborers from the countryside while expanding urban areas; in turn, immigrants further promote the speed of urbanization. The urban population expanded from 172 million in 1978 to 379 million in 1997 and surged by more than 45 percent by 2011. According to the Chinese Academy of Social Sciences, China's urbanization is expected to hit over 71 percent by 2040, accounting for 1.12 billion urban residents by that time. Only about 150 million Chinese people will live in rural areas by 2087.[6]

The implication of urbanization is multifaceted. First, more and more large cities have merged in China. According to China's official media, China has 655 cities, 118 megacities with a population of over one million, and 39 super cities with over five million people, including Shanghai, Beijing, Chongqing, Wuhan, Tianjin, Guangzhou, Xian, Nanjing, Chengdou, Qingdao, Kunming, Wuxi, and others. Many Chinese cities have become over-inhabited, and so there are great shortages of water, fresh air and green land. Accordingly, the quality of people's living environment has been decreasing. Second, rapid urbanization has directly contributed to the decline of arable land, rural laborers and output of grain. While losing land, they do not have any other choice but to move into the city. Third, urbanization also creates various job opportunities, especially in manufacturing and construction projects and housing markets, which enable local peasants to take non-agricultural job positions. The fast expansion of urbanization attracts domestic and foreign capitals to help develop the Chinese economy, but, at the same time, the size of arable land for China's total population is rapidly shrinking, and as more urban residents rely on less arable land, it will be more difficult for the Chinese government to use the minimum size of arable land to feed the Chinese people.

## CHARACTERISTICS OF CHINA'S POPULATION

As early as the second century during the Han dynasty, China had a population of about 60 million, making up 25 percent of the world's population. The size of China's population during that period of time was even larger than it is today in terms of its percentage of the world's total population. Historical fluctuations of population growth and decline kept China's population between 37 and 60 million over a period of at least the next 1,000 years before dramatically increasing in modern China. The rapid growth of China's population occurred especially in the eighteenth century. China's population reached 210 million in 1700, 295 million in 1800, and 400 million in 1900. The growth of China's population was relatively slow during the republican era from 1911 to 1949, partly because of frequent wars, including the three civil wars and the war against Japan. According to China's census, China had a population of 583 million in the 1950s, 766 million in 1966, 933 million in 1976, and 1.34 billion in 2011. As the world's population surpassed 6.7 billion, China's population represents more than 20 percent of the world's total population. It is projected that China's population will continue to grow and will reach its peak by 2030 (about 1.53 billion) and, then, begin to decrease, if the Chinese government continues to implement the one-child policy.

Among China's total population, about 320 million Chinese people make up the youth population under the age of 14, which is 26 percent of the total population. According to a new survey released in April 2011, 180 million people are within the elderly population over 60 years of age, making up about 13 percent of the total population, up from 10.3 percent in 2000. This trend of population growth will place greater burdens on the working young who must support their elderly kin, as well as on government-run pension and health-care systems. It raises legitimate questions of whether China has enough people and whether China has enough laborers to support the entire society and elderly people.

The quality of China's population needs to be improved. The majority of the Chinese population still lives in the countryside. Objectively, the majority of rural Chinese population is relatively poor and less educated. The Chinese government has implemented the 9-year compulsory education system, but school dropout rates have been on the rise since the reform movement because after young rural people immigrated to urban areas, a high percentage of peasant families lacked labor for helping with farm work. The development of social services is lagging far behind the pace of the development of urbanization. In China, streets are crowded, traffic jams are some of the worst in the world, there is a great shortage of water, electricity and medical facilities, air and water are seriously polluted, and food safety scandals are on the rise. All these factors have affected people's daily life and the quality of the population.

China is one of the world's most populated countries. Yet, unlike Bangladesh, Japan, and India, China's population density is not the highest in the world. The world population is currently 6.8 billion and the Earth's area is about 510 million square kilometers (197 million square miles). On average, the world population density is 13.1 people per kilometer or 34.0 people per square mile. By this standard, China's population density ranks eleventh in the world. However, several issues should be mentioned. First, the population density in some regions in China is very high, such as in Macau and Hong Kong. There are 18,811 people residing per square kilometer in Macao. The population density in Macao is even higher than the most densely populated country, Bangladesh, in which there are only 14,737 people per square kilometer. Secondly, the general migratory trend is from western China to eastern China, from northern China to southern China, and from undeveloped areas to developed areas. As a result, 94 percent of the population inhabits 46 percent of China's territory in the eastern and southeastern parts of China. This means that although the average population density in China is about 137 people per kilometer, the population density in the developed areas, especially in the east coast areas, is much higher than in other areas. While some large Chinese cities are overpopulated, such as Shanghai, Beijing, Guangzhou, Shenzhen and Chongqing, the population density in some areas such as Tibet and Qinghai is very low, less than 10 people per kilometer. Although most Chinese people still live in rural areas at the present time, China has the largest urban population in the world.

# CHINA'S POPULATION AND CHINESE CULTURE AND GOVERNMENT POLICY

Several factors contribute to the population growth. First of all, the conception of sex life contributes to population growth. Despite rapid social changes and influences from Western countries, traditional Chinese sexual beliefs still persist in contemporary Chinese societies. According to Confucian tradition, sex is for married couples to produce children. A girl should remain a virgin until her marriage. Sex must be compatible with principles of Confucianism and other traditional ethics. Sex for pleasure and outside marriage are prohibited. In other words, Confucian sexual philosophy emphasizes procreation and maintains the patriarchal social order.

Daoist tradition takes a different view toward sex based on the *yin-yang* doctrine. The Chinese have used *yin* and *yang* to refer to sexual organs and sexual intercourse. Daoist sexual philosophy is about the balance between *yin* and *yang* and personal health. Sexual disorder, like other illnesses, is viewed as an imbalance of *yin* and *yang*. Semen is valued as a source of vitality and needs to be preserved by avoiding ejaculation during intercourse. Both Confucianism and Daoism share something in common: that sex should take place between a man and a woman and encourage healthy sex and, thus, birth control is not an issue in their eyes.

The topic of sex was a taboo subject during the Mao regime. Sex education was prohibited. Whoever openly talked about the sex issue was regarded as a bad person, or a capitalist. Parents also seldom talked to their children about sexual matters even within the family. As a result, the majority of unmarried people were ignorant about sex life and had to acquire sex knowledge after marriage, including knowledge about birth control and abortion. A recent study on sex-related folk beliefs in different regions of China shows that Chinese people still believe that controlled sexual activity protects health, excessive masturbation weakens the body, and sex with a menstruating woman causes illness.

Second, the age of marriage affects population growth rates. In Western societies, it is not abnormal for couples to enter marriage at a late age, which slows down population growth. In contemporary China, Chinese females were eligible to marry at age 18 according to the Marriage Law of 1950 and at age 20 based on the marriage law of 1980. If women got married later, they could try to give birth soon after marriage in order to make up for a lost time.[7] According to the Chinese government, "The rate of early marriage for women has come down and their average age at first marriage has gone up. In 1992, the proportion of women entering first marriage before the age of 20 dropped to 12.9 percent of the total number of first marriage women. In 1970, women's average age at first marriage was 20.2 years, while in 1993 it was 22.67 years, up 2.47 years."[8]

In addition to the marriage age, an important factor that directly affects population growth rate is the average age that women first give birth. Generally speaking, influenced by the traditional culture, married women usually first gave birth between one and two years after marriage. In present-day China, a growing number of married couples prefer to postpone having a child. The number of Chinese women who bear children from the ages of 20 to 29 has exceeded 100 million each year, because they want to enjoy their freedom after marriage. In a 2008 survey conducted by *163.com*, about 39.7 percent of female respondents said they would consider having a baby at 35, compared with 32 percent who said they would not. Twenty eight percent of survey participants thought age is not a big issue when it comes to having children. The number of women who give birth after the age of 35 is growing fast in urban China. Most of older new mothers are graduates of higher education and have high incomes and hold senior white-collar posts. This is an indication of an inevitable trend that China's population growth will continue to slow down with the development of modernization and the enhancement of education.[9]

Third, government policy directly contributes to population growth rates. Population policy is a sum of laws and regulations which are used to influence population movement and demographic changes. National population policy influences the natural population movement and migration movement, and also affects both population quality and distribution. When the CPC came to power in 1949, China began implementing family planning policies, but the policies were optional.[10] The government began to realize that if no restrictions were implemented, the Chinese population would be 4.26 billion by 2080. This number was close to the world population at the time.[11] Thus, it was necessary to strictly implement the one-child policy.

The Chinese government made the one-child policy mandatory in 1979. The policy set guidelines for marriage, child bearing, and birth control methods for the Chinese population. This policy is based on "a projection that the country's population would continue to grow for a long time if every couple had two children."[12] According to the one-child policy, a woman who did not have a child before 1979 was permitted to have one child. If she already had children before 1979, she was not permitted to produce additional children. There are some exceptions for families to give birth a second time, if they meet the guidelines. For example, if the first-born child is disabled, or the parents work in dangerous jobs (e.g., mining), the family may have a second child.[13] The government takes flexible attitudes towards minorities. There are fifty-five ethnic minority groups in China and they make up only 8.4 percent of the total population.[14] Ethnic minorities are allowed to have more than one child because they make up such a small part of the total Chinese population.[15] While the one-child policy is widely carried out in China's cities, it has been more flexibly enforced in rural areas because peasants need additional labor at home. The government allows them to have a second child five years after the first. However, in some areas the first child must be a girl in order to be allowed to have a second child.[16]

Since 1979, the government has imposed a penalty if one is in violation of the policy. The consequences of breaking the policy include heavy fines, confiscation of personal property, low ratings in the work place, or the loss of a job.[17] Whoever violates the one-child policy is subject to financial penalty. China is the only country in the world that has penalized people specifically and directly for violating population policy. The financial penalties for having a second child without a permit typically range from 10 to 50 percent of the annual income of both the husband and wife, imposed each year for a period ranging from 5 to 14 years. People can also receive administrative disciplinary sanctions, such as loss of party membership, demotion from their current positions, deduction of salary, exclusion from opportunities, such as job promotion and political advancement, or even discharge from public employment. Some families, especially the wealthy, may be able to afford a financial penalty, but the majority of Chinese people cannot afford to have more children.

## UNDERSTANDING THE ONE-CHILD POLICY

The one-child policy is one of the most controversial population policies in the modern world. The Chinese people view the one-child policy differently. Those parents whose first child is a girl and second is a boy are expected to stop having children. Those who live in urban areas and are better educated, are less likely to show a preference for sons and more likely to comply with the one-child policy. Peasant women are much more likely to have second and third children, because they want larger families, particularly more sons. Prior to the implementation of the one-child policy Shanghai's total fertility rate ranged from 1.03 to 1.30.[18] Why were the urban fertility rates so low prior to the introduction of the policy? One of the common explanations is that in the majority of urban families, both parents were employed and had no free time to enjoy their personal lives after more than one child, so they were reluctant to have a second child. Most married couples in urban areas do not have trouble accepting the one-child policy. By contrast, rural families want to have as many children as possible, and preferably boys, because they largely rely on their offspring to take care of the parents due to their lack of savings.[19]

There is no doubt from both Chinese and Western perspectives that the purpose of birth control is to manage population growth and simply "achieve nothing less than the wholesale transformation of childbearing patterns of the largest country in the world."[20] The policy has undoubtedly contributed to reduced childbearing.[21] If the one-child policy is scrutinized in a historical Chinese context, it is a necessary strategy to serve the interest of the nation in a specific period of time. China is a developing country, lacking in arable land, housing, water, and other resources. In this sense, the majority of Chinese people could not fully enjoy human rights without controlling the birth rate. High birthrates would hinder social and economic development. If the government did not implement the birth control policy, it would have at least 400 million more people to take care of today. According to a Chinese official report, since 1978, China's GDP has increased almost ten times, but the population growth rates dropped from 3 percent in 1960 to 0.5 percent in 2011. Obviously, the birth control policy is helpful in making Chinese people rich and making the nation strong.

Some Western scholars try to make a case that the one-child policy is a violation of human rights, because the policy kills female fetuses and creates social problems, such as abuse, abandonment, and the killing of baby girls. Theoretically, women should have the right to make their own decision on their own family size. However, human rights not only pertain to the rights of the human body, but also the right to live, to work and to receive an education. It is common sense that if there were more people in China, there would be less opportunity for each Chinese individual. Overpopulation is an obstacle to China's modernization. Although the one-child policy has prevented 400 million births since the policy's implementation in 1979, China's population will continue to grow until it reaches its population peak by 2030. This requires the Chinese government to continue to implement the one-child policy. With the rapid growth of China's population, China will face four great challenges regarding agriculture-food, employment, urbanization, and the aging population. Due to the fact that the growth rate of China's population will be faster than the increase of grain production until 2040, the government will not be able to provide the Chinese people with sufficient food. China will face a serious food shortage problem in the future and will have to import grain from the international market to meet part of the domestic demand.[22] In addition, with the rapid development of urbanization, the pressures of employment demands will be great. About 40 percent of rural laborers will need to be employed in non-agricultural sectors in the next three decades. However, the current unemployment rate is as high as nine percent. It is almost impossible for China to create sufficient job opportunities for Chinese people without birth control.

China's population policy has controlled the growth rate of the Chinese population, improved the quality of life for Chinese people, enhanced gender equality, relieved the high demands on the social welfare system and natural resources, and provided more job opportunities for the Chinese people. The one-child policy has improved health services and relieved the burdens on Chinese women. With fewer children, they have more time to invest in their careers and increase their quality of life. The one-child policy has enabled married parents to support their elderly parents, to pour their resources into their children's education, and to prevent themselves from falling into unemployment and poverty. In addition, the one-child policy is important for stabilizing the global population growth. With 1.34 billion people, a fifth of the world's population, China must be a major part of the solution to the global population crisis. There is nothing wrong with Chinese women voluntarily having an abortion in the Chinese context, but it is wrong for the government to force Chinese women to have an abortion. In June 2012, Feng Jianmei, a twenty-three-year-old Chinese woman, was forced by the local government officials to have an abortion while seven months pregnant. Both Chinese people and world media were shocked by this horrible incident. Western media views the case of Feng Jianmei as much about state violence as about abortion. However, this case cannot justify that the one-child policy is a bad policy, but only a reminder that the government must lawfully carry out the one-child policy. The one-child policy itself differentiates from the process of implementing the one-child policy. Unlawfully implementing the one-child policy is wrong, but the policy itself is historically necessary.

## NEGATIVE CONSEQUENCES OF THE ONE-CHILD POLICY

A good government policy does not only produce positive outcomes, but also creates negative side effects at the same time. The one-child policy is no exception. The one-child policy involves many issues—political, social, economic, ethical, and health issues—and it unavoidably creates some negative consequences in various aspects of Chinese society.

First of all, the one-child policy contributes to the shrinking of the labor pool.[23] Under the one-child policy, China is getting older faster than it's getting richer compared with the United States. The United Nations defines an aging society when adults aged 65 or older exceed 7 percent of the total population. In 2011, the country's population of those over 65 years old already reached 180 million, accounting for 13 percent of China's total population. China is already an aging society by the United Nations' definition. If current population trends persist, the aging population will grow faster.[24] China's manpower will peak by 2016 and will thereafter commence an accelerating decline. If current childbearing trajectories continue, each new generation will be at least 20 percent smaller than the one before it.[25] According to a UN projection, by 2040, the proportion of elderly people in the Chinese population will rise to 28 percent, which is higher than what it predicts for the United States.

The implication of the increase of aging people is two-fold. On the one hand, the rapid growth of the aging population reflects a country's advancement in science and technology and higher standards of living. On the other hand, it reduces the size of the working population, consisting of the age group between 18 and 59 years old for women and between 18 and 64 years old for men. The negative consequence of an aging society is obvious. When developed countries encountered an aging population, their per capita GDP was between $5,000 and $10,000, but China's was below $4,000 in 2011. In 2040, China's annual per capita income will be about $11,000, but by that time the aging population in China will roughly reach 420 million. The situation is even more severe in the countryside. While about 70 percent of the people aged 60 or above in China live in the countryside, more than 10 million people move from rural to urban areas every year, about 95 percent of these domestic immigrants being young people. This means the number of aging people in rural areas is increasing faster than in urban areas. Thus, the agenda of developing social security for aged people in rural areas has become more urgent in China.

It is uncertain if China will have enough working people to support the entire society or enough funds to support the aging population in the future. The Chinese welfare system is at the beginning stage.[26] China now needs another 1.3 trillion *yuan* ($196 billion) to ensure that its aged people get enough pensions to have a decent life. Apart from more pension funds, China also needs more human and material resources to provide for its aging population. The country has about 38,000 care homes with about 2.4 million beds for the elderly. That means only about 15 beds are available for every 1,000 senior citizens in China compared with 50 to 70 in Western countries. Ironically, 20 percent of the available beds in China lie vacant because the aged people in the country cannot afford them.

The shrinkage of the labor force will reduce China's capabilities in international competition. According to Cai Fang from the Population and Labor Economic Research Institute under the Chinese Academy of Social Sciences, China has benefited from its demographic dividend with the number of working-age people contributing to 24 percent of the economy's growth between 1978 and 1998. China will see the growth of its working-age population coming to a halt around 2013 and might begin experiencing labor-force shortages.[27] However, the dividend of the cheap labor force is close to its end. China will soon face a shrinking labor force in 15 years. In the first 50 years of the twenty-first century, China, India and the United States will be the three most populous countries in the world. Nevertheless, China's working-age population, between 15 to 64 years old, will reach its peak in 2020 with a total of 940 million people. After that, it will decline and be overtaken by India. Under the current Indian government population policy, India's population structure will become better than China's in 15 years. By 2050 India will have 200 million more people of working age than China's.

To strengthen China's international competition ability, the Chinese government will be forced to change the one-child policy.[28]

Second, the one-child policy and Chinese tradition contribute to a gender imbalance. Between 1982 and 2000 the gender ratio of male to female babies increased from 1.085 to 1.169.[29] According to the latest statistics, the sex ratio in present-day China is 100:118. A recent survey has found that there are at least 32 million more boys than girls under the age of 20 and overall ratios of boys are much higher everywhere, especially in rural areas, where it peaks at 126 for every 100 girls. Petra Löfstedt observes that "China has the most severe shortage of girls compared to boys of any country in the world."[30]

Although the one-child policy cannot be held solely responsible for the gender discrepancy in China, it is definitely a main contributor. The one-child policy may induce many families to use selective abortion and abandon female infants under the influence of the preference for a son. Many Chinese women use ultrasounds to determine the gender of their unborn child. If they find out their unborn baby is female, they simply abort it. Abortions performed for the purpose of eliminating female fetuses are illegal under the Law on Maternal and Infant Health Care of 1994. In reality, many couples find ways to learn the sex of their unborn child. The result of this selective discarding of female children is increasing the unbalanced sex ratio between boys and girls.

Under the pressure of the one-child policy, many Chinese people, especially in rural areas, prefer to have a son. The preference for a male child has been proven to lead to sex-selective abortion and failure to report the true female population—females born outside of the one-child policy are commonly unreported.[31] Many girls are not legally registered, and are "hidden" in various ways in their home. Large numbers of girls are also believed to be living secretly with their parents in their natal villages without benefit of registration. In China, there are an estimated 15 million "unregistered children" who have been born outside the framework of the family planning program. Children without family registrations have trouble receiving formal education and will also have difficulty securing employment. Under the pressure of the one-child policy and the influence of male-preference, an increasing number of daughters become unwanted, and an increasing number of unwanted daughters are simply abandoned. Some infant girls are being neglected compared with infant boys. One of the most striking things about this is that nearly all the infants and children in orphanages are females. Many of these girls suffer "handicaps" ranging from minor birthmarks to severe retardation, though increasingly girls are being deposited at these places without any disabilities. Rarely are boys found in orphanages today.

The parental preference for sons over daughters is a common phenomenon in many parts of the world, but it is particularly pervasive in developing countries among more traditional couples and among couples of lower soci-oeconomic status. In the Philippines, sons are preferred as the first child. A moderate degree of son preference was found in Malaysia, Thailand, and Sri Lanka, and son preference was extremely strong in Bangladesh, Nepal, Paki-stan, India, and South Korea. The degree of son preference is affected by several factors: the level of the country's economic development, social norms, religious practices, marriage and family systems, degree of urbaniza-tion, and the nature of social security systems.

There are various reasons why son preference is common in China. Ac-cording to Chinese tradition, sons carried a family's name and daughters could not glorify the family through official appointment or the family name. Chinese tradition required sons to perform the ancestral rite and daughters were not allowed to offer ancestral sacrifice. Sons were of overwhelming importance to the family because of their potential role as providers of the family income through office-holding, commerce, landownership or labor and handicraft skill. Sons in rural families may have been thought to be more helpful in farm work. Sons were long-term members of the family and of-fered more support to their parents, especially old-age security. By contrast, daughters consumed rice, needed clothes, and their weddings are usually a drain on the family resources. Daughters could repay their parents only by helping around the house, and, usually, they were often expected to sacrifice for all their younger siblings and leave school at a very early age. After her marriage, she became the exclusive property of the husband's family. Thus, among parents with limited resources, daughters were subject to low-invest-ment contracts, while sons enjoyed high-investment contracts.

An imbalanced gender ratio causes the negative consequence of social and cultural problems. It makes searching for wives more difficult for Chi-nese men and some of them will not be able to find wives at all. Of course, the anxiety of some sexually frustrated men contributes to the rise of crime. The shortage of females also means that the girls who are not aborted or abandoned have more opportunities to choose husbands, a privilege rarely available to them in earlier times. Due to the fact that most Chinese families have only one child, there is a psychological impact on the child's education. This results in the "little emperor" effect, wherein a whole family places all of its hope and attention on only one child, thereby spoiling their child and creating a self-centered child psyche. As a result, the new generation of Chinese people who are born under the one-child policy may have high IQs, but be weak in social and practical ability.

Since both the one-child policy and Chinese tradition contribute to gender imbalance, to improve the gender imbalance, it is necessary to change the one-child policy and remake Chinese traditional culture and customs. Start-ing in the 1990s, some provinces in China began to allow parents to have two children. Henan, China's most populous province, was the last province to approve the alteration to the policy in 2011. This effort has been present across China in order to encourage a younger generation to increase family size. In challenging China's controversial one-child policy, some regional leaders have asked for permission from the central government to relax the policy in their areas. Zhang Feng, the head of Guangdong's population commission, requested that some families be allowed to have a second child (specifically families in which one of the parents is an only child). A similar baby-step was implemented two years ago in Shanghai—under which parents who were both only children were allowed, and even encouraged, to have two children—did not lead to a surge in additional children. Some provincial leaders have taken an even bigger step, asking the central government to lift the one-child policy.[32]

## CONCLUSION

The growth of the Chinese population was especially rapid during the Mao era and almost doubled in the first twenty-nine years under the communist regime. The Chinese government began to develop new national population policies and implemented the one-child policy, which has slowed the rapid growth of the Chinese population, promoted Chinese economy and modernization, and served China's national interests. Success cannot, however, come without consequences. In addition to many violent incidents during implementing the one-child policy, in the long-term, aging and gender imbalance will also negatively affect the normal structure of Chinese society and healthy social development. China's National Population and Family Planning Commission recently expressed deep worries about the looming demographic transformation. Zhang Weiqing, the minister in charge of the National Population and Family Planning Commission, called the population problem a "time bomb" facing the country that could explode any time, implying that China might relax its three-decades-old one-child policy.[33] It is time for the Chinese government to look at all of the negative consequences of the policy. The country needs to focus on the future population and make sure it is evenly distributed, healthy, and well motivated. It is also time for the government to shift the emphasis from quantity control to quality improvement. However, the government should carefully review the current national population policy and cautiously take necessary measures in revising the one-child policy. It is best to think about the next two or three generations. If China allows the birth rates to go up now, then 60 years from now China will be faced with another baby boom. Thus, the Chinese government should gradually adjust the one-child policy to avoid any misstep during the process of adjusting the population policy.

# NOTES

1. Stanley Toops, "China: A Geographic Preface," in *Understanding Contemporary China,* ed. Robert E. Gamer (Boulder, Colo.: Lynne Rienner Publishers, 2008),19.

2. Jianfa Shen, "China's Future Population and Development Challenges," *The Geographical Journal* 164, no. 1 (March 1998): 32.

3. "China's Population: The most surprising demographic crisis," *Economist,* May 11, 2011.

4. Ma Rong, "Population Growth and Urbanization," in *Understanding Contemporary China,* ed. Robert E. Gamer (Boulder, Colo.: Lynne Rienner Publishers, 2008), 242.

5. Edward H. Schafer, "The Glory of the Tang Empire," in *The Making of China: Main Themes in Premodern Chinese History,* ed. Chun-shu Chang (Englewood Cliffs: N.J.: Prentice-Hall, Inc., 1975), 170.

6. Jianfa Shen, "China's Future Population and Development Challenges," *The Geographical Journal* 164, no. 1 (March 1998): 34.

7. Hirschman, Charles, and Ronald Rindfuss, "The Sequence and Timing of Family Formation Events in Asia," *American Sociological Review* 47, No 5 (October 1982): 663.

8. The State Council Information Office, "White Paper: Gender Equality and Women's Development in China ," *China Daily,* 24 August 2005.

9. Zhang Xiwen, "Chinese Women Putting off the Family Way," *China Today*, September 4, 2009.

10. Vanessa L. Fong. "China's One-Child Policy and the Empowerment of Urban Daughters," *American Anthropologist* 104, no. 4 (December, 2002): 1100.

11. Yilin Nie and Robert J. Wyman. "The One-Child Policy in Shanghai: Acceptance and Internalization," *Population and Development Review* 31, no. 2 (June, 2005): 313.

12. Jianfa Shen, "China's Future Population and Development Challenges," *The Geographical Journal* 164, no. 1 (March 1998): 33.

13. Therese Hesketh, Li Lu, and Wei Xing Zhu, "The Effect of China's One-Child Family Policy After 25 Years," *The New England Journal of Medicine* 353, no. 11 (September 15, 2005): 1172.

14. Fuhua Zhai and Qin Gao, "Center-Based Care in the Context of One-Child Policy in China: Do Child Gender and Siblings Matter?" *Population Research and Policy Review* 29, no. 5 (October, 2010): 746.

15. Therese Hesketh, Li Lu, and Wei Xing Zhu, "The Effect of China's One-Child Family Policy After 25 Years," *The New England Journal of Medicine* 353, no. 11 (September 15, 2005): 1172.

16. Fuhua Zhai and Qin Gao, "Center-Based Care in the Context of One-Child Policy in China: Do Child Gender and Siblings Matter?" *Population Research and Policy Review* 29, no. 5 (October, 2010): 746.

17. Therese Hesketh, Li Lu, and Wei Xing Zhu, "The Effect of China's One-Child Family Policy After 25 Years," *The New England Journal of Medicine* 353, no. 11 (September 15, 2005): 1172.

18. Yilin Nie and Robert J. Wyman, "The One-Child Policy in Shanghai: Acceptance and Internalization." *Population and Development Review* 31, no. 2 (June, 2005): 314.

19. Penny Kane and Ching Y Choi, "China's One Child Family Policy," *British Medical Journal* 319 (October 9, 1999): 993.

20. Nicholas Eberstadt, "China's Family Planning Goes Awry," *Far Eastern Economic Review*, 4 December 2009.

21. Daniel M. Goodkind, "China's Missing Children: The 2000 Census Underreporting Surprise," *Population Studies* 58, No. 3 (November, 2004): 293.

22. Jianfa Shen, "China's Future Population and Development Challenges," *The Geographical Journal* 164, no. 1 (March 1998): 36.

23. Scott Zhou, "China's reverse population bomb," *Asia Times,* 1 November 2006.

24. Therese Hesketh, Li Lu, and Wei Xing Zhu, "The Effect of China's One-Child Family Policy After 25 Years," *The New England Journal of Medicine* 353, No. 11 (September 15, 2005): 1177.

25. Nicholas Eberstadt, "China's Family Planning Goes Awry," *Far Eastern Economic Review*, 4 December 2009.

26. Therese Hesketh, Li Lu, and Wei Xing Zhu, "The Effect of China's One-Child Family Policy After 25 Years," *The New England Journal of Medicine* 353, No. 11 (September 15, 2005): 1177.

27. Antoaneta Bezlova, "China's Choice: Baby Boom or Bust," *Asia Times*, March 21, 2006.

28. Ibid.

29. Shixiong Cao and Xiuqing Wang, "Unsustainably Low Birth Rates: A Potential Crisis Leading to Loss of Racial and Cultural Diversity in China," *Journal of Policy Modeling* 32, no. 1 (January/ February, 2010): 159-62.

30. Petra Löfstedt, Luo Shusheng and Annika Johansson, "Abortion Patterns and Reported Sex Ratios at Birth in Rural Yunnan, China," *Reproductive Health Matters* 12, No. 24 (Nov., 2004): 86.

31. Sten Johansson and Ola Nygren, "The Missing Girls of China: A New Demographic Account." *Population and Development Review* 17, no. 1 (March, 1991): 25-51.

32. Emily Rauhala, "A Powerhouse Province Wants to Relax China's One-Child Policy-But Don't Bet On a Baby Boom," *Time*, 12 July 2011.

33. Antoaneta Bezlova, "China's Choice: Baby Boom or Bust," *Asia Times*, March 21, 2006.

*Chapter Four*

# The Status of Chinese Women

Women make up half of the population and constitute over 42 percent of the production force in China. China's modernization involves many aspects of Chinese society; and women's participation is one of the aspects of the process of modernization. According to a 2000 United Nations report, women are now responsible for two thirds of the total work load of the world. Seventy-five percent of the rice in the developing countries is produced by women. It is impossible for China to achieve the goal of China's modernization without the full participation of Chinese women. Many Chinese scholars believe that Chinese women fully enjoy women's rights and that their status is higher in comparison to women in Western societies.[1] Yet Western feminist scholars strongly suggest that the status of Chinese women is very low based on the international standard. Chinese women's liberation is unfinished.[2] Can these two different perspectives be reconciled? This chapter will discuss different standards in evaluating women's social status, examine the status of Chinese women during the four historical periods (premoden China, the Republican era of China, the Mao regime, and the post-Mao era) to see the changes of Chinese women over 2,000 years, and argue that the status of Chinese women in contemporary China has been greatly improved, but women's liberation is a dynamic process without an end.

## APPROACHES FOR THE STUDY OF WOMEN'S STATUS

A variety of approaches are employed by feminist scholars to study Chinese women, but each approach has its own disadvantages. First is the language approach. This approach studies women's issues through an interpretation of the Chinese language. The Chinese writing form is not a Romanized language system, but a vocal symbol system which has experienced historical changes reflecting human relationships in the Chinese historical context. Robin Tolmach Lakoff has examined the relationship between language and gender difference and concluded that "women's language" expresses power-lessness that continues to this day.[3] The Chinese language treats Chinese women "as an oppressed group that is subjugated by men," and offers a "striking illustration of the male as norm syndrome, which was the center of the society."[4]

Chinese scholars also suggest that Chinese language reflects that Chinese culture is anti-women in terms of the structure of the language. For instance, about 238 Chinese characters come with the radical "woman" (in Chinese symbol 女) and can be divided into six categories: name, marriage and birth, relatives and social status, appearance, feeling and behaviors, and disease. However, about 70 percent of these Chinese characters, except neutral terms, have derogatory natures. All these derogatory terms are related to the meaning of disobedience, disrespect, greed, unhappiness, anger, quarrelling, gossip, stupidity, arrogance, and promiscuousness.[5] The term "woman" in the Chinese language is composed of two characters, 婦 女. The left part of the first character refers to female. This is a photographic ancient Chinese character that vividly pictures ancient Chinese women's gesture, kneeling on the ground, indicating the lower status of Chinese women. The right part of the first character literally refers to the word "broom." When the two parts are put together, 婦 portrays a woman holding a broom, cleaning the house. This Chinese character clearly signifies Chinese women were assigned to domestic work and women's position in their family. In addition, the pronunciation of the character 婦 is the same as both Chinese characters 服 and 伏 (*fu*). This indicates that 婦 and 服 and 伏 derived from the same origin. 服 refers to obedience, and 伏 refers to kneeling on the ground, thus, Chinese women must absolutely obey their father and husband.[6] However, the linguistic approach may help in discovering the status of Chinese women in ancient China but it is hardly applied to the study of Chinese women in contemporary China, due to the fact that contemporary Chinese language has basically inherited ancient Chinese language without fundamental changes. Thus, this approach cannot reflect the significant changes of Chinese women in present-day China.

Second is the religious approach. This approach can offer two opposite interpretations concerning women's status. The first interpretation insists that everyone, including women, is equal before God; whoever believes in God can be saved. This interpretation is based on the Old Testament, in which "Eve is created directly by God, totally equal with Adam. Adam's reference to woman as flesh of his flesh, bone of his bone, is not degrading to Eve. Both of them stand before God."[7] The second type of interpretation views God's existence as rooted in the existence of men, not women. In pre-Christian Greece, women were commonly regarded as evil and untrustworthy. In the Bible, both Adam and Eve were punished, because they disobeyed God. Although human beings can be redeemed through a union with Jesus Christ, redemption, for a long time, was defined as man's attainment of moral and ethical elevation. Redemption excluded women. Some Western theologians called women the gate of Hell. In Islamic faith, women hold an inferior social status and Islamic stricture makes "religious professions almost exclusively a male preserve."[8] Moreover, "women are considered ritually polluting and unclean" for many religious rituals in many societies, because of their "dirty bodies," referring to menstrual blood, semen, urine, feces, and pus.[9] Thus, women are prohibited to worship God at Islamic mosques in some countries. The religious approach is apparently not the best way to study Chinese women, not only because the two opposite arguments can both find their theological basis in the Bible, but also because the majority of the Chinese people who are deeply influenced by humanist culture are not easily convinced by this religious interpretation.

The third approach is biological. Based on biology, women in many ways—including the body's structure, physique system and physiological function—are different from men.[10] When scholars extend the biological methodology to women's studies, they believe that women's distinguishing biological factors determine women's basic roles in the family and society. According to the biological approach, the oppression of women is rooted in the nature of men. However, sexual difference is a permanent phenomenon; thus women's liberation becomes an impossible task. Phyllis Andors notes, "Many social scientists, perhaps influenced by Freudian psychology, apparently have assumed that biological factors prevent women from successfully integrating their sexual biological roles with economic or political roles outside the family."[11] As Lynda Birke observes, "Biology is relevant to feminism,"[12] but feminism cannot be replaced by biology, because their starting points are different.

Fourth is the gender approach. The gender approach has two dimensions. Distinctions between men and women are associated with biological factors, but human beings are social animals by nature. The gender perspective is more social than biological. The distinction between sex and gender is "an important step in the understanding of women's position."[13] Gender is a cultural construct: the distinction in roles, behaviors, and mental and emotional characteristics between females and males developed by a society.[14] Thus, gender analysis does not simply divide human beings into two biological groups, male and female, but adds unique social meanings to the characteristics and behaviors of each gender group. In the Chinese context, *yin yang* theory is the earliest philosophical notion to explain gender. Chinese scholars distinguished male and female by using the terms *yin* and *yang*. This theory provides a philosophical basis for labor divisions between men and women. Chinese feminists adopted the gender perspective in their writings in the

Republican era, but this perspective was forbidden during the Mao era, in which feminism was treated as a capitalist idea, a negative term; and in the post-Mao era, feminism has been reinterpreted, using it to denote the advocacy of women's rights and the women's movement. The feminist approach integrates with socialism, becoming a Marxist feminism. Furthermore, feminism overemphasizes the oppression of women by men, giving less attention to the structure of social oppression and to the explanation of the complexities of class, race, sex, nation, age, and sexual orientation. [15]

Fifth is the Marxist approach. The Marxist approach holds that men and women should be equal, but the principle of equality between the sexes can only be fulfilled in the Communist society. According to Marxism, in capitalist societies, the exploitation of female labor was derived from the ruling class, capitalists, ultimately from the capitalist economic and political system. Socialist society brings women to the first stage of women's liberation, and the Communist society—a classless society—provides a sufficient condition and delivers women into the highest stage of women's liberation. When feminism works with both Marxism and the Communist government, it becomes an established Marxist feminism. In fact, the theory of women's liberation does not exist in Marxism, because Marxism views women as "workers" and "class," but not as "women." [16] In this sense, Marxism is sex and race blind. A lack of theory on women's liberation is the shortcoming of Marxist approach.

Sixth is the modernization approach. This approach suggests that economic development is a decisive factor that promotes women's liberation, and that the resolution of the women's liberation is "dependent upon the future success of economic modernization." [17] Claudie Broyelle in 1976 pointed out that modernization does not always mean liberating women. [18] Nowadays, many scholars observe that while modernization creates more job opportunities, it has in effect brought more trouble to women than benefits. The reform movement helps modernization; in turn, it creates new problems for women. The reform movement even sacrificed women's interests and made women's problems worse. [19]

There is not a unified standard to evaluate the status of women in the international society. In 1931, Tseng Pao-sun suggested that "with such a historical background, we may consider the typical Chinese woman from three aspects: education, marriage, and social status." [20] Seventy years later, Tan Lin has developed a similar set of standards, which include four categories—education, employment, marriage, and reproduction. [21] Liu Shuang puts women's health at the top of her categories, followed by education, women's employment, marriage, and the percentage of housewives among married women. [22] In 2001, the All-China Women's Federation (ACWF) conducted a sample survey of Chinese women's social status. The questions on the survey included nine categories: economy, politics, education, marriage, family, health, lifestyle, law, and gender conceptions. The result of the survey suggested that the first standard should be women's legal rights.[23] The Chinese Academy of Social Sciences has also developed a model of standards to evaluate the status of women's lives and views women's rights to education as the basic criteria for evaluating women's status.[24]

It will reach different conclusions if different standards are applied to evaluate the status of Chinese women. At the Conference of Montreal Canada in 1988, the status of Chinese women was categorized at number 132 among 160 countries. This evaluation was based on six categories, including attitudes toward baby girls, school enrollment rates, employment rates, the percentage of females in civil service and government positions, women's position in the family, and the percentage of women's property in society. Interestingly, in the same year, when the Committee of Population Crisis of the United States analyzed world's women's status, Chinese women's status was listed number 51 among 99 countries. This evaluation is based on a different evaluating standard, which consisted of five standards. Women's health is at the top of the five categories, followed by marriage, education, employment, and social justice and equality.[25]

What is the most important aspect among different categories in evaluating the status of Chinese women in the Chinese context? There are many components to women's lives, but the standard of living is the most basic aspect of them. China is still a developing country. A great number of Chinese women still live in poverty. The top priority for Chinese women is to make China prosperous and therefore to make Chinese women affluent. This explains why some popular Western feminist issues are not the top priority of Chinese feminism, including abortion, single motherhood, body image, eating disorders, gender stereotypes, lesbian issues, and sexuality. According to the Conference of China Women's Forum held in Beijing in August 2005, six themes were the hottest topics among Chinese feminists, including women and management, women and economy, women and education, women and health, women and law, and women and environment.[26] Obviously, the goal of eliminating poverty and improving the living standard of Chinese women remains an urgent priority.

## CHINESE WOMEN IN THE PRE-COMMUNIST ERA

The conventional idea in the Chinese academy is that in pre-communist China women occupied a very low place and were the "moral and intellectual inferiors of men and require guidance, care, and control."[27] They were oppressed, powerless, passive, and silent. Regardless of a woman's class background or geographical location, the chance of her escaping all of the preceding women's experiences was rare.[28] Tao Jie, in his introduction of the recent book *Holding Up Half the Sky*, a collection of essays written by China's most distinguished women scholars, points out that "during China's long history of feudalism, women were always a marginal group deprived of political and economic rights. They were excluded from social life, confined to the household, and reduced to a state of dependence on men."[29]

Chinese women only played a marginal role before the Revolution of 1911.[30] Chinese women suffered the most from the male-dominated culture, a prejudiced legal system, an inhuman ethical code, and a patriarchal social structure that reinforced men's political power, physical power, and psychological power over women. The four powers of the society—the authority of the clan, the authority of the divine, the authority of the husband, and the authority of political power—sustained the unequal relationship between Chinese men and women. For more than 2,000 years, the double chains—footbinding and inhuman ethical codes—caged Chinese women in the domestic sphere. Before marriage, women as daughters were the property of their parents; after marriage, women as wives were subject to the authority of their husbands; and after their husbands died, women as widows had to obey their sons or mother-in-laws. In addition, traditional ethical codes, such as the Four Virtues—proper speech, modest manner, diligent work, and filial piety—were social shackles to strictly prohibit Chinese women from social activities, and furthermore, they forced Chinese women to be good daughters, good wives, good mothers, and good mother-in-laws. All human rights, such as property rights, divorce rights, work rights, educational rights, and political rights, were the Chinese man's patent. A Chinese woman did not even have the right to marry the person she loved, or to divorce a person she did not love. A Chinese saying states, "If you marry a chicken, you must stay with the chicken; if you marry a dog, you must obey the dog."[31] Therefore, if you wanted to be a human being, you had to be a man in premodern China.[32]

In recent years, both Western and Chinese scholars have challenged the victim theory. In Western societies, feminist scholars have attempted to explore the contributions of Chinese women to Chinese society. Francesca Bray discusses women's power through a study of the women's handcraft industry, especially spinning and weaving. According to Bray, because Chinese women greatly contributed to the textile industry, they had power, which was not only economic power, but also a moral power in the family.[33] Based on a study of how female poets established a literature position during the seventeenth century, Dorothy Ko points out that it is too simplistic to summarize the nature of Chinese women only by using the term "victim."[34] Du Fangqin and Margery Wolf explain that women gained a mother's power in the patriarchal family through giving birth to a son. A mother's power strategically challenged the male's rule and strengthened the traditional male's power at the same time. This argument points to a new research direction making a distinction between the term "women" as a general group of women and the term "mother" as a specific group of women. The mother-in-law had more power, including three rights: the right to admonish her husband, educate their children, and regulate their daughter-in-law. If a daughter-in-law wanted to be a mother-in-law and exercise the power, she must have improved herself in four areas, including moral integrity, her abilities to manage her home, housework skills, and contribution to the family.[35]

In China, a long time ago, Hu Shih argued that Chinese women in pre-communist China made significant contributions to Chinese political life, to the world of scholarship and literature, and to children's education.[36] Modern Chinese writer Lin Yutang argued that the idea that Chinese women were oppressed was originated by Western people without careful investigation.[37] Ye Xiaochuan argued that Chinese women had civil rights and in some respects, traditional Chinese law protected Chinese women's rights. For example, both men and women were required to pay taxes, to participate in large labor projects, to join the army, and to receive an informal education. Traditional law prohibited sexual harassment, severely punished sexual criminals, and promoted the spirit of filial piety. In ancient China, both mothers and fathers were called parents and received respect from their children. Whoever killed his/her parent would be punished by death. Traditional Chinese law also treated female criminals leniently and protected women's birthrights. In the Han dynasty the Chinese government carried out the system of probationary suspension for pregnant women, meaning they would not have to take the instrument of torture and were not subject to the death penalty.[38] Fang Xuejia, through his recent folklorist inspection tour in Meixian in Eastern Guangdong province, has collected a wealth of ancient documents about changes in women's property rights that lead him to conclude that Meixian's women in the traditional clan society held a significant status level in that ancient society.[39]

## CHINESE WOMEN IN COMMUNIST CHINA

There is a significant divergence of views on the issue of women's status in contemporary China. Chinese official gender ideology suggests that the main causes of women's oppression are private ownership, a low level of social production, and traditional culture.[40] The Chinese government has declared since the CPC came to power in 1949, the fundamental cause of women's oppression has been removed. Chinese women are being given more guarantees of enjoyment of equal rights and opportunities.[41] According to China's *White Paper: The Situation of Chinese Women*, since the mid-nineteenth century, Chinese women along with the entire nation waged a dauntless struggle, including the Taiping uprising in 1850s, the reform movement of

1898, and the Revolution of 1911, but they all failed to bring about funda-mental change in the situation of women. After the establishment of the People's Republic of China, Chinese women have achieved truly historic advances toward the goal of equality, development and peace.[42]

The mainstream of Chinese scholars agrees that Chinese women have achieved liberation in the legal, economic, political, educational, and marital spheres. For example, *Overview of Social Status of Chinese Women* (1993) conducted by a research group, Yongping Jiang's *Women's Status in Con-temporary China* (1995), Ping Zhang's *The Current Situation of Chinese Women* (1995), Xiaoling Zhang's *Women and Human Rights* (1998), and Li Xiaojiang assert that the level of Chinese women's liberation is higher than that of Western women and that the task of liberating women had been accomplished under the leadership of the CPC. They argue that "the status of Chinese women in social life and the level of recognition by society has been relatively high" as "compared with the status of women in the West,"[43] because Chinese women and men have equal rights legally and practically.

However, the assessment of the overseas Chinese scholar is significantly different. Wen Lang Li suggests that there is no evidence to support the assessment that "Chinese women have drastically improved their status under the communist regime."[44] In fact, the gap between the rhetoric of women's liberation and the reality of gender discrimination has widened.[45] Some Western scholars observe that "the Chinese revolution merely reconsti-tuted gender inequality in a different form,"[46] because the Communist Revo-lution of 1949 in essence was a peasant revolution. The victory of commu-nism actually meant that patriarchal tradition prevailed again in China. The party made efforts in women's liberation, especially in the brief period of 1952-53.[47] To get popular support, the CPC launched the Land Reform Movement in the beginning of the 1950s and distributed land to peasants, including women. Not long after Chinese women had the right to possess land, the new government in 1953 launched the Collective Movement that collectivized peasants' land into Soviet-style collective farms. Consequently, the Great Leap Forward and the Commune Movement resulted in the col-lapse of the Chinese economy and a great shortage of food. More than10 million Chinese people starved to death in the early 1960s. The CPC did not draw a lesson from that cost. Instead, Mao called for another political and ideological campaign—the Cultural Revolution (1966-76), which brought China into unprecedented and overall chaos. The Cultural Revolution "oblit-erated natural sex difference" and stripped "women of their female nature and by default masculinzing the feminine."[48]

The essential standard for women's liberation is human freedom and overall development, whereby women's liberation is both a social issue and an individual one. The concept of "overall development" covers many areas, including personal, material, and spiritual life, as well as legal rights to employment, property, political participation, education, and religion. By using this definition to examine the level of women's liberation, it is undeniably true that the status of women in China has increased in some spheres in the post-Mao era, especially in education, social welfare benefits, employment, and political participation. However, the Reform Movement is not always favorable to women's liberation. The next chapter will continue to discuss the relationship between women's life and the reform movement.

More importantly, women's rights are part of human rights in a global context. After World War II, the United Nations proclaimed the *Universal Declaration of Human Rights* "as a common standard of achievement for all peoples and all nations,"[49] and required all nations to "place social, economic and cultural rights on the same level as civil and political rights."[50] In 1979, the General Assembly adopted th*e Convention on the Elimination of All Forms of Discrimination against Women* (CEDAW), which addresses the most important issues for women's lives: poverty, employment, participation, religion, non-government sector, family, population, communication, and health. Because all of these issues contain universal values, since 1979 more than 120 countries "have ratified the UN's Convention for the Elimination of Discrimination against Women (CEDAW)."[51]

The CPC has reviewed the Universal Declaration of Human Rights and the CEDAW as Western rigths. The CPC argues that China maintains the socialist political system with it as the sole leadership of the country. Women's rights must be practiced under the guidance of Marxism. The goal of Marxism is to emancipate all humankind, but the idea of human rights is to meet the needs of individual egos. The Chinese government gradually changed its tone toward women's rights, after China launched the Reform Movement. In 1995, China hosted the Fourth World Conference on Women in Beijing. The Declaration of the Fourth World Conference on Women recognizes women's rights as an inalienable and an integral part of all human rights; determines to empower and advance women's rights, including the rights to freedom of thought, conscience, religion and belief, and participation on the basis of equality in all spheres of society; reaffirms the right of women to control all aspects of their health; eliminates all forms of discrimination against women; promotes women's economic independence; and ensures women's equal access to economic resources, including science and technology, vocational training, information, communication, and markets. However, there is still a large gap between the Chinese government's goals and reality. Even the Chinese government has acknowledged that "the condition of Chinese women is still not wholly satisfactory. There exist various difficulties and resistances which have prevented the full realization of equal rights to women with respect to their participation in political and government affairs, employment, access to education, as well as marriage and family."[52]

# CONCLUSION

Since gender study is a multidisciplinary project, it is necessary to adopt a comprehensive approach to examine the status of Chinese women. Chinese women were deeply oppressed in pre-communist China. The status of Chinese women has significantly improved under the Communist regime. Some scholars question whether the CPC changed the direction of women's liberation after the party came to power in 1949. Judith Stacey affirms that socialist China is a patriarchal system[53] and Kay Ann Johnson points out that the road of socialist China "has restored, preserved and utilized traditional rural communities and traditional family orientations and obligations."[54] Socialist China actually is built on a feudal social base, because the nature of the communist revolution is a peasant revolution. It is safe to say that women's liberation is a dynamic but slow process in contemporary China. While acknowledging the achievements the CPC has made, the era of women's liberation in China is unfinished. Instead, there is a long way to go before Chinese women fully enjoy liberation. It is a misconception that Chinese women have fully achieved liberation. The future of women's liberation in the Chinese context does not only depend on feminism, but largely depends on women's own efforts combined with the process of China's modernization and democratization.

# NOTES

1. Xiaojiang Li, "Economic Reform and the Awakening of Chinese Women's Collective Consciousness," in *Engendering China: Women, Culture, and the State*, ed. by Christina K. Gilmartin (Cambridge: Harvard University Press, 1994).

2. Phyllis Andors, *The Unfinished Liberation of Chinese Women, 1949-1980* (Bloomington: Indiana University Press, 1983), 2.

3. See Robin Tolmach Lakoff, *Language and Woman's Place: Text and Commentaries* (Oxford: Oxford University Press, 2004).

4. Kate Burridge and Ng Bee-Chin, "Writing the Female Radical: The Encoding of Women in the Writing System," in *Dress, Sex, and Text in Chinese Culture*, eds. Antonia Finnane and Anne McLaren (Australia: Monash Asia Institute, 1999), 110.

5. Li Huayuan, "Han zi suo fan ying de fu nü xing xiang," *Beijing Shi Fan Da Xue Xue Bao*, Special Issue (2003), 18.

6. Tang Yaping, "Cong bu fen nüpang gou xing de han zi guan gui gu dai fu nü de she hui de wei," *Xue Shu Tan Su* 8 (2003): 64.

7. Shui Jingjun, "In Search of Sacred Women's Organizations," in *Chinese Women Organizing: Cadres, Feminists, Muslims, Queers,* eds. Ping-Chun Hsiung, Maria Jaschok and Cecilia with Red Chang (London: Berg, 2001), 110.

8. Maria Jaschok and Shui Jingjun, *The History of Women's Mosques in Chinese Islam: A Mosque of Their Own* (Richmond, England: Curzon Press, 2000), 242.

9. Emily M. Ahern, "The Power and Pollution of Chinese Women," in *Women in Chinese Society,* eds. Margery Wolf and Roxane Witke (Stanford, Calif.: Stanford University Press, 1975), 193.

10. Li Jin Feng, "Yu yan xing bie li lun fa zhang yu xi fang nü xing zhu yi si chao," *Fu N ü Yan Jiu Lun Cong* 6 (2004): 50.

11. Andors, *The Unfinished Liberation of Chinese Women, 1949-1980*, 2.

12. Lynda Birke, *Women, Feminism and Biology: The Feminist Challenge* (New York: Methuen, 1986), vii.

13. Michele Barrett, *Women's Oppression Today: Problems in Marxist Feminist Analysis* (London: Verso Editions and NLB, 1980), 43.

14. Quoted in Dorothy Ko, *Teachers of the Inner Chambers: Women and Culture in Seventeenth-Century China* (Stanford, Calif.: Stanford University Press, 1994), 5.

15. Carol Ehrlich, "The Unhappy Marriage of Marxism and Feminism: Can it Be Saved?," in *Women and Revolution: A Discussion of the Unhappy Marriage of Marxism and Feminism*, ed. Lydia Sargent (Boston: South End Press, 1981), 110.

16. Lydia Sargent, "New Left Women and Men: The Honeymoon Is Over," in *Women and Revolution: A Discussion of the Unhappy Marriage of Marxism and Feminism*, ed. Lydia Sargent (Boston: South End Press, 1981), xxi.

17. Andors, *The Unfinished Revolution of Chinese Women, 1949-80*, 168.

18. Claudie Broyelle, *Women's Liberation in China* (Atlantic Highlands, N.J.: Humanities Press International, 1977), 9.

19. Sharon Wesoky, *Chinese Feminism Faces Globalization* (New York: Routledge, 2002), 58.

20. Tseng Pao-sun, "The Chinese Woman Past and Present," in *Chinese Women: Through Chinese Eyes*, ed. Li Yu-ning (Armonk, New York: M.E. Sharpe, 1992), 76.

21. Tan Lin, "Quan qiu hua de tiao zhan: she hui xing bie shi jiao de fen xi." *Ha Er Bing Shi Wei Dang Xiao Xue Bao* 1 (2004): 31-34.

22. Quoted in Liu Hongyan and Jie Zhenming, "Zhong guo fu nü wen ti yan jiu," *(Study on Chinese Women's Problems)*. http://www.cpirc.org.cn/paper5.htm (12 June 2005).

23. The Group of the Research Project, "The Social Problems of the Second Generation of Chinese Women," *Fu Nü Yan Jiu Lun Cong (Journal of Women's Studies)* 5 (2001): 5.

24. According to the Chinese Academy of Social Sciences, women's rights to education are the key to evaluating women's status, including schooling age and years, the female enrollment rate at schools, and the percentage of women receiving professional training. The second standard is women's rights to employment, including women's employment age, level, and satisfaction. The third standard is women's income, including the percentage of women who receive income, and the source of women's income. The fourth standard is women's marriage, including freedom of marriage and divorce, remarriage, and women's power in family business. The fifth standard is women's rights to determine their family size, the rights to make a decision to have a baby, and the rights to use contraception. The sixth standard is women's rights to manage family property, income, and inheritance. The seventh standard is women's rights to make decisions about buying homes, building homes, moving, and supporting their parents and relatives. The seventh standard is women's housework, and the percentage of time spent doing housework.

25. According to the Committee of Population Crisis of the United States, the standard consists of five components. Women's health is at the top of the five categories, including infant mortality rate, the broader population mortality rate, female life expectancy, and the difference between male life expectancy and female life expectancy. The second standard encompassed many aspects of marriage, including female child marriage rate, birth rate, the rate of contraception among married women, the divorce rate, the proportion of unmarried men and women, and the proportion of widows and widowers. Women's educational level is the third standard, which included female teacher rates in schools, female enrollment in elementary and middle schools, and illiteracy rates for men and women, respectively. The fourth standard pertained to women's employment, including female employment rates above age 15, paid job rates above age 15, and percentage of female management positions above age 15. The fifth standard is women's social justice and equality, which included economic, political, legal, and social equality.

26. See *Dou Wei News*, http://www7.chinesenewsnet.com/gb/Main News/SinoNews/ Mainland/zxs_2005-08-05_608444.shtml (10 October 2005).

27. Lisa Raphals, *Sharing the Light: Representations of Women and Virtue in Early China* (Albany, New York: State University of New York Press, 1998), 2.

28. Quoted in Lin Yu-tang, "Feminist Thought in Ancient China," in *Chinese Women Through Chinese Eyes*, ed. Li Yu-ning (Armonk, N.Y.: M. E. Sharpe, 1992), 35.

29. Tao Jie, "Introduction," in *Holding Up Half the Sky*, eds. Tao Jie, Zheng Bijun, and Shirley L. Mow (New York: The Feminist Press, 2004), xxii.

30. Tonglin Lu, "Intruduction," in *Gender and Sexuality in Twentieth-Century Chinese Literature and Society*," ed. by Tonglin Lu (New York: State University of New York Press, 1993), 1.

31. Ziyun Li, "Women's Consciousness and Women's Writing," in *Engendering China: Women, Culture, and the State*, 301.

32. Lu, "Intruduction," 1.

33. See Francesca Bray, *Technology and Gender: Fabrics of Power in Late Imperial China* (Berkeley: University of California Press, 1997).

34. See Ko, *Teachers of the Inner Chambers: Women and Culture in Seventeenth-Century China*, 1994.

35. Wang Bing and Lin Jie, "Lun zhong guo gu dai de pu quan," *Shan Xi Shi Da Xue Bao* 1 (2003), 102.

36. Hu Shih, "Women's Place in Chinese History," in *Chinese Women Through Chinese Eyes*, ed. Li Yu-ning (Armonk, N.Y.: M.E. Sharpe, 1992), 3-15.

37. Wang Fengxian, "Dui mu qing she hui xing bie de si kao," *Zhe Jian Xue Kan* 2 (2000), 99.

38. Ye Xiaochuan, "Nü xing yu zhong guo chuan tong fa lü wen hua," *Zhong Hua Nü Zi Xue Yuan Xue Bao* 1 (2004), 59.

39. Fang Xuejia, "Guan yu nü xing zai chuan tong she hui zhong di wei de si kao," *Fu N ü Yan Jiu Lun Cong* 4 (2004), 46.

40. Ma Yan, "Gai ge kai fang yi lai fu nü jie fang ji ben li lun guan dian zong shu," *Fu Nü Yan Jiu*, 6 (2002), 4.

41. State Council of China, *White Paper: Gender Equality and Women's Development*, August 24, 2005, 1.

42. *White Paper: The Situation of Chinese Women*. Released by The Information Office of the State Council Of the People's Republic of China June 1994, Beijing, China, 1.

43. Li, "Economic Reform and the Awakening of Chinese Women's Collective Consciousness," 379.

44. Wen Lang Li, "Changing Status of Women in the PRC," in *Changes in China: Party, State, and Society*, ed. Shao-chuan Leng (New York: University Press of America, 1989), 219.

45. Emily Honig and Gail Hershatter, *Personal Voices: Chinese Women in the 1980s* (Stanford: Stanford University Press, 1988), 309.

46. Quoted in Lisa Rofel, "Liberation Nostalgia and a Yearning for Modernity," in *Engendering China: Women, Culture, and the State*. 234.

47. Kay Ann Johnson, *Women, the Family and Peasant Revolution in China* (Chicago: The University of Chicago Press, 1983), 218-19.

48. Barlow, "Politics and Protocols of Funu: (Un) Making National Woman," in *Engendering China: Women, Culture, and the State*, 347.

49. A. I. Melden, ed. *Human Rights* (Belmont, Calif.: Wadsworth Publishing Company, Inc. 1970), 45.

50. Asbjorn Eide, ed. The Universal Declaration of Human Rights: A Commentary (New York: Scandinavian University Press, 1993), 6.

51. Dorothy McBridge Stetson and Amy Mazur, eds. *Comparative State Feminism* (London: SAGE Publications, 1995), 4.

52. *White Paper: The Situation of Chinese Women*. Released by Information Office of the State Council of the People's Republic of China June 1994, Beijing, China, 2.

53. See Stacey, *Patriarchy and Socialist Revolution in China.*

54. Johnson, *Women, the Family and Peasant Revolution in China*, 218-19.

*Chapter Five*

# Globalization and Chinese Women

Since China reopened its door to the rest of the world in 1978, it has become part of globalization, which has inevitably influenced every aspect of Chinese women's lives in the post-Mao era. Western feminist scholars believe that under the party's moderate policy, independent women's movements and non-government women's organizations have emerged in Chinese society,[1] so the reform movement has made Chinese women's lives better during globalization.[2] The majority of Chinese feminist scholars suggest that Chinese women have gained many more opportunities, including political participation, access to valuable information, and rights to education and employment, making women's lives much better. However, questions remain: What does globalization mean to Chinese women? What are the negative consequences of the reform movement and globalization on Chinese women? How do Chinese women handle the challenges of globalization in the twenty-first century? In order to address the question of what really happens to Chinese women during globalization, this chapter will emphasize the relationship between globalization and Chinese women in a global context through discussing the basic criterion to evaluate women's lives in the Chinese context and examining the negative impacts of globalization on Chinese women.

## WOMEN'S EMPLOYMENT AND WOMEN'S LIVES

The right to employment is the precondition for women to survive and have better lives. Women's employment rights refer to women who have working capabilities, are willing to work, have legal rights to apply for jobs and have equal rights to gain employment without being discriminated against. If women's employment rights are deprived, they cannot secure their daily livelihood and cannot enjoy their rights to property, education, and political

59

participation.[3] Employment provides the means for a woman to be an independent person. If women have regular incomes, they have a voice in the family. However, the status of a woman in the family does not necessarily have to be directly proportional to the level of economic growth. For example, both Sweden and Japan are developed countries, but a Swedish woman's status in the family is the highest in the developed countries while a Japanese woman's status is the lowest. The percentage of Chinese women's income in the family increased from 20 percent in the 1950s to 40 percent in 2008. Women's income in some peasant families even reached 70 percent of the total family income.[4] As a result, Chinese men are no longer the sole power of a household, and "consultation between husband and wife on family decisions was more natural in households where the woman earned."[5] In a survey conducted by *Synovate*, 90 percent of married Chinese female participants claimed that they had at least an equal say in big-ticket purchases, coming in third behind women in the United Kingdom and France. About 77 percent of Chinese women said that they can afford what they want without having to ask for money from their partners, second behind UK women.[6]

Women's employment is important for improving their social status. When a working woman is married, "she is treated with more respect than a jobless woman would be."[7] By being employed, women have a greater chance of having their voice heard in society rather than being a housewife as they were in traditional China. Women, through employment, can build their own self-confidence, allowing them to effectively fight against domination by a patriarchal society. In a recent survey of 300 women at the Department of Education in Shenzhen University, 80 percent of the women expressed that they did not want to lose the equal status they had with their husbands, or to rely on another person to support them. These women wanted to be independent.[8]

However, a higher percentage of women in the work force does not necessarily reflect a higher level of liberation. Li Xiaojiang argues that the level of women's liberation in China is seen as relatively higher than in the West, because the percentage of Chinese women who participate in productive labor is higher than the world average.[9] In fact, bringing women into production is only the first step in giving them meaningful social tasks and control over their own lives.[10] In order to assess the quality of women's lives during globalization, it is imperative to look at factors other than the percentage of female employees, including the type of work they perform, their wages, their working conditions, benefits, promotions, and the social factors associated with women in the workforce. In premodern China, Chinese women were assigned domestic work. In the Republican era, Chinese women began participating in paid jobs, but middle-class women remained at home. The CPC has viewed "the entry of women into the labor force as the key to the liberation."[11] The CPC deserves the credit for opening up ways for Chinese women to participate in productive activities.

Under the Mao regime, Chinese official gender ideology overemphasized participation in labor outside the home.[12] Being a housewife was shameful and was no longer considered a noble profession but a form of a capitalist lifestyle. Women had no choice but to take part in social production. In fact, Chinese women during the Mao era needed to work to make money because their husbands' salaries were not enough to sustain the family's expenses. Although the government issued equal employment guidelines in the early 1960s, men were overwhelmingly assigned to technical jobs and women to non-technical, auxiliary, and service jobs, regardless of their educational level.

In the post-Mao era, the employment rate of Chinese women remains relatively high in comparison with other countries. If more Chinese people are becoming wealthy, why do Chinese women continue to participate in social production in the post-Mao era? In short, Chinese women wanted to maintain the family's financial situation and to have the chance to be independent from their husbands' incomes. By having full-time jobs, women were no longer financially bound to their husbands or families. If they chose to get a divorce or if something unfortunate was to happen to their husband, the job might secure their social and familial status. In addition, the majority of grandparents are happy to take care of their grandchildren, so married Chinese women are able to keep their jobs instead of staying at home to take care of their children. The social welfare system also affects women's employment rate. If a government provides good childcare service, women's employment rises. In the Mao era, every work unit was required to set up a childcare center in order to encourage the participation of Chinese women in social production. Parents would get reimbursement if the work unit did not provide childcare services. Today, some employers continue to carry out this policy.

## THE NEGATIVE IMPACT OF GLOBALIZATION ON CHINESE WOMEN

Scholars generally agree that globalization is the great transnational integration of the world's economies, social norms, cultures, and political systems. Yet, there are different visions of globalization in current academia. Francis Fukuyama claims that the "West is best" in terms of history and economy.[13] However, Samuel P. Huntington purports the theory of "the West versus the rest."[14] Despite their differences, both Fukuyama and Huntington agree that globalization means one-sided Westernization. The rapid development of contemporary technology, transportation, and communication is the precondition of globalization, and expanding capitals and seeking maximum profits are the fundamental driving forces behind it. The flow of capital promotes comprehensive flux, including the flow of invisible information and visible products, relocation of factories, floating populations, and cultural influences. This overall flow creates a variety of opportunities, but brings misfortunes as well, such as disease, pollution, poverty, alienation, and the separation of family members. Chinese women are not only beneficiaries in the process of globalization, but also the greatest victims because female laborers are the first target for capitalists to seek maximum profits.

Globalization has increased women's unemployment rate. The expansion of foreign investment has sped up the process of China's privatization and marketization, especially in the areas of finance, insurance, credit, medical services, the tourist industry, restaurants, hotels, and the cultural industry. Chinese women have more employment opportunities in these areas, and can access valuable information, receive education, exercise their rights, and participate in public affairs while taking care of the home. However, while some people get jobs, other people lose jobs.[15] A significant number of Chinese women are forced into *xia gang* (layoffs). Women constitute over 60 percent of the total unemployment rate. After *xia gang*, they have experienced difficulty in finding new jobs, because they have fewer professional skills. Women's appearances, including weight and height, also affect their chances for employment.[16] Even female college students have great difficulties finding jobs, especially when they have the same qualifications as male college students.[17]

Globalization has created great wealth and but has also sped up the relative poverty of women. Poverty is not a gender neutral phenomenon. The financial situation of women in China has been getting worse in terms of employment benefits, wages, and working conditions. Women are discriminated against in recruitment selection, occupation, pay, promotion, and in the termination of employment. Although the Chinese Constitution stipulates equal pay for equal work, no concrete laws have been laid down to ensure the execution of this mandate.[18] Women earn less than men, but they must pay the same expenses in education, communication, medical treatment, housing, and expense for children. In addition, the gap between the living standard of women in urban areas and rural areas has been widening. According to a nationwide survey conducted by the Women's Federation, 82.6 percent of urban women had pensions versus. 5.6 percent of rural women; 71 percent of urban women had medical coverage versus eight percent of rural women; 79.9 percent of urban women had paid sick leave versus 9.2 percent of rural women; and 85.3 percent of urban women had paid maternity leave versus 12.1 percent of rural women.[19]

Globalization has changed the structure of the labor force. Foreign direct investment has played an important role in reshaping the structure of the labor force in China. The purpose of foreign investors in developing countries is to reduce cost and make maximum profits. In comparison with male workers, female workers are obedient and are more willing to work in poor conditions with low pay. While some "enterprises and government departments often opt to hire men over women figuring men do not require paid maternity leave or days off to deal with family affairs,"[20] some companies, especially in the sectors of finance, insurance, real estate, and science service, have a preference for women workers between the ages of 18 and 30, in order to make more profits.[21] The majority of working Chinese women are relatively less educated. In the manufacturing industry, more than 60 percent of female workers do not have a high school education, but most companies provide no training programs for them and pay little attention to women's potential talents.

Globalization has intensified the competition between workers. Because the "iron rice bowl" (a permanent job in a state-sponsored enterprise) has been smashed, Chinese women feel deeply conscious of the crisis and seriously worry about their financial situations and their children's education. A large number of women have postponed marriage and spend less time with their family members. The dual role of mother and worker can be an obstacle to promotion in the workplace, because "the greater responsibility at home may hinder women from participating in work related activities, such as study meetings organized by work units."[22] Under this circumstance, Chinese women rarely achieve the maximum success, regardless of the task or their ability.[23]

Globalization also results in many social problems, such as domestic violence, adultery, intoxication, addiction to drug and human trafficking, kidnappings, suicides, concubines, and prostitution.[24] Metropolitan areas seem prosperous, but the urban residents are lonely. They heavily rely on cell phones and the Internet in seeking friendship and love. The suicide rate in China is above the world average, and the suicide rate of Chinese women is much higher than Chinese men. Some forms of cultural industry and entertainment that merged during the reform era have basically served only Chinese men. For example, the majority of consumers of KTV, body massage, and foot massage are men.

Chinese women face new challenges in education. Women are doubly burdened with both productive labor and housework after China carried out the household responsibility system. This situation forced some female students to withdraw from schools to take care of their families. In recent years, the tuition fees have increased dramatically. According to an official Chinese report, based on the Standard of the Shanghai Education Department, the tuition fees are as follows: 14,000 *yuan* for three years of kindergarten, 15,000 *yuan* for five years of primary school, 30,000 *yuan* for seven years of secondary school, and 46,000 *yuan* for four years of college. Therefore, a family needs to pay tuition fees of 105,000 *yuan* for one child to complete an education from kindergarten to college.[25] This amount does not include the daily expenses of the student.

## GLOBALIZATION AND FEMALE MIGRANT WORKERS

Globalization promotes the Chinese market economy. In turn, the market economy has produced great domestic urbanization and immigration movement. According to the results of China's Fifth Population Census, the urban population expanded from 172 million in 1978 to 400 million in 2000.[26] The urbanization level in China is expected to reach 50 percent by 2020.[27] If women are the most disadvantaged gender in China, it is the female migrants who are the most disadvantaged population among women. Most Chinese migrants come from the western and central inland regions of China and go to the eastern and coastal urban areas, such as Beijing, Shanghai, and Guangdong provinces.[28] Although women are less likely than men to migrate to urban areas than men, women still represent almost half of this group.[29] Temporary migrants "are attractive to global capitalist investors. Peasant migrants' institutional and social inferiority, and severe labor surplus in the countryside, leave them with few options other than to pursue and tolerate low-paying urban jobs."[30]

Female migrant workers are the cheapest labor in the workforce. Female migrant workers not only receive less pay in comparison with urban workers, but also receive less pay than male migrant workers. Thus, some of the urban jobs are more open to female migrants than their male counterparts, especially in some areas, such as domestic service, textiles, and the trading sector.[31] Since 1978, the number of female migrant workers has dramatically increased and constituted as much as 90 percent of the work force in some factories in special economic zones. The majority of these female employees are unmarried girls (*dagongmei*).[32] Due to the fact that female migrant workers are poorly educated and have fewer working skills, they are more likely to take low quality jobs that seem below the standards of urban Chinese. Female migrant workers are also regarded as easier to control and less likely to prove troublesome.[33]

Female migrant workers face difficult working conditions. In order to pursue maximum profits, the companies usually do not improve the work environment. Noise, dust, and harmful gas have become serious dangers. Employers do not provide clinics, breast feeding rooms, shower rooms, or enough bathrooms for women. A significant number of private and joint venture companies provide no work protection or workers' insurance. Health and safety rules are not properly observed, resulting in frequent accidents.[34] An example of one of these accidents was the 1993 fire at a Shenzhen toy factory that killed seventy-eight female workers.[35] About 60 percent of private employees have not participated in social welfare system. Overtime is enforced in some companies, but the employers do not offer overtime pay. They usually work 12 hours per day, sometimes seven days a week, for 25 cents an hour.[36] Anyone who challenges her employer is most likely to be fired because she can be easily replaced due to a surplus of female labor in China.

Most female migrant workers have not received social benefits from the government. Many of these manufacturing factories are private and do not provide social services. Migrant workers officially hold a rural *hukou* and are generally excluded from social security and welfare benefits that are given to urban workers. According to a 2003 study on a group of almost 5,000 migrants in Shanghai, only 14 percent were provided health insurance whereas 79 percent of urban or permanent residents received this service.[37] While in some cases it is possible to purchase temporary or even permanent residency cards, it is extremely expensive and the majority of migrant women do not earn enough to do so. Even if a rural migrant woman marries an urban resident, she does not gain urban residency status. Furthermore, if the couple has children, they inherit their mother's *hukou*, making it difficult for mothers to find decent education for her children. While some wealthier rural migrants are able to purchase an urban *hukou*, the majority of migrants will never make enough to be able to change their *hukou.*

Female migrant workers always face both gender and social discrimination. Migrants are often thought of as being poor, dirty, ignorant and prone to violence. Female migrant workers also suffer from other issues. Sexual disease is one of the main concerns for female migrant workers. Young female migrants feel a sense of freedom after leaving their often conservative families in the countryside, and adopt different ideas about premarital sex. However, most of these Chinese women don't receive proper education about these issues when they migrate to cities. If they contract a sexual disease, they are reluctant to visit a doctor because they believe that they will be looked down upon in these urban health centers.[38] In addition, the majority of female migrants are young and single women. After they arrive in urban areas, they are confronted with a shocking new world of modernity and find themselves completely isolated from familiar social networks. In this new environment, it is common for these women to have feelings of loneliness, alienation, low self-esteem, and feel disconnected from social relationships. Consequently, most female migrant workers may not be aware of their mental health issues if they have them, and do not seek psychiatric consultation in the initial stages of psychiatric illness.[39]

## KEYS TO IMPROVING CHINESE WOMEN'S LIVES

It is a comprehensive project to improve women's lives in a global context. First and foremost, Chinese women must nurture their full self-consciousness. Women's rights are inalienable rights, which are neither created by any great man nor bestowed by the CPC. The government and law-makers only legalize and protect women's rights. Self-consciousness without financial resources does not help women achieve full liberation. Financial independence is one of the preconditions for better lives for women. However, many Chinese people, including Chinese women, believe that women are only helpers and men are the real bread-winners, and suggest that women should sacrifice their careers to become virtuous wives and good mothers.[40] Some still do not believe a woman can have a real profession and run a good home at the same time.[41] The voice of "women staying at home" has reemerged in China. According to a survey, about 43.8 percent of men and 37.4 percent of women supported the idea that men are responsible for public work and women are responsible for domestic work.[42] During the meetings of the National People's Congress and the National Political Consultative Conference in 2001, Wang Xiancai, delegate of the National Political Consultative Conference, put forward a proposal in which he suggested that women return home. Some other delegates echoed his proposal. Feminist scholars suggest that the idea of "women going home" actually deprives women of their rights and duties.[43] The majority of Chinese women believe that serving society is more important than doing housework, so they would rather endure the double burdens of housework and public work.

The Chinese government should take all necessary measures to promote the women's movement. In the centralized countries, the role of government in improving women's lives is critical. Under the centralized political system, government policy has gender implications and effects on the social status of women,[44] although the process of improving women's rights must still go through the government and legislation. The government can do many good things for women, e.g., provide childcare, enforce equal pay and equal opportunity, defend a women's right to choose abortion, legislate maternity leave policies, and protect reproductive freedom. Some other issues must also be put on the political agenda, like the legalization of abortion, child custody and access rights, domestic violence against women, rape, incest, pornography, and antidiscrimination legislation.[45] The Chinese government should provide sufficient financial resources to support women's organizations and other feminist activities. China is still a developing country. The government is more concerned with economic growth than with social justice and women's rights. In all communist societies, "the matter of women's liberation has taken second place to the seemingly larger goal of class struggle."[46] With the development of the market economy, the Chinese government is increasingly sensitive to women's affairs.[47] To obtain funding, women's organizations have to comply with Marxist ideology and principles. This inevitably leads to the emergence of "bread feminists"[48] who do not represent women's interests, but rather represent themselves for money. As a result, the role of feminist activities is marginalized in China.

Feminist scholars view the government agency's role in the women's movement as state feminism, which employs administrators and bureaucrats in positions of power, including female politicians advocating gender equality politics.[49] State feminism originally refers to both institutionalization of feminist interests and the activities of government organizations that are charged with women's affairs.[50] In the past thirty years, many democratic societies have established agencies for women and governments have given these institutions the responsibility to achieve what H.M. Hernes calls "feminism from above, or state feminism."[51]

Government agencies for women basically play two major roles. The first role of the government agency is to influence policy. In other words, government agencies must participate in "the formation of feminist policies that promote the status of women and/or undermine patterns of gender hierarchy."[52] The second role is to promote policy access, which is "the degree to which women's policy machineries develop opportunities for society-based actors—feminist and women's advocacy organizations—to exert influence on feminist policies."[53]

Women's rights and the government's goals are not always the same. The central goal of feminism is to gain women's rights, but the goal of government is to develop economy and maintain social stability. Many governments, including democratic societies, do not view women's interests as a top priority. Thus, the conflict between feminism and government is obvious. Sometimes, a government agency for women is "more symbolic than material" and may have "failed to generate the means to ensure the effective use of the new policy instruments to help women."[54]

Generally speaking, democratic government helps women more; non-democratic government helps women less, or even harms the feminist movements. Thus, it is very important to develop a civil society for state feminism to play more important roles in improving lives for Chinese women. A well-developed civil society can ensure an independent women's movement representation of women's interests in working with government agencies. A civil society is a vital ingredient for the development of feminism.[55] Under the current Chinese political system, the government offers very limited freedom to non-governmental organizations. The relationship between the feminist movement and the ACWF (All-China Women's Federation) is only symbolic. Ellen R. Judd notes that the Chinese feminist movement is very different from similar movements in the West because it is dominated by the ACWF.[56] When Jude Howell studies the relationship between the communist state and feminism, she uses the term "state-derived feminism" instead of the term "state feminism," in order to make a distinction between feminism within a democratic system and feminism within the communist political system.[57] Although there are approximately 6,000 women's organizations in China today, all these organizations are controlled by the leadership of the CPC. The largest women's organization, the ACWF, is actually a branch of the CPC because the heads of the ACWF are appointed by the CPC and the task of the ACWF is to implement the party's policy.[58] Under these circumstances, how can the ACWF represent Chinese women's interests and fight for women's rights? How can women's organizations "carry out independent, autonomous and effective work to satisfy the needs of the majority of women?"[59]

It should be noted that there is no direct relationship between the number of women's seats in legislative assemblies and women's liberation. Some Western feminists think that more seats held by women in congress result in more power for women and that more female politicians will result in governance that is more responsive to women because women can only have an influence when they have the numbers.[60] In China, about 20 percent of the representatives in the National People's Congress are female, yet they have no way of representing women's interests. The female representatives of the Congress in communist China have no real political power, but are only filling a quota—"creating the illusion of equality."[61] Female political participants primarily serve the interests of the Chinese government, and the political dependence of women is reinforced for structural and ideological support.[62]

## CONCLUSION

There are different perspectives in evaluating the status of Chinese women, but right to employment is the precondition for women to survive and have better lives in a developing country. By this standard, the status of Chinese women during globalization has generally improved, but the living standard of Chinese women relatively has decreased in comparison with Chinese women and women in developed countries. Poverty is not a gender neutral phenomenon; and women are the poorest among the poor, because they are the first victims of global capital during globalization. Globalization has both positive and negative impacts on Chinese women. The reform movement provides great opportunities for Chinese women, but it creates misfortunes for Chinese women as well. Some women are losing jobs while some are getting jobs. To improve the status of Chinese women, in addition to nurturing the self consciousness of women's rights, the Chinese government must take all necessary measures to promote the women's movement and protect women's rights. In this sense, state feminism will play a vital role in improving Chinese women's status and enhancing their power during globalization. However, it is unrealistic to expect Chinese government to support an independent women's movement within the current political system, because the government views the independent women's movement as a threat to the stability of the regime. Nevertheless, it is impossible for Chinese women to fully enjoy women's rights without an independent women's movement.

## NOTES

1. Wesoky, Sharon, *Chinese Feminism Faces Globalization* (New York: Routledge, 2002).

2. Brian Hoepper, Brown Hennessey, Deborah Henderson, and Walton Mills, eds. *Global Voices: Historical Inquiries for the 21st Century* (John Wiley and Sons Publisher, 2005).

3. Zhang Lixia, "Shi lun wo guo fu nü jiu ye quan de fa lü bao hu," (*Legal Issues of Chinese Women's Employment*) He Nan Da Xue Xue Bao (*Journal of He Nan University*) 1 (2004), 105.

4. Li Yinhe, "Fu nü, jia ting yu sheng yu," (*Women and Family*) Jiangsu She Hui Ke Xue 4 (*Social Science of Jiangsu*) (2004): 170.

5. Delia Davin, *Woman-Work: Women and the Party in Revolutionary China* (New York: Oxford University Press, 1980), 150.

6. Quoted in Yu Zhong, "Women master men . . . and their wallets," *China Daily,* 23 January 2005.

7. Davin, *Woman-Work: Women and the Party in Revolutionary China*, 150.

8. Mary Erbaugh, "Chinese Women Face Increased Discrimination," *Off Our Backs: A Women's News Journal* 20, No. 33 (March 1990): 9.

9. Xiaojiang Li, "Economic Reform and the Awakening of Chinese Women's Collective Consciousness," in *Engendering China: Women, Culture, and the State*, 376.

10. Marilyn B. Young, *Women in China: Studies in Social Change and Feminism*. (Michigan: Center for Chinese Studies, the University of Michigan, 1973), 164.

11. John Bauer, "Gender Inequality in Urban China," *Modern China* 18, no. 3 (1992): 333.

12. Chris Berry, "Representing Chinese Women: Researching Women in the Chinese Cinema," in *Dress, Sex and Text in Chinese Culture,* eds. Antonia Finnane and Anne McLaren (Australia: Monash Asia Institute, 1999), 201.

13. See Francis Fukuyama, *The End of History and The Last Man* (New York: Maxwell Macmillan International, 1992).

14. See Samuel Huntington, *The Clash of Civilizations and the Remaking of World Order* (New York: Simon & Schuster, 1996). L.H.M. Ling, "Sex Machine: Global Hypermasculinity and Images of the Asian Woman in Modernity," *Positions: East Asia Cultures Critique* 7, No.2 (1999): 279.

15. Tan Lin, "Quan qiu hua de tiao zhan: she hui xing bie shi jiao de fen xi," (*Challenges of Globalization: Analysis of Social Gender*) Ha Er Bing Shi Wei Dang Xiao Xue Bao (*Journal of the Party School of Ha Er Bing*) 1 (2004): 32.

16. Liu Meng, Wang Zhonghui, and Dong Ou, "Zhong guo jiu ye shi chang zhong de xing bie qi shi," (*Problems of Chinese Women's Employment in the China's Job Market*) Zhong Hua Nü Zi Xue Yuan Xue Bao (*Journal of Chinese Women's College*) 6 (2004): 7.

17. Pan Jintang, "Beijing nü da xue sheng jiu ye gong qiu yi xiang diao cao feng xi," (*Analysis of Female College Students' Employment Opportunities in Beijing*) Beijing She Hui Ke Xue (*Beijing Social Science*) 3 (2004): 7.

18. Gina Lai, "Work and Family Roles and Psychological Well-Being in Urban China," *Journal of Health and Social Behavior* 36, no. 1 (March 1995): 15.

19. Wang Zheng, "Gender, Employment and Women's Resistance," in *Chinese Society: Change, Conflict and Resistance*, eds. Perry, Elizabeth J. and Mark Selden (New York: Routledge, 2002), 64.

20. Kathy Chen, "Workplace: A Nervous China Awaits Women of the World: China's Women Face Obstacles in the Workplace," *Wall Street Journal* (1995): 2.

21. Hu Hao, "Lun guo ji zhi jie tou zi dui fa zhang zhong guo jia fu nü jiu ye de ying xiang," (*Impact of Foreign Investment on Chinese Women's Employment*) *Shanghai Xing Zheng Xue Yuan Xue Bao* (*Journal of Administrative Studies of Shanghai*) 4 (2003): 47.

22. Gina Lai, "Work and Family Roles and Psychological Well-Being in Urban China," *Journal of health and Social Behavior* 36, no. 1 (March 1995): 24.

23. Phyllis Andors, *The Unfinished Liberation of Chinese Women, 1949-1980* (Bloomington: Indiana University Press, 1984), 44.

24. Tan Lin, "Quan qiu hua de tiao zhan: she hui xing bie shi jiao de fen xi," (*Challenges of Globalization: Analysis of Social Gender*), 32.

25. *People's Daily*, 13 July 2001.

26. Cheng Li, *Rediscovering China: Dynamics and Dilemmas of Reform* (New York: Rowman & Littlefield Publishers, 1997), 56.

27. Wu Bangguo, "Chinese Economy in the Twenty-first Century," *Presidents and Prime Ministers* 9 (Jan. 2000): 16.

28. Daniel Fu Keung Wong and Leung, Grace. "Mental health of migrant workers in China: prevalence and correlates," *Social Psychiatry Epidemiol* 43 (2088): 483.

29. Lu Li Wang, Hong-mei, and Ye, Xue-jun. "Mental health status of Chinese rural-urban migrant workers: Comparison with permanent urban and rural dwellers," *Social Psychiatry Epidemiol* 42 (2007): 716.

30. Cindy C Fan. "The State, the Migrant Labor Regime and Maiden Workers in China," *Political Geography.* 23 (2004): 288.

31. Song Lina, "The Role of Women in Labor Migration: A Case Study in Northern China," in *Women of China: Economic and Social Transformation,* eds. Jackie West, Zhao Minghua, Chang Xiangqun, and Cheng Yuan (New York: St. Martin's Press, 1999), 72.

32. See Phillis Andors, "Women and Work in Shenzhen," *Bulletin of Concerned Asian Scholars* 20, No. 3 (1988): 22-24.

33. Pun Ngai, "Becoming *Dagongmei* (Working Girls): The Politics of Identity and Difference in Reform China," *The China Journal* 42 (1999), 14.

34. Delia Davin, "The Impact of Export-Oriented Manufacturing on Chinese Women Workers." *United Nations Research Institute for Social Development.* (2001): 15.

35. Pun Ngai, *Made in China: Women Factory Workers in a Global Workplace.* Durham and London: Duke University (2005): 15.

36. Medea Benjiamin, "50 Years Later, Chinese Women Still Oppressed," *San Francisco Chronicle*, 1 October 1999.

37. Daniel Fu Keung Wong, Li Chang Ying, and Song, He Xue. "Rural migrant workers in urban China: living a marginalised life." *International Journal of Social Welfare* 16 (2007): 35.

38. Taryn N. Tang and Oatley, Keith. "Impact of Life Events and Difficulties on the Mental Health of Chinese Immigrant Women." *Immigrant Minority Health* 9 (2007): 287.

39. Xiaoming Li and Stanton, Bonita. "Health Indicators and Geographic Mobility among Young Rural-Urban Migrant in China," *World Health Population* 8 (2006): 19.

40. Emily Hong, and Gail Hershatter. *Personal Voices: Chinese Women in the 1980s* (Stanford: Stanford University Press, 1988), 13.

41. Tseng Pao-sun, "The Chinese Woman Past and Present," in *Chinese Women: Through Chinese Eyes*, ed. Li Yu-ning (Armonk, New York: M.E. Sharpe, 1992), 85.

42. Ma Meiling, "Nan zhu wai nü zhu nai xian xiang hui chao," (*Men are Responsible for Public Affairs and Women Are Responsible for Housework*), *Wen Hui Daily,* 9 November 2001.

43. Yang Hexia, "Hui gu zhong guo xian dai li shi shang fu nü hui jia lun de si ci zheng lun," (*Four Debates on Women Back to Kitchen in Chinese History*) *Zhong Hua Nü Zi Xue Yuan Xue Bao* (*Journal of Chinese Women's Colle*ge) 3 (2003): 9.

44. Haleh Afshar, "Introduction," in *Women, State, and Ideology: Studies from Africa and Asia,* ed. Haleh Afshar (New York: State University of New York Press, 1987), 3.

45. Joyce Outschoorn, "Administrative Accommodation in the Netherlands," in *Comparative State Feminism*, 177.

46. Jude Howell, "Women Politicians and Change: Women's Political Participation in China: Struggling to Hold Up Half the Sky." Unpublished Paper for the Fiftieth Annual Meeting of Association of Political Studies, 12 April 2001, Manchester, United Kingdom, 50.

47. Heleh Afshar, "Introduction," in *Women and Politics in the Third World*, ed. Heleh Afshar (New York: Routledge, 1996), 1.

48. Joyce Outschoorn, "Administrative Accommodation in the Netherlands," in *Comparative State Feminism*, 80.

49. Sevenhuisen Siim, "Welfare State, Gender Politics, and Equality Polices: Women's Citizenship in the Scandinavia Welfare States" in *Equality, Politics, and Gender*, eds. E. Meehan and S. Sevenhuisen (London: Sage, 1991), 189.

50. Dorothy McBride Stetson and Amy Mazur, eds. *Comparative State Feminism*, eds. *Comparative State Feminism* (London: Sage Publications, 1995), 267.

51. H.M. Hernes, *Welfare State and Woman Power: Essay in State Feminism* (Oslo: Universitetsforlaget, 1987), 11.

52. Ibid., 273.

53. Ibid.

54. Amy G. Mazur, "Strong State and Symbolic Reform: The Minstere des Droits de la Femme in France," in *Comparative State Feminism*, 76-77.

55. Robinson, "Women, the State, and the Need for Civil Society: the Liga Kobiet in Poland," in *Comparative State Feminism*, 205.

56. *The Chinese Women's Movement Between State and Market* (Stanford, Calif.: Stanford University Press, 2002), 175.

57. Howell, "Women Politicians and Change: Women's Political Participation in China: Struggling to Hold Up Half the Sky."

58. Barlow, "Politics and Protocols of Funu: (Un) Making National Woman," 341.

59. Liu Bohong, "The All China Women's Federation and Women's NGOs," in *Chinese Women Organizing: Cadres, Feminists, Muslims, Queers* by Ping-Chun Hsiung, Maria Jaschok and Cecilia Milwrtz with Red Chang (United Kingdom: Berg, 2001), 154.

60. Marian Sawer, "The Representation of Women in Australia: Meaning and Make-Believe," in *Women, Politics, and Change*, 17.

61. Stanley Rosen, "Women and Political Participation in China," *Pacific Affairs* 68, no. 3 (Autumn 1995): 315.

62. Wang Qi, "State-Society Relations and Women's Political Participation," in *Women of China: Economic and Social Transformation*, eds. Jackie West, Zhao Minghua, Chang Xiangqun, and Cheng Yuan (London: Macmillan Press, 1999), 39.

*Chapter Six*

# Chinese Economy

Economy and politics are two major support systems of Chinese society. The Chinese economy is the basis of the political system; and the political system supports its economic development. This chapter will discuss the Chinese economy, and Chapter 7 will discuss the by-product of the Chinese economic development—environmental problems. Chapter 8 will discuss the Chinese political system, and Chapter 9 will discuss the by-product of current Chinese politics—corruption. Since the Chinese government launched the reform movement, China's economy has been taking off with extraordinary speed for more than three decades. In 2010 China surpassed Japan to become the second largest economy in the world. It is widely believed that China will replace the United States as the largest economy between 2025 and 2040. While the Chinese government is very confident that China will continue to steadily develop its economy, Western scholars and media are skeptical about the development of the Chinese economy. Ten years ago, Gordon Chang concluded that China's political and economic system was unsustainable and predicted that China's economy would collapse in ten years.[1] Recently, Albert Edwards, a leading analyst in London, pointed out that China will have a financial and economic crisis soon, and that the economic crisis will possibly climax in the next 12 months.[2] What is going on with the Chinese economy? What will happen to China's economy in the near future? This chapter will examine the development of the Chinese economy from a historical perspective, discuss the development of the Chinese economy in the past three decades, assess the current status of the Chinese economy, and examine both the strengths and constraints of the Chinese economy in order to understand the issue of whether or not the growth of the Chinese economy is sustainable.

## WHY CHINA LOST ITS LEADING ECONOMIC POSITION

Both Western and Chinese scholars acknowledge that China was the most developed country in the world in terms of its GDP before the seventeenth century. According to Mark Elvin, after the Qin dynasty (221 B.C.), China made considerable progress in the improvement of transportation, communications, and military techniques. China's economy and its technology also made significant progress during the period A.D. 800 to 1300 and had the world's earliest mechanized industry by the tenth century.[3] China was the largest economy in the world during the first half of the Qing dynasty in terms of its GDP, but dramatically fell beginning in the first half of the nineteenth.

Why did China lose its leading position in economic and technological development? In summary, Chinese agriculture was family based, small-scale, and scattered over China's huge land mass. This type of inland agriculture made Chinese farmers easily satisfied with their harvest and their daily life, and it was easier for them to lose the stimulation to seek something new. The Chinese people were subjected to harsh taxation and slave-like servitude.[4] Politically, a highly centralized government acted as both a political and an economic agent and tightly controlled the Chinese economy. Thus, local governments and basic economic units lacked the incentive to increase productivity by improving production and technology. Derk Bodde observed that such centralism may have been harmful to science.[5] Ideologically, China emphasized oneness, together with the bureaucratic form of government that maintained this oneness. In the seventeenth century, *wen zi yu* (execution of an author for writing something against the government) became an important tool by which the ruling class sought to control the soul of the Chinese people. No one dared to go one step beyond the limit. Educationally, China institutionalized the civil service examination, beginning with the Sui dynasty, but this educational system did not serve as the development for the Chinese economy, because this system "provided little opportunity or incentive for scientific research."[6] Culturally, science was separated from technology in ancient China.[7] The sciences and technology were pursued by two different groups. Science was pursued by the Confucian scholars, who obtained knowledge only from books and criticized technology. Technology was pursued by artisans, who were generally less-educated people. Because artisans made their living by their skills, Confucian scholars treated them as "the small men," the ruled class. Therefore, the development of technology was not encouraged. Yet science was divorced from the needs of society. Bodde notes that "Han mathematicians, unlike their Greek and Hellenistic opposites, showed little interest in explaining their techniques."[8] Geographically, the Chinese people in ancient times lived inland and were stimulated little by the outside world. In addition, Western countries invaded China, plundered her property, forced her to accept many unfair treaties, and developed the dirty trade with China—the opium business. At the end of the Qing dynasty, China's economy was burdened by horrible drug addiction, population pressures, and political corruption.[9]

During the period of the Republican era from 1912 to 1949, China was a so-called sovereign and independent country, but the Nationalist government seldom exercised its sovereign rights to develop its home economy. China certainly had a double burden in economic affairs—it was very difficult to reconstruct the traditional economy and build a new economic system in such a short period of time. Under imperialist pressures, China found it difficult to establish its own national industry. Modern factory production was dominated by handicraft manufacturing. In addition, the ruling class only took care of its own interests and was never concerned for the nation and the common people. The top priority of the government agenda was to rule all of China, not to promote economic development. Because of his military background, Jiang Jieshi was never "capable of pushing the Chinese economy off the dead center of stagnation."[10] Without a doubt, the war with Japan between 1937 and 1945 also interrupted the normal development of China economy. Thus, the Chinese economy neither grew in size nor altered in structure to any significant degree under the Nationalist government.[11]

When Chairman Mao declared the establishment of the People's Republic of China in October of 1949, the new China became an independent country and began to truly exercise its sovereignty. Mao Zedong profoundly transformed the ownership system, the kinship structure, the class structure, and the political culture. His main achievements were laying the foundations for heavy industry, eliminating foreign control of Chinese industry, eliminating all major property-based inequalities, and providing for the basic needs of the people.[12] Mao believed that Marxist revolutionary theory could be used not only in politics, but also in economic activities. Guided by Mao's slogan "promote social production while campaigning revolutionary mobilization," class struggle was regarded as the sole driving force for socialist China to develop its economy. From the first day of the founding of the People's Republic of China, Mao never stopped campaigning for class struggles. In the 1950s, through the Great Leap Forward, the People's Commune, Mao called for the Chinese people to catch up with the economic levels of Britain and the United States. In the 1960s, Mao launched the Cultural Revolution, a mass political movement, to mobilize the Chinese people to destroy the existing social order and bring the Chinese economy to the verge of collapse.

Mao stressed centralized government within a large bureaucratic system, utilized ideology to legitimize the communist systems, and maximized party control over the government and the economy. Mao destroyed the market system, implemented a socialist planned economy, and abolished private ownership. In industry, Mao borrowed the heavy-industry-oriented development strategy of the Soviet Union and destroyed the balance between heavy-industry and light-industry. While 45 percent of government investment went to heavy-industry, Chinese agriculture received less than 10 percent of state investment between 1950 and 1979. In agriculture, Mao organized the commune system and virtually destroyed the peasants' incentive to work. Mao also prohibited all commodity economic activities, in order to pursue a pure communist system; also he closed China's door to the outside world in order to carry out a self-reliant and self-sufficient policy. As a result, Maoism failed at all aspects of Chinese society and the Chinese economy collapsed. [13] Thus, it was Mao's extreme revolutionary-centered model that brought the Chinese economy to the verge of collapse.

## SIGNIFICANCE OF THE REFORM MOVEMENT

After Mao died in 1976, the only choice for the party was to correct Mao's mistakes and shift the emphasis of the party from the political campaign to development of the economy in order to put it back on the right track. However, it is not easy to make such a large change. Radical change in policy first requires change in the theoretical foundations of that policy. [14] Deng Xiaoping successfully reinterpreted Marxism/Maoism by using Marxism. He campaigned in a new Marxist movement and set forth two slogans: "To seek truth from facts" and "The practice is the sole criterion to test truth." He implied that the economy was the sole criterion by which to judge the party's policy and the socialist system, and that the living standard of the Chinese people was the basic criterion for evaluating the level of the socialist system. This ideological campaign paved the way for an economic reform movement and provided a new theoretical foundation for the party to shift its emphasis from the class struggle to economic development.

The Chinese reform movement began in the rural regions. Deng reversed the emphasis from heavy industry to agriculture, greatly increasing agricultural productivity and producing enough grain to feed the Chinese people. In 1981, the government officially promoted a household responsibility system that "covered 98 percent of the rural population" within three years. [15] Under the new party policy, land was distributed to single households, each of which became a basic work unit that contracted with its production team. With land distribution and better policy, farmers gained much more incentive to work hard and showed less need for supervision.

The main obstacle to economic growth during the Mao regime was the planned economic system. State ownership is the unshakable foundation of the socialist system, which also includes collective ownership. China had more than 100,000 state-owned enterprises that occupied about 78 percent of China's total enterprises during Mao's regime. "Ownership" is the right to utilize assets and the right to transfer this right to another agent through gift or sale.[16] Under the Constitution of the People's Republic of China, state-owned enterprises are owned by the Chinese people. In reality, it is impossible for 1.34 billion Chinese people to own the firms and exercise the right of control over state-owned enterprises directly, so the central government and local governments inevitably own the real control rights. The state enterprises are like puppets and have no autonomy in the employment of workers, the use of profits, the planning of production, the supply of inputs, or the marketing of their products. Under this ownership system, the state-owned enterprises' total industrial output fell from 77.6 percent in 1980 to 40 percent in 2002 and declined further, to 29 percent in 2007.[17]

In order for the Chinese economy to grow out of the plan, the Chinese government began to implement the new policy—a dual-track system in the reform era.[18] The dual-track system allows state-owned enterprise to retain dominant ownership in the Chinese economy, while allowing private enterprises limited control over the other sectors. First, the government allowed the entrance of massive non-state enterprises, largely without privatization of state enterprise, but through new setups. China now has six types of ownership systems: state-owned enterprises, collective enterprises, private enterprises, stock-share enterprises, foreign-invested enterprises, and joint-venture enterprises. State-owned enterprises, which accounted for 77.6 percent of the gross industrial product in 1978, dropped to about 35 percent by 2012.[19] Second, the Chinese government restructured state-owned enterprises. Instead of privatizing state-owned enterprises, the Chinese government restructured enterprises by consolidating enterprise property rights and giving enterprises the needed autonomy to generate incentives. Third, the government allowed some state-owned enterprises to separate ownership from management, giving them some degree of commercial freedom and independence, including ensuring their rights to lay off workers. The government also leased some small and medium-sized state-owned enterprises to individuals. Fourth, it provided opportunities and let state-owned enterprises merge in joint ventures and shareholding companies. The Chinese government also passed the Bankruptcy Law, which allowed more state-owned enterprises to be dissolved, and sold some state-owned enterprises to domestic or foreign-owned companies.

At the beginning of the 1980s, the government introduced the concept that "the planned economy would be primary and the market economy would be secondary." Then, the CPC decided to take another step and implemented a socialist commodity economy in 1984. Finally, Deng persuaded the Fourteenth National Congress of the CPC to officially accept a socialist market economy in 1992.[20] A year later, *Issues Concerning the Establishment of a Socialist Market Economy* was promulgated. The most important measures were the government lifted some restrictions on nonstate industries, gradually liberalized the state material allocation system, further expanded the household production responsibility system, established Sino-foreign joint ventures, decentralized the administrative system (especially the fiscal system), and enabled local governments to retain and allocate more of the tax revenues they collected.

State ownership and planned economy are two sides of the same coin. According to Marxism, planned economy is opposite to market economy and is associated with the socialist system, while a market economy is associated with the capitalist system. The acceptance of a market economy is the central symbol of modern capitalism.[21] To justify a market economy in China, the party argues that the purpose of introducing a market economy is not to carry out a capitalist system, but to build a market economy with Chinese characteristics.[22] Without a doubt, the nature of public ownership reform is the process of decentralizing power. Precisely, it is the most profound revolution to shift power from the party and the central government to local governments and economic entities, from the government to individuals.[23]

While some scholars suggest that China's economy has already moved decisively toward privatization,[24] most surveys indicate that the state continues to play an important role in the commercial sphere.[25] Louis Putterman has noted that ownership reform in China has indeed been much less radical than the changes in the role of markets.[26] He adds, "Limited reform in the ownership of enterprises is a key element of the evolutionary reform model that is associated with China."[27] *The Decision on State-Owned Enterprise Reform and Development*, which was promulgated by the Fourth Plenary Session of the Central Committee of the Communist Party in September 1999, tends to be conservative and repeatedly affirms that state ownership must take a dominant position in the socialist economy. Obviously, the CPC is not ready to fully give up its positions of governance and ownership.

## ACHIEVEMENTS OF THE CHINESE ECONOMY

The reform movement has transformed China from a poor country to an industrialized one, ended the history of China's poverty, opened up China's doors to the world, and made it part of the global village. Deng's impact on China was no less profound than Mao's because he brought China into a new economic stage. In the first 25 years of the reform era, the growth rates of the Chinese economy have been about 10 percent on average per year.[28] China's economy today is ten times larger than it was in 1978 and three times that of India, making up about 13 percent of the world's economy in terms of GDP.[29] China is the fastest growing economy in the world and has become the world's second largest economy. In 2008, Fareed Zakaria, in the cover story of *Newsweek,* confirmed that the advent of China as a global power was no longer a forecast but a reality.[30] The recent world economic crisis has not affected the Chinese economy much. China was able to keep its economy growing and retained 7.9 percent growth rate in the second quarter of 2009, while the global economy grew by 1.6 percent in the second quarter. China's economy expanded 9.3 percent in 2011, but slid to 7.8 percent in 2012 and 7.5 percent in 2013.[31] About 40 percent of all growth in the global economy has occurred in China since the financial crisis.[32] French newspapers claim that China's economy is like a light in the dark. The German *Nulunbao Daily* claims that the hope of the world economy is in China.[33]

China is a giant of world incorporation. China is the largest maker of toys, clothing, and electronic products, and is now making additional efforts to develop in automobiles, computers, biotechnology, aerospace, and telecommunications.[34] Some Chinese products dominate the U.S. market—about 90 percent of toys, 30 percent of furniture, and about 90 percent of Wal-Mart products are made in China. Today, China assembles about 80 percent of the world's notebook and desktop computers and has become the world's largest notebook manufacturer.[35] China has become the second largest vehicle market after the United States. She also has become the sixth-biggest foreign investor in the world and overtook the United States as Africa's top trading partner last year.[36] This signifies that China is making great efforts to integrate itself into the world economy and will possibly purchase more U.S. companies in the near future.

China was the second largest global trader with its foreign trade totaling 3.75 trillion U.S. dollars in 2011 and grew 6.2 percent in 2012. It is expected that China's foreign trade for 2013 will be slightly better than 2012.[37] According to the World Trade Organization, China, for the first time, became the world's biggest exporter in the first half of 2009. According to the General Administration of Customs of China, China's total volume of imports and exports had reached $1,703.67 billion from January to June 2011, of which the export volume was $874.3 billion and the import volume was $829.27 billion. The accumulated surplus was $44.93 billion. The U.S. goods trade deficit with China was $201.5 billion in 2005, $232.5 billion in 2006 and reached $295.5 billion in 2011, accounting for 41 percent of the overall U.S. goods trade deficit in 2011.[38]

China's foreign reserves hit $3.197 trillion at the end of June of 2011, becoming the largest in the world.[39] China is second only to the United States as the recipient of foreign direct investment with $650 billion in foreign direct investment, which reflects that China's economy has been integrated into the world economy.[40] China is moving rapidly to dominate the global market, not just for labor-intensive manufactured goods, but also for more advanced products, including mobile telephones, laptop computers, and digital cameras.

The majority of Chinese people are becoming wealthier. About 300 million Chinese people joined the middle class in 2010. Chinese families with assets valued from 150,000 *yuan* ($24,193) to 300,000 *yuan* ($48,387) are classified as middle class. The number of people in the middle class is expected to increase to 40 percent by 2020. Chinese consumers' confidence has noticeably increased, as evidenced by the fact that the consumer confidence index in China stood at 109 in 2010, the highest point, but declined to 103 in 2011 while it was 82 in the United States. Chinese consumers scoop up 12 percent of the world's luxury goods compared to U.S. consumers' 17 percent. There are 238 Wal-Mart supercenter stores and 103 Trust-Mart Hypermarkets in China, targeting China's upper middle class. With the economy booming, China has become the fourth largest tourist destination, with about 16 million foreigners among a total of 120 million tourists. China has built 34,000 kilometers of highway, which will double by 2020. China plans to build 70 new airports in the next few years and to expand 100 existing airports. It is expected that that Chinese carriers will operate around 4,700 planes and the number of airports will reach more than 230 by the end of 2015.[41]

A strong nation is usually supported by a strong military force and advanced education and technology. The total defense budget for 2012 was increased to $106 billion from $95.6 billion in 2011.[42] China's total education expenditures increased from 2.1 percent of its GDP in 1999 to 3 percent of its GDP in 2006. China's public budget on education during the first eleven months of 2011 was 1233.2 billion *yuan*, up 25.8 percent compared to the same period of 2010. China devotes more and more energy and resources to developing its space program. China aims to enable its astronauts to engage in extra-vehicular operations, conduct experiments on spacecraft rendezvous, and make breakthroughs in developing basic technologies for sending astronauts to the moon.[43] The Chinese government plans to establish a space station by 2020 and eventually put a man on the moon.[44] In December of 2011, the Chinese government announced a space plan that would include the use of space labs, space stations and manned ships over the next five years. The five-year plan for space exploration would move China closer to becoming a major rival at a time when the American program is in retreat.[45] In January 2007, China used a ground-based missile to destroy one of its aging satellites orbiting more than 500 miles in space. This is a strong signal to the international society that no one country owns space and China has the capability to compete with other countries during war times.

In short, "China has entered the most robust stage of its industrial revolution."[46] Since the reform movement, "China has experienced the same degree of industrialization, urbanization and social transformation as Europe did in two centuries."[47] If the Chinese economy continues to grow at such astronomical levels, China will be in the position to supersede the United

States in the next few decades. Some eminent Western scholars claim that the American era is coming to an end,[48] and the twenty-first century is China's century.[49]

## IS CHINA'S ECONOMIC PROGRESS SUSTAINABLE?

Some Western scholars argue that China's economic progress is not sustainable. They believe that China is on the verge of collapse,[50] and predict that a terminal crisis in China will break out within the next ten to twenty years.[51] The majority of Chinese citizens agree that the Chinese reform movement creates an economic miracle, but at the same time, it produces serious problems, which indicates that there are many uncertainties in the future of the Chinese economy, including a population problem, a low level of scientific and technological development, underdeveloped infrastructure in transportation and communication network, political system, corruption, inflation, unemployment, crime, monetary instability, bottlenecks in energy, foreign exchange, and raw materials.[52] Sarah Tong and John Wong point out that the Chinese are facing great challenges and constraints including the constraints of human resources, natural resources, and social problems.[53] To sustain economic progress in years to come, China will have to overcome the challenges and constraints and deal with all these natural, social and political problems. Obviously, it is not an easy task.

One of the most serious problems is that the gap between the rich and the poor is increasingly widening. China is becoming rich. The number of rich Chinese people is listed at number four in the world, just next to Japan, and it is expected to be in first place in 2013. Meanwhile, the gap between the rich and poor is widening significantly. Investigations have shown that about 0.4 percent of Chinese rich families possess 70 percent of China's property. While China becomes rich, the number of poor people increases. The middle class is the foundation of developed countries, but low income people are the majority in China. In Shanghai, the most developed city in China with 13 million residents, 10 percent of its total population or 1.4 million people have a monthly income below 450 *yuan.* However, medical expenses and educational expenses for low-income people are the same for high-income people. Basic healthcare is simply unaffordable for millions of Chinese people. If they become chronically ill, they could face bankruptcy. Basically, medical insurance only covers urban employees and not rural farmers. Anywhere from 45 to 60 percent of urban residents and 80 to 90 percent of the rural population do not have any form of medical insurance. Because medical expenses for the majority of the Chinese people are too expensive, 36 percent of patients in cities and 39 percent in rural areas choose not to see a doctor when they fall ill, and about 28 percent of those who are admitted to the hospital have no other option.[54] Although 700 million rural people across China have signed up for new rural health care insurance, only a small percentage of medical bills can be covered in some cases.[55] In addition, the Chinese medical system is abused by some doctors who overprescribe medicine and conduct unnecessary tests to increase profits. Pharmaceutical companies know that doctors' incomes are low, so "they offer them incentives to sell more of their medicines."[56] When the World Health Organization (WHO) ranked the public health system of 190 countries in 2007, China was placed at 144, behind some of Africa's poorest countries.

The wide gap between the rich and the poor is partly the result of government corruption. Recent reports have revealed that 91 percent of the wealthy people who own more than 100 million *yuan* are the children of Chinese senior officials. In present-day China, the rich get richer and the poor get poorer. A survey by the Chinese Academy of Social Sciences last year found that nearly half of the 7,063 families polled thought the rich had acquired their wealth illegally.[57] Some businessmen and corrupt officials have worked together and become extremely rich, while the working class becomes relatively poor. In order to protect their special interests, the rich people do not only seek their representative in the political sphere, but also expand their influence to the academic sphere by using their financial power. Money speaks loudly. As a result, the economic law dysfunctions and government regulation always sides with the rich. China's corruption has become systematic and institutionalized. This rampant corruption severely damages the CPC's reputation, ruins the faith of its members, and reduces the capability of its power.

There are some structural problems with the development of the Chinese economy. First of all, the development of China's economy is unbalanced. China's reform movement lacks coordination between economic and social development, between high GDP growth and social progress, between upgrading technology and increasing job opportunities, between keeping development momentum in the coastal areas and speeding up development in inland China, between fostering urbanization and nurturing agricultural areas, between attracting more foreign investment and enhancing the competitiveness of indigenous enterprises, between deepening reform and preserving social stability, between opening domestic markets and solidifying independence, and between promoting market-oriented competition and taking care of the disadvantaged people. The huge difference is obvious between rural and urban China, northern and southern China, and western and eastern Chinas. All these differences imply that many areas of China are undeveloped and China is fragile and this could also easily trigger social conflicts.

Second, China's natural resources are insufficient to meet its growing demands. Only about 15 percent of China's land is arable, but the Chinese government is required to feed a population of 1.34 billion. China will soon become the largest aging country in the world. It is a very difficult task for the Chinese government to keep such a large population fed, clothed, and sheltered, and to satisfy the basic needs of the people without discontent. In addition, China's output has more than doubled in size in the past three decades. Overcapacity causes waste, losses and even closures, and also leads to rising unemployment.[58] China's limited resources cannot afford the over-heated economic growth. China's economic growth is driving its thirst for energy and it has become the world's second-largest oil consumer. Today, China consumes six million barrels everyday and this will double in ten years, but the output of China's oil does not meet the needs of China's consumption. China imported 178.9 million metric tons of crude oil in 2008, up from 91 million tons in 2003.[59] If China's economy continues to expand at 8 percent per year for two decades, by that time, 1.45 billion Chinese people will consume the equivalent of two-thirds of the current world grain harvest and use 99 million barrels of oil a day, but the world currently produces only 84 million barrels daily.[60] Finally, it should be noted that China's rise is parallel to environmental degradation. While the Chinese economy develops, China's environmental problems become one of the most serious obstacles to the development of Chinese economy. This problem will be addressed in the next chapter.

## CONCLUSION

In 1978, China launched economic reforms and made significant progress in agricultural, industrial, and international trade reform. China has already fulfilled the first two steps: doubling the GNP to meet the basic needs of the Chinese people by the year 1990 and helping the Chinese people to live a more comfortable life at the end of the twentieth century. The third step is to raise the per-capita GDP up to the level of moderately developed countries by the middle of the twenty-first century. However, the reform movement has produced a lot of economic and social problems, while creating an economic miracle. Thus, the future of China's economy is still uncertain. The Chinese economy has already slowed down since 1998 and will slow down further. Chinese officials explain that the slowdown is caused mainly by internal problems, such as industrial overcapacity and increasing unemployment. China merely needs a period of time to readjust its industry and further reform the financial system. None of the causes of economic downfall are connected to political and cultural factors. In fact, many political and cultural factors affect the development of economy. To sustain the Chinese economy, the Chinese government must deal with not only the issues of the Chinese economy, but also handle all other major cultural, social and political problems. Gordon White notes that "democratization is an essential precondition for solving the developmental problems of developing countries in general and China in particular."[61] Whether or not China is able to sustain its economy largely depends on how the government wisely balances political and economic reform.

## NOTES

1. Gordon Chang, *The Coming Collapse of China* (New York: Random House, 2001).

2. Larry Elliott, "China's collapse 'will bring economic crisis to climax in 2012'," *Guardian.co.uk*, January 11, 2012.

3. Mark Elvin, *The Pattern of the Chinese Past* (Stanford, Calif.: Stanford University Press, 1973), 180.

4. H. Stephen Gardner, *Comparative Economic Systems* (New York: The Dryden Press, 1998), 656.

5. Derk Bodde, *Chinese Thought, Society, and Science: The Intellectual and Social Background of Science and Technology in Pre-Modern China* (Honolulu: University of Hawaii Press, 1991), 363.

6. Justin Yifu Lin, "The Needham Puzzle: Why the Industrial Revolution Did Not Originate in China," *Economic Development and Cultural Change* 43 (January 1995), 269-92.

7. Bodde, *Chinese Thought, Society, and Science*, 3.

8. Ibid., 362.

9. Gardner, *Comparative Economic Systems*, 657.

10. Ibid., 48.

11. Albert Ferwerker, *The Chinese Economy: 1912-1949* (Ann Arbor, Mich.: Michigan Papers in Chinese Studies, 1968), 1.

12. Mark Selden, *The Political Economy of Chinese Development* (Armonk, N.Y.: M.E. Sharpe, 1993), 17.

13. Justin Yifu Lin, Fang Cai, and Zhou Li, "The Lessons of China's Transition to a Market Economy," *Cato Journal* 16, No. 2 (Fall 1996): 212.

14. Gordon White, *Riding the Tiger: The Politics of Economic Reform in Post-Mao China* (Stanford, Calif.: Stanford University Press, 1993), 158.

15. Gardner, *Comparative Economic Systems*, 657.

16. Louis Putterman, "The Role of Ownership and Property Rights in China's Economic Transition," *China Quarterly* 144 (December 1995), 1049.

17. *China Statistical Yearbook.* National Bureau of Statistics of China, Beijing, 2009.

18. See Barry Naughton, *Growing Out of Plan: Chinese Economic Reform, 1978-1993* (Cambridge University Press, 1995).

19. Keith Bradsher, "China's Grip on Economy Will Test New Leaders," *New York Times,* November 9, 2012

20. Gardner, *Comparative Economic Systems*, 678.

21. William H. Overholt, *The Rise of China: How Economic Reform Is Creating a New Superpower* (New York: W.W. Norton & Company, 1994), 149.

22. Shaomin Li, Mingfang Li, and J. Justin Tan, "Understanding Diversification in a Transition Economy: A Theoretical Exploration," *Journal of Applied Management Studies* 7 (June 1998), 77-95.

23. Andrew G. Walder, "China's Transitional Economy: Interpreting Its Significance," *China Quarterly* 144 (*December* 1995), 967.

24. Jeffrey D. Sachs and Wing The Woo, "Structural Factors in the Economic Reforms of China, Eastern Europe, and the Former Soviet Union," *Economic Policy* 18, No. 1 (1994): 102-45.

25. Terry Sicular, "Redefining State, Plan and Market: China's Reforms in Agricultural Commerce," *China Quarterly* 144 (December 1995): 1020.

26. Putterman, "The Role of Ownership and Property Rights in China's Economic Transition," 1053.

27. Ibid., 1058-63.

28. David Pan, "Damn Lies and Chinese Statistics," *Asia Times*, 19 August 2006.

29. Nicholas R. Lardy, "China's Economy: Problems and Prospects," *China Digital Times*, February 7, 2007.

30. Fareed Zakaria, "The Rise of a Fierce Yet Fragile Superpower," *Newsweek* (December 31, 2007-January 7, 2008): 6.

31. "China's GDP growth eases to 7.8% in 2012," *China Daily.* http://www.chinadaily.com.cn/bizchina/2013-01/18/content_16137028.htm ( February 9, 2013)

32. Graham Allison, "China Doesn't Belong in the BRICS," *The Atlantic,* March 26, 2013.

33. Tony Blair, "We Can Help China Embrace the Future," *Wall Street Journal,* 26 August 2008.

34. Ted Fishman, *China, Inc.: How the Rise of the Next Superpower Challenges America and the World* (New York: Scribner, 2005).

35. Tom Miller, "Trading with the Dragon, Part 1: Manufacturing that Doesn't Compute," *Asia Times*, 22 November 2006.

36. Christian Lowe, "Expansive China Faces Grass-Roots Resentment," *Reuters,* 17 August 2009.

37. "China's foreign trade grew 6.2 percent in 2012," *China Daily,* http://www.chinadaily.com.cn/bizchina/2013-01/10/content_16101628.htm (February 9, 2013).

38. The data is provided by The Office of the United States of Trade Representative. http://www.ustr.gov/countries-regions/china (Accessed on February 9, 2013)

39. "China's foreign reserves hit $3t in June," *China Daily*, 12 July 2011.

40. Lardy, "China's Economy: Problems and Prospects."

41. "China to build 70 airports by 2015," *The Telegraph,* June 11, 2012.

42. Jane Perlez, "Continuing Buildup, China Boosts Military Spending More Than 11 Percent," *New York Times*, March 4, 2012.

43. John Ng, "Aiming for the Stars," *Asia Times*, 14 October 2006.

44. "China's Space Program," *The New York Times,* 1 September 2009.

45. Binoy Kampmark, "ET Wars with China: Future Engagements in Space," http://www.scoop.co.nz/stories/HL1201/S00004/et-wars-with-china-future-engagements-in-space.htm.

46. Joseph Kahn and Jim Yardley, "As China Roars, Pollution Reaches Deadly Extremes," *New York Times*, August 26, 2007.

47. Zakaria, "The Rise of a Fierce Yet Fragile Superpower."

48. John Ikenberry, "The Rise of China & the Future of the West," *Foreign Affairs*, January/February, 2008.

49. Quoted in James Kynce, *China: Shakes the World* (Boston: Houghton Mifflin Company, 2006), xiii.

50. Gordon Chang, *The Coming Collapse of China* (New York: Random House, 2001), 91.

51. Jack A. Goldstone, "The Coming Chinese Collapse," *Foreign Policy* 99 (Summer 1995): 43.

52. Penelope B. Prime, "China's Economic progress: Is It Sustainable?" In *China Briefing*: *The Contradictions of Change,* ed. William Joseph (New York: M.E. Sharpe, 1997).

53. Sarah Tong and John Wong, "China's Economy," in *Understanding Contemporary China,* edited by Robert E. Gamer (London, Lynne Rienner Publishers, 2008), 151.

54. "The Medical Reform Controversy," *Beijing Review* 48, no. 38 (September 2005).

55. "China's Punctured Health Care System," *BBC News,* 8 June 2008.

56. Michael Dobie, "Why China's Health Care System Needs Fixing," *International Development Research Center*, Ottawa, Canada, 2 February 2001.

57. Quoted in Kent Ewing, "Resentment Builds Against China's Wealthy By Kent Ewing," *Asia Times*, March 1, 2007,

58. Peter S. Goodman, "Too Fast in China? Stunning Growth May Have a Built-In Problem," *Washington Post,* 26 January 2006.

59. "China crude oil imports grow 9.6 percent in 2008," *Market Watch*, January 13, 2009.

60. Lester R Brown, "A New World Order," *The Guardian*, 25 January 2006.

61. Gordon White, *Riding the Tiger: The Politics of Economic Reform in Post-Mao China* (Stanford, Calif.: Stanford University Press, 1993), 240.

*Chapter Seven*

# China's Rise and Environmental Degradation

While maintaining a rapidly growing economy, China's environment has been getting worse. The environmental degradation is the byproduct of the growth of Chinese economy in the reform era. Today, China has become one of the largest and most polluted countries in the world. According to the 2010 Environmental Performance Index released by Yale and Columbia Universities at the World Economic Forum, China ranked 121 out of 163 countries on the list.[1] The dominant viewpoint in Western societies suggests that the rest of the world cannot ignore China's environmental degradation because, ultimately, the whole world is affected by many of the devastating catastrophes originating in China.[2] To push the Chinese government to do more in improving China's environment, the U.S. Embassy in China has set up a monitoring point on the embassy roof and posts hourly air-quality data on its popular Twitter feed. However, a senior Chinese official demanded in May 2012 that foreign embassies stop issuing air pollution readings, saying it was against the law and diplomatic conventions.[3] This reflects the differences between China and the Western societies on some critical issues: Do China's environmental problems threaten the international society? Is it possible for China to avoid environmental degradation while it is on the rise during globalization? What is the central cause of China's environmental problems? How should China cope with its environmental problems? Will China be able to solve its environmental problems in a short period of time? This chapter will re-assess China's environmental problems, analyze their main causes in a global context, and argue that the current environmental degradation in China is actually an unavoidable result of China's modernization during globalization. Coping with China's environmental problems is a comprehensive project, and it may take a long time to accomplish the project's goal.

## ENVIRONMENTAL DEGRADATION IN CHINA

China is facing almost all of the world's ecological challenges: climate change, desertification, deforestation, declining water resources, acid rain, soil erosion, air and water pollution, and biodiversity loss, along with other challenges. Pollution is the basic problem amid all other environmental issues. The pollutants are broadly divided into seven types, including contaminated water, polluted air, solid waste, radioactive substances, noise, soil pollution and others.

Polluted air is everywhere and no one can escape it. Sixteen of the world's twenty most polluted cities are in China. According to Min Shao, "The air quality of nearly 70 percent of urban areas [does] not meet the country's national ambient air quality standards (NAAQS)" and "nearly 75 percent of urban residents [are] regularly exposed to air considered unsuitable for inhabited areas."[4] It is "in every major northern city and many urban areas in the south are exposed to air pollution levels that are three to seven times higher than World Health Organization guidelines."[5] Air pollution level literally went off the charts in Beijing in January of 2013. *The Economist* reports that "Saturday [January 12] evening saw a reading of 755 on the Air Quality Index (AQI). That index is based on the recently revised standards of the American Environmental Protection Agency (the EPA), which nominally maxes out at 500. For more perspective, consider that any reading above 100 is deemed 'unhealthy for sensitive groups' and that anything above 400 is rated 'hazardous' for all."[6]

The water quality is also decreasing. China supports 22 percent of the world's population with only 8 percent of the world's water. Although China ranks fifth of all nations in water resources on a per capita basis, China's water supply is 25 percent below the global average, and it has only one-fifth as much water per capita as the United States.[7] The shortage of water has resulted in a lack of drinking water, especially in metropolitan areas. According to a survey of more than 600 Chinese cities, two-thirds of them had inadequate water supplies, while one out of every six experienced severe water shortages.[8]

Recent studies suggest industrial pollution contributes more to China's water shortages than previously assumed.[9] More lakes suffer from sedimentation and diminishing water surfaces as a result of physical and human factors.[10] About 70 percent of China's lakes and rivers are polluted to some degree. In a survey taken in 2004, it was found that 28 percent of 412 monitored areas on seven major rivers were rated of no practical use.[11]

Between 2001 and 2005, about 5 percent of Chinese wells contained more than 50 micrograms per liter of arsenic, which affected over 580,000 people.[12] Seventy-five percent of surface water flowing through urban areas of China is not suitable for drinking, and 90 percent of urban ground water is contaminated. Nearly 500 million people lack access to safe drinking water.[13] Chinese officials have acknowledged that 300 million people drink contaminated water on a daily basis, and of these, 190 million people drink water that is so contaminated, it makes them sick. The Yangtze River and Yellow River provide drinking water for tens of millions of Chinese people, but more than 10,500 chemical companies are located along their banks. Any single accident could lead to disastrous consequences.[14] The United Nations has already listed the harbors of the Yangtze River and the Yellow River as dead zones—low oxygenated areas and de-oxygenated zones.

China's ocean has also become polluted. China's coastline extends 18,400 kilometers and borders four seas: the Bo Hai, the Yellow Sea, the East China Sea, and the South China Sea. In 2006, China's seas generated $270 billion GDP, but the booming economy has increased the degradation of the ocean. Red tides are becoming a common occurrence in China, killing off marine life and adversely affecting the surrounding coastal communities. The ocean pollution comes from industries, agriculture, domestic sewage, oil and gas exploration, and fish farming.[15]

Land in China is also polluted. About 1.03 million square kilometers of land degraded by soil erosion. Land erosion in certain areas, such as the Yunnan, Guizhou, Jiangxi, and Hubei provinces, has ranged between 40 percent and 70 percent of the cultivated area.[16] Land erosion immediately raises food security concerns and directly results in arable land shrinking. China has 22 percent of the global population, but just 7 percent of the world's arable land. China loses up to 5 billion tons of soil due to erosion every year. The nutrients lost are equivalent to 40 million tons of fertilizer, which in turn equals the amount of chemical fertilizer used annually by Chinese agriculture. About 40 million *mu* of cultivated land has been destroyed by erosion since 1949. The Ministry of Land and Resources predicts that grain-producing land will decline by 0.18 percent annually. China will have to import 300 million tons of grain by 2030. However, there will be only 200 million tons of commercial grain available in the world by that time.

China's forest is diminishing while desertification is expanding. Official Chinese statistics indicate that in 2003, China's forest covered 18.21 percent of the country's total area. Today, forests only cover 14 percent of China's land. In recent years, they have decreased at an annual rate of 5,000 square kilometers.[17] Residents have been forced to abandon their villages because desertification is so severe. Although the desertification has been curbed in some areas, it is still expanding at a rate of more than 3,000 per square kilometer every year.

China's environmental problems are severe but they do not necessarily threaten the international society. There is a theory that China's rise inevitably damages distributions of international resources, and imposes a serious threat to global economy, energy resources, and the environment. It is true that more than half the world's population has entered industrial society and it has seriously impacted the system of global resources and ecology. As a result, it creates an issue of the distributions of the rights to global environmental development and the responsibilities to global environmental governance. One Chinese perspective suggests that the theory of China's environmental threat reflects that Western countries are worrisome about the current pattern of the global natural resources and hope to maintain their dominant position through global environmental governance.

China is the the world's biggest energy consumer and greenhouse gas emission contributer because of its large population and economy. However, China's carbon dioxide pollution is largely caused by the manufacturing of goods for developed countries.[18] In fact, it is not China, but the United States that is the biggest country to consume energy and produce greenhouse gas emissions in terms its per capita. Since the 1990s, the American people have largely consumed goods produced overseas, mainly in China and other Asian countries. It is hard to justify that China's environment threatens the international society. Instead, the United States and other developed countries should take major responsibility in global environmental governance because they largely contribute to the current environmental problems. In addition, environmental degradation is a by-product of industrialization. No country can avoid a certain level of environmental degradation during the process of modernization. Thus, it is not surprising that China's environmental degradation has become severe since the Chinese economy took off in the early 1980s, as environmental problems were even more severe in some European countries during the Industrial Revolution between the seventeenth and nineteenth centuries.

## THE CONSEQUENCES OF CHINA'S ENVIRONMENTAL DEGRADATION

Poverty, disease and environmental problems are the three greatest challenges nations face in the twenty-first century. The three problems are interrelated, but the environmental problem is the most serious and costly one. China's environmental problems have a negative impact on her domestic development and the global community.

China's environmental degradation hinders the development of the Chinese economy and bites into economic growth. For example, China has a big acid pollution problem, which covers over 30 percent of the country.[19] Acid rain is estimated to cause more than $4 billion a year in crop damage, as well as close to $1 billion in material damage. In September 2006, the State Environmental Protection Administration of China (SEPA) and the National Bureau of Statistics of China (NBS) jointly released the first green GDP report that indicated that environmental pollution cost China 511.8 billion *yuan* (USD 64 billion) in economic losses in 2004, accounting for 3.05 percent of the country's GDP.[20] In recent years, in fact, overall costs to China's economy from environmental degradation are estimated at 8 to 12 percent of GDP annually.[21]

China's environmental problems have directly damaged Chinese people's health. Air pollution affects respiratory systems and the visibility of the atmosphere.[22] Much of the indoor air pollution in China is caused by the use of solid fuels in simple household stoves. Although China has been experiencing great urbanization, more than 65 percent of the population is still rural, most of which still uses biomass and coal fuels that produce substantial pollution.[23] Coal and biomass are difficult to burn in simple household devices without emitting pollutants. The burning of these solid fuels poses a great health risk to those cooking with the materials. With this inability to pre-mix, anywhere from 10 to 38 percent of what is being burned off become dangerous pollutants that harm those who inhale them.[24]

Air pollution is a major cause of lung cancer, as harmful particles enter the lungs and cannot be discharged.[25] Particle pollution from the burning of coal causes approximately 50,000 deaths per year in China. Air pollution is estimated to be the main cause of nearly 50 percent of all respiratory ailments. The number of pollution-related deaths has already reached 750,000 per year.[26] Keith Florig notes that "today, diseases linked to air pollution are among the largest threats to public health in China, ranking with smoking as the most frequent cause of death."[27] A World Health Organization report in 2007 suggested that pollution was responsible for about 656,000 premature deaths annually.[28] According to the most recent data, air pollution actually contributed to 1.2 million premature deaths in China in 2010.[29]

China's environmental problems have intensified the conflicts between the government and society. Official Chinese data demonstrates that unrest began rising rapidly between 1993 and 1995. The government admits to a nationwide increase of 268 percent in mass incidents from 8,700 in 1993 to 32,000 in 1999,[30] and from 58,000 incidents in 2003 to 87,000 in 2005.[31] In 2010, the number of protests in China was alarmingly high, reaching a total of about 180,000. China is entering a peak period for mass incidents and in the next several years may face even more conflicts that will greatly test the governing abilities of all levels of the CPC.[32] About 10 percent of China's social protests are related to pollution. Obviously, environmental problems are serious sources of localized social instability and violence.

The growing environmental problems have damaged China's image in the international society, and have become the world's problems too. Sulfur dioxide and nitrogen oxides, spewed by China's coal-fired power plants, fall as acid rain on Seoul and Tokyo. According to the Journal of Geophysical Research, much of the particulate pollution over Los Angeles originates in China. The environmental issue is one of the hottest topics between China and the United States because it is applies to all other issues. For example, why is the cost of Chinese products so low? Not only do Chinese enterprises use cheap labor, but they also save on the cost of environmental protection. Under the Obama administration, the United States government has paid more attention to climate changes and made climate change a national priority.[33] If the Chinese government does not handle the environmental issue well, it will hurt its relations with other countries.[34]

## WILL CHINA BE ABLE TO SOLVE ITS PROBLEMS IN A SHORT PERIOD OF TIME?

A high percentage of Chinese people are pessimistic in response to this question. First of all, China's environmental degradation is a common issue in a global context. During the Industrial Revolution, European countries experienced the same environmental problems that China is currently facing. There are many environmental issues in the global community today, including biodiversity protection, desertification control, nuclear safety, protection of the ozone layer, marine pollution by dumping wastes, the trans-boundary movements of hazardous wastes, climate change, conservation of wetland ecosystems, and the international trade of endangered wildlife. It is impossible for China to tackle its problems alone without international cooperation. Since China reopened its door to the rest of the world, it has signed 17 international environmental treaties, which are related to 11 global environmental issues, such as biodiversity protection, desertification control, nuclear safety, protection of the ozone layer, marine pollution by dumping wastes, global climate change, conservation of wetlands, and prior informed consent procedure. The Chinese government made an announcement before the Copenhagen Climate Conference that the government would pledge to cut the amount of carbon dioxide emitted for each unit of national income 40 to 45 percent by 2020. According to the Xinhua Agency, this is a voluntary action taken by the Chinese government based on its own national conditions and it is a major contribution to the global effort in tackling climate change.[35]

Government involvement plays a critical role in battling environmental problems. However, there are so many domestic problems in China. Among all the domestic problems China faces, the environmental problems rank neither on the top nor at the bottom. Some scholars suggest that "the limited capacity of the political system, combined with the plethora and scope of environmental problems, mean that not all problems receive the same level of policy attention."[36] The Chinese government is able to invest only limited efforts in improving its environmental degradation. The environmental protection battle involves many aspects of government affairs, such as public health, business, labor, and trade. Thus, the central government is required to consult with various departments at the national level, in order to set an effective proposal for solving environmental problems.

China's environmental problems are derived from multiple sources that are not easily eradicable in a short period of time. It should be noted that a country's level of environmental degradation is unrelated to the level of economic development and the nature of the political system. At present, environmental problems are critical in Asia, especially in developing countries, such as India, Vietnam, and China. In comparison, Africa is an undeveloped region, but environmental problems there are worse than people thought. India has a democratic system, but environmental problems are severe. Conversely, Singapore has an authoritarian regime, but the country is as clean as a beautiful park. The nature of the Chinese political system does not necessarily negatively affect China's environmental problems. Instead, the highly centralized administrative system makes it even easier to create laws and put them into practice.

To be sure, industries are major polluters. Since the foundation of the PRC in 1949, their ultimate goal has been to industrialize China. In 1950, Mao Zedong made it clear that his plan was to build factories with smokestacks around China. To respond to Mao's call, in a short period of time China has absorbed most of the major industries that once polluted the West. In the early years of the post-Mao era, Chinese leaders embraced the principle of "growth first," which was best reflected by a famous slogan of Deng Xiaoping: "No matter if it is a white cat or a black cat; as long as it can catch mice, it is a good cat." Since the reform movement, China has not just become the world's factory, but also its smokestack.[37] China's pollution comes directly from domestic sewage, chemical fertilizers and pesticides, motorized boat oil, human and animal wastes, and industrial batteries.[38]

Air pollution is directly derived from industrialization. For example, 80 percent of air pollution in Hong Kong came from Guangdong's factories and power plants.[39] Industrial waste directly contributes to the shortage of good water quality in China. The industries that contribute the most to pollution in China are chemical, electric power, waste recycling and disposal, non-ferrous metals, petroleum, ferrous metals, non-metallic mineral products, food, coal mining and washing, paper products, plastic textile, and leather industries. They produce an annual 820 million tons of solid waste, with an integrated utilization rate of 46 percent. Chinese cities dump 140 million tons of domestic waste annually, of which only 10 percent is disposed of in a safe way. Industry waste, on the other hand, has dramatically increased from 13.1 billion tons in 1995 to 22.1 billion tons in 2000.[40] Plastic packaging and the plastic sheeting used in agriculture have created "white pollution," which has spread throughout the entire country.

Chinese factories are still using old technology and many manufacturers lack measures to protect the environment. Some 2,000 tons of mercury from more than 2 billion tons of coal burned every year enter the soil and pose threats to agricultural production and human health. Air-borne pollution particles have cut rainfall in many regions of China, particularly in the northeast and northwest. China's emissions increase is 2-4 times greater than expected. China's $CO_2$ emissions reached 19.95 million tons, more than any other country.[41] Experts estimate that $CO_2$ emissions must be reduced by at least 40 percent if they are to meet the environmental capacity of China's atmosphere. The International Energy Agency predicted that China's carbon emissions would not reach those of the United States until 2020. These factors suggest the old production technologies produce more polluters, but environmental degradation cannot be solved by modern technology itself.

Rapid population growth also contributes to China's environmental problems.[42] China's population will continue to grow and will reach its peak at 1.53 billion in the 2030s despite the one-child policy.[43] Population growth reduces arable land and directly increases demands for more production of food, fibers, housing, and other materials.[44] The rapid growth of China's population is side by side with the development of urbanization. China's urban population increased from 132 million people in 1992 to 665.57 million in 2010.[45] Cities produce a great amount of waste on a daily basis, including industrial waste (IW), municipal solid waste (MSW), and hazardous waste (HW). The majority of waste in China is MSW, totaling 2.3 billion tons in 2009 and 190 million tons of solid waste annually and amounts to 29 percent of the world's municipal solid waste. Only 31 percent of collected MSW is handled in an environmentally friendly manner.

Another factor is that the development of urbanization demands more automobiles on the street. Since China became a large consumer of automobiles, about 14,000 new cars hit the streets daily, and it is predicted that China will have more than 130 million cars on the road by 2020. As a result, "Chinese developers are laying more than 52,700 miles of new highways throughout the country."[46] Because of the lack of government regulation, air quality in cities has become extremely poor. Before the 2008 Beijing Olympic Games, the Chinese government removed roughly two million vehicles from city streets and shut down many factories in Beijing in order to meet the anti-pollution standards of the United Nations.[47] As a result, the number of days with a blue sky in 2008 was more than the total number of "blue sky days" in the past ten years.

China's urbanization has been unavoidably accompanied by water and energy shortages. About 400 of the 668 cities in China suffer from some degree of water shortage.[48] It is estimated that urban sprawl and transportation networks take up 1.4 million hectares annually.[49] Moreover, Chinese buildings rarely have thermal insulation, and about 95 percent of new buildings do not meet China's own codes for energy efficiency. Thus, they require twice as much energy to heat and cool as those in similar climates, such as the United States and Europe.

The ultimate source of environmental degradation is human behaviors. Some countries in South America, such as Peru, Brazil, Argentina, and Columbia, are developing countries, but their environmental problems are not as severe as some developing countries in Asia. One explanation for this is that environmental problems are related to people's behaviors toward environmental protection. Since 1950, the temperature on earth has increased more than 0.5°C. Environmentalists suggest that about 74 percent of this global climate change is caused by human behavior.[50] Some scholars suggest that "China's worsening environmental crisis is, at its core, a crisis of policies and perceptions."[51] Ultimately, human activities are responsible for the problem in the first place.

It is a very complex task to remove all these pollution sources, because it involves various issues, such as government policy, employment and the technologies for treating the factories' wastes, and people's awareness of environmental protection. The success of environmental protection really depends on the joint efforts of the entire society. Every member of society has the responsibility to share in the common goal of protecting the environment.[52] It is impossible to fundamentally improve environmental degradation in China without altering human behavior, both individually and collectively.[53]

## RESOLUTIONS TO IMPROVE CHINA'S ENVIRONMENT

China faces a dilemma. As China's economy has developed, the living standard of the Chinese people has dramatically increased and also produced serious environmental problems. Chandran Nair has made a bold argument that Asia cannot both have a high standard of living and be free of environmental problems, due to the simple fact that the world cannot survive the consequences of the growth of highly populous Asian economies to levels of development reached by industrialized countries. Thus, Asian countries should not simply duplicate the Western model of consumption-led economic growth, because there are too many people in Asia, and there are not enough resources on the planet. Asia must do something differently.[54] In this sense, Asian values and the model of governance should be an alternative to Western capitalist lifestyles. Nair believes the authoritarian regime is a good system to help global environmental problems, such as Singapore-style "guided democracy" or China's authoritarian approach. It is not true that consumption-driven capitalism can deliver wealth to all. In fact, it can only deliver short-term wealth to a minority; in the long term, it can only deliver misery to all. Economic growth is an evil to the natural environment and Western capitalism is incapable of solving the environmental problems in Asia. However, Asian values do not prevent the high economic growth from causing environmental disaster. Japan tried to maintain Asian traditional values while its economy was taking off, but it has not prevented it from joining the top five in carbon emissions. China's environmental degradation also indicates that the combination of authoritarianism and Asian values does not guarantee any different results than the Western model. China must develop its economy by avoiding any catastrophic consequences of the development model, using every possible means, such as bans on some forms of consumption and re-pricing of resources.[55]

In order to effectively improve China's environmental degradation, fundamentally, it is necessary to increase the people's awareness of environmental protection. Theoretically, the Chinese government has implemented environmental protection for more than three decades. The first National Conference of Environmental Protection, held in 1973, marked the start of environmental protection in China.[56] In reality, environmental awareness in China is relatively weak. The public attitude toward environmental protection includes environmental awareness and the actual behavior of protecting the environment. Environmental awareness refers to people's knowledge about environmental protection and environment realities, including environmental conditions and problems and government policies regarding them. According to a survey, while about 30 percent of Chinese people know a lot about environmental laws and regulations, about 42 percent of respondents have only heard of it and 26 percent have never heard of it. Although the majority of people acknowledge that they have roles to play in environmental protection, they believe that government and enterprises, not citizens, should take the major responsibility to protect the environment.

Chinese people tend to show passivity and apathy towards activities that damage the environment.[57] Even though many people are discontent with other people's environmentally unsound behavior, they are unwilling to choose environmental protection over economic growth. Instead, they refuse to change their behavior to protect the environment, and also pollute the environment without guilty consciences.[58] For example, a great number of urban residents do not reuse plastic bags and do not often practice waste separation and recycling.

The government's decisive action is the most important measure in dealing with environmental degradation. The Chinese government has realized the severe consequences of environmental degradation and has launched the second economic transformation from a polluted economy to a green economy. At the United Nations General Assembly in September 2009, Hu Jintao promised that the CPC will fulfill its responsibility and will improve China's environment.[59] The Chinese government has established government agencies to handle the country's environmental problems. The State Environmental Protection Administration (SEPA) is the single largest government agency overseeing the country's environmental problems on the "macro" scale, a full-fledged ministry with the power to implement regional supervising programs, to enact national environmental policies, and to research the environmental impacts of major industrial projects. For years the Chinese government has participated in global summits, supported climate change campaigns, and studied the problems that exist in China. China's Eleventh Five-Year Plan specifically addresses energy efficiency and infrastructure improvements as key goals, and the Twelfth Five-Year Plan addresses environmentally sustainable economic growth as an important aspect of development.

However, the government still faces great challenges in handling environmental issues. First of all, it should reassess the guiding principle of China's development—the economy-centered principle—and make well-balanced between economic development and environmental protection. It is a misconception that Western industrial countries began dealing with environmental problems when they became rich, but China is still a developing country, so it is not urgent for China to speed up the process of environmental protection. The historical context of the environmental degradation arising from China's modernization is different from the environmental degradation arising from the Industrial Revolution. Developed countries took centuries to fix environmental degradation, and it was a costly process. China should learn from the lessons of other countries, instead of using them as an excuse to delay their own problem-solving process. In some respects, China should be more capable of handling environmental issues in terms of the advantages of science and technology. There is no basis to justify the argument that China should concentrate on economic growth and then, when it is rich, solve the environmental problems afterwards. China must effectively treat its environmental problems while promoting its economy. In fact, both environmental protection and economic development are integrated parts of modernization. In comparison with the technologies that developed countries adopted to treat environmental problems a century ago, China should be able to more effectively cope with its environmental degradation using modern technologies, including scientific methods for treating environmental degradation and mass media for increased public environmental awareness.

Because China is still a developing country, ideally, it is the best for her to secure both environmental protection and economic development. In reality, the protection of the environment frequently conflicts with development objectives. If economic development is overemphasized, environmental protection is unavoidably sacrificed. If people have strong environmental awareness, they try to reduce the damage to the environment when they develop their economy.[60] On the one hand, Chinese people want to improve their living standard and enjoy a decent quality of life through promoting economic development; on the other hand, the process of economic development itself creates a great deal of polluters. At the present time, the top priority of the government is to improve the living standard of the Chinese people and make the nation rich. In this sense, it is possible that China's environmental issues will become worse before getting better.

Poverty is one of the main causes of environmental degradation in developing countries, because the lack of financial resources makes it more difficult for the people to protect their environment. Usually, a developing country only has limited funds for the projects of environmental protection. China remains a developing country. Yet, lack of funding is not an excuse for the government to ignore environmental degradation. China will need to invest large amounts of capital into projects designed to strengthen and address many environmental issues. China has spent five billion U.S. dollars per year dealing with the consequences of its environmental problems. Although solving environmental problems is a heavy burden for China, this amount of money is still very small in comparison to the 250 billion dollars America spends per year. China will invest nearly 450 billion *yuan* (Chinese currency), or roughly 1.5 percent of the country's annual GDP, to ultimately go toward environmental protection efforts. However, some Chinese nationalists are opposed to the concept of environmental reform, due to the potential economic setbacks.[61]

The government should make efforts to formulate more specific policy for national environmental issues and to strictly enforce its implementation. For example, the government should regulate waste. It should take the responsibility to build a comprehensive sewage system with primary waste water treatment and impose waste water management fees on all water users. The waste needs to be disposed of in municipally appointed locations; the government should be responsible for the environmental management of domestic waste, and for maintaining sanitation within cities. Local governments should be required to provide these services, as well as enforce regulation regarding waste disposal. Recyclables are presently either collected by scavengers, sorted and brought to a local transport station, or mixed with other waste.[62] The government needs to regulate toxic waste and invest in a newer, safer water system. Food inspections also need to check animals for toxic infection. Due to the fact that China has a large population and limited arable land, the main goal of Chinese agriculture is to increase the output of its production. The majority of farmers in China prefer to use chemical fertilizers and pesticides because they are cheaper and more readily available. Thus, the government should encourage peasants to explore a new way to increase their agricultural production and also help them reach their goals.[63]

The most difficult job for the government is to convince its citizens to become more environmentally conscious. Until each Chinese citizen takes responsibility for his actions, there will continue to be environmental disasters. Because the major polluters come from industries, it is especially important for the leaders of industries to increase the consciousness of environmental protection. There is a big gap between the government's regulations and the people's actions. Some Chinese enterprises have no incentive to minimize their impact on the environment. To maximize profits, many Chinese companies try to circumvent government's regulations. A significant percentage of companies, especially private companies, are not aware of the urgency of dealing with environmental problems.[64]

Various factors affect people's environmental awareness. Selfishness is an issue in China. Quite a few Chinese people focus on their own interest, but pay much less attention to public common good. People's environmental awareness and behavior are influenced by age, gender, educational attainment, income, living location, and political orientation.[65] Though females are generally more sensitive to pollution problems, unmarried young females with a higher level of education and household income are even more inclined to have a stronger environmentalist orientation than others. They often practice more environmentally-friendly behaviors than others.

Zhongjun Tang conducted a survey in Wuhan and took a sample group of a region reflecting the average national household composition, income, and economic development. The study group consisted of households with parents between the ages of 35 and 45 and children. According to the survey, all recycling taking place in the region involved selling recycling to scavengers who profited from trading waste to a dealer, or traveling far distances to directly sell recyclables to a dealer. The study shows how recycling is predominantly undertaken by the elder residents, most often women, and people with less education, corresponding to lower incomes, recycle at higher rates than better educated or more affluent citizens.[66] Usually people are most inclined to engage in recycling, if recycling behavior is rewarded or required by the community, or if they have the environmental knowledge.[67]

Generally, urban residents exhibit higher environmental awareness than rural people. This suggests that it is necessary to promote environmental education and to enhance norms around pro-environmental behavior in order to improve people's recycling behavior, especially in rural locations. Education has a critical role in increasing environmental participation, in developing environmental management systems, and in changing people's values and behavior to protect the environment.[68] When people have received higher education and have more environmental knowledge, they better understand the urgency of environmental protection and are more willing to be involved.

## CONCLUSION

China's remarkable economic success is accompanied by environmental degradation. China is facing almost all major environmental problems during globalization. These problems have serious natural and social consequences, damaging the Chinese economy, harming people's health, and escalating the conflicts between the government and the people. If the Chinese government cannot appropriately handle the environmental issues, the negative consequences could not only damage the Chinese economy and social stability, but also harm China's relations with the international community. Considering that China's environmental problems are derived not from a single source, but from multiple sources, solving them is a comprehensive project. It is not realistic to expect to fundamentally improve China's environmental degradation in a short period of time. Most likely, China's environmental problems may get much worse before getting better. Therefore, either ignorance of environmental problems or unrealistic expectations could damage the battle against China's environmental degradation. The key for the government to solve the problems is to take decisive actions through policy making, implementation and investing all necessary funding in mobilizing national projects to help local projects as well. To be sure, nurturing people's consciousness of environmental protection and changing people's attitudes toward the environment are inseparable parts of the process to control environmental degradation. It is time for schools to make greater efforts toward environmental education. Mass media also has great power to influence people's environmental awareness and behavior, as well as government environmental policy implementation.

## NOTES

1. Yale Center for Environmental Law and Policy and Center for International Earth Science Information Network at Columbia University, "2010 Environmental Performance Index," at http://epi.yale.edu.

2. Simona Alba Grano, "China's Environmental Crisis: Why Should We Care?" Working Paper, no 28, Centre for East and South-East Asian Studies, Lund University, Sweden. http://www.ace.lu.se/images/Syd_och_sydostasienstudier/working_papers/albagrano_final.pdf

3. "China tells US Embassy to stop reporting Beijing pollution," msnbcnews.com. http://worldnews.msnbc.msn.com/_news/2012/06/05/12061702-china-tells-us-embassy-to-stop-reporting-beijing-pollution?lite

4. Min Shao, Xiaoyan Tang, Yuanhang Zhang and Wenjun Li, "City Clusters in China: Air and Surface Water Pollution," *Frontiers in Ecology and the Environment* 4, No. 7 (Sep., 2006): 353.

5. Smil Vaclav, "Environmental Problems in China: Estimates of Economic Costs," *East-West Center Special Reports* no. 5 (April, 1996): 3.

6. "Beijing's Air Pollution: Blackest Day," *The Economist*, January 14, 2013.

7. Jerry McBeath and Jenifer Huang McBeath, "Environmental Degradation and Food Security Policies in China," in *China's Environmental Crisis: Domestic and Global Political Impacts and Responses,* eds. Joel Jay Kassiola and Sujian Guo (New York: Palgrave Macmillan, 2010), 97.

8. Min Shao, Xiaoyan Tang, Yuanhang Zhang and Wenjun Li. "City Clusters in China: Air and Surface Water Pollution," *Frontiers in Ecology and the Environment* 4, No. 7 (Sep., 2006): 355.

9. Richard Louis Edmonds, "China's Environmental Problems," in *Understanding Contemporary China,* ed. Robert E. Gamer (Boulder, Colo.: Lynne Rienner Publishers, 2008), 274.

10. Yong Chen and Wang Yiqian. "Qionghai Lake, Sichuan, China: Environmental Degradation and the Need for Multidimensional Management." *Mountain Research and Development* 23.1 (2003): 69.

11. Min Shao, Xiaoyan Tang, Yuanhang Zhang and Wenjun Li. "City Clusters in China: Air and Surface Water Pollution," *Frontiers in Ecology and the Environment* 4, No. 7 (Sep., 2006): 357.

12. Yu, Guangqian, Dianjun Sun, and Yan Zheng, "Health Effects of Exposure to Natural Arsenic in Groundwater and Coal in China: An Overview of Occurrence." *Environmental Health Prospective* 115 No.4 (2007): 636.

13. Wei Liang, "Changing Climate: China's New Interest in Global Climate Change Negotiations," in *China's Environmental Crisis*, eds. Joel Jay Kassiola and Sujian Guo (New York: Palgrave Macmillan, 2010), 64.

14. Associated Press, "China Risks Environmental Collapse," *Washington Post,* 12 March 2006.

15. Jerry McBeath and Jenifer Huang McBeath, "Environmental Degradation and Food Security Policies in China," in *China's Environmental Crisis: Domestic and Global Political Impacts and Responses,* eds. Joel Jay Kassiola and Sujian Guo (New York: Palgrave Macmillan, 2010), 101.

16. Jikun Huang and Scott Rozelle, "Environmental Stress and Grain Yields in China," *American Journal of Agricultural Economics* 77, No. 4 (Nov., 1995): 853.

17. Jerry McBeath and Jenifer Huang McBeath, "Environmental Degradation and Food Security Policies in China," in *China's Environmental Crisis: Domestic and Global Political Impacts and Responses,* eds. Joel Jay Kassiola and Sujian Guo (New York: Palgrave Macmillan, 2010), 93.

18. Duncan Clark, "West Blamed for Rapid Increase in China's $CO_2$," *the Guardian*, 23 February 2009.

19. Carin Zissis, "China's Environmental Crisis," *Council on Foreign Relations,* 4 http://www.cfr.org/china/chinas-environmental-crisis/p12608#p1 (Accessed on 20 December 2011)

20. Carin Zissis, "China's Environmental Crisis," *Council on Foreign Relations,* 4 August 2008, http://www.cfr.org/china/chinas-environmental-crisis/p12608#p1 (Accessed on 12 December 2011)

21. *China from Inside*, http://www.pbs.org/kqed/chinainside/nature/greengdp.html (January 9, 2013)

22. Timothy Ka-ying Wong and Shirley Po-san Wan, "Environmental Awareness and Behavior in Hong Kong: A Decade of Development." http://web.thu.edu.tw/g96540022/www/taspaa/essay/pdf/environment.pdf

23. Jim Zhang and Kirk R. Smth, "Household Air Pollution from Coal and Biomass Fuels in China: Measurements, Health Impacts, and Interventions," *Environmental Health Perspectives* 115, No. 6 (Jun., 2007): 848.

24. Ibid., 850.

25. Nathan Nankivell, "China's Pollution and the Threat to Domestic and Regional Stability," *Asia-Pacific Journal Japanese Focus* http://www.japanfocus.org/-Nathan-Nankivell/1799 (12 December 2011)

26. Wei Liang, "Changing Climate: China's New Interest in Global Climate Change Negotiations," in *China's Environmental Crisis*, eds. Joel Jay Kassiola and Sujian Guo (New York: Palgrave Macmillan, 2010), 64.

27. H. Keith Florig, "China's Air Pollution Risks," *Environmental Science & Technology* 31, No. 6 (1997): 274A.

28. Kevin Holden, "Chinese Air Pollution Deadliest in the World." *National Geographic News*, 9 July 2007.

29. Edward Wong, "Air Pollution Linked to 1.2 Million Premature Death in China," *New York Times*, April 1, 2013.

30. Murray Scot Tanner, "China Rethinks Unrest," *Washington Quarterly* 27.3 (2004): 138.

31. Thomas Lum, "Social Unrest in China," *Congressional Research Service ~ The Library of Congress,* CRS Report for Congress, 8 May 2006.

32. Jane Macartney, "China Fears Year Of Conflict As Millions Struggle To Find Jobs," *Times Online,* 7 January 2009.

33. "Obama Makes Climate Change a National Priority," *America.gov.* 27 January 2009 http://www.america.gov/st/energy-english/2009/January/20090127161856lcnirellep9. 743899e-02.html (Accessed on 12 December 2011)

34. Tania Branigan, "China Pays High Environmental and Social Price for Reliance on Coal Pollution," *The Guardian,* 27 October 2008.

35. "China Announces Targets On Carbon Emission Cuts," *www.Chinaview.cn,* 26 November 2009 http://www.xinhuanet.com/english/ (27 November 2009)

36. Xibing Huang, Dingtao Zhao, Colin G. Brown, Yanrui W and Scott A. Waldron, "Environmental Issues and Policy Priorities in China: A Content Analysis of Government Documents," China: *An International Journal* 8, no. 2 (Sep. 2010): 220.

37. Wei Liang, "Changing Climate: China's New Interest in Global Climate Change Negotiations," in *China's Environmental Crisis*, eds. Joel Jay Kassiola and Sujian Guo (New York: Palgrave Macmillan, 2010), 72.

38. Yong Chen , and Wang Yiqian. "Qionghai Lake, Sichuan, China: Environmental Degradation and the Need for Multidimensional Management," *Mountain Research and Development* 23.1 (2003): 65.

39. Timothy Ka-ying Wong and Shirley Po-san Wan, "Environmental Awareness and Behavior in Hong Kong: A Decade of Development." http://web.thu.edu.tw/g96540022/www/taspaa/essay/pdf/

40. Min Shao, Xiaoyan Tang, Yuanhang Zhang and Wenjun Li. "City Clusters in China: Air and Surface Water Pollution," *Frontiers in Ecology and the Environment* 4, No. 7 (Sep., 2006): 355.

41. Jerry McBeath and Jenifer Huang McBeath, "Environmental Degradation and Food Security Policies in China," in *China's Environmental Crisis: Domestic and Global Political Impacts and Responses,* eds. Joel Jay Kassiola and Sujian Guo (New York: Palgrave Macmillan, 2010), 96.

42. Richard Louis Edmonds, "China's Environmental Problems," in *Understanding Contemporary China.* ed. Robert E. Gamer (Boulder, Colo.: Lynne Rienner Publishers, 2008), 271.

43. Jerry McBeath and Jenifer Huang McBeath, "Environmental Degradation and Food Security Policies in China," in *China's Environmental Crisis: Domestic and Global Political Impacts and Responses,* eds. Joel Jay Kassiola and Sujian Guo (New York: Palgrave Macmillan, 2010), 89.

44. Artur Victoria, "Environment and Human Behavior," http://ezinearticles.com/?Environment-and-Human-Behavior&id=2536742

45. "China's urban population surges to 665.57 million," *Xinhuanet.com* http://news.xinhuanet.com/english2010/china/2011-04/28/c_13849936.htm (Accessed on 12 December 2011)

46. Elizabeth Economy, "The Great Leap Backward?: The Costs of China's Environmental Crisis," *Foreign Affairs,* 86, No. 5 (September, 2007): 38.

47. Jim Yardley, "China Announces More Pollution Controls," *The New York Times,* 1 August 2008.

48. Xiaoliu Yan, and Jinwu Pang, "Implementing China's 'Water Agenda 21'" *Frontiers in Ecology and the Environment* 4, No.7 (2006): 362.

49. Jerry McBeath and Jenifer Huang McBeath, "Environmental Degradation and Food Security Policies in China," in *China's Environmental Crisis: Domestic and Global Political Impacts and Responses,* eds. Joel Jay Kassiola and Sujian Guo (New York: Palgrave Macmillan, 2010), 90.

50. Eileen B. Claussen, "US Foreign Policy and the Environment: Engagement for the Next Century," *SAIS Review* 17.1 (1997): 93.

51. Hong Jiang, "Desertification in China: Problems with Policies and Perceptions," in *China's Environmental Crisis*, eds. Joel Jay Kassiola and Sujian Guo (New York: Palgrave Macmillan, 2010), 26.

52. Timothy Ka-ying Wong and Shirley Po-san Wan, "Environmental Awareness and Behavior in Hong Kong: A Decade of Development."

53. Aiman Siddiqui, "Human Behavior and Environmental Degradation." http://www.ecoinsee.org/6bconf/Theme%20E/E.3.4%20Aiman.pdf

54. Chandran Nair, *Consumptionomics: Asia's Role in Reshaping Capitalism and Saving the Planet* (New York: Wiley, 2011).

55. Ibid.

56. Xiaolin Xi and Lihong Fan, "Public Environment Awareness in China: An Analysis of the Results of Public Surveys," http://www.andrew.cmu.edu/user/kf0f/Envir_Awareness_Report.pdf

57. Xiaolin Xi and Lihong Fan, "Public Environment Awareness in China: An Analysis of the Results of Public Surveys," http://www.andrew.cmu.edu/user/kf0f/Envir_Awareness_Report.pdf

58. Timothy Ka-ying Wong and Shirley Po-san Wan, "Environmental Awareness and Behavior in Hong Kong: A Decade of Development," http://web.thu.edu.tw/g96540022/www/taspaa/essay/pdf/environment.pdf

59. "Hu Jintao's Speech on Climate Change," *New York Times,* 22 September 2009.

60. Xiaolin Xi and Lihong Fan, "Public Environment Awareness in China: An Analysis of the Results of Public Surveys," http://www.andrew.cmu.edu/user/kf0f/Envir_Awareness_Report.pdf

61. Abigail R Jahiel, "The Contradictory Impact of Reform on Environmental Protection in China," *The China Quarterly* 149 (1997): 81.

62. Yong Geng, "Developing the circular economy in China: Challenges and opportunities for achieving 'leapfrog development,'" *International Journal of sustainable Development & World Ecology* 15 (2008): 235.

63. Mei Chengrui and Harold E. Dregne, "Silt and the Future Development of China's Yellow River," *The Geographical Journal* 167, No. 1 (Mar., 2001): 7.

64. Justin Zackey, "Peasant Perspectives on Deforestation in Southwest China: Social Discontent and Environmental Mismanagement," *Mountain Research and Development* 27, No. 2 (May 2007):153.

65. Jones RE Dunlap, "The Social Bases of Environmental Concern: Have They Changed Over Time?" Rural Sociology, 57 (1992): 28-47.

66. Shichao Li, "Recycling behavior Under China's Social and Economic Transition : The Case of Metropolitan Wuhan," *Environment and Behavior,* 35, No. 6 (2003) : 794.

67. Zhongjun Tang, "Determining Socio-Psychological Drivers for Rural Household Recycling Behavior in Developing Countries: A Case Study from Wugan, Hunan, China," *Environment and Behavior* 43, No. 6 (2011): 865.

68. Artur Victoria, "Environment and Human Behavior," http://ezinearticles.com/?Environment-and-Human-Behavior&id=2536742

*Chapter Eight*

# Chinese Political System

Economic systems and political systems are closely intertwined. Whether or not China is able to sustain its economic growth in the future largely depends on Chinese political reform because Chinese political reform lags far behind economic reform. After discussing the Chinese economy and environmental issues, it is necessary to explore the Chinese political system. The Chinese political system refers to the affairs of the government, which includes the Communist Party and its military, the People's Liberation Army, the State, and the National People's Congress (NPC), which is China's legislature. According to the Constitution of China, the People's Republic of China was founded by the Communist Party of China, which is the country's sole political party in power. There is an ongoing debate about what political system is best for China. The CPC has firmly rejected implementing the Western political system and has insisted that the communist political system is the best for China, a so-called socialist system with Chinese characteristics. The Eighteenth National Congress of the Communist Party of China reaffirms that "the path of socialism with Chinese characteristics, the system of theories of socialism with Chinese characteristics and the socialist system with Chinese characteristics are the fundamental accomplishments made by the Party and people in the course of arduous struggle over the past 90-plus years. We must cherish these accomplishments, uphold them all the time and continue to enrich them."[1] While some Chinese scholars agree that the one-party system has proven to be remarkably adaptable to changing times,[2] many Westerners believe the modern democratic system to be superior, "because the rotation of political parties by voting allows the flexibility required for the government to make policy changes that meet the demands of changing times and thereby better reflect the will of the people. In contrast, China's one-party system is rigid, and the CPC's monopoly on power disconnects it from the people."[3] This chapter will examine the changes of Chinese political systems through the centuries of revolution, discuss the nature of the current Chinese political system, compare the current political system with the modern democratic system, and assess the attitudes of the CPC toward modern democracy to see the possibilities of the Chinese political system in the future.

## CHINESE REVOLUTIONS THROUGH A CENTURY

In the last century, the four revolutions—the Revolution of 1911, the May Fourth Movement of 1919, the Communist Revolution of 1949, and the second communist revolution of 1978 (the reform movement)—were major revolutions of Chinese society in the twentieth century. The Revolution of 1911 was led by Sun Yat-sen, the first president of the Republic of China.[4] Sun was the first man in Chinese history to systematically advocate democratic principles, arguing that it was not enough to acknowledge the sovereignty of the country and the end of the revolution could not win without a democracy.[5] The Revolution of 1911 aimed to topple the Chinese feudal system and to establish a modern nation-state. Although the Revolution of 1911 overthrew the last emperor, it made little impact on common Chinese people, especially in the rural areas.[6] Wang Zheng notes that "the 1911 Revolution failed to establish a strong modern nation-state. Instead, it ended in a shamble of warlordism."[7] The reason for the failure, on the one hand, was that the Revolution of 1911 was not a bourgeois revolution, because most of its revolutionaries were high-ranking officials, landowners, military officers, the heads of secret societies and armed bands.[8] Thus, the revolution "could not get the genuine support from the people."[9] On the other hand, the feudal forces were too strong, and the fruit of revolution was usurped by feudal warlords. This revolution failed to establish a capitalist democratic system. On March 12, 1925, Sun died of liver cancer and his will, stated from his deathbed, was that since the revolution was not successful, comrades must keep going on.

The May Fourth Movement of 1919 was directly triggered by the Paris Peace Conference. On April 30, 1919, Woodrow Wilson, President of the United States, Lloyd George of Britain and Clemenceau of France, decided to transfer all of Germany's interests in Shandong province to Japan. When Chinese students heard the decision made by the Conference, thousands of University students, for the first time in modern Chinese history, walked on Tiananmen Square to protest the decision and ended up committing violence against the corrupt Chinese government. Unlike the Revolution of 1911, the May Fourth Movement was not a radical revolution for changing the Chinese political system, but it was a cultural movement, attempting to promote science and democracy by introducing Western culture. The May Fourth Movement stressed the cultural aspects of the movement rather than the patriotic aspect.[10] Because China's problems were "profoundly cultural,"[11] the May Fourth Movement, as a cultural movement, was very meaningful to resolving China's problems and also paved a way for introducing the experience of the Russian Revolution of 1917 to China.

The Communist Revolution of 1949 refers to the communist movement from its beginning up to the founding of the People's Republic of China. The revolution, which was led by the CPC and guided by Marxism, transformed China from a semi-feudal and semi-capitalist society to a socialist country and from a semi-colony to an independent country. When Jiang Jieshi suppressed the communist movement in 1927, all communist forces withdrew from every city and began developing the Red Army in the countryside. According to Mao Zedong, the basic and reliable force of the revolution was the Chinese peasants and that the best way to seize power in the Chinese context was to steer the revolution from the countryside to the city. The headquarters of the CPC before 1949 was in Yanan, a poor and remote area located in Northwest China. The Red Army controlled the nearby areas of the Shan Gan Ning Border Region, the so-called "liberated base." The leaders of the communist revolution were deeply influenced by Chinese peasants. Today, the party as the sole leadership does not govern through its 80 million members, but through the party's select leaders. According to Kenneth Lieberthal, the top power elite, comprising about 25 to 35 individuals, controls China, and so party rule represents the interests of only a small group, not of the people.[12] Mao believed that socialist revolution and class struggle were the ways to develop a new China, so he never stopped mobilizing political campaigns during his lifetime. The Cultural Revolution in 1966 brought China into unprecedented and overall chaos and brought the Chinese economy to the verge of collapse. After Mao's death in 1976, in order for the party to regain its legitimacy, the party had no choice but to launch a reform movement with the goal of improving the living standard of the Chinese people.[13] The reform movement has not fundamentally changed the Chinese political system but altered the central task of the CPC from political campaign to economic development.

## CORE OF THE CHINESE POLITICAL SYSTEM

The core of politics is the relationship between the state and the individual. In democratic societies, private ownership is the foundation of the political system, and the individual is at the center of society. By contrast, public ownership is the foundation of the Chinese communist political system and the individual is controlled by the state in China. In democratic societies, political parties are agents to drive politics forward and keep politics in balance. An elected president represents an entire nation, not a single party. Yet, the Communist Party of China is not a voluntary political association, but a political and administrative entity. The party holds sole power over government and all other organizations, so Western scholars view the Chinese government as party/state.

Chapter 1 indicates that patriarchal culture is the basic characteristic of Chinese history. In the Chinese peasants' revolutionary tradition, whoever seized the state power sat on the throne. Following this old tradition, Mao Zedong became the paramount leader of the country after the party took power. Mao withdrew from the forefront of Chinese politics twice because of his failures during his tenure, but he never gave up his control of the party. Deng held the position of the president of the Central Military Commission in order to control his successor after he retired from the party. Jiang Zemin followed Deng's example and took over the presidency of the Central Military Commission to control his successor. Surprisingly, Hu Jintao discontinued this model of the power transition and resigned both positions of the General Secretary of the Party and the General Military Commission at the Eighteenth National Conference of the Chinese Communist Party which was held in November 2012, so that the new leader Xi Jinping does not have to live under the shadow of retired communist leaders.

The nature of China's party leadership is that the party controls the entire country through its organization, its ideology, and its structural system. In other words, party controls the government, the society, and the individuals. In order to guarantee its monopolistic power, the party organized a highly centralized hierarchical government, society, mass organizations, economic activities, the military, and media.[14] The state in China is the party/state and is a product of the party.[15] Shiping Zheng points out that "nothing is more crucial than the party's relationship with the state institutions."[16] Under the leadership of the party, the state is unable to function as an independent organ; the state is dependent on the CPC. Theoretically, China has the three powers of judicial, legislative, and executive branches, but the three powers and all other national organs, including the Chinese People's Political Consultative Conference and the military institution, according the Constitution of China, are under the leadership of the Communist Party of China. All the top leaders at the national level—the National People's Congress, the Judicial Department, the State Council, the Chinese People's Political Consultative Conference, and the Central Military Committee—are the members of the party politburo. Every head of the political and administrative branches at the national level, including the State Planning Commission, the State Education Commission, the State Commission for Reconstructing Economy, the National Economy Commission, propaganda bureaucracies, personnel bureaucracies, and civilian coercive bureaucracies, is overseen by a member of the Political Bureau of the Central Committee of the CPC. Most of the important government posts from the national to the local level, including legislative, judicial, administrative, and military institutions—even mass organizations such as the Youth League Committee, All-China Women's Federation, and All-China Worker's Federation—are occupied by members of the party leadership. The party system is pyramidal. All of the party's decisions are made by a small group that is part of the member of the Standing Committee of the Political Bureau.

In the post-Mao era, the party relaxed some of its controls, giving the government more autonomy. After Deng died in 1997, the position of a single leader over the party is weakened, but the party refuses to practice multiparty politics. The era of party control is not over, because party rule does not strongly depend upon a paramount leader, but rather, upon the party's controlling system, including the organizational system, the military forces, and ideological principles.[17] Although the charismatic leaders, Mao and Deng, have gone, the party's controlling system remains, and works. The general secretary of the party still plays a central role in the decision-making process and is able to exercise his personal powers over the government and society through the party system.

Most political scientists suggest that modern democracy is the most advanced political system in the world, because modern democracy guarantees individual rights, moderates conflicts, regulates political competition, makes government more legitimate, improves the quality of government, and recruits political leaders from a large pool.[18] The democratic movement has become global in scope since the third democratic wave began in 1974.[19] Since then, more than thirty countries have shifted from authoritarianism to democracy. According to Francis Fukuyama, modern democracy is the best social and political system; it may constitute the "end point of mankind's ideological evolution," the "final form of human government" and the "end of history."[20] He has predicted that "free democratic governments [will] continue to spread to more and more countries around the world."[21]

In premodern China, the Chinese people were ruled by absolute monarchical government and they had no experience with democratic ideas until modern times.[22] No school of thought in premodern China referenced modern democracy. Mencian ideas of *min-ben* (for the people) and Confucian ideas of benevolence completely differ from democratic principles. Kang Youwei (1858-1927) and Liang Qichao (1873-1929), the first and most influential political reformers in modern China, believed that constitutional monarchy was the best form of government. In 1906, the Chinese government was inspired by the political reforms in Japan and issued an imperial edict calling for a constitutional government. The May Fourth Movement of 1919 was the first public call for modern democracy in Chinese history, but the nationalist government made little efforts to modern democratic system.

During the thirty-five years after the Nationalist government left the main-land for Taiwan, the Nationalist Party continued to exercise an authoritarian power under a one-party system in Taiwan until October 1986, so the Taiwa-nese never got a chance to enjoy real modern democracy during the time of Jiang Jieshi.

In mainland China, Mao also did not give modern democracy a chance to succeed. Instead, Mao implemented a new socialist democratic system. Western scholars believe that socialist democracy bears little resemblance to modern democracy.[23] Deng's economic reform movement promoted eco-nomic development and triggered a democratic zeal of the Chinese people as well, and finally reached its peak—the Tiananmen Square Protest of 1989. Unfortunately, Deng did not hesitate to sacrifice his previous supporters and suppressed the democratic movement by ordering the PLA to kill the protes-tors in Tiananmen Square. Political reform was stagnant during the adminis-tration of Jiang Zemin and Hu Jintao. Some top Chinese leaders, such as Wen Jiabao, advocated political reform, but never took serious actions.

One of the main arguments for the party to refuse democracy is that China learned its lessons from the reform movement in the former Soviet Union. Unlike the situation in China, at the beginning of economic reform, Mikhail Gorbachev introduced the kind of political reform and dissolved the commu-nist party that would make economic reform possible. However, "the conse-quences of Gorbachev's bold strategy were political chaos and economic failure."[24] By contrast, Deng "took a more cautious approach of introducing economic reforms without political reforms."[25] From the viewpoint of the CPC, China must follow a gradual reform model, beginning with economic reform, so that China can go through the transitional period smoothly. How-ever, it is widely believed by the majority of the Chinese people and Western scholars that the main reason for the CPC to refuse political reform is to protect the special interests of a small group—the interests of some Chinese officials and their families.

## HAS CHINA CHANGED ITS POLITICAL IDENTITY?

According to official Chinese documents, the reform movement is the second socialist revolution. The purpose of the first socialist revolution in 1949 was to transform political power and ownership, yet the purpose of the second socialist revolution was to realize a socialist modernization with Chinese characteristics. The party has realized there is a fundamental conflict be-tween a free market economy and the socialist system, but in order to save the socialist system, it pursues the pragmatic formula of stimulating econom-ic reform by adopting both socialist principles and capitalist means. In this sense, what changed for the party in the post-Mao era is not the political system, but only economic measures. Deng's philosophy of the reform movement may look like a new idea, but obviously it is a refurbished version of the slogan—"Chinese learning is for basis, Western learning is for use," adopted by the Self-Strengthening Movement in the nineteenth century.

The Chinese people are becoming rich. When their living standard reaches a certain level, they demand political participation and democracy. Without a doubt, China's rapid economic growth would generate other changes in all social aspects, and China has begun to depart from communism and state socialism.[26] Ideologically, Marxism and Maoism have been reassessed. Economically, China is moving from an agricultural country to an industrial country. The traditional planned economy is moving into the socialist market economy, and sole public ownership has been replaced by six types of ownership. Politically, since the death of Deng Xiaoping, a single charismatic leader no longer holds all power and controls the entire country.

The central government is losing control at the local level because of decentralization, but government authority at the provincial level is gaining power. China is moving from a Lenin-state to an authoritarian system. Spiritually, all citizens are legally permitted to practice their personal religious faith as long as they do not organize independent religious groups that threaten the state. At present, at least five types of culture—Chinese traditional culture, Marxism-Maoism-Dengism, Western culture, religious culture, and nationalism—are coexisting and developing. The cultural development of recent years could be described as the decline of Marxism, the renaissance of Western political science, other non-Marxist thoughts, and the renaissance of Chinese traditional thought.[27] Because China's transitions appear imbalanced, some scholars have even noted that China really consists of many different Chinas, linguistically and ethnically.[28] The Chinese people in advanced areas are more concerned about culture and politics. Young people are inclined to reject Chinese traditional culture and the new Confucian nationalism, while thirsting for Western thought. Some observers are surprised by China's impressive changes and argue that China is becoming a capitalist society, that China is no longer a meaningful communist country, and that what communism is left in China is only the Communist Party itself. Moreover, some scholars believe that the party is dead. They think that as China becomes more like Western societies, it is on the verge of becoming a democratic system.

However, lifestyles and living standards cannot represent the nature of a nation. A nation's identity is determined by the nature of the state. China is a socialist country, as determined by the nature of the state/party. A careful observation of the Chinese way of life—including religious freedoms, human rights, censorship, the elections, and legislative systems—will show that the majority of the Chinese people still live with the communist political system. At present China "remains unchanged in its political nature."[29] Although official Chinese documents do not clarify the identity of China, the major Chinese official documents, such as the Constitution of the People's Republic of China, the Constitution of the Chinese Communist Party, the constitutions of all mass organizations, continue to insist that China is a socialist country with Chinese characteristics. According to J. Howard W. Rhys, "national identity does not depend on racial heritage," but on cultural factors and political systems.[30] Therefore, China's transitions from state socialism, including the political system, economic development, and ideological censorship, "are far from complete,"[31] even though China has achieved significant progress in many areas.[32] The state/party nation remains stable,[33] though China is no longer the typical Lenin-state.

## IS THE CPC READY FOR MODERN DEMOCRACY?

If the CPC were ready for modern democracy, it would acknowledge the basic principles of democracy. Modern democratic society is ruled by the people through law, not by a single political party or a single person. In China, legitimacy is what conforms to the top leader of the CPC. The party does not govern China by law but, rather, by party policy and the will of its top leaders. The personal decision of leadership is above the law. Under the Mao regime, the constitution and law together served as a rubber stamp. Mao was at the center of Chinese politics and served in an absolute dictatorship role. He exercised unfettered personal authority over the party, government, society, the military, the economy, and ideology. He promulgated his theory as ultimate truth and infallible dogma. The Chinese political system under the Mao regime was actually personalism, nepotism, and authoritarianism functioning together. After Mao died, China began decentralizing personal power during the reform movement, but still emphasized personal loyalty as the criterion for appointment. Chinese politics is essentially personal politics by nature.

The National People's Congress (NPC), founded in 1954, never played an independent role in the Mao era, but was only a tool for the party. The NPC was completely paralyzed during the ten years of the Cultural Revolution. In order to increase the new government's acceptance and heighten government efficiency, the post-Mao government began to restore the NPC's normal activities in 1978.[34] In the past thirty years, the NPC has become stronger, and Chinese legislatures have made considerable progress. However, the CPC still has much power to interfere in NPC affairs through its power of appointments. The delegates of NPC have no requirement to speak for the people because the candidates for delegate are not really elected by the people. Structural reforms in the NPC, such as free elections, campaigning, longer sessions and meaningful votes, were rejected.[35] Other issues, such as legislative checks and balances, "were discussed but never adopted."[36] Another serious legal problem in China is that law enforcement officials break the laws they are in charge of enforcing. For instance, arbitrary arrest and detention for political purposes remain serious problems. Police continue to hold individuals without granting them access to their family or a lawyer, and trials continue to be conducted in secret.[37] All of these legal problems come from the party and serve to override juridical autonomy and interfere with the police, the courts, and legal proceedings.[38] Therefore, "party interference and the destruction of the judicial system" are the main obstacles to Chinese legal reform.[39]

Modern democratic society is based on a well-developed civil society. Law is legalized consensus, the formation of the public will. A lawful country is based on a well-developed civil society because its legal system relies upon civil society as the source to improve the legal system and to make the state more legitimate. In turn, the civil society is the basic supporter of legitimate government. Therefore, a high degree of civil society is always associated with a democratic system. The degree of civil society is the criterion used to measure the degree of separation between the state and society.[40] Although the emergence of civil society is not a sufficient condition for democratization, it is a necessary precondition. Democratic institutions have little meaning without a well-developed civil society.[41] The term civil society can be considered to describe the realm of institutional social life, which is "self-generating, self-supporting, and autonomous from the state."[42] In China, civil society is a new phenomenon. In premodern China, there was neither a public realm between the state and society, nor the separation of the state and society. The Republic of China was "a sheet of loose sand" with no basic foundation for a civil society before 1949.[43]

In the Mao era, the party thoroughly penetrated society, controlled the economic system and public opinion, and shaped individuals' political conduct by means of secret police forces.[44] Mao also isolated China from the rest of the world, forbade the Chinese people to listen to shortwave radio under penalty of criminal law, cut off connections between the countryside and the city by the rigid registration system, and prohibited peasants from moving from the countryside to the city, while urban residents were prohibited from moving from one place to another. Since the economic reform began in 1978, the market economy has weakened the vertical party/state control of society.[45] Consequently, professional and mass organizations have developed rapidly. However, among these associations, the mass organizations sponsored by the state are still the most influential and popular force. The most important positions in mass organizations are appointed by the party; and the mass organizations eventually become part of the government authority, and they are unwilling to break off formal relations with the party to seek autonomy from the party/state because they want to keep their own political and economic privileges. Dissident activities are prohibited and are strictly suppressed. The conflict between the state and society has not been resolved.[46]

Individual rights are guaranteed in a democratic society. The role and status of the individual is the gauge used to evaluate the degree of social civilization. *The Universal Declaration of Human Rights*, promulgated by the United Nations in 1948, identified human rights as "a common standard of achievement for all peoples and all nations."[47] In theory, the Chinese people fully enjoy all fundamental rights. In practice, the CPC views "political rights and equality" the same as Western rights. The CPC argues that China is a sovereign country and Western countries should not impose Westernized human rights on China. Chinese society would become disordered if the Chinese people practiced Westernized human rights on Chinese soil. The CPC insists that China has a population of almost 1.34 billion and it will take a long time for the Chinese people to learn democracy and fully implement the principle of human rights. According to Chinese official logic, it would destabilize society if China accepted the principle of human rights unconditionally.

Finally, political participation is part of the process of democratization. The degree of participation is determined by two factors—how much political interest the people have, and how much law permit the people's participation. Under the Mao regime, most Chinese people blindly followed Mao and participated in mass politics. Although the political system has gradually improved in the post-Mao era, the Chinese people have only limited opportunities for political participation. In the countryside, Chinese peasants were granted rights to vote for their village leaders nine years ago. The Chinese government exaggerated this progress and called this village election democracy with Chinese characteristics. Some American scholars view village elections as a good start for China's future. Even former U.S. President Jimmy Carter made a special trip to China to monitor the village elections in 2001. As a matter of fact, the Chinese village, usually composed of twenty to fifty families, or less, is not a government authority, but a small work group. At this point, village elections could be good practice for democracy, but they insignificantly affect Chinese politics. In urban areas, residents generally have only the right to participate in politics in their *danwei* (work unit) and to vote for the representatives of the local People's Congress. They still do not have the right to elect the head of the *danwei*. In contrast with the villages, *danwei* in cities play a more important role in influencing social and governmental affairs, so the party wants to preserve its right to appoint the head of *danwei* choosing from those employees who are loyal to the government and the party. Samuel Huntington suggests that the criterion of a democracy is whether power is turned over from one party or group to another through the general elections.[48]

Real participation must be involved in decision making. In China, the decision-making process is divided into three stages: agenda setting, decision making, and policy implementation.[49] Political participation in China is only permitted in the implementation stage, for example, in village elections and *danwei* elections. Multiparty and independent campaigns are prohibited; appeals and adversarial activities are considered dissident activities; and political resistance is regarded as an anti-government activity that must be suppressed. The Chinese common people have no way to influence the first two stages of the decision-making process directly, nor are they allowed to publicize their democratic ideas in public squares. In China, no opposition party is allowed to campaign for office. All mayors, governors, and the president are appointed by the party. All candidates for the NPC at all levels are nominated by the government. Recently, some self-nominated candidates have emerged, but the government has prohibited their political campaigns. In order to restrict political participation within the official framework, the government has suppressed dissident activities by eliminating organizational activities and reshaping "people's psychological orientation" through political education and various punishments,[50] such as reeducation through the labor system. The Chinese government has announced that it will reform the program of reeducation through labor system in 2013, but it is still unclear how the government reforms the notorious program. Many scholars assert that the Chinese people participate in politics without influence.[51] Some even reject the notion of participation in the Chinese Communist regime.[52]

## CONCLUSION

China's political system has been changed through the centuries, but China still carries out the one party system. Chinese political reform is a very slow process, while the Chinese economy has been growing rapidly since early 1980s. Despite the demands for political change from the majority of the Chinese people, the CPC has made it very clear that China does not need Western democracy. Can China continue its economic growth without political reform? Will China automatically move toward democratization if it fulfills its economic goals and becomes a developed country? Obviously, the answers to both questions are no. An integrated reform movement includes both economic reform and political reform. Political change has lagged far behind economic reform, not because the Chinese people have had no desire to promote political reform, but because the CPC believes that China should maintain harmony between the market economy and the socialist system.[53] However, the market economy and the socialist system are essentially opposite forces. The development of China's economy and the market system unavoidably conflict with the present Chinese political system. Theoretically, the market economy is an irresistible force that sooner or later will lead to a democratic society. Practically, "democratization is not a natural process, but a political one."[54] Political reform in present-day China has become urgent, but is a very difficult task and it may take a long time to do.

## NOTES

1. *Hu Jintao's report at 18th National Congress of Communist Party of China.* Beijing China, 2012.

2. Eric X. Li, "China's political system is more flexible than US democracy," *Christian Science Monitor*, 10 17, 2011.

3. http://hnn.us/articles/eric-x-li-chinas-political-system-more-flexible-us-democracy

4. Harold Z. Shiffrin, *Sun Yat-sen, Reluctant Revolutionary* (Boston: Little, Brown and Company, 1980), 4.

5. A James Gregor, *Marxism, China & Development: Reflections on Theory and Reality* (New Brunswick, N.J.: Transaction Publishers, 1995), 233.

6. Michael Gasster, *Chinese Intellectuals and the Revolution of 1911* (Seattle: University of Washington Press, 1969), 229.

7. Wang Zheng, *Women in the Enlightenment* (Berkeley, Calif.: University of California Press, 1999), 10.

8. Jonathan D. Spence, *Chinese Roundabout: Essays in History and Culture* (New York: W.W. Norton, & Company, 1993), 269.

9. Ren Zhongping, "Great Awakening of Chinese Nation-marking 90th Anniversary of 1911 Revolution," *People's Daily*, 9 October 2001.

10. Chow Tse-tsung, *The May Fourth Movement: Intellectual Revolution in Modern China* (Cambridge, Mass.: Harvard University Press, 1960), 1.

11. Benjamin I. Schwartz, "Introduction," in *Reflections on the May Fourth Movement: A Symposium*, ed. Benjamin I. Schwartz (Cambridge, Mass.: Harvard University Press, 1972), 7.

12. Kenneth Lieberthal, *Governing China: From Revolution through Reform* (New York: W.W. Norton & Company, 1995), 181.

13. James A. Dorn, ed. *China in the New Millennium* (Washington, DC: CATO Institute, 1998), 1.

14. Quoted in Tai-Chun Kuo and Ramon H. Myers, *Understanding Communist China: Communist China Studies in the United States and the Republic of China, 1949-1978* (Stanford, Calif.: Hoover Institution Press, 1986), 17.

15. Shiping Zheng, *Party vs. State in Post-1949 China: The Institutional Dilemma* (New York: Cambridge University Press, 1998), 17.

16. Ibid.

17. Zheng said, "Once the paramount leader is gone, the revolutionary ideology becomes bankrupt, and the organizational discipline erodes, the party as we know it is over." See Zheng, *Party vs. State in Post-1949 China: The Institutional Dilemma*, 263.

18. Andrew J. Nathan, *Chinese Democracy* (New York: Knopf. 1985), 225.

19. Samuel P. Huntington, *The Third Wave: Democratization in the Late Twentieth Century* (Norman: University of Oklahoma Press, 1991), 5.

20. Francis Fukuyama, *The End of History and the Last Man* (New York: Maxwell Macmillan International, 1992), 34.

21. Ibid.

22. Mingchien Joshua, *Modern Democracy in China* (Shanghai, China: Commercial Press, 1923), 1.

23. Suzanne Ogden, *China's Unresolved Issues: Politics, Development, and Culture* (Englewood Cliffs, N.J.: Prentice Hall, 1995), 202.

24. Susan L. Shirk, *The Political Logic of Economic Reform in China* (Berkeley: University of California Press, 1993), 333.

25. Ibid., 334.

26. This viewpoint forms the central argument of the following two books: Edwin A. Winckler, ed., *Transition from Communism in China* (Boulder, Colo.: Lynne Rienner Publishers, 1999); and Yanqi Tong, *Transitions from State in Hungary and China* (New York: Rowman & Littlefield Publishers, 1997).

27. Werner Meissner, "Western Political Science in China," in *Chinese Thought in a Global Context,* ed. Karl-Heinz Pohl (Boston: Brill, 1999), 359.

28. Robert W. McGee and Danny Kin-Kong Lam, "Hong Kong's Option to Secede," *Harvard International Law Journal* 33, no. 3 (Spring 1992), 438.

29. Bernstein and Munro, *The Coming Conflict with China,* 15.

30. J. Howard W. Rhys, "Religion and National Identity," *Faculty of Religious Studies* 19 (Spring 1991), 47.

31. Tong, *Transitions from State in Hungary and China,* 234.

32. Minxin Pei, *From Reform to Revolution: The Demise of Communism in China and the Soviet Union* (Cambridge, Mass.: Harvard University Press, 1994), 7.

33. Edward Friedman, *National Identity and Democratic Prospects in Socialist China.* (Armonk, N.Y.: M.E. Sharpe, 1999), 319.

34. Kevin J. O'Brien, *Reform without Liberalization: China's National People's Congress and the Politics of Institutional Change* (New York: Cambridge University Press, 1990), 126.

35. Ibid., 177.

36. Ibid.

37. Bureau of Democracy, Human Rights, and Labor U.S. Department of State, *1999 Country Reports on Human Rights Practices.*

38. Victor C. Falkenheim, ed., *Chinese Politics from Mao to Deng* (New York: Paragon House, 1989), 9.

39. Ibid.

40. Stanley Lubman, "Introduction: The Future of Chinese Law," *China Quarterly* 138 (March 1995): 16.

41. Arthur Lewis Rosenbaum, *State and Society in China: The Consequences of Reform* (Boulder, Colo.: Westview Press, 1992), 9.

42. Edward X. Gu, "Cultural Intellectuals and the Politics of the Cultural Public Space in Communist China (1979-1989): A Case Study of Three Intellectual Groups," *Journal of Asian Studies* 58, No. 2 (May 1999): 392.

43. Alan P.L. Liu, *Mass Politics in the People's Republic: State and Society in Contemporary China* (Boulder, Colo.: Westview Press, 1996), 17.

44. Barrett L. McCormick, *Political Reform in Post-Mao China: Democracy and Bureaucracy in a Leninist State* (Berkeley: University of California Press, 1990), 7-8.

45. White, Howell, and Shang, *In Search of Civil Society,* 209-11.

46. McCormick, *Political Reform in Post-Mao China,* 201.

47. Quoted in A. I. Melden, ed., *Human Rights* (Belmont, Calif.: Wadsworth Publishing Company, 1970), 145.

48. See Christopher Marsh, *Making Russian Democracy Work: Social Capital, Economic Development, and Democratization* (Lewiston, N.Y.: Edwin Mellen Press, 2000), 14.

49. Tianjian Shi, *Political Participation in Beijing* (Cambridge, Mass: Harvard University Press, 1997), 8-22.

50. Ibid., 27.

51. Nathan, *Chinese Democracy* (New York: Knopf, 1985), 227.

52. Shi, *Political Participation in Beijing,* 5.

53. X.L. Ding, *The Decline of Communism in China: Legitimacy Crisis, 1977-1989* (New York: Cambridge University Press, 1994), 3.

54. Bruce J. Dickson, "China's Democratization and the Taiwan Experience," *Asian Survey* 38 (April 1998), 350.

## Chapter Nine

# Rampant Corruption and the Chinese Political System

Chinese political change is lagging far behind the pace of economic development. The rampant corruption in China is a symptom of the lack of political change. The CPC has realized that if China cannot effectively minimize corruption, it could seriously damage the legitimacy of the CPC and even trigger social chaos as well. However, the CPC is reluctant to admit that the current Chinese political system is the primary source of corruption and take decisive actions against corruption. Western political scientists point out that corruption is political behavior in nature because "corruption is behavior of public officials which deviates from accepted norms in order to serve private ends."[1] By contrast, Marxists believe that if corruption is found in socialist societies, "it must be a residue of the feudal past or a by-product of the polluting influence of the West."[2] Some Chinese scholars argue that the deep roots of corruption are derived from the economic system, although corruption is a political phenomenon.[3] They believe that the source of corruption is neither the CPC nor the communist political system, but the economic system in the post-Mao era. It is common sense that corruption is not confined to one particular place in the world and has existed in every country throughout history.[4] However, why is corruption more common in some societies than in others and more common at some times in the evolution of a society than at other times?[5] Under what conditions does corruption thrive? Why has corruption become so rampant in the post-Mao era? This chapter will examine the epidemic corruption in China, analyze the relationship between China's corruption and its highly centralized political system, argue that the primary source of corruption is not the reform movement, but the current political system, and find workable solutions of combating China's corruption.

## SYSTEMATIC CORRUPTION IN CHINA

In 1985, the Supreme People's Court described corruption as activities conducted by government officials who "use their position to acquire public property by misappropriation, embezzlement, theft, fraud or other illegal methods."[6] Corruption refers to the misuse of their power by public officials for private gain, thus deviating from the public good.[7] Yan Yiming points out that corrupt activities aim to gain private profits by using public power.[8] Thus, corruption "only involves the behavior of an official in his or her public role."[9] When public officials misuse their power for private gain, they are certainly in violation of the legal codes which regulate public officials.

In the annual survey of the Transparency International Corruption Perceptions Index published by the Berlin-based organization Transparency International, a score of 5.0 is considered the borderline figure that distinguishes countries that do or do not have a serious corruption problem. China received 3.6 points in 2012, ranking 80th among 174 countries in the world.[10] China's corruption is at one of the highest levels in all Asian countries.

Corruption has permeated into every sphere of society in the post-Mao era.[11] In present-day China, money can buy power to be converted back into money. Power lubricates business, e.g., changing registration (*hukou*), processing law suits, leasing land, obtaining loans, getting promotions, promoting the stock market, reducing taxes, and winning public bids to get contracts. The level of corruption is in direct proportion to the expense of enterprise in dealing with officials. The terminology *guandao* is well-known to the Chinese people. It refers to all government officials who run businesses by using their power to conduct business, thus making unlawful profits.[12] Zengke He observes that "officials engaged in speculation ("Guan Dao" and "Guan Shang") emerged as the newest new rich becoming one of the major objects of public indignation in the 1989 anti-corruption demonstration."[13] Corruption is also visible in the judiciary area, including embezzlement and bribery, abuse of fair procedures and misuse of power for personal gains. Money can facilitate the process of prosecution, reduce sentences, and buy special services in jail, such as special rooms, care, and sex. About 470 judges were punished for corruption in 2004 and about 218 judges were prosecuted in 2007.[14]

In 2003, the Chinese procuratorate oversaw some 335 corruption cases, 79 of which were cases involving over one million *yuan*.[15] Between 2003 and 2008, Chinese courts convicted more than 120,000 officials on corruption charges, an increase of 12 percent over the preceding five year period.[16] The Anti-Corruption Department investigated 142,893 corruption cases in 2011.

In the past three decades, more than 4,000 corrupt Chinese officials fled from China to foreign countries, carrying with them more than $50 billion.[17]

In 2011, corrupt Chinese officials took $123 billion overseas, accounting for 2 percent of 2011's total GDP.[18] Top destinations for high-level thieves included the United States, Canada, Australia, the Netherlands and West European countries. Due to the fact that there is no extradition treaty between China and major developed countries, some developed countries have become safe harbors for corrupt Chinese officials. For example, Lai Changxing masterminded a network that smuggled everything from cigarettes to cars and oil, and he bribed dozens of government officials between 1996 and 1999. His smuggling operation was valued at $10 billion. Lai became China's most-wanted man after he fled to Canada in 1999 and fought extradition for 12 years until he was deported in July of 2011.[19] In 2012, the Chinese government expressed in 2012 that the government will strengthen the measures to recover illicit assets transferred abroad, but, at the same time, it acknowledged there are obstacles to doing so.[20]

## CONSEQUENCES OF CHINA'S CORRUPTION

The consequence of massive corruption in China is grave, undermining the government's legitimacy, causing the government's inefficiency, restricting the development of economy, disturbing market order, widening the disparity between the poor and the rich, and creating serious social discrepancies and conflict. Corruption undermines the legitimacy of the party/state by reducing public trust.[21] Legitimacy is a necessary precondition for every government to maintain authority and social stability. A legitimate government should represent the majority of the people, but corrupt activities result in the CPC's loss of credibility and accountability. Corruption and organized crime are two serious challenges in the CPC. In the post-Mao era, the two separate challenges have merged into one—group-oriented corruption activities. The organized corruption is not for individual gain; rather, members of a group share information, risk, and mutual benefits in order to "enhance organizational performance and efficiency for the benefit of the organization's employees."[22]

Corruption damages the stability of Chinese society and delays the process of China's democratization by eroding the people's trust, shrinking civil society, reducing the effective domain of public participation, and creating inefficiencies in deliveries of public services.[23] Corruption has become the principal affliction leading to social upheaval,[24] so significantly contributes to wider social unrest and makes politics more fragile.[25] Many peasant riots in the past several years were triggered by anger over land confiscation, in which "country officials took money from business developers in return for favorable deals."[26] It should be noted that corruption among the Chinese government and party officials is a major reason for dissatisfaction among the 1.34 billion Chinese people.[27]

Corruption directly damages the development of the Chinese economy. Corrupt Chinese officials concentrate on their personal profits instead of serving the people. As a result, corrupt activities undermine rational economic choices, hurt the banking system, and increase unemployment rates. It is estimated that from 1989 to 1999 the number of corrupt Chinese officials increased by 1 percent. During that period of time, China lost anywhere between 223.3 and 1,271 billion *yuan*.[28] Corruption, including bribery, smuggling, tax fraud, and embezzlement, has cost about 98.8 billion *yuan* every year over the past two decades, making up between 13.2 percent and 16.8 percent of China's total GDP.[29] In addition, corrupt officials use public money for their own personal interests. According to Professor Wang Zhen at Beijing University, every year about 600 billion *yuan* flows into gambling places in Hong Kong, Macao, Vietnam, and Russia. About 30 percent of this amount of money comes from corrupt officials, originating from people's tax dollars. The former Mayor of Shen Yan City, Ma Xiandong, went more than ten times to Hong Kong and Macao to gamble between 1998 and 1999 and lost more than 4 million *yuan*. Former Director of the Transportation Bureau of Ji Ling Province, Cai Haowen, went abroad to gamble and lost more than 3 million *yuan*. New research found that Chinese officials' appetite for money has dramatically grown. Before the reform movement, a 10,000 *yuan* bribery case was the biggest and deserved the death penalty. The average bribe in 2008 was 8.84 million *yuan*, more than three times the 2.53 million *yuan* amount in 2007.[30]

Corruption significantly reduces inward foreign direct investment.[31] Outsiders investing in China, as compared with an uncorrupt country, would spend an additional 20 percent tax on their investment.[32] The corrupt social environment has also influenced foreign investors and driven international companies to follow hidden Chinese rules. For example, in order to secure a major real estate deal in Shanghai, Morgan Stanley offered cash and gifts to Chinese officials, although this violated the United States Foreign Corrupt Practices Act.[33] According to the U.S. Justice Department in August 2009, U.S.-based valve manufacturer Control Components Inc. (CCI) was involved in a bribery case. From 2003 through 2007, CCI paid approximately $4.9 million in bribes to officials of various foreign state-owned companies and approximately $1.95 million in bribes to officers and employees of foreign companies.[34] China National Offshore Oil Corp, along with eight other Chinese firms, accepted bribes from CCI.[35] In 2013, GlaxoSmithKline was accused of bribing to increase sales of Glaxo products in China.

Corruption has destroyed the CPC's credibility. The CPC cannot survive without the triumph of anti-corruption.[36] The most serious threat to Chinese society is not social unrest but social collapse.[37] The signs of social collapse have been appearing in China: the hidden rules have become a common phenomenon; the bottom line of moral behavior has disappeared; a group of special interests has emerged; and the systematic falsification of statistic data indicates that the entire information system of Chinese society has been fundamentally distorted. According to a survey conducted by an official Chinese magazine, *Xiao Kang*, the CPC is losing its credibility. About 90 percent of participants believe China's prostitutes are to be trusted more than Chinese politicians, just next to farmers and religious workers.[38] By comparison, in the 2007 survey, only 79 percent of the respondents said they did not trust government statistics. The sharp increase in distrust indicates a "significant drain" of government credibility.[39] It is not strange for the Chinese people to trust peasants and religious workers, but this is the first time for prostitutes to receive such an honor.

The consequences of China's corruption could be grave, although China's corruption "does not yet pose an imminent threat to its ruling status."[40] If one takes a look at the collapse of every dynasty in imperial Chinese history from the first dynasty, the Qin Dynasty, to the Qing Dynasty, it is easy to find that every dynasty's collapse was accompanied by government corruption, although every dynasty had different failures in addition to their corruption. The Revolution of 1911 benefited from the Qing government's corruption but, unfortunately, the nationalist government could not avoid the same mistake. Jiang Jieshi, the top leader of the nationalist party and government, was not accused of corruption, but he did nothing to prevent the corruption of others. This is one of the most important reasons why the nationalist government lost popular support from the Chinese people and withdrew from mainland China.

## THE REFORM MOVEMENT AND CORRUPTION

Every legitimate government should take responsibility to campaign against corruption. But what are the effective measures that can control corruption? Since corrupt activities are conducted by officials, the question should be turned into this: what are the most effective measures to prevent officials from becoming corrupt? Anti-corruption battles under the Mao regime basically relied on mass movement, political education, and party and administrative disciplinary measures. Since China launched the reform movement, the central government has tried to minimize corruption in order to restore the reputation of the government, but there has been little achievement of anti-corruption. Many scholars feel that the measures of anti-corruption are not adequate to clean up the government's mess, and the majority of the Chinese people feel hopeless to institute anti-corruption methods.[41] Chinese scholars have examined the causes of corruption and offered constructive suggestions for anti-corruption, including developing independent judiciary systems and supervisory systems, perfecting the legal system, increasing government employees' salaries, cultivating people's moral standards, deepening the reform movement, promoting citizen participation, introducing a competition mechanism into the hiring process to improve the quality of government officials, and increasing corruption costs.[42] However, the scholars' analysis is guided by Marxism and they are unable to extend their analysis under the party censorship.

Some Western scholars suggest that corruption may be more prevalent during the transition of modernization.[43] The poor economic condition only provides few accessible targets for corruption, but the reform movement creates more opportunities and sources of wealth and power for corruption.[44] When a country buys modernization at the price of decay of political institutions, corruption "becomes alternative means of making demands upon the system."[45] The economic crime rate was 30 per 100,000 people in 1956. At that time, whoever earned bribes over ten thousand *yuan* (about $1,600) would be sentenced to death. The level of corruption remained low in the 1960s and early 1970s, with the corruption rate averaging about 50 per 100,000 in early 1970s.[46] The corruption rate was very low during the first 26 years of the communist regime, but corruption has become epidemic during the post-Mao era.[47] One of the explanations for this interesting phenomenon is that the party members and government officials disciplined themselves under the Mao regime.

In the post-Mao era, corruption has become "more widespread than during the Guomindang period."[48] Some Western observers have also noticed that corruption has grown hand in hand with the reform movement.[49] During the transition period, the Chinese market economy remains irrational and lacks basic rules and regulations for competition, thus providing officials with new opportunities to cheat. Unlike the government of Singapore, Hong Kong, and Taiwan, Hilton Root notes, the Chinese government has failed to draw the distinction between the private and public roles of officials.[50] Chinese officials have access to a great amount of government capital. Under this circumstance, the party's power is not outside the market because the Chinese market economy is not a typical market economy, but party-corporatism. Businessmen seek help from government officials in order to make maximum profits; the government officials can trade their power in exchange for profits. Whoever has power can use market resources to make profits. All Chinese people are trying to become rich during the reform era, but many Chinese officials simply choose the easiest and most profitable way to become rich. Obviously, it is Chinese officials who use their political power to make their own profits within the current political system. The reform movement and market economy only provide a platform for them to fulfill their goals. The way to fix loopholes is not to stop the reform movement, but to deepen the reform movement, especially by developing a market control system, blocking the way for Chinese officials to exchange their power for profits, separating the party from the government and market economy, establishing a modern enterprise system to control enterprise's corruption, and changing the Chinese political system. In short, the problems of the reform movement should be resolved through the process of both economic and political reforms.

## POLITICAL REFORM AND THE ANTI-CORRUPTION BATTLE

Some Chinese scholars believe that politics is the central reflection of an economic system based on Marxism, so the deepest roots of corruption derive from the economic system.[51] Wang Chuanli argues that corruption has nothing to do with the political system either.[52] Generally speaking, three conditions—opportunity, motivation, and dysfunctional supervisory and checking systems—provide opportunities for officials to conduct corrupt activities. Thus, the question is how to make the motivation true. In other words, what kind of social and political systems make officials able to fulfill their greedy desires?[53] The economic perspective cannot provide a satisfactory answer for these questions. The subject of every form of corruption is the officials, including officials in governments, enterprises, and different kinds of institutions. Where there is power, there is corruption. Absolute power often results in absolute corruption. Although every case of corruption is different, the nature of corruption is the corruption of power. Corruption in China is essentially the crisis of the current political system.

First, the highly centralized political system creates corrupt officials. Jean-Jacques Rousseau believed that it is not corrupt men who destroy the political system, but the political system which corrupts men.[54] China's rampant corruption indicates that the Chinese government "has deficient legal and supervisory mechanisms to control corruption."[55] China's corruption is deeply rooted in hierarchical social and political systems,[56] in which the individuals are relatively weak.[57] In other words, a less individualistic society usually has a higher level of corruption.[58] Power without check tends to corrupt; and "corruption of kingship is tyranny."[59] The current Chinese political system is a highly centralized structure in which the CPC's power is monopolized at both the national and the grassroots levels and easily produces corruption. The most corrupt industries in China are real estate, electric power, tobacco, banking and financial services, and infrastructure, because these industries are monopolized by the CPC/state. Usually, in these areas, a big contract is worth more than 10 million *yuan* or more. In order to get one, some businessmen do whatever they can, including bribing those who are in charge of the contract. In order to get the contract, a contractor's bribe is usually anywhere between 10 percent and 20 percent of the total project budget. When officials manage socialist market economy by abusing power, they become corrupt. Crony capitalism is the biggest source of China's corruption.

Second, Chinese officials have a lot of power over the people. Although China has begun a process of separating the party from the government and market, the party/government officials have interfered with the market economy and commercial business, so they can also easily misuse their power to pursue their self-interests.[60] As long as the officials have the right to interfere in economic activities, officials' power still has market value and they can trade their power for personal gain.[61] Among the top fifty corrupt officials of the country between 1990 and 2004, Yu Zhengdong, whose bribery totaled 4 billion *yuan*, was on the top of the list. The last person on the list was Wu Genyue, whose bribery totaled 6 million *yuan*.[62] Money speaks loudly, and rich people have penetrated governments, trying to control politicians and direct the development of the economy in China. Government officials become their puppets, laws and government regulations become their instruments for serving their interests, and mass media becomes their voice of propaganda. Hu Angang believes that 90 percent of Chinese officials of local governments are corrupt.[63] Many high level Chinese officials have been imprisoned for corruption. According to official Chinese newspaper, more than 880,000 officials were punished for misconduct between July 2003 and December 2009.[64] Bo Xilai, the Communist Party secretary of Chongqing municipality, was ousted from his post in March 2012 and is expected to be prosecuted in 2013. Apparently, the CPC has become the largest and the most corrupt organizational machine. The most serious corruption cases in China come directly from this political machine—the Party. In order to minimize official corruption in China, the first and the foremost thing for the CPC to do is to clean up the house of the CPC.

Third, the current judiciary system for corruption does not work well. Unlike democratic societies, the CPC does not allow an independent anti-corruption agency to exist. In China, anti-corruption agencies are neither independent, nor free from political influence. There are three organizations that are responsible for supervision, including the Central Commission for Discipline Inspection of the CPC, the Government Supervisory Committee, and the Procuratorate. Each of these three institutions has played a role in anti-corruption, but they are actually under the leadership of the CPC, so they have to obey the party's instructions instead of being able to conduct independent investigations and prosecutions.[65] In practice, whether or not one is punished depends on who that person is. The CPC often replaces legal code with party policy, judiciary power with party power, and legal punishment with party discipline.[66] Some scholars observe that wining and dining investigation teams and false reporting are very common practices to curry superiors' favors.[67] Chinese officials can even "short-circuit corruption investigations by appealing to their protectors in the party hierarchy."[68]

Fourth, an unchecked party system also makes the Chinese legal system dysfunctional. Law is one of the most important forms of a social control system to safeguard the interests of the dominant group. The Chinese government pays attention to the leading officials' corrupt activities, but gives little attention to the anti-corruption regulations.[69] The government relies on unwritten laws. Under the Mao regime, China had a lack of written regulations on corruption among the administrative ranks.[70] In the post-Mao era, China still lacks clear legal and commercial codes to regulate market activities and to make distinctions between criminal and lawful activities.[71] Although the Chinese government has made some good regulations curbing corruption during the reform movement, this does not necessarily mean that the government has enforced that Chinese officials follow the regulation. Under this unchecked one-party system, the CPC has the right to dismiss the judge or change policy to change the legal process. Chinese courts and judges either make their decisions as instructed by the CPC or based on their personal interests instead of laws. Some judges abuse the laws and have become corrupt too.

Finally, the centralized political system also results in an inadequate information system. The cases of government corruption are often covered by the CPC. Senior official's cases were mainly exposed by investigation of other cases. Among the 39 researchable cases, 19 cases were exposed by other case involvement, accounting for 80.6 percent of total corruption cases, and five cases exposed by informant reports, while one case was discovered through confession, with the remaining case detected by suspicion. This shows that supervision of senior officials was weak, both by the CPC and by the public.[72] Under the party's censorship, the Chinese people, including journalists and correspondents, are not allowed to freely publish articles which criticize the government's corruption. Root points out that "inadequate information about the creditworthiness of national financial institutions and unpredictable behavior by government make long-term business calculations difficult."[73] Without public supervision through free media, no one can check the behavior of corrupt officials, or even of the anti-corruption institution.

In short, it is the current political system that makes it possible for Chinese officials to conduct corrupt activities and to "obtain a share of the new wealth being produced by the reforms."[74] Huntington believes that corruption is one symptom of the absence of effective political institutionalization.[75] Anti-corruption efforts must focus on institutionalization, among other issues. Bryan W. Husted uses the term "power-distance" to describe how scandals involving people in authority are always covered up as long as the person remains in power.[76] This high-power-distance in China has allowed many government officials to go unpunished. The party's judgment is always final. Thus, the reform movement cannot be limited to economic reform but must include profound political reform.

## CONCLUSION

China's corruption has become an epidemic and systematic in the post-Mao era. China's corruption has seriously damaged the CPC's legitimacy, undermined social stability, and harmed the Chinese market economy. The CPC has clearly seen that corruption threatens the party's ability to stay in power.[77] The top leader of China warned that corruption undermined the party's hold on power and urged the government to remove the soil that generates corruption.[78] President Hu Jintao points out that fighting against corruption is the key to maintaining the "advanced nature" of the CPC and its survival.[79] Xi Jinping has warned that corruption could lead to the collapse of the party and the downfall of the state. Although Xi has made the fight against corruption his No. 1 mission since he became the General Secretary of the CPC in November of 2012, he has not touched the source of China's corruption—the current Chinese political system. Instead, in order to protect the special interests of the ruling class, the CPC has tried every possible means to detour the process of China's democratization. It is urgent for the CPC to place political reform as the top priority among other reforms and take one step further to introduce institutional checks and balances, as well as allow scrutiny from the media and independent anti-graft agencies.[80] The CPC should also endorse political strategies for fighting against corruption: carry out the democratic election system to improve the quality of Chinese officials; separate the party from the government and market; reform government-sponsored ownership; establish various independent supervisory institutions to check the party's power and prevent the party leaders from abusing power; expand the supervisory power, including the right to punishment, impeachment, and hiring;[81] maintain the sacred purity of the Constitution; perfect legal and judiciary systems to increase the costs and risks of corrupt activities; publicize officials' and their families' incomes by filing the property declaration form;[82] and guarantee freedom of speech and press to publicize corrupt officials.

## NOTES

1. Samuel P. Huntington, "Modernization and Corruption," in *Political Corruption: Concepts & Contexts*, ed. Arnold J. Heidenheimer and Michael Johnston (New Brunswick, N.J.: Transaction Publishers, 2002), 253.

2. Liu Cuiping, "On the Identity Between Opposing Bourgeois Liberation and Anti Corruption," *Guangming Daily*, 30 June 1990.

3. Liu, "Zhong Guo she hui zhuan xing qi de xing zheng fu bai j qi zhi li" (Corruption and its Control During the Transition in China), 75.

4. Kate Gillespie and Gwenn Okruhlik, "The Political Dimensions of Corruption Cleanups: A Framework for Analysis," *Comparative Politics* 24, no. 1 (Oct., 1991): 77; Richard Levy, "Corruption, Economic Crime and Social Transformation since the Reforms: The Debate in China," *The Australian Journal of Chinese Affairs* 33 (Jan., 1995): 1.

5. Huntington, "Modernization and Corruption," 253. S. T. Quah asks, "How do we explain the different levels of corruption in Asian countries?" See Jon S.t. Quah, "Responses to Corruption in Asian Societies," in *Political Corruption: Concepts & Contexts*, ed. Arnold J. Heidenheimer and Michael Johnston (New Brunswick, N.J.: Transaction Publishers, 2002), 514. John Girling asks, "Why does corruption occur on a massive scale in some countries and much less so in others?" See Girling, *Corruption, Capitalism and Democracy*, 7.

6. Quoted in Richard Levy, "Corruption, Economic Crime and Social Transformation since the Reforms: The Debate in China," *The Australian Journal of Chinese Affairs* 33 (Jan., 1995): 4.

7. According to Julia Kwong, corruption refers to misuse power in one's public office for personal gains. See Julia Kwong, *The Political Economy of Corruption in China* (New York: M E Sharpe, 1997), 24. According to Kate Gillespie and Gwenn Okruhlik, "Corrupt behavior involves misuse of public authority for private gain." See Kate Gillespie and Gwenn Okruhlik, "The Political Dimensions of Corruption Cleanups: A Framework for Analysis," *Comparative Politics* 24, no. 1 (Oct., 1991): 77. John Girling defines corruption as a "'deviation' from the public good" and "the abuse of a public position of trust for private gain." See John Girling, *Corruption, Capitalism and Democracy* (New York: Routledge, 1998), 2 & 10.

8. Yan Yiming, "Fu bai gen yuan de shen ceng li lun tan jiu" (Study on the Roots of Corruption), *Zhong Guo Qing Nian Zheng Zhi Xue Yuan Xue Bao* 4 (2004): 74.

9. John Gardiner, "Defining Corruption," in *Political Corruption: Concepts & Contexts*, ed. Arnold J. Heidenheimer and Michael Johnston (New Brunswick, N.J.: Transaction Publishers, 2002), 26.

10. "Corruption Perceptions Index," http://www.transparency.org/cpi2012/results (15 January 2013).

11. Hilton Root, "Corruption in China: Has it Become Systemic?" *Asian Survey* 36, no. 8 (August 1996): 749.

12. See Yan Sun, "The Chinese Protest of 1989," The Issue of Corruption, The Regents of the University of California, 1991.

13. Zhengke He, "Corruption and Anti-corruption in Reform China," *Communist and Post-communist Studies* 33 (2000): 250.

14. Eric Chi-yeung Ip, "Judicial Corruption and its Threats to National Governance in China," *JOAAG* 3. No. 1 (2008): 82.

15. "Former Provincial Secretary Probed," *China Daily,* 19 February 2004.

16. "Justice System Reports Surge in Corruption Convictions," *China Justice News Update*, No. 45 November 2008.

17. "Party Demands Full Asset Disclosure to Curb Graft," *China Daily,* 21 September 2009.

18. James T. Areddy, "Report: Corrupt Chinese Officials Take $123 Billion Overseas," *Wall Street Journal,* 16 June 2011.

19. Gillian Wong, "Suspect confesses to biggest China corruption case," *Xinhua News Agency,* 30 December 2011.

20. "China targets corrupt officials' overseas assets," *China Daily*, June 28, 2012. http://www.chinadaily.com.cn/china/2012-06/28/content_15528385.htm (January 15, 2013)

21. David C. Nice, "The Policy Consequences of Political Corruption," *Political Behavior* 8, no. 3 (1986), 287.

22. John M. Kramer, "Political Corruption in the U.S.S. R.," *The Western Political Quarterly* 30, no. 2 (June, 1977): 213.

23. Mark E. Warren, "What Does Corruption Mean in a Democracy?" *American Journal of Political Science* 48, no. 2 (April 2004): 329.

24. Michael Johnston & Yufan Hao, "China's Surge of Corruption," *Journal of Democracy* 6, no. 4 (1995): 80.

25. Kent Ewing, "Step by Step to Democracy in China," *Asia Times,* July 25, 2008.

26. Edward Cody, "China Takes Aim at Corruption," *Washington Post,* 8 January 2006.

27. Edward Cody, "Hundreds Are Reproved By China for Corruption," *Washington Post,* December 17, 2004.

28. Cheng Liwei and Zhang Bing, "Fu Bai dui Zheng fu de xiao li de ying xiang ji fan fu bai zhi li du she ji, " (Impact of Corruption on Government's Efficiency and Designing the Regulation of Anti-corruption), *Ha Er Bing Gong Ye Da Xue Xue Bao* 7, no. 3 (2005): 20.

29. Liu Wenge, "Dao De Wen Hua, fu bai he jing ji zhuan xin" (Moral Culture, Corruption and Economic Transition), *Jing Ji Yan Jiu* 12 (2003): 26.

30. "Officials' 2008 Appetite for Graft 3 times larger than 2007," *China Daily,* 24 February 2009.

31. Shang-jie Wei, "Local Corruption and Global Capital Flows," *Brookings Papers on Economic Activity 2* (2000): 303.

32. Daniel Kaufmann, "Corruption: The Facts," *Foreign Policy* 107 (Summer, 1997): 120.

33. David Barboza, "Morgan Stanley's Chinese Land Scandal," *New York Times,* 1 March 2009.

34. "CCI's Bribery Case Adds Another 3 Chinese Companies," *Global Times,* 20 August 2009.

35. "Bribery cases prompt call for probe," *People's Daily,* 17 August 2009.

36. Albert Keidel, "China's Social Unrest: The Story Behind the Stories," *Policy Brief* 48, September 2006.

37. Sun Liping, The Biggest Threat to China is not Social Turmoil but Social Decay," *China Digital Times,* http://chinadigitaltimes.net/2009/03/sun-liping-%e5%ad%99%e7%ab%8b%e5%b9%b3-the-biggest-threat-to-china-is-not-social-turmoil-but-social-decay/ (18 September 2009).

38. "China trusts prostitutes more," *BBC News,* http://news.bbc.co.uk/2/hi/asia-pacific/8183502.stm (16 August 2009).

39. Wu Zhong, "Sex and China's credibility gap," *Asia Times,* 12 August 2009.

40. C. Fred Bergsten, Bates Gill, Nicholas R. Lardy, and Derek Mitchell. *China: The Balance Sheet: What the World Needs to Know Now About the Emerging Superpower* (New York: Public Affairs, 2006), 45.

41. Yufan Hao and Michael Johnston, "Corruption and the Future of Economic Reform in China," in *Political Corruption: Concepts & Contexts,* ed. Arnold J. Heidenheimer and Michael Johnston (New Brunswick, N.J.: Transaction Publishers, 2002), 596.

42. Liu Shuqian, "Zhong Guo she hui zhuan xing qi de xing zheng fu bai j qi zhi li" (Corruption and its Control During the Transition in China), *Guang Zhou Da Xue Xue Bao* 1 (2004): 76. Tian Jun, "Gou jia gui fan ji zhi, ti gao fu bai chen ben" (Establishing Standard Mechanisms to Increase Corruption Costs), *Shanghai Shi Fan Da Xue Xue Bao,* 6 (2004): 42.

43. J.C. Scott, "Corruption, Machine Political Corruption," *American Political Science Review* 63 (December 1969): 42.

44. Daniel Kaufmann, "Corruption: The Facts," *Foreign Policy* 107 (Summer, 1997): 120.

45. Huntington, "Modernization and Corruption," 251.

46. Kwong, *The Political Economy of Corruption in China,* 83.

47. Kwong, *The Political Economy of Corruption in China,* 145.

48. Kwong, *The Political Economy of Corruption in China,* 85.

49. Al Jazeera, "Corruption is Endemic and has Grown Hand in Hand with Reforms," http://english.aljazeera.net/HomePage (14 September 2006).

50. Hilton Root, "Corruption in China: Has it Become Systemic?" *Asian Survey* 36, no. 8 (August 1996): 752.

51. Liu, "Zhong Guo she hui zhuan xing qi de xing zheng fu bai j qi zhi li" (Corruption and its Control During the Transition in China), 75.

52. Wang Chuanli, "Tou Shi fu bai gai nian di si ge shi jiao" (Four Perspectives on Study of Corruption), *Beijing Ke Ji Da Xue Xue Bao* 3 (2004): 18.

53. Wu Jinglian, "Zhong guo fu bai de zhi li" (Anti-corruption in China), *Zhan Lue Guan Li* 2 (2003): 22.

54.  Carl J. Friedrich, "Corruption Concepts in Historical Perspective," in *Political Corruption: Concepts & Contexts*, ed. Arnold J. Heidenheimer and Michael Johnston (New Brunswick, N.J.: Transaction Publishers, 2002), 19.

55.  Quah, "Responses to Corruption in Asian Societies," 515. Hao and Johnston, "Corruption and the Future of Economic Reform in China," 586.

56.  John Hagan, *Structural Criminology* (New Brunswick: Rutgers University Press, 1989).

57.  Kenneth J. Meier and Thomas M. Holbrook, " 'I Seen My opportunities and I took 'Em:' Political Corruption in the American States," *Journal of Politics* 54, no. 1 (Feb., 1992): 138.

58.  Bryan W. Husted, "Wealth, Culture, and Corruption," *Journal of international Business Studies* 30, no. 2. (1999): 344.

59.  Arnold J. Heidenheimer and Michael Johnston, "Preface," in *Political Corruption: Concepts & Contexts*, ed. Arnold J. Heidenheimer and Michael Johnston (New Brunswick, N.J.: Transaction Publishers, 2002), 3.

60.  Kwong, *The Political Economy of Corruption in China*, 80.

61.  Yan Yiming, "Fu bai gen yuan de shen ceng li lun tan jiu" (Study on the Roots of Corruption), 73.

62.  "Who is the Most Corrupt Officials in Mainland China," *Shanghai Qiao Bao*, 16 July 2004.

63.  Quoted in Julie Chao, "Amid Reforms, China Is Losing Its Battle With Corruption," *Cox News Service,* 30 November 30, 2002.

64.  "Party Demands Full Asset Disclosure to Curb Graft," *China Daily,* 21 September 2009.

65.  Li Haihong, "Lun xin shi xia fu bai xian xiang di fang zhi gui ce" (On the Strategies of Anti-corruption under New Circumstances), *A Bei Shi Fan Gao Deng Zhuan Ke Xeu Xiao Xeu Bao* 1 (2005): 44.

66.  Deng Xiquan and Fen Xiaotian, " Fu bai zhu ti zhongqing nian qu di xian xian xiang di yuan ying feng xi " (Analyzing the Causes of Corruption among Young Chinese), 190.

67.  Kwong, *The Political Economy of Corruption in China*, 30.

68.  Root, "Corruption in China: Has it Become Systemic?" 750.

69.  Xinhua, "Voice from the Top: No Mercy for Corruption," *China Daily*, 14 February 2004.

70.  Kwong, *The Political Economy of Corruption in China*, 131.

71.  Hao and Johnston, "Corruption and the Future of Economic Reform in China," 594.

72.  Noah J. Smith, "China's Corruption Crackdown Sifts out Select Targets," *The Christian Science Monitor,* 19 February 2000.

73.  Root, "Corruption in China: Has it Become Systemic?" 741.

74.  Jean-Louis Rocca, "Corruption and Its Shadow: An Anthropological View of Corruption," *China Quarterly*, 130 (June 1992): 402.

75.  Samuel Huntington, *Political Order in Changing Societies* (New Haven, Conn.: Yale University Press, 1968), 9.

76.  Bryan W. Husted and Instituto Tecnologico Y de Estudios, "Wealth, Culture, and Corruption," *Journal of International Business Studies* 30, no. 2 (2cd Qtr., 1999): 343. According to Husted, power distance refers to "the extent to which the less powerful members of institutions and organizations within a country accept and accept that power is distributed unequally."

77.  Chen Chunren, "Jia qiang zhi du wen ming jian she: e zhi fu bai di gen ben tu jing" (*Strengthen Institutional Reform: the Fundamental Way to Minimize Corruption*), *Hu Nan Ke Ji Da Xue Xue Bao* 6 (2004): 72.

78.  Josephy Kahn, "China's Leader Pushes Doctrine While Warning of Corruption," *The New York Times*, 1 July 2006.

79.  Joseph Kahn, "China's Leader Pushes Doctrine While Warning of Corruption," *The New York Times,* 1 July 2006.

80.  Willy Lam, "Hu's Anti-Graft Drives Lack Institutional Checks and Reforms."

81.  Li, "Lun xin shi xia fu bai xian xiang di fang zhi gui ce" (On the Stratagies of Anti-corruption under New Circumstances), 8.

82.  Chen, "Jia qiang zhi du wen ming jian she: e zhi fu bai di gen ben tu jing" (*Strengthen Institutional Reform: the Fundamental Way to Minimize Corruption*), 74.

## Chapter Ten

# Traditional Chinese Religion

Religion and politics are inseparable in modern democracy and inevitably work together.[1] In Western societies, religion in fact is a sub-political system, in part because the majority of people are religious believers and religion has significantly influenced politics in Western societies. Jacques Gernet has referred to these two aspects as the "political sovereign" and the "doctrinal sovereign."[2] Although the percentage of religious people among China's total population is relatively low and religion has played much less of a role in politics in comparison with Western societies, Chinese religion also comes with a political dimension. When Chinese religions have increasingly grown under government's liberal policy in the post-Mao era, the Chinese government has become more sensitive to religion. Thus, it is necessary to examine the relationship between Chinese religion and politics, in order to understand the way of people's lives in contemporary China. Chinese religion includes two groups: traditional Chinese religions and imported religions. This chapter focuses on traditional religions, and Chapter 11 will discuss imported religions. There are two core questions in discussing Chinese traditional religion: Are the Chinese people a religious people? Do Chinese religious believers have rights to enjoy freedom of religion under the current political system? There has been a misunderstanding for a long time in Western societies that the Chinese people are not a religious people, and the Chinese people only have very limited freedom to enjoy religious practice. This chapter will examine the development of religions in China, analyze the characteristics of Chinese traditional religion as part of the Chinese belief system, and discuss the relationship between traditional Chinese religion and the government, and explore the issue of how religions shape Chinese people and society through religious education. It will also argue that the Chinese people are a religious people and the government's attitude toward traditional

Chinese religions is different from imported religions, and that traditional religious believers enjoy more religious freedom than imported religious believers.

## CHINESE RELIGIOUS TRADITION

Beginning about 2,500 years ago, Buddhism, Christianity, and Islam emerged, gradually becoming the three dominant world religions. These three religions dominate the three main cultural circles of the world. Christianity dominates the European cultural circle, which began in ancient Greece and Rome; Islam dominates the Arab cultural circle, which began in ancient Egypt and Babylon; and Buddhism dominates the Asian cultural circle, which began in India. Beginning with the Han dynasty, the three religions—one after the other—began their difficult journeys in China and were confronted with traditional Chinese culture. However, in the past 2,000 years, no one foreign religion has been able to conquer Chinese culture and become the dominant religion. Confucianism, as the mainstream of culture as well as religion, dominated China before 1919. The failure of the three world religions to dominate Chinese culture does not mean that there is no room for religion to develop on Chinese soil. Rather, different countries nurture different religions in a diverse world.

China's religious heritage is made up of three religious traditions—Confucianism, Daoism, and Buddhism,[3] which together depict the "religiousness of the Chinese people."[4] It is impossible to understand Chinese traditional culture and contemporary China without comprehending the three Chinese traditional religions. Some scholars do not see the three Chinese traditional religions as religions, but as humanism and philosophy. Derk Bodde notes that "religion, in Western terms, means of course Christianity. When the Chinese use this term, they make no distinction between the theistic religions and purely moral teachings."[5] Chinese traditional religion is very unique from a historical perspective.

Etymologically, there are different meanings in Chinese for the terms "religion" and "teaching." The word religion did not have an equivalent term in China until the late nineteenth century.[6] Based on the word's basic meaning in the West, the Chinese created the word *zong-jiao* for the term religion. *Zong* refers to clan, tribe, and ancestors; *jiao* refers to teaching. When the Chinese people put the words *zong* and *jiao* together for the equivalent of "religion," they reinforced the Chinese understanding of the role of patriarchal religion. The term "teaching" for most Chinese refers "to pass on knowledge," like history, art, science, and technology. The term religion in any contemporary Chinese dictionary means "belief in god," "holy spirit," "retribution for sin," and "a hope of heaven." Obviously, the term religion has the same basic meaning in China as it does in Western countries.

According to official reports, there are more than 100 million religious believers in China, but "most profess Eastern faiths."[7] To ignore the three religions is to disregard the fact that the Chinese people have been religious practitioners. Theoretically, the three Chinese religions have served religious aims. Of China's three traditional religions, Confucianism is arguably the foundational one. Confucius (551–479 BCE) was one of China's first great teachers and philosophers, and his words were studied by centuries of Chinese scholars. Confucius taught the principles of benevolence, loyalty, righteousness, propriety, and knowledge, and dealt with the five relationships— between ruler and subject, between father and son, between husband and wife, between elder brother and younger brother, and between friend and friend.

Some scholars refuse to call Confucianism a religion, because Confucius did not perform miracles or discuss death or the existence of gods, and because Confucianism does not have religious texts, systematic rituals, and formal religious organizations. In fact, *The Analects* records Confucius's prayers, fasting, and regular attendance of worship services. Confucius discusses God using the terms *shàng dì* ("heavenly god") and *tiān* 天. Confucius as a sage was worshipped by the vast majority of Chinese people in imperial China. Confucian temples were established everywhere. In a Confucian temple, religious rituals were held twice a year, in mid-spring and mid-autumn, to worship the ancestors of Confucius, but these ritual services were not convened by priests, rather by state officials and Confucian scholars. Chen Jingpan affirms that Confucius was a "true heir of [the] best religious heritage." He concludes that Confucius was "not a teacher of religion, but a religious teacher."[8] According to Julia Ching, in China the term state religion has always referred to Confucianism. Confucianism has served both secular and religious functions throughout history.[9] Chapter 12 will continue to discuss Confucianism as Chinese ideology.

In comparison with Confucianism, Daoism and Buddhism have served far greater religious functions in Chinese history. Daoism is composed of many disparate components, including witchcraft, yin-yang theory, ideas regarding ghosts, the theory of Chinese medicine, and the religious ideas of Laozi. Daoists synthesized these sources and formed a unique religious system, which is reflected in the Daoist canon, composed of about 1,120 volumes. Daoism is a salvation religion that guides its believers beyond this transitory life to a happy eternity, but in the third century, it shifted its emphasis from the present world and its concerns to the transcendental values.

Buddhism began its difficult journey in China in the first century and it gradually became integrated into the Chinese way of life after its concepts were made understandable through the use of Daoist terminology. As Buddhist scriptures and teachings were translated into Chinese, Buddhism opened the way of Buddhahood to Chinese believers. By the fourth century, Buddhism had penetrated into the highest social and economic circles; wealthy Buddhists began founding Buddhist temples, supplying the monks with necessities, and paying for the translation of Buddhist texts. Buddhist scholars became advisers for the imperial court. Although Buddhism faced resistance from supporters of Confucianism, it continued to develop and spread rapidly among the populace. Buddhism in China reached maturity during the Tang dynasty and reached its peak at the beginning of the Song dynasty, after which it began to decline.

The four most important factors contributing to this decline were the moral corruption of high-level clergy, the institution of civil-service examinations that forced Chinese scholars to seek office through a study of the Confucian classics, diminishing support of Buddhism from India, and the introduction of Western culture. Yet, few scholars deny that Buddhism is "one of the world's three major universal religions, along with Christianity and Islam."[10] According to Chinese official reports, by 1997, there were 25,000 Daoist priests, 1,500 Daoist temples, 13,000 Buddhist temples, and 200,000 monks and nuns in China. Among them were 120,000 lamas and nuns, more than 1,700 living Buddhas, 3,000 temples of Tibetan Buddhism, nearly 10,000 Bhiksu and senior monks, and more than 1,600 temples of Pali Buddhism.[11]

Since the Han dynasty, the three Chinese traditional religions have assimilated aspects of one another and developed peacefully together. The development of the three religions constitutes the main picture of Chinese culture and contributes significantly to Chinese history. Some scholars point out that the three religions share one body and merge into one.[12] At the popular level, there are no divisions or mutually exclusive groups, because most believers do not sign an oath of affiliation with a particular religion. Many believers hold several religious faiths at the same time. But each of the three religions has its own fixed system of thought at the intellectual level, so their mutual exclusivity exists at this level. For more than 2,000 years, Buddhism has been an integral part of the Chinese culture. It is not so much that Buddhism conquered Chinese culture, but, rather, that Buddhism was gradually assimilated into Chinese culture.

## CHARACTERISTICS OF CHINESE RELIGIONS

Chapter 1 points out that the patriarchal system is the basic characteristic of premodern China. Accordingly, Chinese traditional religion is essentially patriarchal. More precisely, patriarchal religion is part of China's patriarchal system. It was a clan-based religion that derived from the primitive clan and formed in the Xia dynasty. The basis of the patriarchal religion was the worship of ancestors, land, sun, moon, mountain, river, and ghosts. The Chinese people believed that their ancestors were still alive in heaven after their death, and had the power to bring harm or good fortune to their descendants. Sacrifices to honor them were a basic part of religious ritual since the Zhou dynasty (1045–256 BCE). China's patriarchal religion classified four types of gods: heavenly god, earthly god, manly ghost, and material god. Correspondingly, there were four types of worship: heaven worship, land worship, ancestor worship, and grain worship.

The patriarchal religion was not only the product of the patriarchal system, but was one of the ideological pillars in the Chinese feudal society to sustain the absolute monarchical system and had a profound impact on other Chinese religions, daily life, culture, and politics. Few scholars, however, are aware that Chinese traditional religion and foreign religions were deeply influenced by the Chinese patriarchal religion. The traditional Chinese patriarchal religion had the most believers of any religion in the world before the twentieth century and was an important base for the fifty-six nations in China to reach a common understanding. This strengthened rather than destroyed some aspects of the clan religious system after China entered the second period of its history. Compared with the rest of the world, China was the only country in which ancient patriarchal religion continued to develop systematically; thus, it became more powerful in Chinese feudal society. The rise and decline of dynasties did not shake the orthodox position of the patriarchal religion. The entrance of Buddhism and the rise of Daoism also did not change the position of patriarchal religion as an established religion. For most Chinese people, including both the nobility and the common people, ancestor worship come first, and belief in other religions was secondary.

The patriarchal religion was unified with the emperor and with the administration system. Important sacrificial rites were national events and were presided over by the emperor, thereby indicating that the emperor's power was endowed by heavenly power. Therefore, the traditional patriarchal religion actually dominated other religions and became an established religion, although it did not have a formal religious structure. Other religions were not permitted to contradict the patriarchal religion in idea, moral code, belief, or rites. It is not difficult to find a connection between Daoism and patriarchal religion through a look at witchcraft, which is a primary religion and one type of patriarchal religion. Many basic Daoist ideas, rites, and ghosts came from witchcraft. Some indigenous Buddhist priests tried to compromise the patriarchal religion by emphasizing the conformity between the two religions and making the distinctions between their content and form. Nestorians came to China in the seventh century, but their mission was not successful because they did not coordinate with traditional Chinese culture. This is one of the reasons why some later Christian missionaries failed in China. By contrast,

when Christian missionary Matteo Ricci came to China in the sixteenth century, he changed the missionary style and applied the concepts of heavenly
god, or *Shang Di* in Chinese, based on Confucian classics and compromised
with some traditional customs and rites, such as the worship of Confucius
and ancestors. Therefore, the Christian missionary movement in the sixteenth
century represented by Ricci was successful. Similarly, the development of
Islam in China essentially was a process by which Muslims learned to compromise with the patriarchal religion and the Chinese moral code.

The patriarchal religion also impacted the daily life of the Chinese nation.
Compared with other types of Chinese culture, the patriarchal religion was
easier to develop among common Chinese people through religious rites,
prayer, festivals, and ceremony. The common Chinese people were more
difficult to teach and less likely to accept formal Chinese culture due to their
limited education. Therefore, the basic ideas of Chinese culture and tradition
came from the patriarchal religion. Ethically, the patriarchal religion maintained moral behavior and social order by ancestor worship, so the model of
human relationships continued generation after generation. Economically,
the patriarchal religion—through grain worship, land worship, and nature
worship—sacralized the periodization of agricultural production and the natural environment required for agricultural production. Because the patriarchal religion was easy to practice, it became the most popular religion. The
important reason why Confucianism had a profound influence on Chinese
society and culture was that the central principles of Confucianism preserved
traditional Chinese familial values, which conformed to the core of the patriarchal religion.

Finally, the patriarchal religion impacted Chinese politics. The development of ancestor worship in traditional Chinese society generally synchron-
ized with the evolution of the patriarchal political system. Patriarchal religion
maintained the emperor's power through the rite of heaven worship. When
the patriarchal religion unified with the political system, the king or the head
of the clan presided over the ceremony of ancestor worship. After the family
separated from the state, the clan and the family held the rituals of ancestor
worship at the family level; the emperor held the rituals of ancestor worship
in national services. The political system provided the social value for ancestor worship and regulated the activities of ancestor worship; ancestor worship, in turn, sustained the political system. As Benjamin Schwartz notes,
"Ancestor worship may have greatly influenced the political system of early
China."[13] The combination of ancestor worship and the patriarchal system
produced the teaching of loyalty and filial piety. In premodern China, filial
piety was not merely an ethical value, but had a "religious resonance."[14]
Therefore, the Chinese political system was very similar to the familial system. In the later feudal societies of the Ming and Qing dynasties, ancestor
worship was more popular and was completely dispersed into every family

as one of the basic familial functions. According to the regulations of ancestor worship, people were permitted to worship only the father before the Ming dynasty, but there was freedom to worship both parents during the Ming dynasty, and all grandparents during the Qing dynasty. Patriarchal religion and politics did not disappear after the feudal system was abolished. Worshipping Mao under the Mao regime, especially during the Cultural Revolution, was a typical mixture of communist politics and ancestor worship.

## TRADITIONAL RELIGIONS UNDER THE COMMUNIST REGIME

The ultimate goal of the Communist Party of China is the creation of a Communist social system. In order to fulfill that goal, the party uses Marxism-Leninism and Mao Zedong's thought as guides. Atheism is a central tenet of Marxism; Marxism holds that God is a mere fabrication, invented by people to soothe the misery of this world, a fabrication exploited by the ruling classes to oppress the working class. Therefore, the abolition of religion and the abolition of the capitalist system go hand in hand. The party requires its members to profess Marxist atheism and to educate the masses in a Marxist perspective.

Legally speaking, Chinese citizens enjoy full freedom of religion under all versions of the Constitution of China, including the versions of 1954, 1975, 1982, 1988, 1993, 1999, and 2004. Article 36 of the Constitution of 1982 reads, "No state organ, public organization or individual may compel citizens to believe in, or not to believe in, any religion; nor may they discriminate against citizens who believe in, or do not believe in, any religion." The state protects normal religious activities. No one may make use of religion to engage in activities that disrupt public order, impair the health of citizens or interfere with the educational system of the state. This indicates that the government pays equal attention to protecting the freedom not to believe in religion. The preference is to support non-believers. The CPC clearly understands that religion is a serious challenge to the CPC, in terms of the role of religious ideological influence, eternal attraction, organizational strength, and variety of financial resources. Thus, the CPC has tried strategically to restrict the function of religion in the political area.

Under the Mao regime, religious activities were discouraged. During the ten years of the Cultural Revolution (1966–76), all religions were denounced, all religious believers were persecuted, all religious meeting places were closed, all religious activities were prohibited, and property belonging to religious institutions was confiscated. After the Cultural Revolution, the Chinese government made efforts to restore freedom of religious belief and reopened sites for religious activities. The CPC remains officially atheist, but it has been growing more tolerant of religious activity for the past twenty years.[15] According to a survey published in a state-run newspaper, 31.4 percent of Chinese adults claim to be religious. According to BBC news, there are 300 million believers in China, and the number of religious believers in China could be three times higher than official estimates.[16] Most Chinese believers profess Eastern faiths.

Because the Chinese government views religious activities as potential threats to the regime, it tightly controls all religious activities, including religious education. One of the important controlling mechanisms is that the CPC controls Chinese religious activities through official Chinese ideology. The Constitution of China continues to insist that the Four Cardinal Principles—Marxism-Leninism-Mao Zedong thought, the leadership of the party, the proletariat dictatorship, and the socialist road—are the theoretical foundations of China. Marxism is the theoretical foundation of the CPC and the official ideology of China. Not only are the Youth League Members and the Party Members required to follow the principles of Marxism, but also all the Chinese people, including church members and seminary students and faculty. In Chinese colleges and universities, Marxism is a required course. Religious education is also required to be guided by Marxism.

The government uses criminal law to limit religious freedom. The Criminal Law of PRC, adopted by the Second Session of the Fifth National People's Congress on July 1, 1979, and amended by the Fifth Session of the Eighth National People's Congress on March 14, 1997, clearly states that "a person who organizes or uses a superstitious sect or secret society or an evil religious organization or uses feudal superstition to undermine enforcement of the state's laws or administrative regulations shall be sentenced to fixed-term imprisonment not less than three years and not more than seven years; and if the circumstance is especially serious, to fixed-term imprisonment of not less than seven years. A person who organizes or uses a superstitious sect or secret society or an evil religious organization or uses feudal superstition to deceive another person and causes death of another person shall be sentenced in accordance with the provisions of the preceding paragraph. A person who organizes or uses a superstitious sect or secret society or an evil religious organization or uses feudal superstition to rape a woman or defraud property shall be convicted of a crime and sentenced respectively in accordance with the provisions of Article 236 or 266 of this Law."[17]

Government/party policy is above the law in China. All religious activities are actually guided by government/party policy instead of laws. On March 31, 1982, the central committee of the Chinese Communist Party issued an important statement of religious policy, Document 19, which called for restoration and administration of churches, temples, and other religious sites, warned that religion must not interfere with politics, education, or marriage and family life, and reaffirmed that the government prohibited criminal and counter-revolutionary activities committed under the cover of religion. In 1994, the government issued two important decrees, No. 144 and No.145, signed by Chinese Premier Li Peng, regulating both foreigners' and Chinese citizens' religious activities within in China.

Regulation Governing the Religious Activities of Foreign Nationals within in China Decree No. 144 stipulates that foreign nationals may participate in religious activities in religious venues in China, including monasteries, temples, mosques, and churches, which are recognized by the Religious Affairs Bureaus of the People's Government at or above the county level. They may invite Chinese clerical personnel to conduct religious rituals as baptisms, weddings, funerals, and prayer meetings. However, they are not permitted to establish religious organizations, liaison offices, venues for religious activities, or run religious schools and institutes within China. They are not allowed to seek to convert members of the Chinese public, or to appoint clergy or undertake other evangelistic activities. When foreign nationals enter China, they may carry printed materials, audio and visual materials, and other religious items for their own use, but if greater quantities are brought in, the materials will be dealt with according to the relevant Chinese customs regulations.

Regulation Governing Venues for Religious Activities Decree No. 145 emphasizes that all religious activities must be registered. Registration requires three things: patriotic association, a fixed meeting place, and activities confined to a specific geographic area. The regulation reaffirms that venues for religious activities shall not be controlled by persons or organizations outside China. Land, mountains, forests, and buildings cannot be used for religious purposes without the government's permission; donations from persons and organizations outside China cannot be accepted; and the publication of religious articles and artwork is forbidden. If violation of the stipulations of this regulation threatens public security, the public security organs are empowered mete out penalties in accordance with the relevant sections of China's Public Security Administration Penal Code; if the violation constitutes a criminal act, the judiciary is to undertake an investigation to determine criminal responsibility.

In 2005 the Chinese government issued the Decree of the State Council of the People's Republic of China, No. 426, Regulations on Religious Affairs, to ensure citizens' freedom of religious belief, maintain harmony between religions, preserve social concord, and regulate the administration of religious affairs. This document once again uses the term "normal religious activities," saying that the government protects normal religious activities and safeguards the lawful rights and interests of religious bodies and sites for religious activities. This document includes seven chapters: general provisions, religious bodies, sites for religious activities, religious personnel, religious property, legal liability, and supplementary provisions.[18]

To control religious activities, Religious Affairs Bureau State Council issued a special document in July of 1996 to enforce the implementation of government laws and policy toward religion, called *Method for the Annual Inspection of Places of Religious Activity.*[19] This document aims to protect the legal rights of places of religious activity, strengthen the management of places of religious activity according to law, and advance the systemization and standardization of the self-management of places of religious activity. This method is established according to the relevant regulations of the Management of Places of Religious Activity Ordinance and the Method of Registration for Places of Religious Activity. The department responsible for the annual inspection of a place of religious activity is the department which is responsible for the registration of that place of religious activity. The purpose of the annual inspection is to ensure that all religious activities in China are obedient to national law, regulations and policies.

## CHINESE TRADITIONAL RELIGIONS AS AN EDUCATION

The three Chinese traditional religions (in Chinese *san jiao*) are closely related to education. The Chinese word for religion is *jao*, which means "teaching" or "system of teaching." When the Chinese use this term, they make no distinction between the theistic religions and purely moral teachings.[20] The moral teaching is thus developed to provide guidance for people to follow, rather than to worship without a desirable ending. Thus, being a Buddhist, a Daoist or a Confucian-style person makes no difference as long as one follows the moral teachings that are generated from these religions, as the West would define them.

Daoism teaching associates human weakness and sickness with sin, tries to heal such ills with the confession of sin and forgiveness, and bridges the gap between human beings and divine beings through the ritual practices of prayer and penance. Buddhism preaches karma, the Four Noble Truths, and the Eightfold Noble Paths, and affirms a spiritual dimension through belief in meditation and transcendence which lie outside of time and history. Robert Thurman calls this process the "inner revolution" toward life, liberty, and the pursuit of real happiness. Buddhist teaching includes three major points: discipline, meditation and wisdom. Buddhist education is based on filial piety. Daoism and Buddhism are inclusive religions so they absorb good elements from the other traditional religions, especially from Confucianism. Thus, the three religions became integrated moral teachings in China. Li Shiqian, a famous Chinese scholar, described the three religions in this way 1,500 years ago: "Buddhism is the sun, Daoism the moon, and Confucianism the five planets."[21]

Confucianism kept expanding its influence through its educational program before 1949. Confucius was the greatest teacher in Chinese history, and made tremendous efforts to develop educational programs. His disciples did the same thing for more than 2,000 years. The content of civil service examination was the Confucian text. Anyone who wanted to be an official was required to study Confucianism and pass the examination. The main concern of most Chinese families was to learn Confucianism and prepare their children for the examinations. This trend created a huge demand for Confucian books and became the stimulus for the development of printing techniques. In turn, the printing techniques promoted Confucianism's spread throughout the country. Therefore, in ancient China, Confucianism became the tool of the Chinese people to fulfill their political dreams, the bridge to cross the gap from the status of common people to official positions, the only source of moral behavior, and the sole standard of social and political values.

It should be noted that the CPC adopts a more tolerant policy toward Chinese traditional religions and has invested solid efforts in promoting Chinese traditional religions, including renovating Buddhist and Daoist temples to attract domestic and foreign tourists. Moreover, in recent years the CPC has tried to use traditional Chinese religious teachings as a vehicle to promote a "harmonious society," in order to retain its ruling party position. Yet, all the restrictions imposed by the party/government certainly have a negative impact on religious education in China. Theoretically, China has implemented a policy of separating religious activities from the government. The Chinese government protects normal religious activities, but no one is allowed to make use of religion to engage in activities that disrupt public order and interfere with the educational system of the state.[22]

According to the Constitution of China, all Chinese people have equal opportunities to receive an education. This is why China has the largest school system in the world, but Chinese schools, including primary schools, middle and high schools, and colleges and universities, are mainly run by the government. Because the CPC was very concerned about political education and ideological control, it did not allow anyone to establish private colleges and universities during the Mao era. Since the reform movement, private primary schools have slowly developed, but very few of them are really funded by private organizations and foreigners.

In China, religion is not a subject taught in state schools, although some institutions of higher learning and research institutes conduct research on religion. According to the U.S. International Religious Freedom Report, some primary and secondary schools, which are operated or funded by religious organizations, may provide religious education, but the government does not maintain statistics on this subject.[23] Generally speaking, religious courses in China are included in the curriculum of Philosophy Departments. For example, the Department of Philosophy at Beijing University offers the following courses: Introduction to Religion, Marxism on Religion, Classic Texts of Chinese Buddhism, Classic Texts of Chinese Islam, Introduction to Quran, Original Text of Daoism, Introduction to the Bible, Religious Philosophy, History of Christianity, History of Buddhism, and Science and Religion.[24] The Department of English Language and Literatures at Chinese universities also offer some religious courses, such as "Reading the Bible," but professors only teach the Bible from a cultural perspective instead of a religious perspective. In this sense, there is no Western-style religious education in Chinese schools and universities.

According to a White Paper published by the Chinese State Council, "religious organizations in China run their own affairs independently and set up religious schools, publish religious classics and periodicals, and run social services according to their own needs. The various religious schools and institutes set up by the different religious organizations teach religious knowledge in line with their own needs."[25] In China, there are over 3,000 religious organizations.[26] However, there are only about 30 Buddhist schools and colleges, 15 Daoist training schools, and 18 registered Christian seminaries and Bible schools. Nanjing Theological Seminary serves as the national seminary of China. Regional seminaries include Huadong Theological Seminary, Yanjing Theological Seminary, Binhe Road Theological Seminary, Dongbei Theological Seminary, Zhongnan Theological Seminary, Sichuan Theological Seminary, Guangdong Union Theological Seminary, Anhui Theological Seminary, Shandong Theological Seminary, Yunnan Christian Theological Seminary, Shaanxi Bible School, Hunan Bible School, Jiangxi Bible School, Henan Theological Seminary, Inner Mongolia Training Center, and Jiangsu Bible School.

Due to the special circumstances in China, the educational goal of religious schools is to train professional religious service people who support the CPC's leadership, love the socialist motherland, possess a rich spiritual life in faith and religious knowledge, unite the majority of religious followers, and develop local independent religious organizations. Obviously, the purpose of religious education in China is somewhat different from that of religious education in Western societies.

## CONCLUSION

China has many religions—not only the three traditional Chinese religions, but also other imported religions. Among all religions in China, Chinese traditional religions remain dominant. Chinese people are religious people. The development of Chinese religions went through more than 2,000 years, but they have never been separated from the Chinese political system. Although the CPC has more tolerant attitudes toward Chinese traditional religions, it still closely monitors and controls these traditional religions. While the CPC tries to minimize the role of Chinese religions, Chinese religions, in fact, shape Chinese society and the daily life of the Chinese people through religious practice. China has a long religious tradition, but religious practice in China appears to be a very complex phenomenon. First, teaching a moral and social code is one of the distinctive characteristics of Chinese traditional religions. Culturally, Chinese traditional religion as an education is still pervasive and influential. The CPC is willing to use Chinese traditional religions to promote family values and the common good because Chinese traditional religions are morally centered. Second, the CPC is very sensitive about the political aspect of religions, so the Chinese government has closely monitored and controlled overt religious activities. Due to various restrictions imposed by the CPC and the government, the influence of religion is very limited. Third, although in the post-Mao era the Chinese government has implemented more liberal policies for Chinese religions, the development of Chinese religion is still slow. At the present time, the direction of the development of the Chinese political system is uncertain, so a rise in religious growth should not be expected anytime soon. Fourth, China has a rich cultural heritage in religious belief, but the development of Chinese religion faces great challenges in the twenty-first century. In the era of globalization religious practice should deal not only with moral and spiritual issues, but also with the threats of war, the crisis of pollution, energy, and diseases. Thus, it has left a large space for religious professionals, scholars, and educators to provide research in this area.

## NOTES

1. Dipesh Chakrabarty, "Postcoloniality and the Artifice of History," *Representations* 37 (1992), 1-26.

2. Jacques Gernet, *China and the Christian Impact: A Conflict of Cultures* (Cambridge, England: Cambridge University Press, 1985), 108.

3. James E. Wood Jr., "Religion and the State in China: Winter Is Past," *Journal of Church and State* 28 (Autumn 1986), 394.

4. John N. Jonsson, "Introduction," in Kwong Chunwah, *Hong Kong's Religions in Transition* (Waco, Texas: Tao Foundation, 2000), ix.

5. Derk Bodde, *Chinese Thought, Society, and Science: The Intellectual and Social Background of Science and Teaching in Pre-modern China* (Honolulu: University of Hawaii Press, 1991), 148.

6. Julia Ching, *Chinese Religions* (Maryknoll, N.Y.: Orbis Books, 1993), 2.

7. Quoted in Bureau of Democracy, Human Rights, and Labor, U.S. Department of State, *1999 Country Reports on Human Rights Practices,* released on 25 February 2000.

8. Chen Jingpan, *Confucius as a Teacher: Philosophy of Confucius with Special Reference to Its Educational Implications* (Beijing: Foreign Languages Press, 1990), 351.

9. Julia Ching, "Ethical Humanism as Religion?" in Hans Kung and Julia Ching *Christianity and Chinese Religions* (New York: Doubleday, 1989), 87.

10. Christian Jochim, *Chinese Religions: A Cultural Perspective* (Englewood Cliffs, N.J.: Prentice-Hall, Inc., 1986), 10.

11. State Council of China, "1997 White Paper," *China's Religion* 12 (Spring 1998), 7.

12. Timothy Brook, "Rethinking Syncretism: The Unity of the Three Teachings and Their Joint Worship in Late-Imperial China," *Journal of Chinese Religions* 21 (Fall 1993), 13-14.

13. Benjamin Schwartz, *China's Cultural Values* (Arizona: Lionheart Press Inc., 1993), 10.

14. Ibid., 8.

15. Preeti Bhattacharji, "Religion in China," Council on Foreign Relations, http://www.cfr.org/china/religion-china/p16272 (30 April 2011).

16. "Survey finds 300m China believers," *BBC News*, http://news.bbc.co.uk/2/hi/6337627.stm (February 20, 2013)

17. *Criminal Law of the PRC*. http://www.procedurallaw.cn/english/law/200807/t20080724_40992.html (February 21, 2013)

18. "Regulations on Religious Affairs," http://www.purdue.edu/crcs/itemResources/PRCDoc/pdf/Regulations_on_Religious_Affairs_no426.pdf ( May 2, 2011).

19. Religious Affairs Bureau State Council, "Method for the Annual Inspection of Places of Religious Activity," http://www.purdue.edu/crcs/itemResources/PRCDoc/pdf/Method_for_the_Annual_Inspection_of_Places_of_Religious_Activity.pdf (6 May 2011)

20. Derk Bodde, *Chinese Thought, Society, and Science: The Intellectual and Social Background of Science and Teaching in Pre-modern China* (Honolulu: University of Hawaii Press, 1991), 148.

21. Quoted in Stephen F. Teiser, "Introduction: The Spirits of Chinese Religion," in *Religions of China in Practice*, ed. Donald S. Lopez (Princeton, N.J.: Princeton University Press, 1996), 1.

22. Chinese State Council, *White Paper: Freedom of Religious Belief in China,* Beijing, 1997.

23. Bureau Of Democracy, Human Rights, And Labor, "China" (includes Tibet, Hong Kong, Macau). International Religious Freedom Report 2010, November 17, 2010. http://www.state.gov/g/drl/rls/irf/2010/148863.htm (10 May 2011).

24. Curriculum for Undergraduate Students in the Department of Philosophy at Beijing University, http://www.pku.edu.cn/education/kcsz/bks/bks.jsp?deptid=023 (2 May 2011).

25. Chinese State Council, *White Paper: Freedom of Religious Belief in China, Beijing*, 1997.

26. *China Country Report on Human Rights Practices for 1997.* http://www.state.gov/www/global/human_rights/1997_hrp_report/china.html (6 May 2011).

*Chapter Eleven*

# Chinese Christianity in the Post-Mao Era

The development of Christianity has become a fascinating phenomenon in the post-Mao era. Some Western observers claim that the Chinese Christian movement has developed rapidly in the past three decades, growing at a rate of about 7 percent annually. They predict that Chinese Christians will follow in Eastern European Christian footsteps and play a pivotal role in the process of China's democratization. While the Chinese economy is rapidly developing, the Chinese government is "still ranked among the most repressive in the world" by Western standards.[1] Under this circumstance, what kind of roles will Chinese Christians play in the process of China's democratization? In the United States, there are two opposing opinions on the relationship between politics and religion in China. The first opinion is that China's democratization will rely on the role of the Chinese Christian movement and that China is actually "in the process of becoming Christianized."[2] The second opinion, represented by the neo-conservative movements, suggests that democratization is the key to religious freedom in China. There is no religious freedom without democratization.[3] According to Jason Kindopp, however, "The rise in importance of church-state relations within China remains largely unexamined either in China or in the United States."[4] This chapter will discuss the development of Christianity in the Chinese context and the new trend of the Chinese Christian movement in the post-Mao era, assess the roles of Chinese Christians in the process of China's democratization, and conclude that Chinese Christianity can only play a marginal role in the democratization process without fundamental changes of the current Chinese political system.

## DEVELOPMENT OF CHRISTIANITY IN CHINA

Chinese Christianity and Islam were imported religions and both of them began their missionary activity in China in the seventh century.[5] The Chinese Christian movement developed with a very slow pace before China was forced to open its doors to the West in the early 1840s. The Persian Bishop Alopen of the Nestorian Christian Church was the first Christian missionary in China, beginning the Nestorian mission in 635 in Chang'an (present-day Xi'an), the capital city of the Tang Dynasty. Emperor Tang Taizong (reigned 627– 49) honored Alopen after his death with a monument outside the city, erected in 678. Although there was considerable collaboration between Buddhists and Nestorians, the Nestorians had little impact on Chinese society. The second wave of the Christian mission was the Franciscan mission, a Roman Catholic missionary movement of short duration. Giovanni da Montecorvino (1247–1328), the first Catholic missionary and a zealous monk, arrived in China from Italy in 1292 during the Mongol Yuan dynasty (1279–1368), which adopted a tolerant religious policy. Catholic missionaries were allowed to build churches and to baptize Chinese believers, but the Catholic mission did not have much influence until Jesuit missionaries came to China in 1583, during the Ming dynasty (1368–1644). At the beginning of the Ming dynasty, foreigners were permitted to establish churches only in Macao, but the Jesuit Matteo Ricci (1552–1610) finally opened the way for Christian missions in the rest of China. Ricci, who was originally from Italy but was ordained in Goa, India, developed the Christian mission in new ways, learning Chinese culture and tradition and using the Chinese concepts of *tiān* and *shàng dì* to explain Christian principles. As a consequence, the Christian missionary movement in the sixteenth century was relatively successful.

Although Christian missionaries worked in China for centuries, the Chinese response was always minimal. Ralph R. Covell observed, "Whether Christian messengers attempted to present a Chinese gospel or one uncritically imported from a distant land, the results were virtually the same. The response to the Christian faith in China was always minimal, and the church never constituted more than a fraction of one percent of the national population. The Chinese masses never perceived that the biblical message addressed their deepest needs."[6] Jason Kindopp held the similar viewpoint that "until recently, most outside observers viewed the Christian missionary enterprise in China as a failure, drowned in the sea of history."[7]

If "the Chinese have always been a religious people,"[8] why has the Christian mission experienced such difficulty in China? Theologically, the central Christian doctrines, such as creation, sin, and incarnation, contradict Confucianism and traditional Chinese culture. Gernet points out that "the concept of a God of truth, eternal and immutable, the dogma of the incarnation—all this was more easily accessible to the inheritors of Greek thought than to the Chinese."[9] Politically, the contacts between Chinese and Western Christianity before the nineteenth century were mutually beneficial, but the Christians were supported by gunships and protected by unequal treaties in the nineteenth century. Foreign churches and foreign missionaries enjoyed extraterritorial privileges in China. Some Western missionaries joined the Eight Power Allied Forces against China in 1900; some participated in the drafting of unequal treaties, including the Sino-British Treaty of Nanking in 1842; and some Western missionaries even called for restoring the Qing dynasty, an inhumane feudal society. Consequently, the Chinese people had little sympathy for Christianity.[10] Culturally, early Christian missionaries frequently rejected Chinese civilization and denounced the Chinese people. The first Protestant missionary, Robert Morrison, blamed the Chinese for being "selfish, deceitful and inhuman among themselves."[11] Some Western missionaries even thought that destroying the traditional Chinese culture was the first task of the Christian mission in China.

After the Nationalist government was finally established in Nanjing in 1927, Chinese Christianity gained more ground. Accordingly, religious education, particularly Christian education, emerged in China, especially in the east coast cities. Due to resistance from the Chinese indigenous religious movement, religious education was mainly limited to the religious schools, which were established by foreign missionaries. During the anti-Japanese War, Chinese Christians combined the Christian movement with the social movement, boycotting Japanese products and supporting the anti-Japanese war to win international recognition. The growth of the Chinese Christian movement slowed down again after the CPC came to power in 1949, because the communist ideology was radically anti-religious and asserted that religion is harmfully false, the foe of science and human progress.[12] Christians in China were seriously persecuted during the Cultural Revolution. After the CPC implemented liberal religious policy in the reform era, Chinese Christian revival has taken place in China.

## RELATIONSHIP BETWEEN THE CPC AND CHINESE CHRISTIANITY

The CPC has restricted the function of religion in the political area in order to maintain the CPC's monopoly of power, but, strategically, its tolerance for Buddhism, Taoism, and Confucianism has been greater than that for Christianity. The three traditional religions often face fewer restrictions.[13] Why is the CPC willing to tolerate the three religions? First of all, the three religions neither have any ecclesiastical organization at the national level, nor form a hierarchical system that controls all temples.[14] Most of the traditional religious temples are scattered in the remote areas, which are far away from the center of politics and even lack regular communication with the outside world. Those temples that are located in the center of major cities or in urban areas have actually become commercialized. Daoists retreat from society and choose to be close to nature. Buddhism and Daoism also have a shortage of intellectual leadership with a modern educational background. Thus, Buddhism and Daoism show their "weakness in the lack of adequate appreciation of science and the new technological environment."[15] In this sense, it is not easy for traditional religions to attract Chinese intellectuals. The three traditional religions show no interest in becoming a secondary political force to challenge the political authority. In Chinese history, some Buddhist priests only occasionally offered advice for emperors and politicians. Some Daoist teachings advocated a new world order, but they were not the real force that provoked rebellion.[16]

Both Islam and Christianity are theistic religions. The Chinese Islamic population is about the same size as the Christian population, but Islam has less influence than Christianity. Most Chinese Muslims belong to about ten minority groups and live in remote border provinces. Chinese Islam has a shortage of prominent advocators at the national level and lacks seats in the government. The Islamic message is hard to get through to the mainstream of Chinese society. Historically, Muslims came to China as immigrants and traders rather than missionary workers. They set up their families and gradually naturalized in China. Chinese Muslims have generally been peaceful. Chinese Islam has been tightly monitored, especially in some regions, such as Xinjiang. The communist government has not seen a real threat from Chinese Muslims.

Unlike Muslims, Western Christians came to China for Christian evangelism. After the Opium War, under the protection of Western power, Western Christians began a new missionary movement in the east coast cities, and then expanded to all of China's major cities. While introducing Western culture into China, Western missionaries established schools, hospitals, manufacturing, and humanitarian services. Chinese society was shaped by the Christian missionary movement and Chinese people, especially urban residents, intellectuals, and officials, were deeply influenced by Christian ideas. This is one of the reasons why the revival of Chinese Christianity is growing rapidly in the reform era. Chinese Christians are very organized with a strong faith and have regular meetings, fellowships, worship services, and other religious activities. Numerically, "Christianity remains a minor religion in China."[17] Yet, the majority of Chinese Christians inhabit developed areas and they can quickly respond to political issues and easily organize social activities. In the CPC's eyes, Chinese Christians might cause social instability within Chinese society.

When the CPC came to power in 1949, it immediately began to suppress Chinese Christians and deport Western missionaries in order to cut off the relations of Chinese Christians with Western society. In 1950, the first Chinese Christian Conference drafted the Christian Manifesto: The Direction of Endeavor for Chinese Christianity in the Construction of New China, indicating that China began to launch the Three-self Movement—self-administration, self-support, and self-propagation. Under the three-self principles, all Chinese religious organizations were cut off from foreign countries and all foreign missionaries were driven out from mainland China. The CPC also propagandized atheism, Darwinism, and Marxism to brainwash the Chinese people, and persecuted house church leaders by eliminating independent churches. For example, Wang Mindao, a fifty-six-year-old pastor of an independent church, was sentenced to fifteen years in prison in the 1950s.[18] It is safe to say that "Christianity was particularly hated by the new Communist rulers,"[19] and that "government persecution is stronger against Christians than other religious groups."[20] In the post-Mao era, the CPC continues to suppress Christianity, while showcasing its tolerance.[21]

## NEW TREND OF THE CHINESE CHRISTIAN MOVEMENT

Christianity is the fastest growing religion in mainland China.[22] There are about 130 million Christians in China, which means that China contains more Christians than party members (74 million).[23] In the post-Mao era, a new trend of the Chinese Christian movement emerged, which indicates that Chinese Christians will play a greater role in the process of China's democratization.

First of all, the growth of the Chinese house church has been faster than the three-self church. The Chinese house church was initially developed in response to the formulation of the TSPM. Under the Mao regime, the Chinese house church was totally restricted and, thus, was illegal and functioned underground. In the post-Mao era, the house church has been spreading widely, largely in the countryside.[24] The house church members come from different occupations and nationalities, including laid off workers, millionaires, professors, students, peasant workers, and other professionals, but they are united in the name of God and they treat each other as brothers and sisters. The major difference between the house church and the three-self church is whether they report to the CPC and whether they have a legal status. The "Three-Self Church" is legally recognized by the government, but the house church has not received government recognition. Many scholars suggest that the government should allow the house church to be registered and presented to the public with a legal identity. If the church had the same legal status as other groups, they could improve their management system, freely organize religious activities, open bank accounts, raise money, be tax exempt, freely deliver religious publications, establish seminaries to train pastors and missionary workers, and provide social services. The Chinese government has realized that the house churches are potentially dangerous to the communist regime, so it continues to tightly control Chinese house churches.[25]

Second, Chinese intellectuals are moving toward Christianity. Since China opened its door to the rest of the world, about ten million Western tourists have visited China every year. More and more Westerners go to China to teach, to study, and to work. Chinese universities are registering a growing number of foreign visiting professors.[26] About 223,500 foreign students from 189 countries are currently studying in China, and more and more Western investors, professionals, and skilled workers come to China to work.[27] There is no doubt that many of those foreigners devote themselves to the Christian mission. Meanwhile, Chinese people also have the opportunity to go to foreign countries. Many Chinese students go abroad to study. About 600,000 Chinese students and their family members live in the United States, and about 200,000 Chinese students and their family members live in European countries. In the United States about half of the overseas Chinese students participate in various church activities, and more than 10 percent of Chinese students and their family members have been baptized. The Christian church has become the second cultural center in which Chinese study English as a second language, hold wedding services, and have their babies baptized. The rest of the students and their family members have generally recognized Christianity, even if they don't participate in church events. These Chinese students and their family members have a certain influence on Chinese politics, after they go back to China.

With the revival of the Chinese Christian movement in the post-Mao era, Chinese intellectual Christians have emerged and become a new phenomenon of the Chinese Christian movement. Chinese cultural Christians have a high level of education and are "not satisfied that either the Marxist interpretation of religion or the standard Western Darwinian understanding of life adequately explained the human condition in general and the Chinese condition in particular."[28] Thus, they have challenged the Marxist interpretation of religion, reinterpreted Christianity in the Chinese context, begun to study Christian theology, and some of them have proclaimed themselves Christians. Intellectual Christians are not necessarily the same as traditional Christians, who have been baptized, attend church service, and regularly pray. The category of intellectual Christians is very broad and can be divided into several groups: some of them are scholars who conduct research on Christianity; some of them are Ph.D. or master students majoring in Christian studies; and some of them are involved in international activities relating to Christianity. In recent years, the urban intellectual house church has grown quickly. However, some Westerners do not see the close association of Chinese students with the churches. Foreign missionaries in China simply complain that the Chinese were the rice Christians, meaning that most of them came to the church for something to eat, rather than for their soul and spirit. The same kind of impression is still around—many Chinese students have their practical reasons for interacting with the churches other than seeking salvation.

Third, boss Christians have emerged. In the post-Mao era, while the private economy is expanding, the number of private enterprise owners has increased. Some of them have converted to Christianity. These Christians are also called boss Christians. They are young, educated, open-minded, and active in both social and church work. [29] They are wealthy and their contributions have become the major economic resource for the development of the churches. They are enthusiastic sponsors, organizers, and participants in public welfare activities and evangelized work. They also play a role as mediators between the church and the government and other non-Christian communities. [30]

Fourth, with the development of urbanization, a great number of peasants go to cities to work for a better life. As a result, peasant worker churches have emerged in urban areas. The term "peasant worker" refers to a migrant worker who came from the countryside. Migrant workers are engaged in non-agricultural occupations and are either self-employed or employed by other institutions, but they do not have urban resident permits, so they experience discrimination in many aspects of life. Some migrant workers became Christians after moving to the city because they had difficulties, such as their own illnesses or illness within their family. When they heard that "you will get well after believing in Jesus Christ," they simply believed it, although they did not know who Jesus Christ was at that time, mainly because they did not have to pay anything if they believed it. If a miracle occurred that helped them get through their crisis, they immediately believed in Jesus without rational thoughts.

Various factors have driven the development of Chinese Christianity in the post-Mao era. The living standard of the Chinese people has dramatically improved, but the Chinese belief system does not meet the needs of their spiritual lives. In the twentieth century, Communism, Confucianism and Christianity were expected to become the mainstream of the Chinese belief system. However, communism fails to enrich the needs of people's spiritual life. Confucianism has been losing its ground in the post-Mao era because it lacks a solid public network and it conflicts with the core principles of modernization and democratization. The majority of people go to church not only in search of miracles, but also to solve spiritual puzzles and answer eternal questions. Christianity is able to answer these questions and solve people's problems. Thus, the rapid increase of Chinese Christians is basically derived from a crisis of faith or spiritual vacuum. Globalization, Western culture, Christian missionaries, and the changes of government religious policy have also contributed to the growth of Chinese Christianity.

## ROLES OF CHRISTIANITY IN CHINA'S DEMOCRATIZATION

The Christian movement can serve China's democratization. There is a distinction between democratization and political liberalization. The process of liberalization can be "defined as a loosening of control by an authoritarian regime without the intention to move immediately toward a democratic transition,"[31] but political liberalization can take place within the framework of an old political system. Under the communist regime, it is necessary to promote political liberalization first and then "build a more solid foundation for an eventual transition to democracy."[32] Democratization is essentially a political process. The Christian movement is part of political liberalization; there can be no Chinese democratization without the coordination of Chinese Christianity. China's democratization may occur only "when the Chinese dragon is tamed by the power of the Christian Lamb."[33]

Chinese Christianity can play many roles in China's democratization. Generally speaking, the divine order tends to regulate the secular order in democratic societies. The principle of freedom of religion ensures religious pluralism, which is a necessary precondition to guarantee individual rights and strengthen a democratic system. Religion can expand civil society, help people to nurture their spiritual lives, promote the common good, and improve moral behavior. Tun-jen Cheng and Deborah Brown note that "the coalescence between religious organizations and the political opposition is a crucial variable in the process of democratic transition."[34] Christianity can provide faith-based ideological support for modernization and democratization.[35] Although Christianity has numerous "pre-modern" ideological elements and structural forms, it can be used for serving the transition from "modernity" to "post-modernity" and guard against social crisis and spiritual collapse. Yet, Christianity will help develop China's modernization more than China's democratization. For the Chinese people, "modernization" is an extremely appealing statement full of hope.[36]

Christianity offers an example of optimistic lifestyle for the Chinese people. In contemporary society, many people are burdened by their work, life, marriage, and family crises. There is a wide range of emotional and behavioral problems in China because of depression, anxiety disorders, autism and other mental illnesses. All these emotional problems are leading factors that contribute to suicides. Recent statistics show that more than 287,000 people end their own lives every year on mainland China. Stress and depression cause 70 to 80 percent of suicides in urban areas. More than 58 percent of suicides are female.[37] When the survey asked why participants wanted to commit suicide, 63.57 percent of participants responded: "spiritual crisis or survival pressure." The other answers were "failure in love and family crisis" and "disease pain."[38] The main factor for the majority of those who committed suicide would be that they were puzzled with the values of life. The Christian faith can resolve the confusion of people's life and values, calm their mind, enrich their spiritual life, and inspire them to love each other.

The principles of Christian ethics help the Chinese people reconstruct the value standard. Ethical principles are very important in restoring the Chinese people's faith as traditional Chinese culture and communism are declining. Some scholars point out that "the material, scientific, and economic progress brought about by the process of modernization goes hand in hand with evils such as moral decay, rampant corruption, selfish pursuit of money, and the deterioration of the environment."[39] A large number of Chinese people have paid more attention to their material lives and ignored their spirit lives. Money has become the most important criteria to measure people's achievements. The motivation of making money drives people crazy and creates serious social problems, such as corruption, prostitution, drug trafficking, kidnapping, suicide, and disease. Christian values could in some way heal these problems, defeat modernization's negative effects, and help them reconstruct the Chinese cultural system.[40]

The growth of the Christian movement will remake China's image and improve the relationship between China and Western societies and make Western societies more comfortable accepting China as an insider in the international society. China is an atheist country according to its constitution. A country without the guidance of religion is dangerous from a democratic viewpoint. Christianity can not only make China stable but also make the world safer and ensure the implementation of international law. Christian values would also help China share a common worldview on many international affairs within the international society.

## THE LIMITATION OF CHINESE CHRISTIANITY WITHIN THE CURRENT POLITICAL SYSTEM

The roles of Christianity in the process of democratization cannot be amplified, mainly because the role of religion is largely determined by the nature of the political system. Under the current Chinese political system, Chinese Christians can only play marginal roles in the process of China's democratization.

First, the CPC's policy toward Chinese religion has changed from time to time, but the nature of the anti-religious mentality has never changed. Kindopp observes that "although the CCP has stepped back from its extreme anti-religion policies of the Mao era, China's leaders have not yet demonstrated the political will to embrace a more accommodative posture."[41] The highly centralized administration system is the basic tool for the CPC to control the Chinese Christian movement. In addition to the United Front Office and the Religious Affairs Bureau (RAB), three other government-sponsored organizations directly control the Chinese Christian movement, the Three-Self Patriotic Movement Committee of Protestant Churches of China (TSPM), the China Christian Council (CCC), and the China Catholic Patriotic Association.[42] The TSPM network is embedded in the Communist Party bureaucratic structure and reports to the Religious Affairs Bureau, a government arm of the Communist Party. According to the Chinese government, the goal of the Three-Self Movement is to assist the party and government in implementing the party's policies. Thus, the Three-Self Movement must accept the leadership of the party; every church must register with the government according to the law; individual religious activities must be reported to the local committee of the Three-Self Movement; all places of religious activity must be reported to the provincial Bureau of Religious Affairs; and all religious groups must submit a written report of their activities to the special committee of the government every six months.[43]

China's current political system has made Chinese Christianity difficult to develop. The government owns all the land, and no one is permitted to build a church without a special government permit. The Chinese government tightly controls the media, including television, newspapers, radio, public forums, and the Internet. The party censorship system makes it impossible for Chinese people to organize private publishing houses or to publish articles that discuss religious rights from a democratic perspective in official magazines. The government continues to crack down on Christian house churches and home religious activities. Within such a controlled system, one scholar asks, "How much freedom will these associations be given in the future to engage in religious activities?"[44]

The size of the Chinese Christian population is still relatively small, which has also hindered development. Among all Chinese Christians, the three-self churches remain the mainstream, especially in urban areas. The impact of the Chinese house church on Chinese politics is limited, due to the fact that they are illegal and largely underground. The three-self church will continue to follow the CPC's principles to provide their services. Some Westerners have overestimated the growth of the population of Chinese Christians. According to David Aikman, nowadays Chinese Christians make up about 7 to 8 percent of China's population, and he believes that some Chinese officials, including military officials and deputy provincial governors, judges, and lawyers, have become Christians.[45] Some Western scholars predict that "with some thirty to seventy million souls and a growth rate of 7 percent annually, the number of Christians in China dwarfs the number of

Christians in most nations of the earth."[46] Therefore, in three decades Chinese Christians will constitute 20 to 30 percent of China's population, which translates to about 450 million Christians.[47] According to Aikman's assumption, China is going to be Christianized soon. These statistics are impressive, but they simply cannot stand up under close analysis because they are backed by no reliable documented evidence.[48]

According to a 2002 Government White Paper, only about 1.5 percent of China's population is Christian. According to the International Religious Freedom Report in 2004, released by the U.S. Department of State, about 4 percent of China's population is Christian, including the members of the registered and unregistered churches. *BBC News* Survey in 2007 suggested about 3 percent of China's total population were Christians.[49] In fact, there is no reliable source on this issue available either in China or outside China. Objectively, less than 2 percent of China's total population are Christians in most big cities, and this figure even falls below below 1 percent in some big cities. On average, the Chinese Christian population does not exceed 2 percent of the total national population. It is not realistic to predict that the Chinese Christian population will reach one-third of China's total population. Although Chinese culture can be compatible with democracy, as the case in Taiwan has shown us, democracy does not necessarily bring rapid growth to the Christian population. Only 5 percent of the Taiwanese population is Christian, although Taiwan has enjoyed democracy since the late 1980s.

In addition, the consciousness of the church is weak. A great number of Chinese house church members lack theological knowledge, including knowledge of the trinity, Christology, and the Bible. Chinese house churches lack the solid foundation of biblical tradition and are relatively far away from the mainstream of Christianity. During globalization, secularization has influenced Chinese church members and church activities are shadowed by material temptation. Some Christian fellowships have become a club for church members to socialize. Overall, the majority of church members are poorly educated, especially in rural churches. Missionaries in rural areas, on average, have only received a middle school education. All they can do in the church service is read the Bible and offer very basic interpretations of the Bible.

While acknowledging that Chinese scholars are interested in Christian theology and practice, it is worth noting that the role of Chinese cultural Christians in communist China is limited. Zhuo Xinping points out that Chinese cultural Christians "consist only of a very small proportion in both Chinese Christian and Chinese intellectual circles."[50] Most Chinese intellectuals who are interested in research projects on Christianity are not Christians themselves. In this sense, the "cultural Christians" are actually not a part of the Christian movement, but are part of the Christian cultural periphery.

Although Chinese cultural Christians acknowledge the Christian truth, they do not profess Christianity, do not belong to Christianity, and do not have the characteristics of Christian faith. Besides, Chinese intellectuals and scholars, including seminary professors, are required to follow Marxist methodology in conducting research on religion. Otherwise, their research achievements are not allowed to be published.

Finally, China's democratization is not the same as Christianization. Why is Western society so powerful? According to Aikman, religion is the driving force of Western society and makes Western societies strong.[51] He believes that it is not just necessary to Christianize China in order to democratize China, but that it is also possible, and that China is actually "in the process of becoming Christianized."[52] The history of the Western missionary movement has proven that China cannot be Christianized easily. Since there is not a single Christianized country in the West, how can Christians Christianize China, which has had a strong humanist tradition for more than 2000 years? In addition, the Chinese people have a longer memory of Western Christian missionaries misleading them than of their own warlords slaughtering them. The history of the Christian movement reminds us that a country can easily become a theocratic power if it is Christianized. A democratic country should come with diverse culture and plural religions.

The idea of Christianization is not only utopian, but it also harms China's democratization. Any attempts to Christianize China could mislead the Chinese people and the international society. China's religious freedom ultimately relies on the efforts of the Chinese people, but support from the international society can accelerate the development of the democratic movement. However, the vast gulf between Western views and the official Chinese viewpoints remains.[53] While the Chinese government is emphasizing its status quo, Western democratic societies are concerned about violations of religious freedom in China. The U.S. annual report on international religious freedom had listed China as a "country of concern." Under the Bush administration, religious freedom became a leading issue in bilateral relations. In meeting with China's president Jiang Zemin in October 2001, President George Bush raised the issue of religious freedom. When President Barack Obama visited China in November 2009, he also made it clear that freedom of worship is a universal right. It must be available to all people, whether they are in the United States, China or any nation. Without a doubt, constructive dialogue between the two governments is very helpful in improving religious freedom in China, but the future of Chinese Christianity fundamentally relies on the Chinese people.[54]

## CONCLUSION

The doctrines of Christianity are relevant to modern democracy. There can be no Chinese democracy without religious coordination. Although the Chinese Christian movement has developed faster in the post-Mao era, the number of Chinese Christians is still small. China is in transition from an authoritarian regime to a democratic one, and it is expected that Chinese religions will play an active role in mobilizing the Chinese people to fight for their future. However, Chinese religion, especially Chinese Christianity, cannot be overestimated, largely because of the political nature of the CPC. Three preconditions are essential for Chinese Christianity to play a bigger role in the process of democratization. First is the separation of the government from the party and of religion from the government/party. As long as the government/party interferes with religious affairs, Chinese religion cannot become an independent force to influence Chinese society and politics. Second, religious believers should have the right to assume public office. Currently, all important posts in China are filled by the members of the Communist Party. According to the party's constitutions, all party members must be atheists; they are not allowed to believe in God. In other words, religious believers do not qualify for important positions in the public arena. Thus, religions in China are unable to directly influence Chinese politics at the policy-making level. The third precondition is the establishment of a pluralistic culture. Chinese religious believers should be allowed to freely express their beliefs through public media, including TV, radio, art, literature, film, journalism, and other public forums. That these three preconditions have not yet been institutionalized explains why religion in China can play only a marginal role within the Communist system.

## NOTES

1. Catharin E. Dalpino, *Deferring Democracy: Promoting Openness in Authoritarian Regimes* (Washington, D.C.: Brookings Institution Press, 2000), 2.

2. David Aikman, *Jesus in Beijing: How Christianity Is Transforming China and Changing the Global Balance of Power* (Washington, D.C.: Regnery Publishing, Inc. 2003), 285.

3. Jason Kindopp, "Policy Dilemmas in China's Church-State Relations: An Introduction," in *God and Caesar in China: Policy Implications of Church-State Tensions*, edits. Jason Kindopp and Carol Lee Hamrin (Washington, D.C.: Brookings Institution Press, 2004), 19.

4. Ibid., 12.

5. David B. Barrett, ed., *World Christian Encyclopedia* (New York: Oxford University Press, 1982), 232.

6. Ralph R. Covell, *Confucius, the Buddha, and Christ: A History of the Gospel in Chinese* (New York: Orbis Books, 1986), 4.

7. Kindopp, "Policy Dilemmas in China's Church-State Relations: An Introduction," 1.

8. Covell, *Confucius, the Buddha, and Christ: A History of the Gospel in Chinese*, 4.

9. Jacques Gernet, *China and the Christian Impact: A Conflict of Cultures* (Cambridge, England: Cambridge University Press, 1985), 3.

10. Kan Baoping, "The Christian Church in its Chinese Context," in *Contemporary Religious Trends within the Socio-Political Climate of East Asia,*" ed. John N. Jonsson (Waco, Texas:, mimeographed, 1996 Baylor University), 12.

11. Quoted in Xiaoqun Xu, "The Dilemma of Accommodation: Reconciling Christianity and Chinese Culture in the 1920s," *Historian* 60 (Fall 1997): 22.

12. Searle Bates, "Churches and Christians in China, 1950-1967: Fragments of Understanding," *Pacific Affairs* 41, No. 2 (Summer, 1968): 211.

13. U. S. Department of State, "International Religious Freedom Report 2004," released by the Bureau of Democracy, Human Rights, and Labor, 6.

14. Holmes Welch, "Buddhism under the Communists," *The China Quarterly* 6 (April-June, 1961), 1.

15. Lucy Jen Huang, "The Role of Religion in Communist Chinese Society," *Asian Survey* 11, No. 7 (July 1971): 694.

16. See Frederick Hok-ming Cheung, ed. *Politics and Religion in Ancient and Medieval Europe and China* (Hong Kong: The Chinese University Press, Chinese University of Hong Kong, 1999).

17. Aikman, *Jesus in Beijing: How Christianity Is Transforming China and Changing the Global Balance of Power*, 287.

18. Francis Jones, ed., *Documents of the Three-Self Movement: Source Materials for the Study of the Protestant Church in Communist China* (New York: National Council of the Churches of Christ in the U.S.A., 1963), xv.

19. Aikman, *Jesus in Beijing: How Christianity Is Transforming China and Changing the Global Balance of Power*, 286.

20. Quoted in Pedro C. Moreno, ed. *Handbook on Religious Liberty around the World* (Charlottesville, Va.: the Rutherford Institute, 1996), 52.

21. H.H. Lai, "Religious Polices in Post-Totalitarian China: Maintaining Political Monopoly over a Reviving Society," *Journal of Chinese Political Science*, 11, no. 1 (Spring 2006): 55.

22. Jacqueline E. Wenger, "Official vs. Underground Protestant Churches in China: Challenges for Reconciliation and Social Influence," *Review of Religious Research,* 46, No. 2 (Dec., 2004):169.

23. "Christianity in China," *The Economist*, 2 October 2008.

24. Jacqueline E. Wenger, "Official vs. Underground Protestant Churches in China: Challenges for Reconciliation and Social Influence," *Review of Religious Research,* 46, No. 2 (Dec., 2004): 173.

25. "China: Twenty-One Pastors Sent to Labour Camps," *Release International Persecuted Voice of Christians,* http://www.releaseinternational.org/pages/posts/china-twenty-one-pastors-sent-to-labour-camps349.php (1 October 2009).

26. Jean-Paul Wiest, "Religious Studies and Research in Chinese Academia: Prospects, Challenges and Hindrances," *International Bulletin of Missionary Research,* 29, no.1 (January 2005): 21.

27. "China Education Yearbook 2009," *CHIWEST* http://www.e-admission.edu.cn/HomePage/2009-09-24/page_261.shtml (12 October 22009).

28. Aikman, *Jesus in Beijing: How Christianity Is Transforming China and Changing the Global Balance of Power*, 17.

29. Chen Cunfu and Huang Tianhai, "The Emergence of A New Type of Christians in China Today," *Review of Religious Research* 46, No. 2 (Dec., 2004) : 184.

30. Ibid.

31. Catharin E. Dalpino, *Deferring Democracy: Promoting Openness in Authoritarian Regimes* (Washington, D.C.: Brookings Institution Press, 2000), 3.

32. Ibid., 3.

33. Aikman, *Jesus in Beijing: How Christianity Is Transforming China and Changing the Global Balance of Power*, 292.

34. Tun-jen Cheng and Deborah A. Brown, "Introduction: The Roles of Religious Organizations in Asian Democratization," in *Religious Organizations and Democratization*, eds. Tun-jen Cheng and Deborah A. Brown (New York: M.E. Sharpe, 2006), 5.

35. Xinping Zhuo, "Christianity and China's Modernization," *Landerburo China*, http://www.kas.de/wf/doc/kas_6824-544-1-30.pdf (6 January 2009)

36. Ibid.

37. Xie Chuanjiao, "China's suicide rate among world's highest," *China Daily*, 11 September 2007.

38. Wang Xin-Lin, sheng Li, and Fang Yao-Qi, "A Survey on Suicide in China during the Past Decade," *Hong Kong Journal of Psychiatry* 8, No. 1. (1998): 9.

39. Wiest, "Religious Studies and Research in Chinese Academia: Prospects, Challenges and Hindrances," 26.

40. See Xinging Zhou, "The Significance of Christianity for the Modernization of Chinese Society," *Crux* 33 (March 1997), 31-37.

41. Ibid., 11.

42. Aikman, *Jesus in Beijing: How Christianity Is Transforming China and Changing the Global Balance of Power*, 136.

43. James E. Wood, Jr., *Church-State Relations in the Modern World* (Waco, Texas: J.M. Dawson Institute of Church-State Studies, 1998), 197-201.

44. Bob Whyte, "The Future of Religion in China," *Religion in the Communist Lands* 8 (1980), 8.

45. Aikman, *Jesus in Beijing: How Christianity Is Transforming China and Changing the Global Balance of Power*, 8.

46. Thomas Alan Harvey, *Acquainted with Grief: Wang Mingdao's Stand for the Persecuted Church in China* (Grand Rapids, Mich.: Brazos Press, 2002), 159. Aikman, *Jesus in Beijing: How Christianity Is Transforming China and Changing the Global Balance of Power*, 291. Also see *Christianity Today* editorial, "Free China's Church" *Christianity Today* Internet edition, 7 January 2002.

47. Aikman, *Jesus in Beijing: How Christianity Is Transforming China and Changing the Global Balance of Power*, 325.

48. Tony Lambert, "Counting Christians in China: A Cautionary Report," *International Bulletin of Missionary Research* 7, no. 1 (January 2003): 6.

49. "Survey finds 300m China believers," BBC News, February 7, 2007. http://news.bbc.co.uk/2/hi/asia-pacific/6337627.stm (March 10, 2013)

50. Zhuo Xinping, "Discussion on 'Cultural Christians' in China," in *China and Christianity: Burdened Past, Hopeful Future.* eds. Stephen Uhalley Jr. and Xiaoxin Wu (New York: M.E. Sharpe, 2001), 283.

51. Aikman, *Jesus in Beijing: How Christianity Is Transforming China and Changing the Global Balance of Power*, 291-292.

52. Ibid., 286.

53. Kindopp, "Policy Dilemmas in China's Church-State Relations: An Introduction," 18.

54. Ibid, 19.

*Chapter Twelve*

# Will Confucianism Be Able to Help China's Democratization?

One of the distinguishing characteristics of China is that the Chinese political system and ideology support each other. Chinese official ideology justifies the legitimacy of the government, and the government ensures the implementation of Chinese official ideology. It is impossible to understand contemporary China without comprehending Chinese ideology. Confucianism was the dominant ideology for over 2,000 years before the Revolution of 1911; the Three Principles of the People dominated in the Republican era between 1912 and 1949; and Marxism has been Chinese official ideology since 1949. This chapter will discuss Confucianism and Chapter 13 will discuss Marxism in China. Due to the fact that mass media play a critical role in Chinese ideology and politics, Chapter 14 will discuss the role of media in contemporary China.

Some scholars avoid using the word "ideology" to describe Confucianism, yet the Confucian doctrine has functioned as an ideology to serve political life in China from the Han dynasty to the end of the Qing dynasty.[1] Chinese liberal intellectuals began to attack Confucianism during the Republican era. Communism's official ideology continued to criticize Confucianism under the Mao regime. In the post-Mao era, the Chinese government has turned around and promoted the renaissance of Confucianism to reshape Chinese cultural identity. Will the revival of Confucianism be able to help China's democratization with Chinese characteristics? Mainstream Western societies are skeptical about the role of Confucianism. According to Samuel Huntington, Confucianism is one of the eight major civilizations in the world, which opposes the progressive ideas and institutions of Western civilization.[2] The decision made by the U.S. State Department in 2012 to tighten visa requirements at Chinese Confucius Institutes in the United States reflects its concern about the influence of Confucianism in the United States. McMaster University will shutter its Confucius Institute in summer 2013, because the university was "uncomfortable, and felt that it didn't reflect the way the university would do hiring"—"building an inclusive community, respect for diversity, respect for individual views."[3] This chapter will attempt to challenge the arguments from both anti-Confucianism and state-sponsored Confucianism and argue that Confucianism is a very complex system, including both positive and negative elements through re-assessing the original Confucian ideology, discussing the core values of Confucianism, and examining the relevance of Confucianism to contemporary China to see if Confucianism is a remedy for China's future.

## CONFUCIUS AND THE PRIMARY SOURCES OF CONFUCIANISM

To reconcile the two opposite viewpoints regarding the role of Confucianism, it is necessary to make distinctions between the original Confucius's teachings and reinterpreted Confucius's teachings, which we know today as Confucianism. Historically, Confucius, or Kong Qiu in Chinese (551-479 B.C.), was the founder of Confucianism and the first great teacher of wisdom in Chinese history. His teaching is called Kong Jiao or Ru Jiao in Chinese, or Confucianism in English. The conventional viewpoint is that the Four Books (*The Analects*, *Mencius*, *The Doctrine of the Mean*, and *The Great Learning*) and the Five Classics (*The Book of Changes*, *The Book of History*, *The Book of Songs*, *The Book of Rites*, and *The Spring and Autumn Annals*) represent the authority of Confucius's teaching. Only these works, which recorded Confucius's teaching, can be categorized as authentic Confucian works. However, Confucius wrote none of them because Confucius, as a transmitter, followed the tradition of *shu er bu zuo* (only teaching without writing). Confucius said, "I am a transmitter, rather than an original thinker. I trust and enjoy the teachings of the ancients. In my heart, I compare myself to old Peng."[4]

*The Analects* is the most revered sacred scripture of Confucius's teaching. It was not Confucius himself, but his disciples who wrote and compiled the manuscript, which recorded conversations with their master. It is difficult to confirm the authorship of *The Great Learning*, but most Confucian specialists agree that Confucius's grandson wrote the book. The current edition of the book differs from the original text, because many Confucian scholars worked on the book after Confucius's death. After the brothers Cheng Hao and Cheng Yi worked on *The Great Learning,* Zhu Xi continued the Cheng brothers' project and added his introductory commentary to the book. In *The Doctrine of the Mean*, there are clear references indicating that the book came from the Confucian school, although it is hard to assign authorship.

Mencius (371-288 B.C.) was not of the same generation as Confucius, but *The Mencius* is categorized as one of the Four Books because Mencius was a loyal disciple of Confucius's teaching and played a pivotal role in the two hundred years that connected Confucius's teaching and Mencius's own time. Thus, "both Confucius and Mencius are represented as having been considerable figures in their day."[5]

The Five Classics were passed down from one generation to another from the Shang dynasty (1700 – 1100 B.C) to the Spring and Autumn period (500 B.C.). *The Book of History* collects a variety of archival documents from the Xia to the Zhou dynasties, reflecting the wisdom of Chinese politics and government and "outlining the responsibilities of the ruling elite toward heaven and the common people."[6] *The Book of Songs*, probably written in the Zhou Dynasty (1122-256 B.C.) and assembled in the Han dynasty by Confucian scholars, is a collection of Chinese poems, portraying daily life in court and countryside. *The Book of Rites*, compiled in the second century, includes more than three thousand ancient social rules and the descriptions of government structure, focusing on community and communication. *The Spring and Autumn Annals* is about the history of a single Chinese province from about 700 to 500 B.C. *The Book of Changes* has been viewed by most scholars in Chinese history as the earliest discussion of the metaphysical structure of the universe. It discusses universal movement and order from its beginning, the Dao, and also sketches the relationships between the universe, society, and human beings through texts and diagrams.

The content of the Four Books and the Five Classics is very rich. Tu Weiming puts it like this: "The Five Classics, as five visions—metaphysical, political, poetic, social and historical—provide a holistic context for the development of Confucian scholarship as a comprehensive inquiry in the humanities."[7] However, since the Song Dynasty, the Five Classics have been reduced to secondary canonical status.[8] Today, only a few Chinese intellectual historians believe that the Five Classics represent the collective teachings of the ancient holy sage-kings.[9]

## BASIC CHARACTERISTICS OF CONFUCIANISM

The original intention of Confucius's teaching was to restore trust in the government, to transform society into a moral community,[10] to bring comfort to the old, to have trust in friends, and to cherish the young through practicing the five constant virtues.[11] In Confucius's time, China was experiencing a great transformation from a heredity system to a hierarchical system. The old social order was broken (*li beng*) as wars and violence started occurring across the land in the Warring States Period. Through Confucius's eyes, the old social order was the best social order because it was compatible with *li* (propriety). Confucius was determined to bring society back to the traditional system (*fu li*). *Ke ji fu li*—conquer yourself and return to ritual [12] —was his primary motivation and central political ambition. Therefore, the ultimate goal of Confucian teaching was to maintain traditional social order. Thus, Confucius's original teaching was not a "precise moral orientation, but a professional training with the general goals of state service." [13] Tu Weimin points out that "Confucianism is hierarchical oriented political ideology which is essentially the same as Marxism in a political perspective." [14]

Most Western scholars view Confucianism as humanism. In Western societies, humanism is a movement advocating individual value and capabilities while respecting scientific knowledge and cultivating classics. Unlike Western humanism, heaven and family are the two cornerstones of an integrated Chinese humanism. Because the individual is a basic element of the family and society, the theory of the union of heaven and the individual is the foundation of Chinese humanism. According to Confucius, to be a *jun-zi* (gentleman) is the precondition to regulate the family and to serve the country. [15] Mind, will, and character were the three most important aspects in developing self. A *jun-zi* is supposed to possess a righteous mind, a strong will, and moral character. [16]

To establish a harmonious social order, the Chinese people were required to follow Confucius's teaching, including the five constant virtues: *jen* (benevolence), *yi* (righteousness), *li* (propriety), *zhi* (knowledge/wisdom), and *xin* (sincerity), the three cardinal guides (ruler guides subject, father guides son, and husband guides wife), Five Relationships (ruled is subject to ruler; son is subject to father; wife is subject to husband; younger is subject to elder; and friends must trust each other), the three obediences (in ancient China a woman was required to obey her father before marriage, her husband during married life, and her sons in widowhood), and the four virtues (fidelity, physical charm, propriety in speech, and efficiency in needlework). All these Confucian principles worked together as a net to maintain Chinese social order and political structure and to restrain the human nature of the Chinese people. "Let the father be indeed father, and the son son; let the elder brother be indeed elder brother, and the younger brother younger brother, let the husband be indeed husband, and the wife wife: then will the family be in its normal state. Bring the family to that state, and all under heaven will be established." [17]

*Tian* (heaven) is the superior power beyond human control. The Chinese emperor was the mediator between heaven and society. The Chinese must obey the will of heaven and the will of the mediator—the emperor. According to Confucius's teaching, all under heaven are of one family, and all nations are of one people. Chief Minister of the Han dynasty Dong Zhongshu (195-105 B.C.) canonized Confucius's teachings, such as "Heaven changeth not, likewise the Way changeth not," and "the imitation of the ancients." He also required the Chinese people "not to do things which do not conform to the rites," to "look at nothing that is not consistent with propriety," "not to listen to things which do not conform to the rites," and "not to say things which do not conform to the rites." Under these principles, a person had to die if the emperor wanted him or her dead.[18] The legitimacy of an absolute monarchical government was based on the unconditional obedience of the common people. Gilbert Rozman points out that one of the important reasons why China failed to complete reforms in the nineteenth century was that the Chinese people were unwilling to abandon their old traditions and customs, such as Dao, Way, and Heaven.[19]

## WHY DID CONFUCIANISM BECOME THE DOMINANT IDEOLOGY?

The first Chinese emperor (259-210 B.C.) only appreciated legalism which advocated that the government should rule by strict law and punishment. The first emperor believed that education would enlighten the common people and thus contribute to unrest. In the emperor's eyes, Confucius's teaching used the past to criticize the present, so he put Confucian writings to the torch and buried 460 of Confucius's disciples alive. In addition, high taxes, conscript labor, and severe persecution contributed largely to the peasant's rebellion at the end of the Qin dynasty.

The first emperor of the Han dynasty learned the lesson from the Qin dynasty and carried out more flexible policies in regard to Chinese peasants. In order to improve the relationship between the ruling class and the ruled class, the Han dynasty began to follow Confucian political philosophy, departing from legalism. Dong Zhongshu suggested that emperor Han Wu Di should worship Confucius's teaching only and abolish all other schools of thought, in order to establish a benevolent government. The emperor Han Wu Di accepted his suggestion and put it into practice and dismissed all non-Confucian scholars from the government.[20]

Confucianism did not come to dominate Chinese life by accident.[21] First, compared with the other nine schools of thought—Buddhism, Daoism, yin-yang, legalist, Mohist (utilitarianism), Political Strategists, Eclectics, Logicians (nominalism), and Agriculturalist—Confucianism was the best for the ruling class to maintain its power over the long term.[22] The founders of Daoism, Lao Zi and Zhuang Zi, emphasized the contradiction between human society and the natural world. According to Lao-Zhuang, human beings created civilization, but lost their morality. In order to avoid evil, one must be willing "either to flee from civilized society or to destroy it."[23] Lao-Zhuang advocated a negative philosophy and preached "do-nothing-ism" and nihilism. In practice, its negative theory neither pleased the ruling class nor fit the needs of the Chinese people. Mocianism claimed that the state was the highest value and humans were only the instruments. Governing is a trade similar to that of a butcher.[24] This political theory was not compatible with Chinese humanism and the hypocritical face of the *ren zheng* (benevolent government). Legalists viewed human nature as wicked and self-seeking and advocated that a centralized government exercise absolute power to impose harsh punishments. In fact, the harsh governance of legalist theory would not help the ruling class gain Chinese people's support. Legalism could be used for a short time, but it could not be used for the state ideology over a long term. Sun Zi was the founder of the strategist or militarist school and his strategy is recognized and applied to military, businesses and administrations worldwide. Although his military strategy contained rich philosophical ideas, it was not comprehensive enough to achieve recognition as an official ideology to regulate the Chinese society.

Second, the civil service examination system expanded the influence of Confucianism and strengthened the dominant position of Confucianism. The Han dynasty began to select officials from Confucian scholars, and the Sui Dynasty institutionalized the civil service examination system. This system offered hope for those who were not of noble origin, but who wanted to have a bright future if they could pass the examination. The content of the examination was the Confucian text. This created a huge demand for Confucian books and promoted Confucianism's spread throughout the country.[25] The competitive examination system became one of the major channels for recruiting government officials and the scholar-officials became the main body of bureaucracy and the main part of the ruling class in the Ming and the Qing Dynasties.[26]

Third, Confucianism is not an exclusive system but an inclusive system, so it constantly strengthened itself by assimilating good ideas from other schools of thought for more than 2,000 years. For example, Confucianism assimilated Buddhist cosmology, modified its theoretical system, and made Confucian ethics and political theory more metaphysical.[27] The most significant neo-Confucian scholars, such as Wang Yangmin, Zhu Xi, Cheng Hao, and Cheng Yi, introduced important conceptions of *qi* (life-force energy) and *li* to reconstruct Confucian theory. Neo-Confucianism also fostered the concepts of the "ethic of thrift, honesty, and effort" from Daoism and promoted productive activities.[28]

## THE DEVELOPMENT OF CONFUCIANISM

After Confucius's death, "his followers split into eight distinct schools all claiming to be the legitimate heir to the Confucian legacy."[29] Obviously, the meaning of the term "Confucianism" being used today is different from

Confucius's original teachings. Michael Nylan points out that not all Confucian scholars "were devoted of the Confucian Way."[30] Thus, the term "Confucianism" is not singular, but plural.

Confucianism has gone through three periods or three epochs throughout history.[31] The first epoch, from Confucius's time to the Tang dynasty (618-907 A.C.), was the formative period of Confucianism. After Han Wu Di issued an edict to dismiss all non-Confucian scholars from the government, Confucius's teaching became popular, his hometown became a sacred place of worship, and Confucian books became the textbooks in schools and the basic content of the civil service examination. To be sure, the influence of Confucius's teachings during this period of time basically served as political and governmental needs through intellectual self-cultivation and the civil examination. Professor Hsu Cho-yun ascribed the beginning of the exegetical tradition to Confucius's followers who combined careers in government service with learning.[32]

Beginning with the Song dynasty (960-1279 A.C.), Confucianism entered a new stage, Neo-Confucianism, or *lixue* in Chinese. Cheng Hao, Cheng Yi, Zhu Xi, and Wang Yang-ming were the major figures whose interpretations represented the basic characteristics of Neo-Confucianism, though their interpretations were "seriously challenged" by contemporary scholars.[33] The development of Neo-Confucianism "was a broad historical process" and attempted to "redefine tradition and reformulate orthodoxy."[34] According to Jian Zang, "Although Song Confucian learning was built on the foundation of Han learning, it differs from the latter in the depth and scope of its exploration into the origins and principles of nature and human society."[35] Confucian scholars made Neo-Confucianism more metaphysical by adding some ambiguous concepts, such as "the Great Ultimate, the heavenly principle, vital energy, nature, mind, and humanity."[36] Neo-Confucianism also emphasized individual learning and "personal cultivation" in the Way (the basic concept of Daoism, the way or path of life) to conduct a moral life and become a Sage.[37] Meanwhile, in the Song dynasty, printing technology became available, making books more accessible.[38] The Four Books and Five Classics were widely circulated.[39] Accordingly, the influence of Neo-Confucianism expanded considerably, not only to the elite, but also to the common people. William Theodore de Bary suggests that following the Song dynasty, traditional Confucian values began to move in a modern direction to become more vigorous.[40]

After the world experienced Nazism in the World War II, the inauguration of democratic systems spread throughout many countries, such as West Germany, Italy, Austria, Japan, and South Korea.[41] Since the 1960s, Western countries have experienced a "great disruption," including family breakdown, rising crime, and loss of trust.[42] Western liberalism, conservatism, and the Third Way tried to resolve the crisis, but without success. Looking across the Pacific Ocean, Western countries found that Confucianism in some Asian countries had become a primary means to shape economic, political, and social structures. Western countries, thus, began paying attention to the role of Confucianism. Then, Confucianism entered into its third epoch—New Confucianism in the 1970s. [43] During the third epoch, Confucianism made a great contribution not only to mainland China, Taiwan, Hong Kong, and other Asian countries, [44] but also to countries outside of Asia, including Western countries.

The influence of Confucianism is still limited, mainly in East Asian countries including Japan and the four other "Mini Dragons" (Taiwan, South Korea, Hong Kong, and Singapore). These Eastern Asian countries have shared Confucian values with China and faced a similar challenge from Western ideas and practices. Peter R. Moody asserts that "Eastern Asian societies are characterized by personalism, familism, and political moralism. [45] In the 1970s both South Korea and Singapore used Confucian ideology to support their authoritarian government and to promote a national economy. Nepotism is also a popular phenomenon in modern Japanese politics. The relationship between the leader and his followers is based on loyalty, favor, and seniority and more than 35 percent of Diet members are sons of past and present Diet members. John E. Ho describes this characteristic of Japanese society as "Japan Inc." [46]

Interestingly, Chinese liberal intellectuals began to challenge Confucianism in the mid-1910s. Mao Zedong followed in the footsteps of the first emperor, and opposed Confucianism reached its peak during the Cultural Revolution between 1966 and 1976. In the post-Mao era, while some Chinese liberal intellectuals still blamed Confucianism for China's domestic chaos, others have revisited Confucianism and returned to traditionalism, arguing that Confucianism is the core of Chinese civilization and trying to make Confucianism the state religion. Kang Xiaoguang, one of the leading advocates for Confucianism in recent years, has called to Confucianize the civil service cadres, the school system, and even the Chinese Communist Party. [47]

As early as the 1980s, the Chinese government started to promote the renaissance of Confucian tradition. According to Anna Sun, the Chinese government has endorsed Confucianism through various efforts. First, in 2004, the party borrowed Confucian political philosophy by using the slogan "harmonious society." Second, the annual formal ceremony of the Qufu Confucius Temple has been broadcast on Chinese national television since 2005. Third, the government established Confucius Institutes around the world. Fourth, the Chinese government promotes Confucian heritage through symbolic means, such as images, test, and artworks. The opening ceremony of the Beijing Olympics in 2008 was the major event that attempted to link China's recent achievements with its Confucian past. Finally, the government uses Confucius as an explicit political tool on the stage of international politics to award the first Confucius Peace Prize in 2010 in response to the 2010 Nobel Peace Prize which was awarded to Chinese political dissident Liu Xiaobo.[48]

Since 2002, the Chinese government has made great efforts to develop Confucius Institutes around the world. At the end of 2010 a total of 322 Confucius Institutes and 369 Confucius Classrooms were put in place in 96 countries and regions.[49] The total number of registered students at Confucius Institutes has reached 360,000, along with about 4,000 Chinese language teachers. According to *Xinhua*, China will establish 1,000 institutes by 2020. Confucius Institutes are the central project of Chinese cultural diplomacy for improving China's image through teaching Chinese language and culture.[50] However, the government-sponsored Confucius Institutes have unavoidably received various criticisms from Western societies. It is widely believed that the establishment of Confucius Institutes represents not just an international-ization of education, but is also a special representation of China's soft power which extends Chinese political power in the international society.[51] Some Western scholars and politicians argue that the government uses Confucius Institutes as a vehicle for its global dominance and for extending Chinese political control activities to Western universities.[52] Essentially, Confucius Institutes serve the central task of the Chinese government to spread commu-nist party culture in the name of Chinese culture.[53] Hartig's research project concludes that next to the promotion of language and culture, Confucius Institutes also have more far reaching political purposes, at least indirectly.[54]

## THE RELEVANCE OF CONFUCIANISM TO CONTEMPORARY CHINA

Many Confucian specialists, such as Lin Yutang, Herrlee Creel, Tu Wei-min,[55] Julia Ching,[56] Wm. Theodore de Bary,[57] and Irene Eber, hold a very positive view on Confucianism and "appreciated Confucius's teachings as virtually ageless."[58] They believe that Confucianism plays a major role in the development of Chinese civilization and remains a model and inspiration. Confucianism can help people "find the wisdom and strength to cope with [problems], including those problems that we shall never understand."[59] They also argue that Confucianism is compatible with modern democracy. Confucian liberal ideas embrace the seeds of the principle of equality among human beings, and are very similar to Western individualism.[60] Tu Weimin suggests that Confucian values—a life of benevolence, justice, ritual, wis-dom, and trust—are merely Asian values, but universal values rooted in East Asian theory and practice.[61] He believes that a new form of Confucianism has "inherited the Enlightenment legacy and became committed to universal values rooted in the modern Western experience: liberty, due process of law, human rights, and the dignity of the individual."[62] In addition, *zhong yong*— the doctrine of the mean—is the resolution of social, cultural, and religious conflicts and a universal path that prohibits people going to extremes. Thus, the doctrine of the mean is the best teaching for the people in the practice of democracy, because democracy itself is a compromise between the state and the individual, and between the state and civil society.[63]

Confucianism has played a positive role in making a good contribution to the economic development in China and to the Asian economic miracle of the early 1990s, as well as to the Pacific Rim.[64] Furthermore, the central principles of Confucianism, *jen* (benevolent or caring) and *li* (ritual), are essentially about caring ethics.[65] In *The Analects*, Confucius mentioned *jen* as many as 105 times.[66] Although Confucius never clearly defined the term *jen*, the meaning of *jen* is obvious: *"jen* is to love others,"[67] bring comfort to the old, have trust in friends, and cherish the young.[68] Thus, the meaning of *jen* in *The Analects* is the same as the meaning of love in the Bible.

Confucian advocates believe that Confucianism can be adapted for China's modernization.[69] The reform movement creates China's economic boom and also produces many social problems as well, such as corruption, the gap between the rich and the poor, care for the elderly, and disaster relief.[70] Under this circumstance, it is especially meaningful to utilize Confucianism in order to address all these issues from a Confucian perspective. If the current state-sponsored Confucian movement succeeds, Confucianism is likely to play a major role in shaping China's cultural identity.[71] Anna Sun predicts that "the twenty-first century may prove to be the Confucian century."[72]

However, it remains questionable as to how and in what way state-sponsored Confucianism is able to enrich the Chinese culture, rescue Chinese people from the moral crisis in present-day China, and help China's modernization and democratization. Actually, the majority of Chinese people do not believe that China is able to solve China's major problems by adopting Confucian values, because Confucianism comes with its historical limitations. First, Confucianism has tended to advocate unlimited authority for the monarchical government and neglect the individual.[73] According to Confucianism, the individual is not the center of society. Instead, the state dominates and shapes society, and the emperor holds absolute power over government.[74] Second, Confucianism has supported patriarchal and hierarchical systems. According to Confucius, "men are not born equal in intelligence, although all people can become moral men." Also, "some are endowed with superior intelligence, others with inferior."[75] The ruled must obey the ruling, and the emperor is on the top of the ruling. Hence, Confucianism as ideology "valued hierarchy in both political and social spheres."[76] Third, Confucianism has insisted that a good society is maintained by a moral obligation, not by an obligatory law.[77] According to Confucius, "Lead the people by laws and regulate them by punishments, and the people will try to avoid wrongdoing but will have no sense of shame. Lead the people by virtue and regulate them by the rules of propriety, and the people will have a sense of shame, and moreover will become good."[78] All these limitations of Confucianism obviously contradict with the basic principles of modern democracy. China may become the world economic superpower without modern democracy, but could not become an international recognized world leader without incorporating modern democracy.

## CONCLUSION

Confucius is the founder of Confucianism. The development of Confucianism is a complicated process, in which some Confucian scholars' interpretations are faithful to Confucius's teachings, and some actually depart from them, such as Neo-Confucianism. From a historical perspective, Confucius's original teaching significantly differs from the general term "Confucianism." There are many interpretations for Confucius's original teaching today; accordingly, there are also many forms of Confucianism. Scholars around the world fail to sufficiently address the differences between Confucius's original teaching and Confucianism today, and to address the question of whether or not Confucianism will be able to help China's democratization in the twenty-first century. However, while it is necessary to acknowledge the great contributions of Confucianism to Chinese civilization, it must be admitted that Confucianism is more compatible with the needs of the Chinese ruling class and the centralized Chinese government. Although Chinese social and family relations remain stable, contemporary China shows a radical departure from traditional Chinese culture. China's materialism is increasing, social relations are becoming superficial, submission to authority is weakening, and adventurism and risk are on the rise.[79] The majority of the Chinese people no longer endorse Confucianism, nor do they submit compliantly to authority as previous generations did. To be sure, Confucianism is the major heritage of Chinese civilization and contains many positive elements that may continue to serve Chinese modernization and global development, though it is necessary to carefully absorb and practice them.

## NOTES

1. John W. Dardess, *Confucianism and Autocracy: Professional Elites in the Founding of the Ming Dynasty* (Berkeley: University of California Press, 1983), 7.

2. Samuel Huntington, *The Clash of Civilizations and the Remaking of World Order* (New York, Simon & Schuster, 1998).

3. "McMaster Closing Confucius Institute Over Hiring Issues," *The Globe and Mail*, February 7, 2013.

4. *The Analects*, 7:1.

5. W.A.C.H. Dobson, *Mencius: A New Translation Arranged and Annotated for the General Reader* (Toronto: University of Toronto Press, 1979), xvii.

6. Michael Nylan, *The Five Confucian Classics* (New Haven, Conn.: Yale University Press, 2001), 8.

7. Tu Wei-Ming, "Confucius and Confucianism," in *Confucianism and the Family*, ed. Walter H. Slote and George A. De Vos (New York: State University of New York Press, 1998), 21.

8. Nylan, *The Five Confucian Classics,* 58.

9. Ibid., 18.

10. Tu, "Confucius and Confucianism," 12.

11. *The Analects*, 5:26.

12. *The Analects,* 12:1.

13. Nylan, *The Five Confucian Classics*, 3.

14. Tu Weiming, "Confucian Spirituality in Contemporary China," in *Confucianism and Spiritual Traditions in Modern China and Beyond.* Edited by Fenggang Yang & Joseph Tamney (Leiden, the Netherlands: Koninklike Brill, 2012), 77.

15. Paul Myron and Anthony Linebarger, *The Political Doctrines of Sun Yat-sen: An Exposition of the San Min Chu I* (Westport, Conn.: Hyperion Press, 1936), 29.

16. Gung-hsing Wang, *The Chinese Mind* (New York: John Day Company, 1946), 18.

17. *The Book of Changes,* Section II.

18. H. G. Greel, "The Eclectics of Han Thought," in *The Making of China: Main Themes in Premodern Chinese History*, ed. Chun-shu Chang (Englewood Cliffs, N.J.: Prentice-Hall, Inc., 1975), 141.

19. Rozman Gilbert, ed. *China's Modernization* (Jiangsu Province, China: People's Publishing House, 1998), 63.

20. Wang, *The Chinese Mind*, 114.

21. Ibid.

22. Vitaly A. Rubin, *Individual and State in Ancient China: Essays on Four Chinese Philosophers* (New York: Columbia University Press, 1976), 116.

23. Ibid, 119.

24. Ibid, 117.

25. John E. Ho, *East Asian Philosophy: With Historical Background and Present Influence* (New York: Peter Lang, 1992), 3.

26. James R. Thomas, *Chinese Politics* (Jiangsu, China: People's Publishing House of Jiangsu, 1992), 34

27. Creel, *Chinese Thought, from Confucius to Mao Tse-tung,* 204.

28. Timothy Brook and Hy V. Luong, eds., *Culture and Economy: The Shaping of Capitalism in Eastern Asia* (Ann Arbor: University of Michigan Press, 1997), 24.

29. Tu, "Confucius and Confucianism," 14.

30. Nylan, *The Five Confucian Classics*, 3.

31. Tu Wei-Ming, "Toward a Third Epoch of Confucian Humanism: A Background Understanding," in *Confucianism: The Dynamics of Tradition*, ed. Irene Eber (New York: MaCmillan Publishing Company), 3.

32. Irene Eber, "Introduction," in *Confucianism: the Dynamics of Tradition*, ed. Irene Eber (New York: MaCmillan Publishing Company, 1986), xii.

33. Tu, "Confucius and Confucianism," 27.

34. Wm. Theodore de Bary, "Introduction," in *The Unfolding of Neo-Confucianism*, ed. Wm. Theodore de Bary (New York: Columbia University Press, 1975), 11.

35. Jian Zang, "Women and the Transmission of Confucian Culture in Song China," in *Women and Confucian Cultures in Premodern China, Korea, and Japan*, 124.

36. Tu, "Confucius and Confucianism," 27.

37. Wm. Theodore de Bary, *The Message of the Mind in Neo-Confucianism* (New York: Columbia University Press, 1989), 1.

38. Lisa Raphals, *Sharing the Light: Representations of Women and Virtue in Early China* (Albany, N.Y.: State University of New York Press, 1998), 295.

39. Quoted in Elisabeth Croll, *Feminism and Socialism in China* (London: Routledge & Kegan Paul, 1978), 14.

40. William Theodore de Bary, *The Liberal Tradition in China* (New York: Columbia University Press, 1983), 43.

41. Samuel Huntington, *The Third Wave: Democratization in the Late Twentieth Century* (Norman, Okla.: University of Oklahoma Press, 1991), 18.

42. See Francis Fukuyama, *The Great Disruption: Human Nature and the Reconstitution of Social Order* (New York: Free Press, 1999).

43. Vitaly Rubin, "Values of Confucianism," *Numen* 38, no. 1 (1981), 72.

44. Tu, "Toward a Third Epoch of Confucian Humanism: A Background Understanding," 19.

45. Peter R. Moody, *Political Opposition in Post-Confucian Society* (New York: Praeger, 1988), 250.

46. John E. Ho, *East Asian Philosophy: With Historical Background and Present Influence* (New York: Peter Lang, 1992), 183.

47. Kang Xiaoguang, "A Study of The Renaissance of Traditional Confucian Culture in Contemporary China," in *Confucianism and Spiritual Traditions in Modern China and Beyond.* Edited by. Fenggang Yang & Joseph Tamney (Leiden, the Netherlands: Koninklike Brill, 2012), 72.

48. Anna Sun, "The Revival of Confucian Rites in Contemporary China," in *Confucianism and Spiritual Traditions in Modern China and Beyond.* Edited by Fenggang Yang & Joseph Tamney (Leiden, the Netherlands: Koninklike Brill, 2012), 316

49. Falk Hartig, "Confucius Institutes and the Rise of China," *Journal of Chinese Political Science* 17, no. 1 (2012): 53.

50. N. J. Cull, "Public Diplomacy: Taxonomies and Histories." *The Annals of the American Academy of Political and Social Science*, 616 (2008:1): 55.

51. Hartig, "Confucius Institutes and the Rise of China," 68.

52. J. Chey, "Chinese 'Soft Power', Cultural Diplomacy and the Confucius Institutes," *The Sydney Paper Summer* 2008: 40.

53. Quoted in J. Steffenhagen, "Has BCTT Sold Out to Chinese Propaganda," *The Vancouver Sun*, April 2, 2008.

54. Hartig, "Confucius Institutes and the Rise of China," 68.

55. See Wei Ming Tu, *Centrality and Commonality: An Essay on Confucian Religiousness.* (Albany, NY: State University of New York Press, 1989).

56. See Julia Ching, *Confucianism and Christianity: A Comparative Study.* (New York: Kodansha International, 1977).

57. See de Bary, *The Message of the Mind, in Neo-Confucianism*, 1989.

58. Wm. Theodore de Bary, *The Trouble with Confucianism* (Cambridge: Harvard University Press, 1991), xii.

59. Julia Ching, "What is Confucian Spirituality," in *Confucianism: the Dynamics of Tradition*, ed. Irene Eber (New York: MaCmillan Publishing Company), 80.

60. Li Chenyang, "The Confucian Concept of Jen and the Feminist Ethics of Care: A Comparative Study," in *The Sage and the Second Sex: Confucianism, Ethics, and Gender*, ed. Li, Chenyang (Chicago: Open Court, 2000), 23-42.

61. Tu Weiming, "Confucian Spirituality in Contemporary China," in *Confucianism and Spiritual Traditions in Modern China and Beyond.* Edited by Fenggang Yang & Joseph Tamney (Leiden, the Netherlands: Koninklike Brill, 2012), 91.

62. Ibid.

63. Li Yu-ning, ed. "Changes in Women's Status, in *Chinese Women Through Chinese Eyes*, (Armonk, N.Y.: M.E. Sharpe, Inc, 1992), 112.

64. Tu Wei-Ming, "Probing the 'Three Bonds' and 'Five Relationships,' in *Confucianism and the Family*, eds. Walter H. Slote and George A. De Vos (New York: State University of New York Press, 1998), 135.

65. Patricia Buckley Ebrey, *Confucianism and Family Rituals in Imperial China: A Social History of Writing about Rites* (Princeton, N.J.: Princeton University Press, 1991), 14.

66. Li, "The Confucian Concept of Jen and the Feminist Ethics of Care: A Comparative Study," 23.

67. *The Analects,* 12: 22.

68. Ibid., 5:26.

69. Joseph B. Tamney, "The Resilience of Confucianism in Chinese Societies," in *Confucianism and Spiritual Traditions in Modern China and Beyond.* Edited by Fenggang Yang & Joseph Tamney (Leiden, the Netherlands: Koninklike Brill, 2012), 127.

70. Robert P. Weller, "Religion, Ritual, and the Public Good in China," Anna Sun, "The Revival of Confucian Rites in Contemporary China," in *Confucianism and Spiritual Traditions in Modern China and Beyond.* Edited by Fenggang Yang & Joseph Tamney (Leiden, the Netherlands: Koninklike Brill, 2012), 329.

71. Tu Weiming, "Confucian Spirituality in Contemporary China," 79.

72. Anna Sun, "The Revival of Confucian Rites in Contemporary China," in *Confucianism and Spiritual Traditions in Modern China and Beyond.* Edited by Fenggang Yang & Joseph Tamney (Leiden, the Netherlands: Koninklike Brill, 2012), 327.

73. Quoted in Tse-tsung Chow, *The May Fourth Movement: Intellectual Revolution in Modern China* (Stanford, Calif.: Stanford University Press, 1967), 301.

74. Peter R. Moody, *Political Opposition in Post-Confucian Society* (New York: Praeger, 1988), 251.

75. Mousheng Lin, *Men and Ideas: An Informal History of Chinese Political Thought* (New York: John Day Company, 1942), 36.

76. Kenneth Lieberthal, *Governing China: from Revolution through Reform* (New York: W.W. Norton & Company, 1995), 7.

77. Benjiamin Isadore Schwartz, *China's Cultural* Values (Mesa, Ariz.: Lionheart Press, 1993), 32.

78. Quoted in Richard W. Wilson, Sidney L. Greenblatt, and Amy Auerbacher Wilson, eds., *Moral Behavior in Chinese Society* (New York: Praeger, 1981), 104.

79. Godwin Chu and Yanan Ju, *The Great Wall in Ruins: Communication and Cultural Change in China* (Albany: State University of New York Press, 1993), 296.

## Chapter Thirteen

# Marxism and Maoism

After the CPC came to power in 1949, the Chinese government officially made Marxism the established ideology. The Preamble in the Constitution of China clearly states that "the successes of its socialist cause have been achieved by the Chinese people of all nationalities under the leadership of the Communist Party of China and the guidance of Marxism-Leninism and Mao Zedong Thought." This indicates that the CPC is the organizational leader of the country, and Marxism is the ideological guide. According to the Constitution of the Communist Party of China, the party "takes Marxism-Leninism, Mao Zedong Thought, Deng Xiaoping Theory and the important thought of Three Represents as its guide to action." The CPC and Marxism are two sides of the same coin working together and ruling the entirety of China. Will Marxism be able to guide the CPC to develop a modern and democratic China in the twenty-first century? In Western societies, Marxism is not dead. There are many Marxist professors on America's college campuses. However, politically, the mainstream of public opinion in Western societies has rejected Marxism, because it has been proven that the ideology failed in developing the economy in Eastern European countries and other communist countries. More importantly, all Marxist states are opposed to the basic cornerstones of modern democracy. Although after the September 11 attacks the ideological distinctions between China and democratic countries have been blurred, the conflict between Marxism and modern democracy remain an obstacle between China and Western societies. This chapter will discuss the original Marxist theories and the characteristics of Chinese Marxism-Maoism, explore the issues of why Marxism won popular support before 1949, discuss why it is losing its vitality in the post-Mao era, and examine the relationship between the CPC and Marxism and Maoism in order to predict the future of Chinese Marxism in China.

## WHO WAS MARX?

Karl Marx (1818-1883) was born into a middle-class family in Trier, Germany. Marx's family lived affluently, but not really wealthy. Marx was educated at home until age thirteen. After graduating from the Trier Gymnasium, Marx enrolled in the University of Bonn in 1835 to study law but transferred to a more academically oriented university in Berlin the following year, in which Marx became more intellectual and turned his studies from law to philosophy. During this period, Marx wrote many poems and essays concerning life and also absorbed the atheistic philosophy of the Young Hegelians. In 1841, he completed his doctoral thesis about contrasts in the philosophies of Deocritus and Epicurus, but the university did not offer him lectureship. In 1847, Marx went to London to attend a Congress of the newly formed Communist League and he wrote the *Communist Manifesto*, the first systematic outline of Marx's theory. During the first half of the 1850s, the Marx family lived in poverty. Marx's major source of income at that time was Engels's support, supplemented by weekly articles written as a foreign correspondent for the *New York Daily Tribune.* His most productive period was in 1857-1858 in which he wrote a draft of *Capital.* In 1867, Marx finally completed the first volume of *Capital.*

With the help and support of Friedrich Engels (1820-1895), Karl Marx founded Marxism, modern communism. Friedrich Engels was born in Barmen-Elberfeld in Germany as the eldest son of a successful German textile industrialist. Engels began writing articles, such as *The Condition of the Working Class in England in 1844*, published in 1845 to support working class movement. After Engels and Marx first met in person in September 1844, they discovered that they had similar world outlooks and decided to work closely together. In 1847, Engels and Marx began writing a pamphlet based on Engels's *The Principles of Communism,* and published it as *The Communist Manifesto* in February 1848. After Marx's death in 1883, Engels devoted much of the rest of his life to editing and translating Marx's writings.

*Das Kapital (Capital* in English) was Marx's main work. The basic theory of Marx's communist thought comes from *Das Kapital.* His thought rested on the fundamental assumption that it is human nature to transform nature, and he called this process of transformation "labor" and the capacity to transform nature, labor power. Egoism, as human nature, is not eliminated by economic reorganization or by material abundance.[1] Although he rejected the idea of an unchanging and universal human nature, Marx believed that a certain social context would be conducive to human fulfillment. Since human relations center on self-creation, a fulfilling society must allow people to make maximum use of their capacity for creative activity. He believed that human history is shaped by our social relations, instead of the way that we think about ourselves.[2]

Marxism includes three types of theory—philosophy, political economics, and socialism—but the core of Marxism is political science in response to the Industrial Revolution and the capitalist system. The goal of Marxism is to overthrow capitalist society and establish communist society. As early as 1844, Marx in his *1844 Manuscript* described communism as the resolution of various conflicts between man and nature, between man and man, between freedom and necessity, and between individual and species.[3] *The Communist Manifesto* was published in 1848 and marked the birth of Marxism, which clearly declared that capitalist society would inevitably collapse and socialist society would inevitably emerge based on the theory of the contradiction between production and productive relations in capitalist societies. In the 1860s, Marx in *Das Kapital* again tried to systematically present his declaration from an economic perspective, in which he advocated materialism, economic determinism, public ownership, violent revolution, class struggle, proletarian dictatorship, one-party system, and the communist society.

According to Marx, the capitalist system collapse is inevitable because it is the result of the conflict between individual free choice and collective outcome. In the market based capitalist society, everyone has the right to choose their own interests, but the final result, in fact, is in no one's interest. The conflict between individual free choice and collective outcome results in class struggles between the ruling class and the laboring class. The mode of production naturally divided social life into antagonistic classes, groups determined by relations to the mode of production. The social classes primarily include two groups—the working class or proletariat, who do not own the means of production and only sell their labor power for living, and capitalists, the bourgeoisie, who own the means of production and exploit the proletariat due to the fact that the worker's labor power generates an added value greater than his salary.

Marx forecasted that the communist revolution and communist society would come first to the most industrially advanced societies. In communist society, due to the establishment of public ownership, planned economy, and new social relationship, the exploitation system would be eliminated, and conflict between nature and human society and between social groups would disappear, and the difference between urban and rural, between intellectuals and laborers, and the poor and rich would be eradicated as well. Marx predicted that the communist revolution would break out soon, but in fact there were only some minor revolutions during Marx's lifetime, such as the German Revolution of 1848 and the Paris Commune of 1871. Marx and Engels never saw a proletarian dictatorship come to power, and thus did not prove the hypothesis of their theory during their time.

After Marx and Engels passed away, their followers became increasingly uneasy about the original Marxism. First of all, some followers believed that the different stages of a capitalist society and the special situations of different countries must also be taken into account. Secondly, Marx left a lot of manuscripts to be explained and his thinking was sometimes ambivalent, so there was room for everyone to interpret Marxism from different perspectives.[4] Third, some socialists and Marxist scholars suspected Marxist theory. According to Marx, socialist revolutions would take place in advanced industrial countries. Marx and Engels both believed that the economic systems of the most advanced industrial countries had already reached revolutionary maturity, but revolutions never took place in developed countries. It may be that the revolutions will never happen. Therefore, wise disciples of Marxism in Western countries wanted to reinterpret Marxism to fit the reality of capitalist societies, while some pushed Marxism to an extreme. Chinese Marxists call these neo-Marxists revisionists and Chinese official ideology firmly rejected the new interpretations of Marxism.

The Russian Revolution of 1917 led to the formation of the Soviet Union, the first socialist country in the world. Vladimir Ilich Lenin (1870-1924) represented the second generation of Marxism, and his interpretation of Marxism was the orthodox Marxism during his time. After Lenin died, Joseph Stalin (1879-1953) replaced Lenin as the leader of the international Marxist movement. Therefore, the Soviet Union became the headquarters of the international communist movement. Lenin and Stalin pushed Marxism to an extreme. They attacked capitalist democracy and assisted proletariat dictatorships. According to Lenin and Stalin, in capitalist societies everyone has equal rights, but everyone does not have equal power. Capitalist democracy is a *façade*, masking class dictatorship. Neo-Marxism in the West and Marxism-Leninism in the under-developed countries play different roles. Neo-Marxism acts as a dissolver of the existing order. Marxism-Leninism aims to establish a totalitarian regime.[5] Chinese Marxism-Maoism derives from Marxism-Leninism.

## MARXISM CAME TO CHINA

Contemporary China has been deeply influenced by Marx's legacy.[6] Some sinologists do not see Marxism as relevant to China because China was too backwards and undeveloped to support a Marxist socialist revolution.[7] In fact, it was not an accidental event for Marxism to come to China. The introduction of Marxism in China was promoted by two important events: the Russian Revolution of 1917 and the May Fourth Movement of 1919. The former was like a hurricane in the way its effects swept across China and brought Marxism there. The latter was the first intellectual and ideological revolution in response to Western democracy, attacking old political institutions (feudal system) and old Chinese culture (Confucianism), introducing

Western ideas of science and democracy to China, and propagandizing Marxism.

The October Revolution directly sent Marxism to China. Mao Zedong inherited many of the ideological legacies of Lenin and, especially, Stalin. Historically, because China was an agricultural society and had a feudal-despotic tradition, in which blind faith and worship of idols were very popular, it was easy for the Chinese people to accept Stalinism.[8] Culturally, it was the right time for Marxism to come into China as cultural guidance during the early nineteenth century. Due to their defeats in the first and the second Opium Wars, the Chinese people were initially shocked by Western military power and technology, and they began to realize the shortcomings of Chinese culture and political system. The first positive response to Western culture was the Self-Strengthening Movement of the 1860s, which Brian Hook views as the first generation of the new Chinese culture.[9] Self-Strengthening reformers advocated that China should learn science and technology from Western societies. At this stage, the reformers took a very positive attitude toward traditional Chinese culture and confirmed that Chinese culture was the foundation of Chinese society and added aspects of Western culture only for their practical uses.

When China was defeated again in the Sino-Japan War in 1895, the Chinese elites realized that China should model itself after not only Western society's science and technology, but also its political science and institutions. This consciousness directly motivated the process of the political reform movement. The Hundred-Days Reform of 1898 was the climax of the reform movement. The main promoters of the movement believed that constitutional monarchy was the best form of government. Liang Qichao realized that the defeat of the Sino-Japan War implied that intellectual strength was more important than physical strength, but that intellectual strength derived from Confucian principles. Their arguments showed that they were Confucian scholars, and that they were the only bridge between traditional Chinese culture and new Chinese culture.

The Revolution of 1911 was essentially a political revolt which transformed the feudal political institution into a republican government. Before the revolution broke out, the revolutionaries did not have a well-prepared theory. After the revolution, the new government did not make efforts to develop a new culture. In the beginning of the republican era, traditional culture still dominated Chinese society, and Confucius remained the icon of the Sage. A new culture did not come of age until the May Fourth Movement, a milestone of the new Chinese culture. The Chinese road to Marxism has been associated with the May Fourth Movement.[10] Professors Chen Duxiu and Li Dazhao of Beijing University had decided to embark on the Marxist road to a socialist, not a bourgeois-democratic, revolution before May 4, 1919.

The journal *New Youth* was the first intellectual forum for criticizing Confucianism and proclaiming new culture. *New Youth* was founded by Chen Duxiu in 1915, who later became one of the founders of the CPC. *New Youth* trained a new generation of new culturalists and radicalists, including Mao Zedong and Li Dazhao, the other founders of the CPC. *New Youth*, as the flag of the movement, guided the Chinese people to call for a new culture. The first issue of *New Youth* highlighted individual freedom and the second issue introduced American liberalism. Chen argued that Confucianism was a product of the feudal society, and it no longer served the needs of contemporary China because it suppressed individual freedom, upheld a caste system, blocked the development of modern economy, and deprived women of rights. Therefore, new culturalists became rebels against the traditional Chinese dominant culture.[11] This can partly explain why some scholars insist that the new cultural movement directly led to the birth of the CPC.

Chen Duxiu published a journal in 1902, called *Patriotic News*, using a new medium—the vernacular language of the common people—to spread his message, and he signaled a development that is distinctive to the Marxian revolution in China. Through the journal, Chen introduced many revolutionary, political and social ideas. He denounced the emperor as confused, and the ministers as treacherous slaves, arguing that unless the people's knowledge was widened, the nation's power would be restricted and the nations' foundation would not be firmed. He declared that the nation belongs to all the people, not the emperor or the elite. The emperor was but one member of the nation, which is very revolutionary thinking indeed.[12]

The May Fourth Movement of 1919 introduced many ideas from Western cultures, such as liberalism, ideas of progress, socialism, Marxism, Social Darwinism and feminism. The May Fourth Movement used all of these "isms" as weapons to criticize the old culture, create a new cultural framework, reconstruct the Chinese political community, and "rejuvenate the spirit of the Chinese people."[13] The May Fourth Movement smashed the icon and thus "was closely connected with iconoclasm," so it "is a unique historical phenomenon from the perspective of Chinese history as well as of world history."[14] The introduction of Western thought and the May Fourth Movement contributed to the spread of Marxism in China and the birth of the CPC.[15] Influenced by Chen Duxiu and Li Dazhao, in 1921 Mao Zedong attended the first party's conference of twelve delegates. Fourteen years later, Mao consolidated his dominant position in the party at the Zun Yi Conference in 1935 and held the sole right to interpret Marxism. Since then, Maoism has become Marxism in the Chinese context.

# MARXISM AND MAOISM

Marxism in China is represented by Mao Zedong, the first generation of Chinese Marxism. Mao Zedong (1893-1976) was born into a moderate peasant family in a village called Shao Shan in Xiangtan county, Hunan Province. During the 1911 Revolution, Mao served several months in a local regiment in Hunan. However, having felt unaccustomed to a life of military service, he returned to school in Changsha. After graduating from the First Provincial Normal School of Hunan in 1918, Mao traveled with Professor Yang Chang-ji, his high school teacher, and his future father-in-law, to Beijing during the May Fourth Movement in 1919. Professor Yang held a faculty position at Peking University. Because of Yang's recommendation, Mao worked as an assistant librarian at the University with Li Dazhao as the curator of the library. At the same time, Mao registered as a part-time student at Peking University and audited lectures and seminars by some famous intellectuals, such as Chen Duxiu and Hu Shi. Mao was influenced by these revolutionaries during these years and became a communist activist. As one of the twelve delegates, Mao attended the first national conference of the Chinese Communist Party in Shanghai in 1921. According to Chinese officials, "the CPC was born in the process of integrating Marxism-Leninism with the Chinese workers' movement. The birth of the CPC was a natural product of the development of modern and contemporary Chinese history as well as the indomitable exploration of the Chinese people for survival of the nation."[16]

Soon after the conference, Mao went back to his home village of Shao Shan. After Jiang Jieshi's massacre in 1927 killed thousands of Chinese Communist Party members, Mao began rethinking his revolutionary ideas and gradually formed a new idea that "political power grows out of the barrel of a gun."[17] Mao organized the famous Autumn Harvest Uprising in Changsha in 1927 and established the Soviet Republic of China in 1934 in which he was elected Chairman of this small republic among the mountainous areas in Jiangxi Province. Afterwards, Mao began his real political career. Unlike Sun, Mao did not receive formal higher education and never believed in Western education, but read a lot of Chinese classic books. He undoubtedly was deeply influenced by Chinese tradition and knew how to mobilize the Chinese people in the Chinese context. He challenged some classical doctrines of Marxism. For example, he rejected the idea that developed industrial capitalism was a prerequisite for socialist revolution, because China was a poor agricultural country. He denied that the industrial proletariats were the bearers of the socialist future, because 90 percent of Chinese people were peasants. According to the reality of China, Mao made out his own road map of the Chinese communist revolution from the countryside to the city. To reach his revolutionary ambition, he utilized the three tools of power—mass movement, ideological campaign, and violent revolution. Mao held fast to three ultimate tools of power—ideology, the army, and his spider's position at the center of the party's factional web. The three supreme elements of Maoist revolutionary purity became personal selfishness, belief in the masses, and belief in Chairman Mao. As a result, Mao succeeded and the communist troops of China defeated five million nationalist troops in 1949.

After the victory of the communist revolution in 1949, Mao used Marxism as an ideological tool and brought it to an extreme. He called the Chinese people to believe in Marxism but his ultimate goal was to guide them to worship Mao Zedong thought. Thus, Marxism as Chinese official ideology was written in the first draft of the Constitution of China. Accordingly, Mao Zedong became the sole leader of China and Maoism became Chinese Marxism. Mao held absolute power and no other leader in the history of China held as much power over so many people. Consequently, his absolute power affected his mental and physical health and decision making process.[18] During Mao's time, he kept all power in his own hands, including power over the party, executive power, military power, and power over the National People's Congress. The centralized government had reached its highest point in Chinese history, and Mao became the absolute dictator of China. His unlimited power created an illusion that Mao believed that he could do everything that he wanted, and that China could catch up with Britain and the United States in a short period of time. Apparently, his failure became inevitable when he continued to rely on Chinese tradition to govern China. In every respect, Marxism and Maoism failed to reach their goals in ideology, economics, culture, religion, and politics. The history of the Marxist movement in China has proven that Marxism is a utopian ideology, because Marx's ideas were divorced from historical realities in China.[19] Under the Mao regime, China was poor and isolated and enjoyed a self-sufficient and self-reliant economy free from foreign capital and foreign control.

China broke off formal ties with the Soviet Union following the introduction of de-Stalinization in the 1960s and encouraged the entire nation to worship him, proclaiming Maiosim to be the sole universal truth. His "little red book" became the revolutionary bible. However, Mao actually was not a theorist, but a radical revolutionary strategist. Some Western scholars call him a romantic revolutionist. He only succeeded in power struggles by using political strategy and violence. His theory was very simple: "fight against whatever Western countries support; support whatever Western countries fight against." According to Mao, poor socialism was better than rich capitalism. He defended his socialism and attacked capitalist economy and democracy. His sole purposes in interpreting Marxism were to eliminate political dissidents, perfect his God/father image, and strengthen his power. Therefore, Marxism in China, the modern political ideology, "is very much a civil religion."[20] In fact, "Marxism is a civil religion, both in theory and in the actual role that it plays in those countries unfortunate enough to be governed by Communist parties."[21]

Before the reform movement, the image of Mao was sacred in China. Maoism was recognized as the absolute correct interpretation of Marxism in the Chinese context. After Mao died in October 1976, the "Gang of Four," Mao's revolutionary disciples, was crushed, but the mistakes made by Mao Zedong were not criticized. Instead, they were insisted upon under the slogan of the "two whatevers." The so-called "two whatevers" was an abbreviation for the expression: We firmly uphold whatever policy decisions Chairman Mao made, and we unswervingly adhere to whatever instructions chairman Mao gave.[22] In order to smash the "two whatevers," Deng campaigned in a new Marxist movement and reinterpreted Marxism/Maoism by using Marxism which paved a way for the reform movement to develop.[23] The hot debate over how to reinterpret Maoism "is not simply post-neo-Marxist, or non-Marxist, but quite distinctively post-Maoist and post "Marxist."[24] The emergence of Dengism indicates that Chinese Marxism goes from one extreme to the other—economy-centered model of social development.

## MARXISM AND THE CPC

Marxism and the CPC are two sides of the same coin. One cannot understand Marxism without understanding the CPC. Marxism is the official Chinese ideology and the guiding principle of the CPC and the CPC is the sole leadership of Chinese people of all nationalities. It is true that the reform movement begins to depart from classic Marxism and Maoism, but Deng Xiaoping, the general designer of the reform movement, was a pragmatist. His ideology was very clear: keep the party in power, but make the Chinese people rich. Thus, the purpose of this reform movement was to develop the Chinese economy and improve the living standards of Chinese people. Deng said that "the purpose of socialism is to make the country rich and strong."[25] This implied that the socialist system and the party system could not be reformed. In order to justify the legitimacy of the CPC, the new Constitution of the CPC in 2007 set up a new goal of the CPC—to establish a "well-off society" by 2021. Hu Jintao points out that over the past 90 years, the CPC has completed the socialist revolution, established the basic socialist system, and carried out a great new revolution of reform by opening up, creating, upholding, and developing socialism with Chinese characteristics. Therefore, "the CPC truly deserves to be called a great, glorious and correct Marxist political party and the core force leading Chinese people in breaking new ground in development."[26]

As long as the CPC is in power, China will keep Marxism as the state ideology. Marxism is the necessary tool for communist leaders to tightly control China. The CPC has no intention of abandoning Marxism and giving up its sole leadership. At the Meeting to Celebrate the Eightieth Anniversary of the Founding of the CPC on July 1, 2001, Jiang Zemin firmly pointed out that Marxism is the fundamental guiding principle of the consolidation of the CPC and the development of the country. According to Jiang, the CPC is the representative for the requirements of the development of China's advanced productive forces, for orientation of the development of China's advanced culture, and for the fundamental interests of the overwhelming majority of Chinese people. At the meeting commemorating the 90th anniversary of the founding of the Communist Party of China, Hu Jintao made it very clear that based on the 90 years of history of the CPC, it is essential for the Party to preserve and develop its advanced nature as a Marxist political party: The Party should free up the mind, seek truth from facts, advance with the times, take a scientific approach toward Marxism, use Marxism as an evolving theory to guide practice in new realities, uphold truth, correct mistakes, blaze new trails, and maintain the motivation that enables the Party to forge ahead in a pioneering spirit. According to Hu, "To make Party building more scientific under the new historical conditions, we must follow the principle of putting people first and governing for the people, firmly adhere to the Marxist viewpoint on the people, purposefully implement the mass line of the Party, and maintain close ties between the Party and the people."[27] In early 2012, Hu Jintao published an article in *Seeking Truth,* a magazine that evolved from a publication founded by Mao Zedong as a platform for establishing Communist Party principles, in which he clearly pointed out that "China must strengthen its cultural production to defend against the West's assault on the country's culture and ideology, according to an essay in a Communist Party policy magazine published this week."[28]

Although the highest power of the party has been switched from Hu Jingtao to Xi Jinping in the Eighteenth National Congress of the Communist Party of China in 2012, a fundamental ideological change is not to be expected. According to a CCTV report in January 2012, Xi Jinping has ordered universities to step up ideological control of students and young lecturers ahead of the keynote Eighteenth Party Congress. Xi said at a gathering of Communist Party representatives from universities that university party organs must adopt firmer and stronger measures to maintain harmony and stability in universities. Daily management of the institutions should be stepped up to create a good atmosphere for the success of the Party's eighteenth congress.[29] There is no point for the party's existence without Marxism. At present, Marxism is still the state ideology, the CPC is still in power, and state ownership still dominates the Chinese economy. The concept that China has become a capitalist society or that China has entered into a post-socialist society is false.

Many scholars suggest that China is actually departing from the classical communist model. Whoever visits China would personally experience that the actual influence of the CPC is declining, although the size of the party is increasing. The signs of the CPC are disappearing. Before the reform movement, the CPC was a supreme power, controlling the entire Chinese society. The authority of the CPC was not only reflected in its organizations; it was also visible. There were picture billboards and posters on roadsides and in public places. The signboards of CPC branches hung at the front of every work unit. Television and movies were also filled with Party images. The Party was everywhere. Its image was as common in China as McDonald's restaurants and gasoline stations are in the United States. However, at present, there is nothing on the roadside except innumerable commercial advertisements visible throughout a cab ride. In hotels, at least forty TV channels can be accessed, including CNN. Most Chinese TV programs follow Western styles, including soap operas, talk shows, and commercial programings. Even news reports are much less political than before. On both sides of the highway in the east coast areas, the visible signs of the party have been completely replaced by commercial buildings, housing, shopping malls, and commercial signs and advertisements. All party signboards at the front of work units, including businesses, factories, hospitals, schools, universities, department stores, grocery stores, and residential committees, have disappeared. The only exception is that the signboards of the Party committees at the district level or above remain. Every city is filled with commercial smells. As a result, the market economy in China is greatly expanding, regardless of whether it is a socialist market economy or a capitalist market economy. When the market is expanding, the CPC loses its territory. If China continues its rapid pace of marketization, the time will soon come when the CPC's monopolized power will be gone.

A large number of Party members no longer believe in Communism. Before the reform movement, Chinese people thought that the CPC was fulfilling mission, and most Party members had serious commitments to the CPC. However, members no longer have serious faith in the CPC and in communism. So why has Party membership increased, up to 82 million by 2012? First, the quality of the Party members is dramatically declining. Second, a large number of Party branches are actually paralyzed. In urban areas, Party branches at small work units do not function at all. About 65 percent of Chinese people still live in the countryside. After China carried out the household responsibility system in 1978, every rural household made the economy its the top priority. In addition, there is a floating population of about 200 million in China. It is certain that some of them are Party members who are no longer active, although it is difficult to get an accurate percentage. Third, the stratum of Party members has been changed. Based on the *Research Report on Social Rank in China*, published by the Academy of

Social Sciences of China, the Chinese people can be divided into ten basic social ranks: (1) government officials at different levels who are decision makers, making up 1.1 percent; (2) middle-and high-level managers in the middle and large enterprises, making up 1.5 percent; (3) big private owners, making up 0.6 percent; (4) professionals, making up 5.1 percent; (5) general office workers, making up 4.8 percent; (6) small business owners, making up 3.2 percent; (7) commercial services people, making up 14 percent; (8) industrial workers, making up 22.6 percent; (9) peasants, making up 44 percent; and (10) the unemployed, making up 3.1 percent. In the post-industrial era, the most advanced social ranks are professionals, managers, big private owners, and general office workers. The four social ranks altogether make up only 12 percent of the total Chinese population. However, those people, in contrast with other social ranks, are less interested in becoming Party members.

Chinese elites have lost interest in joining the Party. The Party established a very high standard for accepting members before the reform movement. Whoever wanted to join had to go through the following stages: submitting an application, handing in confessional reports, being evaluated and interviewed, having an extensive background investigation, filling out the formal application, being voted into the Party branch, and, finally, becoming a reserved Party member. One qualified to become a formal Party member after the oath ceremony if she or he made no mistakes over the course of one year. Although it was a very complicated and long process, the majority of the Chinese people tried very hard to seek the possibility to join the CPC, because *dang piao* (the title of "party member") is critical for professional advancement. Nevertheless, fewer Chinese people are interested in joining the CPC. The reason is very simple: The reform movement has opened up many ways for the Chinese people to reach their goals. Becoming a Party member is only one of the ways, yet, this way is uncertain in the future. In order to have a stable and good life, most Chinese people believe that three things—intelligence, education, and money—are the most important. The slogan "time is money" has already become popular. The Chinese people look upon Party activities as "extra tax." They like to spend their time not on Party activities, but on receiving education, making money, and having fun. Many Chinese people are capable of making their lives comfortable without *dang piao*; they do not want to be restricted by political and spiritual shackles. Obviously, *dang piao* is no longer attractive to the Chinese people, especially to talented people and the younger generation. Under these circumstances, the CPC must persuade people to become Party members through different means, including reducing the requirements to become a Party member.

Party branching at work units is becoming paralyzed. In work units, there is no regular Party meeting; Party members are not required to write confessional reports; Party offices are absent of visitors; and Party jobs no longer attract the people. The Party in work units exists in name only. Most of the time, Party cadres at the grassroots and district levels stay in their offices and do nothing. The public opinion in China is that full-time Party cadres are not necessary at work units. However, some Party cadres who work at provincial levels are still very confident and work very hard, focusing on ideological work. They believe that the CPC is the sole leadership of China and will survive into the twenty-first century, though they have realized that they have great difficulty in implementing its policy on the grassroots level. As they say in Chinese, *pi zhi bu cun mao jiang yan fu* (With the skin gone, to what can the hair attach itself?). Moreover, the Party's reputation has seriously been hurt by widespread corruption among the Party cadres. Thus, it is a real question whether the CPC can represent the will and the interests of the majority of the Chinese people.

## CONCLUSION

Influenced by the Russian Revolution of 1917, Marxism came to China in the 1920s. Under the special circumstances of China, Marxism gradually won popular support from the Chinese people. Guided by the principles of Marxism, the CPC achieved the victory of the Communist Revolution of 1949. However, the CPC failed to prove that Marxism was a remedy for a new China when it used Marxism as a tool to develop a socialist economy. In the post-Mao era, the CPC has reinterpreted Marxism and Maoism and altered its emphasis from political struggle to economy. As a result, China faces a dilemma: rapid economic development, but political stagnation. How will the CPC reconcile both economic development and political enhancement? Marxism is the product of the Industrial Revolution in the nineteenth century and emphasizes the basic political principle of fulfilling the goal of the communist revolution through the proletariat dictatorship and the one-party system. Marxism does not offer an existing answer for China's future in the twenty-first century. The CPC is still in power, and is not ready to carry out a multi-party system. Nor is it willing to give up the authority over interpreting Marxism. It means that Marxism is a state orthodox and the CPC has monopolized the power of interpreting Marxism. This leaves a very small space for Marxism to rejuvenate its vitality and for the reform minded people to truly practice the slogan—seeking truth from the facts. In this sense, China's future, in some respects, is up to how they view and use Marxism. Because of the incompatibility of Marxism with the mainstream of Western culture, if the CPC continues to maintain Marxism as the state orthodox, it may help the CPC retain its power for a short period of time, but it would damage the CPC's governance in a global context in the long term.

# NOTES

1. Peter Singer, *Marx: A Very Short Introduction* (New York: Oxford University Press, 2000), 94.

2. Roger Gottlieb, *Marxism, 1844-1990: Origins, Betrayal, Rebirth.* (New York: Routledge, 1992), 8.

3. Quoted in Singer, *Marx*, 79.

4. See David McLellan, *Marxism after Marx: An Introduction* (New York: Harper & Row, 1980).

5. Milorad M. Drachkovitch, ed., *Marxist Ideology in the Contemporary World: Its Appeals and Paradoxes* (New York: Pall Mall Press, 1966), xiv.

6. Peter Singer, *Marx*, 2.

7. Adrian Chan, *Chinese Marxism* (New York: Continuum, 2003), 10.

8. Shaozhi Su, *Marxism and Reform in China* (Spokesman Books, 1993), 33.

9. Brian Hook, "The Modernization of China: 19th and 20th Century Comparisons and Contrasts," in *Changes in China: Party, State, and Society*, ed. Shao-chuan Leng (New York: University Press of America, 1989), 6.

10. Adrian Chan, *Chinese Marxism* (New York: Continuum, 2003), 29.

11. Wang Zheng, *Women in the Enlightenment* (Berkeley, Calif.: University of California Press, 1999), 10.

12. Chan, *Chinese Marxism*, 25.

13. Yu-Sheng Lin, "Radical Iconoclasm in the May Fourth Period and the Future of Chinese Liberalism," in *Reflections on the May Fourth Movement: A Symposium*, ed. Benjiamin I. Schwartz (Cambridge, Mass.: Harvard University Press, 1972), 23.

14. Lin, "Radical Iconoclasm in the May Fourth Period and the Future of Chinese Liberalism," 26.

15. Yi Danping, "Si fang si xiang de chuan ru yu zhong guo nü xing zhu yi de jue qi," *Wuhan Da Xue Xue Bao* 4 (2004), 482.

16. Hu Jintao, " Speech at a Meeting Commemorating The 90th Anniversary Of The Founding Of The Communist Party Of China," 1 July 2011.

17. Mao Zedong, *Selected Works,* Vol. II, 224.

18. Andrew I. Nathan, "Forward," in Li Zhisui, The Private Life of Chairman Mao (Random House: New York, 1994), x.

19. Maurice J. Meisner, *Marxism, Maoism, and Utopianism: Eight Essays* (Madison: University of Wisconsin Press, 1982), 7- 10.

20. Richard J. Bishirjian, *A Public Philosophy Reader* (New Rochelle, N.Y.: Arlington House, 1978), 25.

21. Ibid., 26.

22. Shaozhi Su, *Marxism and Reform in China* (Spokesman Books, 1993), 42.

23. Gordon White, *Riding the Tiger: The Politics of Economic Reform in Post-Mao China* (Stanford, Calif.: Stanford University Press, 1993), 158.

24. Kalpana Misra, *From Post-Maoism to Post-Marxism: The Erosion of Official Ideology in Deng's China* (Taylor & Francis, 1998): 15.

25. Gregor, *Marxism, China, and Development*, 238.

26. Hu Jintao, " Speech at a Meeting Commemorating The 90th Anniversary Of The Founding Of The Communist Party Of China," 1 July 2011.

27. Ibid.

28. Edward Wong, "China's President Lashes Out at Western Culture," *New York Times,* 3 January 2012.

29. Stephen Chen, "Thought Control Called for at Universities," *South China Morning Post*, 5 January 2012.

## Chapter Fourteen

# Media in China: The Internet and Chinese Cinema

Media is a platform for people to spread different cultures, including ideology. In contemporary societies, media has played critical roles in developing economy, influencing politics, and shaping belief systems and cultural identity. Regarding the relationship between the media and democracy, while some scholars do not suggest that media produces democratic political cultures in the transition of Eastern European countries,[1] most scholars and commentators agree that the media has contributed to the emancipation of oppressed peoples by playing a watchdog role to check on government's power, increasing the credibility of the government and weakening the centralization of the major political parties; it serves as a transmission belt between society and its government, acting as a participant in the policymaking process.[2] Although there are various types of media, the Internet and film are the two most popular forms of media. This chapter will examine the development of media by focusing on the Internet and Chinese film, explore the roles of media in China's modernization and democratization, and provide three case studies on selected Chinese films in order to help the Western audience further understand Chinese culture, politics and society in the post-Mao era.

### THE ROLE OF INTERNET TECHNOLOGY

The term "media" refers to the aggregate of the public mass distributors of news and entertainment and other information, including three forms of media: print media, such as newspapers, journals, and books; electronic media, such as radio broadcasting and television; and recently information technologies, such as the Internet, podcasting, and blogging. The media is not only a mirror reflecting society, but also actively reshapes people's way of life and the structure of society.[3] According to Fred S. Siebert, media can play six roles in society.[4] The media can serve the transition from a non-democratic society to democratic one.[5] The emergence of the Internet has further contributed the process of democratization. Western scholars and politicians predicted that the arrival of the Internet would ultimately topple the one-party system and inevitably and swiftly set China free.[6]

The invention of the Internet is a major component of the information revolution. Only about 2,000 Chinese had access to the Internet in early 1994, but the Internet industry began booming after China's Internet entered into the commercial sector that year. By 2005, 100 million Chinese people regularly connected to the Internet.[7] According to the China Internet Network Information Center, the number of Chinese Internet users already reached 134 million at the end of June in 2006,[8] 298 million in 2008, 300 million in 2009,[9] and 538 million by June 2012.[10] China has become the world's biggest Internet market.[11] China also has the largest number of cell phone subscriptions in the world and is the world's second-largest PC market.[12]

By adopting a multi-interactionist perspective, Guobin Yang found that Chinese netizens have been increasingly gaining power in developing a diverse culture, civil society, trans-nationalism, finance and business, and democracy through Internet activities.[13] The Internet has played an increasingly important role in Chinese public affairs. For example, in 2008, after a young Chinese man was sentenced to life imprisonment for stealing money from a bank by taking advantage of a malfunctioning ATM machine, Chinese netizens posted massive comments asserting that the verdict was ridiculously too heavy. A court in Guangzhou, provincial capital of Guangdong, dramatically reduced the previous verdict of life imprisonment to a five-year jail term. Obviously, this change of verdict in such a case was made under pressure of public opinion.[14] After Zhao Lianhai's three-year-old son was poisoned by contaminated milk, he was scared and needed advice, so he created a website for parents of children hurt or killed by contaminated milk. Unexpectedly, more than 4,000 families signed up in several days and soon the discussion evolved into many topics. In trying to cover up the contaminated milk scandal, the government quickly shut down the website and cracked down on his group, but more groups fought back. As a result, the government had no choice but to acknowledge the scandal.[15]

The Internet is a kind of catalyst for freedom, justice and democracy. In a traditional civil society, a participant is called citizen. In the eighteenth century, Europeans met each other in coffee shops and the English pubs to chat about social events and produce public opinion. In the information society, a participant is called a netizen. Coffee shops and pubs along with today's Internet are part of civil society.[16] The recent technology of the Internet has expanded the role of the media in people's social, cultural, and political life. The Internet, along with mobile phones, has contributed to the development of a better economy, education and healthcare,[17] direct relations to freedom of assembly, freedom of expression, and alternative sources of information, cultivation of civil society, and enhancement of government accountability through online discussions and the spread of information.[18]

The Internet has provided Chinese citizens with an unprecedented capacity to express their voices, expose corrupt Chinese officials and call for social justice, despite heavy government censorship.[19] Under these circumstances the Chinese people are disinclined to take their grievances to the streets but prefer to roar dissent online expressing their voices. In the Internet age, most opposition and subversive ideas can be found in Chinese cyberspace, which forms "a sharp contrast to the official newspapers and television channels."[20] Therefore, "online activism is emblematic of a long revolution unfolding in China today, a revolution intertwining cultural, social and political transformations."[21]

The Internet is now the main propaganda channel for the CCP, but it is also used by common citizens to engage in political activities. The 538 million Chinese netizens obviously are China's new rebels. About eighty-four high level Chinese officials have stepped down from their posts after their misconduct was published online.[22] The majority of netizens believe the Internet is "a forum to express their political opinions and as a source for political information."[23] The Internet allows anonymous communication without distance limitation. Citizens can post critical messages with less fear, organize gatherings and protests in response to social events, and offer the perfect tool for increasingly sophisticated political discourse. When a breaking news story emerges, thousands of follow-up posts spring up within minutes in cyberspace.[24] In addition, "the Internet has played a role in bringing international attention to China."[25] Although China has between 30,000 and 50,000 Internet monitors, Chinese Internet users always find it still possible to discover ways to get news past the censors. Sometimes, Chinese netizens use humor and political satire in the blogosphere to promote freedom of speech. Some netizens are willing to risk a jail sentence in order to obtain information blocked by the Chinese government. Internet technology has made it more difficult for the government to unify traditional ideological propaganda. The Deputy Director of the State Council Information Agency, Wang Guoqing, publicly acknowledged that it is a dead-end road for the Chinese government to block government information. As time goes by, the Internet will eventually become a popular medium serving as a democratization tool in China and the CPC will ultimately lose its battle of controlling the Internet, because CPC's harsh control over it can only slow down the process of democracy but cannot stop it.

The role of the Internet in the process of China's democratization cannot be overestimated. This role is largely determined by two preconditions: politically-minded users and free access environment. The Internet will only produce little political consequence without these two preconditions. In China, first of all, "the majority of Internet users in China use the Internet for entertainment purposes."[26] Although some people use the Internet for organizing, criticizing, and protesting, the majority of the netizens use it for socializing, debating, gathering information about educational service, health, entertainment, making friends, playing games, shopping, posting humorous and clever messages, and having fun. According to a survey conducted by the Chinese Academy of Social Sciences, 71.8 percent of netizens use the Internet for checking email, 57.3 percent for reading news, 52.3 percent for hobbies, 50.6 percent for chatting, 45.2 percent for listening to music, 32.6 percent for playing games, 31.4 percent for searching the information of knowledge, 29.8 percent for searching the information of entertainment, 19.1 percent for subscribing to electronic journals, 12 percent for studying, trading in the stock market, searching for jobs, shopping, and advertisement, and about 8 percent for office work. Jeffrey Wasserstrom and Kate Merkel-Hess argue that a lot of what happens on the Chinese Internet is not political because most Chinese Internet cafes are packed with students playing online video games, chatting, and trading stock.[27]

Second, due to the fact that it is necessary to have certain knowledge of literacy and computer skills, the Chinese middle class makes up the most important group of the netizens. About 91 percent of all netizens are between 18 and 30 years old, although some are under age 18. High school students are the fastest-growing segment of new users.[28] The vast majority of Internet users are young male urban citizens with more than average education. More than 75 percent of them have a senior high school degree or higher and are from the new urban middle class families. Their parents have more than the average income and have benefited from the economic reform in the post Mao era.[29] Obviously, the majority of Internet users are not highly politicized and critical. Surfing the Internet is part of their consumption and lifestyle.[30]

Third, unlike the democratic societies, the Internet is not developed within an independent academic sphere in China but by government agencies.[31] The hardware and infrastructure remain very centralized. This makes it easy for the government to implement its censorship policy from the national level to the bottom of society. The Chinese government spent a tremendous amount of money to create a new system to control political activities on the Internet. According to Xiao Qiang, "About 10 percent of all sites in Chinese cyberspace are directly set up and run by the government. Over 150 main news sites are established by the central and local government directly."[32] Although many netizens are still very interested in using the Internet for political purposes, the political consequences are minimal.[33] Thus, there is little reason to believe that the Internet could trigger significant social and political changes within the communist regime.[34]

## DEVELOPMENT OF CHINESE CINEMA

Chinese cinema was born in 1905. Over the last one hundred years, especially during the post-Mao era, Chinese cinema has developed rapidly and China's film industry now is the third largest in the world in terms of the number of films produced and box office earnings.[35] According to the State Administration of Radio, Film and Television, China's box office receipts exceeded $1.6 billion in 2010.

In contemporary society, film is an effective vehicle for developing culture, enhancing education and elevating the quality of people.[36] The term "Chinese cinema" refers to the film which is produced by Chinese filmmakers or foreign filmmakers depicting the Chinese people and society. From a geographic perspective, Chinese cinema includes Mainland Chinese cinema, Taiwanese cinema, and Hong Kong cinema. Therefore, Chinese cinema as a general term is often applied to films made in mainland China, Hong Kong, and Taiwan. Some scholars use *"liang'an sandi,"* literally, two sides of the Taiwan strait and three regions.[37] The three cinematic traditions have developed in different directions but all of them represent Chinese cinema.

The most ancient inventions originated in China, but cinema as a new technology and form of art originated in the West.[38] The United States is the birthplace of this modern technology. Eadweard Muybridge (1830-1904) was an early photographer and inventor and he photographed the first successful serial images of fast motion in 1878 in Palo Alto, California. His work laid the groundwork for the development of motion pictures. The world's first film studio was built on the grounds of Edison's laboratories in West Orange, New Jersey, in 1893. Edison's Kinetoscope began commercial operation in April of 1894. The first movie theater opened at 1155 Broadway in New York City and exhibited movies commercially.

Chinese filmmakers had no indigenous traditions to follow when making films. There was not even an equivalent term for "film" available in the Chinese language before film was introduced into China, so several different expressions, such as "electrical shadow play" or "electric shadow," were deployed to refer to the modern technology "cinema." Chinese cinema did not emerge in China until 1905, during the eve of the Republic Revolution of 1911. Scholars in Chinese cinema studies generally agree that the first Chinese film, *Dinqjun Mountain* (in Chinese *Dingjun Shan*), was made by Ren Jingfeng at his photography shop in Beijing in 1905. In the film, a staged Beijing opera is performed by the well-known actor Tan Xinpei in front of a stationary camera. After successfully screening the film at Dagualou Theater, the film's producer, Ren Qingtai, and his photographer, Liu Zhonglun, continued to make "shadow opera" pieces.[39]

China was experiencing a transformation from a feudal society to a modern nation-state in the early twentieth century. Chinese cinema became part of Chinese culture from its inception, and served as the representative of the nation-state and new culture movement. As a result, the central themes of early Chinese cinema are modernity, nation-building, anti-nationalism, anti-imperialism, anti-feudalism, and new gender identities. Chinese filmmakers' efforts remained sporadic and of little significance until the mid-1920s when China enjoyed a brief prosperous period, in which it began developing its national industries such as railroads, machinery, textiles, and communication.[40] Under the Jiang Jieshi regime, Chinese filmmakers began to develop their own indigenous cinema in Shanghai and other large cities. Three film companies, Mingxing, Lianhua, and Yihua, represented the "Left Tendency" work of studios.[41] This period is called the golden age of Chinese cinema, especially during the period of 1933-1949. However, the rapid growth of an indigenous film industry in the mid-1920s did not fundamentally alter the foreign domination of China's film market.[42] Hollywood presence in Shanghai remained a significant factor in the Chinese film market from the 1920s to the 1940s.

Under the Mao regime, Chinese cinema was deeply influenced by Marxism and the CPC, and became the most popular form of cultural entity with the potential to reach the most people. Through the lens of Chinese film, the party leaders could reach the widest possible audiences with a message presented on film, and could do so without any intermediary between producers and viewers. Because film educates people through its images, Chinese people could easily understand the meaning of the film, even if they were illiterate. Thus, the Chinese government has strictly controlled the movie industry since the establishment of communist China.

By 1950, the Chinese government had not only established firm control over the film industry nationwide, it also owned and operated three major film studios, producing 80 percent of the country's total output. The government published *Temporary Regulations Regarding the Importation of Foreign Films* in July of 1950, and began to purge Western films, especially Hollywood productions. By October 1950, American films totally disappeared from China. To propagandize socialist ideas, however, the government never stopped importing foreign films from socialist countries, such as North Korea, Romania, Albania, and Vietnam. Meanwhile, the CPC sought to build an indigenous "revolutionary cinema" to promote revolutions and class struggle.

During the ten years of the Cultural Revolution from 1966 to1976, China witnessed its most radical and bloody political turmoil, as Chinese film production came almost to a standstill. Revolutionary film-making became extreme, and every film produced during the Cultural Revolution was propaganda for the radical revolution. Chinese film moved away from the international cinema, and the distance between Chinese film and the rest of the world's production was widened during that period.

New Chinese cinema in the 1980s was primarily a national cinema, and the predominant theme was a critique of the Cultural Revolution and traditional Chinese culture. A group of young filmmakers, the fifth generation of Chinese filmmakers, emerged in China and produced a great amount of Chinese films. The fifth generation of Chinese filmmakers includes Zhang Yimou, Chen Kaige, Tian Zhuangzhuang, Wu Ziniu, Zhou Xiaowen, Zhang Junzhao, Huang Jianxin, and Hu Mei. To respond to the needs of the new era and to meet the demands of the new audience, Chinese filmmakers also began to work with producers outside of the Mainland. Many of the fifth generation filmmakers started to target their films towards international audiences. For example, Chen Kaige's *Farewell My Concubine* and Zhang Yimou's *To Live* received warm welcomes from international film festivals. Chinese cinema during this period of time can be characterized by transnational films that target both domestic audiences and international film festivals. In 1988, Zhang Yimou's first film, *Red Sorghum*, received the Golden Bear Award at the Berlin international film festival. It was the first Chinese film to receive a major award from a Western film festival.

The Chinese government began implementing a market economy in the 1980s and further expanded it in the early 1990s. Accordingly, Chinese society was characterized by the expansion of consumerism, the spread of popular culture, and the commercialization of cultural production. With the development of marketization, Chinese film makers face new challenges: there was little domestic audience for serious films; and Chinese art film suffered from the rapid commercialization of popular culture. The profitability of films at the box-office was not a major issue between 1949 and the 1980s because the government took care of the loss due to state ownership, but the Chinese film industry could not survive under the market system if they could not make profits. Chinese filmmakers began to explore a new way to solve problems—producing commercial film. The sixth generation is the commercial filmmaker. Chinese cinema started a new chapter in the 1990s, the era of commercial film. Since then, commercial film has become the mainstream of the Chinese film industry. Although China is the third largest filmmaker, Chinese films have not made a significant impact on the world, partly because of government censorship and the gap between Chinese culture and Western culture.[43]

## THREE FILM STUDIES

### 1. From the First Emperor to the Last Emperor

Since Ying Zheng (the first emperor) unified China in 221 B.C., the country has spent more than 2,000 years going through three different periods—the feudal society, the Republican era, and the communist regime. *The Emperor's Shadow*, directed by Zhou Xiao-wen in 1999, and *The Last Emperor*, directed by Bernardo Bertolucci in 1987, allow audiences to get a sense of the political legacy of historical China.

The film *The Emperor's Shadow* is worth watching not only because the film boasts two of China's most famous actors, Jiang Wen (*Red Sorghum*) and Ge You (*To Live*, and *Farewell My Concubine*), but also because it comes with meaningful social and political implications. The film illustrates the life of the emperor Ying Zheng beginning with his childhood days. Ying Zheng and his friend Gao Jianli are raised by the same mother as foster brothers, but they have completely different lives. The former finally becomes an absolute tyrant through numerous battles, killing thousands of innocent people. The latter is forced to become Ying Zheng's court composer. The emperor wants him to write an anthem to play throughout the entire country in order for the emperor not only to unify the entire country, but also to control the heart and soul of all the Chinese people. One of the interesting political implications of the film is that the emperor can enforce his will upon anyone. Whatever the emperor says must be accounted; whoever disobeys his personal will is subject to severe punishment. Nobody is an exception. His daughter Yueyang, for instance, has fallen in love with Gao, but she is not allowed to marry him. After Ying Zheng seizes power, he uses the power to kill his political rivals and common peoples without checking. Because of his ruthless and autocratic rule, the Qin dynasty is overthrown by the peasant uprising fifteen years after Ying Zheng established the first highly centralized government, but Qin's political system continues to develop in the following centuries and reached its highest point in the Qing dynasty (1616-1911).

*The Last Emperor*, the 1987 Oscar-winner, is an irresistible movie. It takes audiences to the Forbidden City—a realm of fantastic historical sites and rituals—and depicts the last emperor of Chinese feudal society Pu Yi's (1905-1967) life for six decades, from the Qing dynasty to the nationalist government (1912-1949) and the Mao regime (1949-1976), reflecting the continuation of Chinese history. When Pu Yi was three years old in 1908, he ascended the throne. Three years later, the Revolution of 1911, led by Sun Yat-sen, broke out in Wuchang in 1911, and the last emperor of China was overthrown, although he was allowed to stay with his wives in the Forbidden City until 1925. After Japanese troops invaded China, Pu Yi shortly restored his rule in Manchuria, as a puppet of the Japanese government. Pu Yi was arrested by the Russian Red Amy after World War II and transferred over to the new communist government of China in 1950. After Pu Yi was released in 1959 from jail, he became a common Chinese citizen. When he came back to visit the Forbidden City—the symbol of emperor's power in feudal China—he was filled with a thousand mixed feelings related to the experience of an emperor and the experience of a common citizen. Pu Yi's transformation from dragon emperor to common citizen is a simple story, but fascinating and thoughtful.

In both films the audience is exposed to forms of unlawful acts and corruption derived from the feudal political system. Both of the films indicate that dictatorship and corruption have been common themes in imperial China for more than 2,000 years. The revolution of 1911 swept the last emperor away a century ago, and the communist party has ruled China for more than 60 years since 1949. However, the emperor's shadows are evidently still present in contemporary China. Like tragedies in all other feudal dynasties, thousands of innocent Chinese people were persecuted, jailed, and killed during the Cultural Revolution of 1976 and in the Tiananmen Square Incident of 1989. Although the CPC has tried to develop a harmonious society at home and a peaceful presence abroad, it continues to try to rule both the land of China and the soul of the Chinese people by using coercive force and censorship. Will the CPC's efforts be successful? Although it is not so easy to answer the questions, the CPC should learn a lesson from Chinese history, and accordingly, reform its political system, in order to survive in the twenty-first cenutry.

## 2. The Clash of Traditional Chinese Culture

Confucian filial piety was a basic social norm that consolidated family ties in pre-communist China. What principles have the Chinese people followed to deal with family relations in the post-Mao era? *The Day the Sun Turned Cold* (*tian guo ni zi*), produced and directed by Yim Ho in 1994, provides an excellent case study that explores this question by demonstrating a complex murder story based on a real-life Chinese criminal case. This film won Best Film and Best Director awards at the 1994 Tokyo Film Festival.

The story is set in rural China in the early 1990s. At the beginning of the film, Guan Jian suggests that the local police captain reopen a case against his mother, Pu Fengying, for the murder of his father, Guan Shichang. He believes he has new evidence that challenges the declaration of innocence in her trial ten years before. The police captain listens to Jian's story, which takes the audience back to the early 1980s where Fengying is in an unhappy marriage with Shichang, but cannot divorce him because of her parents. One day, Fengying, along with her son, falls into an icy river. A young woodsman, Liu Dagui, passing by, saves them from drowning. This incident eventually evolves into a secret love affair between Fengying and Dagui. Shichang becomes suspicious when he hears talk in the village. He comes home and beats Fengying with a thick stick and insists they go to see Dagui immediately. To avoid public disgrace, Fengying cooks dinner, puts rat poison in it, and serves her husband. After eating the dinner, Shichang becomes mysteriously ill and dies. Ten years later, the adult Jian, upon reading a French story of a woman who poisoned her husband with arsenic, realizes that his mother did murder his father. As he had done before Fengying's first trial, once again Jian turns his mother in to the police for murder. However, when a test for arsenic is negative, Jian is not satisfied with the test results and continues his investigation. Bone testing indicates Schichang died from rat poison. As a consequence, Fengying and Dagui are tried and executed.

The title of the movie in Chinese, *Tian Guo Ni Zi* (Unfilial Son in Heaven), denotes exactly the meaning of Jian's legal action. From the Confucian view, the roof of the empire is the State, but the root of the State is the family. Thus, the purpose of Confucian teaching is to strengthen family relationships. High respect for paternal authority was the distinguishing characteristic of Chinese tradition. In traditional China, both mothers and fathers were legally regarded as parents and had to be respected. Based on ancient Chinese legal codes, whoever wanted to bring their parents to justice would be punished first. On the surface, Jian betrays his mother and violates the principle of Confucian filial piety.

However, based on Jian's family relationships, it is difficult to find a satisfactory answer as to why Jian turned against his mother. His father never really showed love—he beat his son and yelled at him, abusing him both physically and verbally. By contrast, his mother was very caring. She cooked for the family, sent the children to school, served her husband, and sold bean curd to supplement the family income. She was the one who brought Jian comfort. Then why did Jian turn his mother in, not once, but twice? The only explanation is that Jian's cultural tradition and political beliefs had not changed. Although Confucianism emphasizes family relations, the core of Confucianism is to justify the rule of the father. In this sense, he is not only a filial son on the earth, being loyal to his father and the government, but he is also a *Tian Guo Ni Zi* (unfilial son in Heaven).

According to Confucianism, the father is the center of the family and family members must obey him. Society can be viewed as an enlarged family; the state is the center of society and is ruled by an emperor. Thus, Confucian filial piety demands unreserved obedience from children to their father in the family and the state/emperor in society. To legitimize the communist state, Mao Zedong manipulated the principle of filial piety and required Chinese people to be loyal only to the state. During the Cultural Revolution, it became a popular phenomenon that family members fought against each other and children turned against their parents to demonstrate their sincere loyalty to the great leader Mao. Many Chinese movies directed by the fifth generation of Chinese filmmakers, such as *To Live*, *The Blue Kite*, and *Farewell My Concubine*, reveal such tragedies.

Emotionally, Jian loved his mother. Before turning her in, Jian asked her to tell him the truth and even begged her to tell him that she did not do it. However, when the conflict between loving his mother and loyalty to his father occurs, ultimately he chose to be loyal to his murdered father, the symbol of the government. In this sense, Jian was truly a filial son. This interpretation obviously contradicted the Chinese title of the film. Yet, as a human being, Guan Jian found himself feeling as if he betrayed his mother, and after the sentencing, he visited his mother in prison showing his emotional crisis. His mother understood why he turned her in and willingly goes off to her execution, telling Jian she feels no anger toward him. His mother's eternal love made Jian feel even worse, and he deeply regretted what he did. By this time, there was no way the verdict could be changed, so he forced himself to accept his actions. While desperately waiting during the few days until her execution, because of his mixed feelings and internal conflicts, Jian discarded a knit sweater which was made by his mother in jail. This was likely the reason the director translated the Chinese title *tian guo ni zi* into *The Day the Sun Turned Cold*, because metaphorically the English title better fit the description of Jian as a human being and helped the Western audience to better understand his actions.

As a rational citizen, Jian fulfilled the goal of his legal action. But he will live the rest of his life with emotional suffering that is more punishing than an execution: his memories cannot be discarded the way he threw away the sweater. The film portrays the internal conflict between Jian seeking justice for his father and eternally loving his mother. The implication of this internal conflict is relevant to China's modernization and democratization, as it mirrors the inner conflict between traditional Chinese culture and China's modernization. Neither Confucian filial piety nor the principle of rule of law can remedy the conflict between Chinese tradition and modern life. Indeed, China needs to incorporate traditional Chinese culture into the modern culture instead of simply burying or manipulating it. *The Day the Sun Turned Cold* inspires students to comprehend some critical questions, such as: How do we wisely absorb good elements from traditional Chinese culture? What is the essential connection between historical China and the current Chinese political system? What is the most important task for the Chinese people to modernize and democratize China?

## 3. Chinese Prostitution through the Centuries

The four films, *Flowers of Shanghai* (directed by Hou Hsiao-Hsien, 2001), *Farewell My Concubine* (directed by Chen Kaige, 1993), *Hua Hun* (directed by Huang Shuqin, 1994), and *Blush* (directed by Li Shaohong, 1994) are not typical women's films from a feminist perspective. They not only depict Chinese people's lives from different perspectives, but also explore sensitive women's topics in China, that is, Chinese prostitution from the flourishing period in the second half of the nineteenth century to the communist era. A bunch of flowers—a group of prostitutes—in *Flowers of Shanghai*, Juxian in *Farewell My Concubine*, Pan Yulian in *Hua Hun*, and Qiuyi and Xiao'e in *Blush* represent the destiny of prostitutes in imperial China, in the Republican era, and in communist China.

Prostitution existed in China as early as in the Shang dynasty (17th–11th century B.C.).[44] After the First Opium War, China was forced to sign the unequal Nanking Treaty, which ceded the Chinese island of Hong Kong to Britain and opened five ports—Guangzhou, Xiamen, Fuzhou, Ningbo, and Shanghai—to foreign trade and residence. All these cities were called treaty ports, which contained large areas called concessions that were leased to foreign powers. After China signed the Nanking Treaty, Western powers, including Russia, Japan, and the United States, soon demanded similar treaties with China. After 14 treaty ports were opened to Western countries in the 1860s, Western people and culture flowed into China. All these cities attracted prostitutes from surrounding provinces. The Chinese sex market reached its peak in the second half of the nineteenth century.[45] According to the health officer of the International Settlement, in 1869 there were 463 brothels with 1,612 prostitutes in Shanghai.[46]

*Flowers of Shanghai* vividly depicts the lavish and luxurious lives of Chinese prostitutes in Shanghai brothels in the late nineteenth century. At the end of the century in Shanghai each of the foreign concessions had a number of luxurious "flower houses," reserved for the male elite of the city. Since Chinese dignitaries were not allowed to frequent common brothels, these fine establishments were the only ones that they could visit. They formed a self-contained world with their own rites, traditions, and even their own language. The women working in these fine establishments were known as the "flowers of Shanghai." The men visited the houses not only for sex, but also for dining, smoking opium, playing mahjong, and relaxing. These flower girls wore elegant clothing, ate the best food, and served rich men with different motivations. Sometimes the girls tried to get the men to pay their debts or buy them gifts. The story of *Flowers of Shanghai* involves a power struggle between "flower girls" for the favors of the richest customers, but *Flowers of Shanghai* only reflects the lives of high ranking prostitutes in the nineteenth century. In patriarchal Chinese society, prostitution was a hierarchal system within different ranks, such as *shuyu* prostitutes (courtesans in a private residence), *yao* prostitutes (prostitutes in a public brothel), *yeji* prostitutes (escorts), and prostitutes in smoke rooms.[47]

Although *Farewell My Concubine* does not highlight the theme of prostitution itself, it indirectly reflects that the Chinese national capitalist industry and market economy stimulates the business of prostitution. This film about the real lives of actors in the Peking Opera depicts the triangular relationship between Xiaolou, Dieyi and the prostitute Juxian. In the film, Xiaolou has an affair with a lowly prostitute, Juxian. As a result, Xiaolou marries her. Afterward, as a good wife, Juxian manages her family affairs well, contributes much to Xiaolou's Beijing Opera business, and as a good sister-in-law, balances the relationship between Xiaolou and Dieyi. Before the Cultural Revolution, Juxian and Xiaolou have a harmonious relationship and a peaceful life. This powerfully convinces the audience that a prostitute can redeem herself. However, Chinese prostitutes had terrible experiences in the Mao era, especially during the Cultural Revolution from 1966 to 1976. Agitated by Mao Zedong's revolutionary ideas and enforced by the Red Guard, both Xiaolou and Dieyi publicly reveal Juxian's background as a prostitute. When Juxian sees her husband, Xiaolou, turn against her, she sinks into the depths of despair and hopelessness and commits suicide. Wendy Larson notes that "she kills herself because [she is] under terrible but historically limited pressure."[48] This story indicates that the Maoist model of the socialist system essentially had no room for Chinese prostitution and tried to eliminate it by using coercive force, but failed.

If the primary objective of *Farewell My Concubine* is not to explore the inevitable fate of Chinese prostitutes, the film *Hua Hun* (*A Soul Haunted by Painting*) enables the audience to see the confrontation between a prostitute's redemption in traditional Chinese culture and the inevitable fate of prostitutes in the historical context of both the Republican era and communist China. Pan Yulian is born in a poor family and becomes an orphan at the age of eight. After her uncle raises her for six years, she is sold to a brothel. Three years later, Pan meets Pan Zanhua, a revolutionary and a kind-hearted man, who sympathizes with her and finally marries her. After marriage, Pan Yulian begins to learn how to paint and goes to the Shanghai Art Academy to study painting. With the help of her husband, Pan Yulian goes to France and becomes the first Chinese student at the National Leon Art School. She also studies at the National Paris Art School where she becomes a classmate of Xu Beihong (1895-1953), the most famous painter in modern China. Through her serious efforts, Pan's works win gold prizes at the Rome International Art Exhibition and the Italy International Fine Arts Exhibition. She is the first Chinese artist who wins international awards in such important art events.

In 1928, Pan Yulian returns to China and becomes a professor at the Shanghai Art School. Soon after, she is invited to be a professor at the art department of the Central University in Nanjing, then director of the department. Although Pan Yulian becomes one of the greatest Chinese artists of the twentieth century and wins a world reputation with her great works and outstanding artistic talent, her colleagues and Chinese popular opinion never recognize her as an artist during her life time because of her past. Under these intolerable prejudices, Pan leaves China for Paris again in 1937. After the Communist Party of China comes to power in 1949, Pan plans to return home, but eventually fails to do so, because she is afraid of persecution by the government's political campaigns. In 1977, she dies in regret and poverty in her small apartment in Paris at the age of 82. Pan Yulian's story once again demonstrates that a Chinese prostitute would always be miserable, once she was a prostitute, regardless of her achievements.

Prostitutes culturally and socially had hard lives in pre-communist China, but Chinese society as a whole had room for prostitutes to survive. Marxist orthodoxy, however, is completely incompatible with prostitution and views prostitution as a disease of the old society and culture of capitalism. As soon as the CPC came to power in 1949, the new government carried out an uncompromising policy and cracked down on every single brothel. The film *Blush* reflects the Chinese government's efforts to rehabilitate Chinese prostitutes at the beginning period of the People's Republic of China. It tells a story about the different destinies of two former Chinese prostitutes, Qiuyi and Xiao'e, through different processes of re-education: self-redemption and communist labor education. *Blush* begins in 1949 with prostitutes from the Red Happiness Inn being rounded up and relocated to a re-education center. Qiuyi escapes across the rooftop, fleeing to the house of her favorite former client, Lao Pu, who invites her to live with him. When Lao Pu's mother discovers Qiuyi's background, she tries to get Qiuyi to leave. Under Lao Pu's mother's pressure, Qiuyi leaves his home and takes refuge in a Buddhist nunnery, but is expelled from the Buddhist temple when she becomes pregnant. Finally, however, Qiuyi restarts her life by marrying a small tea house owner. Through her self-cultivation based on her common daily life, Qiuyi becomes a good citizen and lives with her family peacefully. By contrast, Xiao'e is brought to the re-education center on that night, and goes through rehabilitation in a silk factory. After she is released from the rehabilitation center, she marries Lao Pu. As time goes by, the marriage between Lao and Xiao'e degenerates into a series of ugly arguments, because Lao Pu is unable to provide her with a luxurious lifestyle. In order to please Xiao'e, Lao Pu embezzles a large sum of money for her to spend. Subsequently, he is caught and executed. Under these circumstances, Xiao'e gives her son to Qiuyi and runs to another man. The two different stories show that the new Chinese government tried to reeducate Chinese prostitutes through physical labor, but the result went in the opposite direction—the education through physical labor in the labor camp did not help in changing the minds of Chinese prostitutes.

Although there is no single Chinese film that directly portrays the situation of Chinese prostitutes in the post-Mao era, prostitutes are visible in present-day China. According to statistics, there are about 10 million sex workers in China.[49] The four films inspire audiences to think about some serious questions: What are the similarities and differences between the flourishing period of Chinese prostitution in the second half of the nineteenth century and the revival period of prostitution in the post-Mao era? What lessons should we learn from the Chinese government's efforts to eradicate prostitutes in the Mao era? Why has prostitution come back in the post-Mao era? Does the market economy inevitably produce prostitutes? How will the Chinese government be able to effectively control the rapid growth of prostitution in the post-Mao era?

## CONCLUSION

The CPC is the sole legitimate party in China and does not allow any opposition party and press to stand. According to Press Freedom Index 2009, China is the eighth worst country for press freedom among 175 countries.[50] The roles of the media are double-edged swords which can serve democracy and yet undermine democracy as well. Under the Mao regime, the CPC solely controlled the media. In the post-Mao era, the market media has begun to challenge the party censorship, but the CPC remains the dominant force and continues to carry out its censorship policy to resist China's democratization. Marketized media is one important step towards the freedom of the media, but is not the full precondition for China's democratization. Although the goal of media freedom ultimately contradicts with the basic principles of the CPC, relative media freedom can be fulfilled as the development of market media and globalization along with the changes of government policy.

The Chinese film industry has a vital role to play in response to China's various problems in politics, culture, and other social issues, such as the sex market. The Chinese film industry has made great achievements during the post-Mao era, but in comparison with the pace of Chinese economic growth, Chinese film industry has a lot to do in the future. At present, China only exports films dealing with limited topics related to martial arts, Chinese traditions and customs, and other documentary films. To narrow the gap between the Chinese film industry and the international film industry, it is necessary to change the Chinese cultural and political value systems. Practically, the Chinese film industry must become a relatively independent sector to accurately reflect the changes of Chinese people and Chinese society.

Chinese filmmakers should continue to explore the serious issues of Chinese society and its people around the world to understand contemporary China. It is only when the world is made completely aware of some troubling aspects of Chinese society that there will be any hope of affecting any change and improving the situation in China as a whole. In this sense, the Chinese government should allow independent films/underground movies to screen in China and the international community.

## NOTES

1. Peter Gross, *Entangled Evolutions: Media and Democratization in Eastern Europe* (Baltimore, MD: The Johns Hopkins University Press, 2002).

2. See Ithiel de Sola Pool, *Technologies of Freedom: On Free Speech in an Electronic Age* (Cambridge: Belknap Press, 1983), 32.

3. Richard Davis, *The Press and American Politics* (New York: Longman Publishing, 1992), 27.

4. Fred S. Siebert, Theodore Peterson, and Wilbur Schramm, *Four Theories of the Press* (Urbana: University of Illinois Press, 1956), 74. According to them, media can play six roles in society: "(1) give service to the political system by providing information, discussion and debate; (2) help to enlighten the general public so that it might self-govern; (3) act as a defender of civil rights by assuming a role as government watchdog; (4) act as a conduit through which the economic sector might be served by bringing together buyers and sellers through advertisements; (5) provide entertainment; and (6) maintain financial independence so that reporting will not be influenced by special interests."

5. Quoted in Marsh, Christopher and Laura Whalen. "The Internet, Electronic Social Capital, and the Democratization Movement in Contemporary China," *American Journal of Chinese Studies* 7, no. 1 (April 2000): 65.

6. Jeffrey Wasserstrom and Kate Merkel-Hess, "Digital China: Ten Thins Worth Knowing about the Chinese Internet," *The Huffington Post*, 7 July 2008.

7. Jehangir Pocha, "China's Press Crackdown: The Broadening of Economic Reforms in China has been met with Greater Restrictions on Journalists," *In These Times*, 12 September 2005.

8. Summer Lemon, "China's Internet population hits 123 million," *IDG News Service*, 19 July 2006.

9. Andrew Jacobs, "Internet Usage Rises in China," *The New York Times,* 14 January 2009.

10. "China's Internet Users Hit 538 Million," *China Daily*, July 19, 2012.

11. David Barboza, "China Surpasses U.S. in Number of Internet Users," *The New York Times,* 26 July 2008.

12. William Thatcher Dowell, "The Internet, Censorship, and China," *Georgetown Journal of International Affairs* 7, no. 2 (Summer 2006): 113.

13. Guobin Yang. *The Power of the Internet in China: Citizen Activism Online* (New York: Columbia University, 2009), 8-12.

14. Wu Zhong, "Courts Withdraw Verdict on ATM Bandit," *Asia Times,* 9 April 2008.

15. Ariana Eunjung Cha, "Grieving Parents Gain Clout in China," *Washington Post,* 28 March 2009.

16. Guobin Yang, "Mingling Politics with Play: The Virtual Chinese Public Sphere," *International Institutes for Asian Studies News Letter* 33 (March 2003), 7.

17. Nina Hachigian, "The Internet and Power in One-Party East Asian States," *Washington Quarterly* 25, no. 3 (2002): 56.

18. Greg Sinclair, "The Internet in China: Information Revolution or Authoritarian Solution?" http//www.oocities.org/gelaige79/intchin.pdf.

19. The Editors, "China's New Rebels," *The New York Times,* 2 June 2009.

20. Yang. *The Power of the Internet in China: Citizen Activism Online*, 2.

21. Ibid., 24.

22. Cristian Segura, "Beijing Hires a Media Guru," *Asia Times,* 10 October 2009.

23. Liang Guo and Wei Bu, *Hulianwang Shiyong Zhuangkuang Ji Yingxiang De Diaocha Baogao* (Survey on Internet Usage and Impact) (Beijing: Chinese Academy of Social Sciences, April 2001).

24. The Associated Press, "China Information minister Rejects Criticism of China's Treatment of Media, Internet Users," *International Herald Tribune,* 25 October 2006.

25. Thomas Lum, "Internet Development and Information Control in the People's Republic of China: CRS Report for congress," Congressional Research Service, The Library Congress, 10 February 2006, http://www.fas.org/sgp/crs/row/RL33167.pdf (20 August 2007).

26. Guo Liang, *Surveying Internet Usage and Impact in Twelve Chinese Cities* (Beijing: Research Center for on Social Development, Chinese Academy of social Sciences, 2005).

27. Jeffrey Wasserstrom and Kate Merkel-Hess, "Ten Things Worth Knowing About the Chinese Internet," *The Huffington Post,* 7 July 2008.

28. David Barboza, "China Surpasses U.S. in Number of Internet Users," *The New York Times,* 26 July 2008.

29. Gudrun Wacker, "The Internet and Censorship in China," in *China and the Internet: Politics of the Digital Leap Forward*, eds. Christopher R. Hughes and Gudrun Wacker (New York: Routledge Curzon, 2003), 72.

30. Jens Damm, "Internet and the Fragmented Political Community," *International Institutes for Asian Studies News Letter* 33 (March 2003): 10.

31. Ibid., 10.

32. Xiao Qiang, "The Development and the State Control of the Chinese Internet," Written Presentation of XIAO Qiang, Director, China Internet Project, The Graduate School of Journalism, University of California at Berkeley. Before the U.S.-China Economic and Security Review Commission Hearing on China's State Control Mechanisms and Methods, 14 April 2005.

33. Damm, "Internet and the Fragmented Political Community," 10.

34. Hachigian, "The Internet and Power in One-Party East Asian States," 56.

35. Kate Hunt, "Can China's film industry ever rival Hollywood?" *BBC News,* 11 December, 2011.

36. Yingjin Zhang, *Chinese National Cinema* (New York: Routledge, 2004), 28.

37. Yingjin Zhang, *Screening China* (Ann Arbor, Michigan: Center for Chinese Studies, the University of Michigan, 2002), 21.

38. Sheldon Hsiao-en Lu, "Historical Introduction: Chinese Cinema (1896-1996) and Transnational Film Studies." *Transnational Chinese Cinemas: Identity, nationhood, Gender*, ed. Sheldon Hsiao-peng Lu (Honolulu: University of Hawai'i Press, 1997), 4.

39. Shuqin Cui, *Women Through the Lens: Gender and Nation in a Century of Chinese Cinema* (Honolulu: University of Hawai'i Press, 2003), 191.

40. Paul Clark, *Chinese Cinema* (Cambridge: Cambridge University Press, 1987), 2.

41. Zhang, *Chinese National Cinema*, 70-71.

42. Sheldon Hsiao-peng Lu, ed. *Transnational Chinese Cinemas: Identity, nationhood, Gender* (Honolulu: University of Hawai'i Press, 1997), 35-36.

43. Kate Hunt, "Can China's film industry ever rival Hollywood?" *BBC News,* 11 December, 2011.

44. Nanette J. Davis, *Prostitution: An International Handbook on Trends, Problems, and Policies* (Westport, CT: Greenwood P, 1993), 88.

45. Teemu Ruskola, "Law, Sexual Morality, and Gender Equality in the Qing and Communist China," *Yale Journal of Law & Feminism* 103, no. 8 (June 1994), 2531.

46. Christian Henriot, "From a Throne of Glory to a Seat of Ignominy: Shanghai Prostitution Revisited (1849-1949)," *Modern China* 22, no. 2 (April 1996), 152.

47. Ibid., 463-71.

48. Wendy Larson, "The Concubine and the Figure of History Chen Kaige's *Farewell My Concubine,"* in *Transnational Chinese Cinemas: Identity, Nationhood, Gender*, ed. Sheldon Hsiao-peng Lu (Honolu: University of Hawai'i Press, 1998), 339.

49. Li Yuguo, "Over 10 Million Sex Workers Estimated in China," *The Epoch Times*, 20 October 2006.

50. "Press Freedom Index 2009," *Reporters Without Borders,* http://www.rsf.org/en-classement1003-2009.html (26 October 2009).

*Chapter Fifteen*

# U.S.-China Relations

China's development is within the international society and contributes to world peace and development; China's problems more or less destabilize the global order; and China's domestic political and economic policies inevitably affect its relations with other countries. In turn, international relations influence the direction of China's development during globalization. After examining China's domestic issues in the previous fourteen chapters, it is necessary to discuss contemporary China in a global context, in order to see the interaction between contemporary China and the international society. Due to the fact that the relationship between China and the United States is the most important issue in the world in the twenty-first century, the following three chapters will mainly discuss U.S.-China relations. Chapter 15 will provide an overview of U.S.-China relations; Chapter 16 will clarify the misconception that China threatens the United States; and Chapter 17 will analyze the cause of the conflicts between the United States and China in order to find a constructive solution for strengthening Sino-America relations. In order to obtain a basic sense of the complex and multi-faceted Sino-American relations, this chapter will briefly examine the development of U.S.-China relations, assess the current status of the relationship between the U.S. and China, discuss the critical issues of improving U.S.-China relations, and predict the dynamic relationship between the two countries in the future through addressing some important questions, such as: What is likely to be the future character of the relationship between the United States and the People's Republic of China? Will it be marked by convergence toward deepening cooperation, stability, and peace or by deterioration that leads to increasingly open competition and perhaps even war? This chapter will conclude that no matter how international scholars and politicians around the world assess current U.S.-China relations, the relationship between the two

countries has become the most important issue in the international community. Aaron L. Friedberg puts it in this way: "The most significant bilateral
international relationship over the course of the next several decades is likely
to be that between the United States and the PRC."[1]

## GENERAL ISSUES OF U.S.-CHINA RELATIONS

There are many reasons that justify the claim that the U.S.-China relationship
is the most important issue in the world and will deeply affect every aspect of
world affairs. China and the U.S. are the two largest economies in the world.
The Chinese economy makes up about 16 percent of total GDP of the world
economy and is expected to surpass the U.S. in 15 years. The two countries
share some common interests in enhancing world security, supporting nuclear non-proliferation, controlling diseases, reducing poverty, improving environmental degradation, and winning the war on terror. It is simply unrealistic
for the U.S. and the international community to make a decision on major
global issues without China's participation; it is also not wise for the U.S. to
block China's rise instead of working with it.

However, "it is a misconception that the importance of China-U.S. relations is based on the two nations' common interests. Few understood that
mutual unfavorable interests make contribution to the importance." Yan
Xuetong points out that "the importance of Sino-American relations lies
mainly in their conflicting interests rather than shared ones."[2] Due to the fact
that there are more mutually unfavorable interests than mutually favorable
ones between China and the United States, the relationship between China
and the United States is so important not only to the two countries, but also to
the world. If the two countries could not appropriately manage their relations, it could have a deadly negative impact on the world.

U.S.-China studies involve many perspectives. Historically, since the first
American boat arrived in China in 1784, the two countries have gone through
both hostile and friendly times. U.S.-China relations can be characterized
differently during different periods of time. Sino-American relations can be
examined from an economic perspective through a discussion of major issues
between the two countries, such as natural resources, currency policy, trade,
investment, environmental issues, and cooperation of sustainable economies.
It can be examined from a political perspective in terms of human rights,
religious freedom, NGO, and China's democratization. It can be examined
from a military perspective in terms of nuclear power, military budget, and
the intention of military development, and military cooperation. It can be
examined from a social perspective to see how population, the welfare system, and immigration affect U.S.-China relations. It can be examined from
an educational perspective to see how China's educational system challenges

the American educational system and influences American views toward China and the Chinese people.

There are various schools of thought in conducting research on U.S.-China relations. According to American scholar Aaron L. Friedberg, most analysts deploy arguments that derive from the three main camps in contemporary international relations theorizing: liberalism, realism, and constructivism. Liberalism expects confrontation and conflict; realists believe that the relationship between the two countries will basically be stable and peaceful; Constructivists think that events could go either way. Each of the three theoretical schools has two variants, one of which is essentially optimistic about the future of U.S.-China relations, the other distinctly pessimistic.[3] Most Chinese people are optimistic realists believing that U.S.-China relations will be peaceful even though both countries face some difficult issues. Most Americans are optimistic liberalists, including U.S. analysts, policymakers, and China watchers, and they "believe in the pacifying power of three interrelated and mutually reinforcing causal mechanisms: economic interdependence, international institutions, and democratization."[4] The Chinese government has promised that China's rise will be peaceful and has also tried to make peace with the United States, but some U.S. analysts believe eventual conflict between the two nations is inevitable.[5]

Being influenced by these three schools of thought, US foreign policy toward China has changed over time and the U.S. has adopted three different approaches in making foreign policy toward China accordingly. The first one is a moderate approach, trying to engage in a less confrontational posture toward China. This policy was largely followed by the George H. W. Bush and Clinton administrations. The second approach has been favored by the George W. Bush and Obama administrations, and is less accommodating to Beijing's concerns. According to this approach, rather than trying to persuade Beijing of the advantages of international cooperation, the United States should keep military forces as a counterweight to China's rising power in Asia, remain firm in dealing with economics, arms proliferation, and other disputes with China, and work closely with traditional U.S. allies and friends in the region to deal with any suspected assertiveness or disruption from Beijing. The current move of returning to the Asia-Pacific region is a typical example demonstrating military muscle in the front door of China. The third one is the more confrontational approach, which is based on the premise that the Chinese political system needs to change dramatically before the United States has any real hope of reaching a constructive relationship with China.

# DEVELOPMENT OF U.S.-CHINA RELATIONS

Since the American ship *Empress of China* arrived in China in 1784, China has had direct relations with the United States. Within the last 200 years, the Chinese political system has fundamentally changed twice through great political revolutions: the Revolution of 1911 that established the first nation-state, the Republic of China, and the Revolution of 1949 that established the People's Republic of China. Accordingly, U.S.-China relations have experienced extraordinary historical changes over the last two centuries. The history of U.S.-China relations can be divided into five periods of time.

The first period of time was from when the first boat *Empress of China* arrived in China to the revolution of 1911. During this period of time, the relationship between the two countries can be characterized as unequal. China and its people were humiliated by the West for more than a century. Especially after the First Opium War, China gradually became a semi-colony of Western powers, particularly the eight Western powers, including the United States. The Chinese government was forced to sign many unequal treaties with the Western governments, in which the Chinese government ceded its lands and paid a huge indemnity to the West. China was also forced to open its port and cities to the West, operating unequal international trades with them. Theoretically, China was a sovereign country, but the government was actually a puppet of Western powers and was almost incapable of making any independent decisions in foreign affairs. The U.S. had privileges in China's territory and U.S. government officials were even exempted from any punishment after killing Chinese citizens in China's land. The United States also played a significant role in suppressing the Boxer Rebellion. Accordingly, at home, the United States Congress passed the Chinese Exclusion Act on May 6, 1882, signed by President Chester A. Arthur, to suspend Chinese immigration, excluding Chinese "skilled and unskilled laborers and Chinese employed in mining" from entering the country for ten years under penalty of imprisonment and deportation. When the Act expired in 1892, Congress extended it for another ten years in the form of the Geary Act, but there was actually no significant change until the Immigration and Nationality Act of 1965, which opened the door to a new stereotype of Chinese as a model minority. The U.S. did not offer an apology until the U.S. Congress issued an apology for the Chinese Exclusion in 2012.[6]

The second period was from the end of 1911 to 1949, in which the two countries tried to develop mutual friendly relations. In order to get support from the CPC and the first socialist country, the Former Soviet Union, and the majority of the Chinese people, the first president of the Republic of China, Sun Yat-sen, developed the policy of accommodating the CPC and working with Russia. However, the successor of Sun, Jiang Jieshi, altered the direction of the Republican Revolution and viewed communism as the biggest enemy. He believed that it was necessary to suppress domestic anti-government forces—the communist movement—in order to make peace with the international community. His policy was compatible with the needs of Western powers, especially the interests of the United States' presence in Asia. The U.S. put in a huge investment to support the nationalist government and worked with Jiang Jieshi, launching wars against the communist movement. Although the Sino-Japan War interrupted the intentions of Jiang, the U.S. and the nationalist government persistently implemented the policy of the anti-Chinese communist party, trying to consolidate Jiang's dictatorship. However, the nationalist government eventually lost the popular support from the majority of the Chinese people. Although Jiang tried to counterattack the mainland after the nationalist government withdrew its troops from the mainland, the influence of his government in the international community gradually diminished. Jiang passed away in Taiwan in 1975, a year before the death of Mao Zedong, Jiang's lifelong political rival.

The third period was full of confrontation between the two countries from the establishment of PRC in 1949 to 1971, when Richard Nixon visited China. Since the establishment of the PRC, China-U.S. relations have gone through different stages from tense confrontation to a "complex mix of intensifying diplomacy, growing international rivalry, and [becoming] increasingly intertwined."[7] The United States tried to disrupt, destabilize, and weaken China for twenty years, from 1949 to 1969.[8] The international community did not view the global significance of U.S.-China relations until China launched the reform movement in 1978. Under the influence of McCarthyism in the 1950s, the U.S. viewed communism as evil and also demonized the image of communist China. Consequently, China's intention was rebuffed by the U.S. government. The world entered into the Cold War era and the conflict between the capitalist and socialist societies increasingly intensified. China launched the anti-imperialist movement and prepared for war against the U.S. In 1950, North Korea invaded South Korea, attempting to unite all of Korea. In response to the Soviet-backed North Korean invasion of South Korea, the United Nations Security Council convened and passed the UNSC Resolution 82 condemning the Soviet Union and North Korea. In the name of the United Nations, the U.S. sent troops to Korea and the Korean War started on November 1, 1950. According to the Chinese government, to prevent the war from coming into the newborn China, the government decided to send approximately one million troops across the Yalu River to help North Korea, fighting against American military forces until a cease-fire was agreed on July 27, 1953. After the Korean War, Chinese nationalism remained strong and the U.S. continued to fear the communist evil spreading from Asia to the West. The Vietnam War broke out in 1959, which was the longest war with a foreign country in American history. China did not officially declare to send their troops to Vietnam. In fact, Chinese military troops closely worked with the Vietnamese against American troops until the war officially ended on April 30, 1975. Mainly because of the hostile relationship between China and the U.S., for much of the first half of the twentieth century, China was "in" but not really "of" the world.[9] China's roles in the international society were marginalized because China was actually isolated. Under these circumstances, China had no other choice but to implement the self-reliance policy to isolate itself from Western societies. Under Mao's self-sufficiency policy, Chinese nationalism became extreme and also created hostility toward Western powers.

During the fourth period both governments tried to change their attitudes from hostility to a normalized relationship between 1971 and 1979. When the U.S. government realized that a less confrontational relationship would be good for both countries, President John F. Kennedy made efforts to improve Sino-American relations.[10] As early as 1963, Roger Hilsman, assistant secretary of state, claimed that that United States was in favor of keeping the "door open" to China, if China gave up its "venomous hatred" of the United States.[11] Because of various reasons, such as Kennedy's assassination, the Vietnam War, and the Cultural Revolution, the process of the normalization of Sino-American relations was interrupted. After Richard Nixon became president in 1969, he immediately declared that "the policy of this country at this time will be to continue to oppose Communist China's admission to the United Nations,"[12] but he soon changed his attitude toward China after secret negotiations between the two countries. The historical turning point for U.S.-China relations came when Secretary of State Henry Kissinger secretly visited China via Pakistan in 1971, making arrangements for Nixon to officially visit China. In July 15, 1971, Richard Nixon announced that he accepted China's invitation to visit China. Nixon was the first U.S. president to visit communist China and shake hands with Mao Zedong in the Forbidden City, and he signed the *Shanghai Communique*, which marked a new chapter in Sino-American relations. To follow the *Shanghai Communique,* China and the U.S. established liaison offices in both countries. In the same year, China regained a seat in the United Nations. In 1975, Gerald Ford visited the PRC and reaffirmed the U.S.'s interest in normalizing relations with Beijing. The Carter administration accepted China's three "non-negotiable conditions" of normalization: "Termination of the United States-Republic of China defense treaty, establishment of diplomatic relations with the government in Beijing instead of with Taipei, and withdrawal of the United States military forces from Taiwan."[13] Since then, the relationship between China and the United States has been officially normalized.

During the fifth period, from 1979 to the present, the two countries have further engaged in international cooperative issues. In 1979, Deng Xiaoping had a state visit to the U.S. and opened a new chapter in engagement and cooperation between the two countries. U.S.-China relations during the ten years between 1979 and 1989 developed smoothly. In response to the Tiananmen Square Incident, while the Bush Administration publically took tougher actions towards the Chinese government, it privately sent secret delegates to China to discuss bilateral relations. Chinese leaders appeared anxious to assure smooth Sino-U.S. relations. The relationship between the two countries finally came back onto a normal track after Deng's south investigation tour to Shenzhen in 1992, re-affirming that China would continue to carry out reform and open up policy. The senior Bush Administration spent its four years from 1989-1992, trying to protect U.S.-China relations and implement the policy of engagement with China against mounting congressional opposition. Former President Clinton also came to favor a policy of engagement with the "one China policy" and divorced international business with China from the Chinese political system, although a group of conservative members of Congress felt that Clinton's policy of 'strategic engagement' in the late 1990s betrayed American interests in the growing threat of China.[14] After the U.S. Congress approved China's most-favored-nation trade status (MFN) in 2001, China became more closely linked in the world economy.[15] China's accession to the WTO implies that China has become a substantial part of global economy and has played more important roles in many aspects of world affairs.

## THE CURRENT AND FUTURE STATUS OF U.S.-CHINA RELATIONS

Before September 11, China had both positive and uneasy relations with the U.S. Sometimes, U.S.-China relations were very shaky, like the 1996 Taiwan Strait Crisis, the bombing the Chinese embassy in Belgrade in 1998, and a Chinese jet-fighter colliding with a U.S. Navy EP-3 in 2001. All these incidents created very difficult times for both sides. However, the September 11 terrorist attacks blurred the ideological distinctions between democratic U.S. and communist China and deepened further cooperation in economy, trade, education, and the war on against terrorists. Some Western scholars suggest that this rosy relationship is only temporary and, in the long term, the two countries will unavoidably become increasingly competitive. In the United States, the debate over how to respond to China's rise and threat is still ongoing.[16] Agreement has not been reached on the current status of U.S.-China relations.[17] Some American scholars believe that China is a strategic partner while others suggest that it is a strategic competitor. Most American people are inclined to agree that China is either a strategic partner or competitor, but the two countries share common interests in various areas. During U.S. President Barack Obama's four-day state visit to China in November 2009, China and the U.S. signed a joint statement and reached an agreement to advance China-U.S. relations in the new era.[18] Both governments have agreed that "China-U.S. bilateral relations are the world's most important."[19] Also, both governments have agreed to use an ambiguous term—neither-friend-nor-enemy (fei di fei you)—for describing the current status of U.S.-China relations. In this sense, some scholars suggest that the current U.S.-China relationship is a superficial one, because there are so many serious conflicts behind the scenes and so many potential crises between the two countries. Nevertheless, this superficial relationship is better than antagonistic attitudes toward each other.

The U.S. is readjusting its foreign policy toward East Asia, especially toward China. Over the past ten years, the U.S. has invested enormous financial and human resources in Iraq and Afghanistan and spent less effort in dealing with China's rise. The power has begun shifting from the West to the East. As the U.S. withdraws its forces from the two countries, over the next 10 years, according to Secretary of State Hillary Clinton, the U.S. will "lock in a substantially increased investment—diplomatic, economic, strategic, and otherwise—in the Asia-Pacific region."[20] Clinton claims that "the region is eager for our leadership." Clinton characterizes this policy as "forward-deployed" diplomacy that attempts to affect every country and corner of the Asia-Pacific region by using any necessary means, including deploying highest-ranking officials, development experts, interagency teams, and permanent assets. The U.S. will take six key lines of action: strengthening bilateral security alliances, deepening working relationships with emerging powers, including with China, engaging with regional multilateral institutions, expanding trade and investment, forging a broad-based military presence, and advancing democracy and human rights.[21] The U.S. will deploy littoral combat ships to Singapore, station American military troops in Australia, and increase U.S. operational access in Southeast Asia and the Indian Ocean region. Why is the U.S. returning to the Asia-Pacific region and deeply involving itself with major issues of the region? Mainly, it is because the region has become a key driver of global politics, due to the fact that it spans two oceans, the Pacific and the Indian oceans, which are increasingly linked by shipping strategies, making the strategic location critical to the U.S. About half the world's population lives in the Asia-Pacific and many of the world's major economies are located in this area. The region will most likely become the center of the global market in the near future. More importantly, major U.S. allies are located in this region, including Japan, South Korea, Australia, Philippines, and Thailand. According to Clinton, the major purpose for the U.S. to return to the Asia-Pacific region is not to contain China's rise, but to balance the power between China and the U.S. and other Asian countries.[22] The Chinese government and the U.S. have different views on whether or not the policy of U.S. returning to Asia is good for the regional peace.

There is no sufficient evidence to accurately foresee the future of the relationship between the two countries for over the next ten or twenty years because there are so many instabilizing factors between the two countries. The future of U.S.-China relations depends not only on the U.S. and China themselves, but also on many other factors, including but not limited to relations between China and Taiwan; the war against terror; both sides' sincerity, trustworthiness, efforts, and understandings; and China's domestic situation, especially China's economic development, political reform, religious and human rights issues and labor unrest. Aaron L. Friedberg points out that "scholars and analysts lack the kinds of powerful predictive tools that would allow them to say with any degree of assurance what the state of relations between the United States and China will be in five years time, to say nothing of ten or twenty. And although options vary about what kinds of analytical advances are possible, there are good reasons to believe that such instruments are, in fact, unattainable."[23] The direction of the future of U.S.-China relations will largely be determined by the actions taken by the two governments in managing all unsettled issues, including national security issues, such as weapons proliferation, allegations of espionage, allegations of cyber-attack plans, economic issues such as trade deficit, the currency exchange rate, restrictions on export products, and intellectual property rights, and sovereignty issues, such as the issues of Taiwan and Tibet.

Despite the Edward Snowden incident, the U.S. is still concerned about cyber attacks on the U.S. military and defense industry. They believe that China has developed cyber espionage capabilities and that many of the attacks are coming from China. Such capability makes the U.S. highly vulnerable. The U.S. has accused Chinese hackers of stealing data on diverse subjects, such as NASA files on the Mars orbiter's propulsion system, solar panels and fuel tanks, planning systems for Army helicopter mission and Air Force flight planning software. China has been able to break into the U.S. military's non-classified NIPRNet, which could give the country the potential capability to delay or disrupt U.S. forces without physically engaging them. Richard A Clarke points out that the U.S. has already lost in the new millennium's cyber battles and warns that the cyber war is a silent threat, but equally dangerous threat to the U.S.[24] Regarding the issue of how the U.S. makes foreign policy towards China, the three schools of thought hold different perspectives, but the mainstream of American international relation academia suggests that no matter what happens in China, U.S. foreign policy toward China should be guided by a clear and firm sense of American national interests. The U.S should also encourage China to become more democratic and to respect the human rights of its own people, particularly on the grounds that democracy and the peaceful resolution of disputes go hand in hand.[25] Regardless of disagreements between the two governments, both have agreed that it is most important for the two countries to search for common ground through cultural exchanges, research projects, education, museum exhibitions, cultural performance, trade, immigration, tourism, and sports.

## TRIANGLE RELATIONS OF U.S.-CHINA-TAIWAN

The relationship between the U.S. and China not only involves the two countries, but also other countries and regions. The triangle relationship between the U.S. and China and Taiwan is the most critical factor that directly affects U.S.-China relations, because it is most relevant to China's sovereignty, the so-called core interest of China. In 1895, the Japanese military defeated China and forced China to cede Taiwan to Japan. Taiwan reverted back to Chinese control after World War II. Following the Communist victory on the mainland in 1949, two million Nationalists fled to Taiwan and settled the nationalist government there. Eleven years after Jiang Jieshi died in Taiwan, the nationalist party began to implement the modern democratic system in 1986. Taiwan underwent its first peaceful transfer of power from the Nationalist Party to the Democratic Progressive Party in 2000.

The term "China" generally refers to the Mainland, Taiwan, Hong Kong, and Macao. Taiwan, Hong Kong, and Macao have adopted different economic and political systems, and so are referred to as "one country, two systems." Since Hong Kong and Macao have returned to the People's Republic of China, the two special regions have established close relations with mainland China under the guidance of the central government. Nowadays, Hong Kong, Macao, and the Mainland are becoming more and more similar, though Hong Kong and Macao Chinese have had quite different experiences.

From China's perspective, the Taiwan issue is a Chinese domestic issue and other countries should not interfere with China's domestic affairs. From a U.S. perspective, Taiwan is a democratic region and needs to be protected. Geographically, Taiwan can be used for checking on China and watching the China Sea, South China Sea, and other Asian countries. Economically, Taiwan is one of the four little dragons and an important international business partner to the U.S. Theoretically, the U.S. continues to hold "one China policy" based on the *Shanghai Communique*, and acknowledges that Taiwan is part of China. Under this umbrella, the U.S. tries to maintain the status quo: one China, but two parts. The U.S. opposes the Chinese government uniting China by using military force, and also opposes that the Taiwanese government goes too far, like Taiwan declaring independence. Meanwhile, the U.S. continues to keep its promise to defend Taiwan's territory because Taiwan serves an exemplar of peace in the region and helps the U.S. and China coexist and work together. Thus, most American scholars suggest that the U.S needs to maintain the present belief among leaders in Beijing that

American intervention in response to the unprovoked use of military force by China is nearly certain.

Under the "one China policy," the Chinese government argues that no high-level officials of the Taiwanese government should be received in the United Sates, so U.S. officials for years have remained unwilling to issue visas to senior Taiwan officials for U.S. visits. This changed dramatically on May 22, 1995, when President Clinton, bowing to substantial congressional pressure, decided to allow Taiwanese President Lee Teng-hui to visit the United States, though it was in his capacity as a private citizen, not as an official representing Taiwan. The Bush Administration had been more accommodating in granting limited visits to senior Taiwan officials. In 2001, Chen Shui-bian was allowed a transit stop in New York City and Houston on his way to Latin America. Under the One China Policy, the Chinese government also protests against the U.S. selling military weapons to Taiwan, because China views the weapon sale as the interference with their domestic affairs. By contrast, the U.S. is concerned about Taiwan's security, and they insist that it is the responsibility of the U.S. to sell military weapons to Taiwan based on the U.S. law—the 1979 Taiwan Relations Act. This dispute has not been resolved yet.

The future of Taiwan remains uncertain. While most scholars agree that Taiwan is part of China, some argue that Taiwan and mainland China are two separate Chinese states. Legally, the ROC has been a sovereign state since its foundation in 1912 and it has not disappeared because of its retreat from the Chinese mainland to Taiwan. Politically, the PRC has never ruled Taiwan for one single day since the CPC took over the mainland in 1949. The two governments have never reached a consensus regarding the definition of "one China," and the two sides still hold different definitions of one-China. The PRC has interpreted the one-China principle to refer to the PRC as the sole legitimate government of China and has continued to insist that Taiwan's future is dependent on the premise of one-China principle. There are also some misconceptions concerning China's relation with Taiwan. Some believe that China will finally allow Taiwan to become an independent country to avoid conflict with the U.S; some believe it is Taiwan's right to establish a sovereign and democratic autonomy; some believe the U.S. has unlimited power and will take the responsibility to protect Taiwan if the mainland takes it over by military force; some believe that China will not attack Taiwan any time soon, because of the vulnerability of east coast cities in China, the deficiencies of China's military weapons, and the fear of U.S. interference. In fact, regardless of the timetable of the unification, the unification of the mainland with Taiwan is the common goal of the Chinese government and the Chinese people. The Chinese government clearly sees the strategic position of Taiwan in the world and wants to unify Taiwan as soon as possible. Mainland China will not give up this mission under any circumstance. This common feeling is produced not only by patriotic nationalism, but also by traditional Chinese culture—the idea of great union.

Without a doubt, there is a big gap between Taiwan and the Mainland in political and cultural systems. Chen Shuibian's election as the President of Taiwan in 2000 indicated that the Taiwanese were trying to drift away from the mainland by that time. The more serious signal sent to the Beijing government was the result of the Parliament election of Taiwan in November of 2001. For the first time the Nationalist Party lost its dominant position after the nationalist government fled the mainland in 1949. Among the 225-seat Legislative Yuan, the Democratic progressive Party improved from 66 seats to 87 as the Nationalists dropped from 123 to 68. The election itself implied that the Taiwanese are uncomfortable with the current political system of mainland China. Although the nationalist party has regained the ruling party position, the relationship between Taiwan and PRC remains the hot debate issue for the Taiwanese general election. However, after Ma Ying-Jeou's re-election as President of Taiwan in January of 2012 is likely to lead to closer ties with the mainland as China seeks to limit political concessions and advance its goal of political unification. [26]

At present, Taiwan is unlikely to be convinced that unification with mainland China can be accomplished peacefully without profound political reform in mainland China. Yet, the Chinese government continues to hold the unchangeably strong position, i.e., if Taiwan declares itself independent, the Chinese government will take any necessary actions to stop it, including military force. According to Chinese officials, any attempt to wage pro-independence policies will fail to get public support. It is a wrong and dangerous perception that China lacks the military capabilities to take over Taiwan and China will likely never have the chance to unify Taiwan because it needs more time to develop sophisticated weapons and military forces. To be sure, the Chinese government will not let Taiwan go, if it declares independence. It seems that the U.S. assumes that if it cannot stop China from taking over Taiwan, China will immediately become the Asian superpower, and nobody in the region will be able to compete with China. Thus, the U.S. promised many times that it would take responsibility for defending Taiwan. The U.S. presumption in fact makes U.S.-China relations more complicated.

## CONCLUSION

As China is on the rise, the relationship between China and the United States has become the most important issue in the world in the twenty-first century. It is almost impossible to resolve important global issues without cooperation between the two countries. Since the normalization of Sino-American relations in the 1970s, the general trend of the relations has been towards engagement and cooperation. However, the future of U.S.-China relations is uncertain, because many unresolved issues lie between the two countries. The direction of Sino-American relations is really up to the two governments' foreign policy on how to resolve unsettled issues. The triangle relations of China and Taiwan and the U.S. are the most critical among all issues from Chinese perspective. It is best for the U.S. to wisely make foreign policy on the most sensitive issue—the triangle relations of Taiwan-U.S.-Mainland China. Meanwhile, it would be advantageous for the CPC to reform its political system in order to peacefully reunite Taiwan with the mainland.

## NOTES

1. Aaron L. Friedberg, "The Future of U.S.-China Relations: Is Conflict Inevitable?" *International Security* 30, no. 2 (Fall 205): 8.

2. Yan Xuetong, "The Instability of China-U.S. Relations," *The Chinese Journal of International Politics* 3 (2010): 263-292.

3. Friedberg, "The Future of U.S.-China Relations: Is Conflict Inevitable?" 9.

4. Michael Doyle, *Ways of War and Peace: Realism, Liberalism, and Socialism* (New York: W.W. Norton, 1997), 260.

5. Susan Lawrence and Thomas Lum, "U.S.-China Relations: Policy Issues: CRS Report for Congress," *Congressional Research Service*, March 2011.

6. Moni Basu, "In rare apology, House regrets exclusionary laws targeting Chinese," CNN http://inamerica.blogs.cnn.com/2012/06/19/in-rare-apology-house-regrets-exclusionary-laws-targeting-chinese/ (December 16, 2012)

7. Carin Zissis and Christopher Alessi, "U.S Relations with China (1949-present)" *Council On Foreign Relations* , http://www.cfr.org/china/us-relations-china-1949-present/p17698

8. Henry Kissinger, "The Future of U.S.-Chinese Relations Conflict Is a Choice, Not a Necessity ," *Foreign Affairs*, March/April 2012.

9. Lowell Dittmer, "China's Search for its pace in the world," *In Contemporary Chinese Politics in Historical Perspective,* ed. Brantly Womack (Cambridge: Cambridge University Press , 1991)

10. Shia-ling Liu, *U.S. Foreign Policy toward Communist China in the 1970's: The Misadventures of Presidents Nixon, Ford and Carter* (Taibei: Kuang Lu Publishing Company, 1988), 3.

11. Quoted in Kwan Ha Yim, ed., *China and the U.S. 1964-72* (New York: Facts on File, 1975), 3.

12. Ibid., 181.

13. Liu, *U.S. Foreign Policy Toward Communist China in the 1970's,* 31-32.

14. William Callahan, "How to understand China: the dangers and opportunities of being a rising power," *Review of International Studies* 31 (2005): 705.

15. Jingping Ding, *China's Domestic Economy in Regional Context* (Washington, DC: Center for Strategic & International Studies, 1995), 2.

16. U.S. Government, China's Foreign Policy and Soft Power in South America, Asia, and Africa ( Books LLC, Reference Series, 2011).

17. Thomas J. Christensen, "Fostering Stability or Creating a Monster? The Rise of China and U.S. Policy toward East Asia," *International Security* 31.1 (2006): 82.

18. Yan Xuetong, "The Instability of China-U.S. Relations," *The Chinese Journal of International Politics* 3 (2010): 263.

19. Yan Xuetong, "The Instability of China-U.S. Relations," *The Chinese Journal of International Politics* 3 (2010): 270.

20. Hillary Clinton, "America's Pacific Century," *Foreign Policy*, November 2011, http://www.foreignpolicy.com/articles/2011/10/11/americas_pacific_century

21. Ibid.

22. Ibid.

23. Friedberg, "The Future of U.S.-China Relations: Is Conflict Inevitable?," 8.

24. Richard A. Clarke and Robert K. Knake, *Cyber War: The Next Threat to National Security and What to Do About It* (New York: Harper Collins Publishers, 2010).

25. *U.S. Policy toward China: Try for the best, prepare for the worst,* by Avery Golstein, Foreign Policy Research Institute, March 30, 2001.

26. Ralph Jennings, "Taiwan and China to grow closer with Ma's reelection," *Christian Science Monitor,* 16 January 2012.

## Chapter Sixteen

# Does China's Rise Threaten the United States?

China's rise has an immediate impact on every aspect of Western societies, both in opportunities and in challenges for other countries. Power transitions usually come with international conflicts. Rising powers usually want to gain more authority in the global system and declining countries are afraid of loss of their dominant position. Over the past decade or so, the "China threat" theory has spread throughout the West, despite Beijing's repeated pledges that China's rise will be peaceful. Many Americans think that China's rise is weakening Western societies and fostering fears in the United States and the Asia-Pacific region, while China is using Western capital to build up its strength.[1] As early as 1997, Richard Bernstein and Ross Munro in their book *The Coming Conflict with China* argued that war between China and the United States was a distinct possibility. In 2005, Robert D. Kaplan contended that whether or not there will be a Sino-American war is no longer a question. The only question, he wrote, is how the United States should fight China.[2] John Mearsheimer warned that "the United States and China are likely to engage in an intense security competition with considerable potential for war."[3] Fareed Zakaria goes further, saying that "when a new power rises, it inevitably disturbs the balance of power."[4] Susan L. Shirk, former deputy assistant secretary for China in the Bureau of East Asia, suggests that "China needs to reassure the United States that China's rise is not a threat and will not challenge America's dominant position."[5] In order to understand the relationship between China and Western societies, one must address the issues on whether China's rise really poses a challenge to U.S. dominance. This chapter will examine the major arguments of the China threat theory in seven aspects, explore the implications of the China threat theory, and conclude that it is not constructive to Sino-U.S. relations for Washington's China policy to be based on the "China threat" hypothesis.

## CHINA HAS NO INTENTION OF CHALLENGING THE U.S.

For one country to pose a challenge or threat to another, it must have the intention to do so. Despite widespread fears about the motivation of China's rise, the Chinese government remains committed to a peaceful rise.[6] The Chinese government does not believe that its future depends on overturning the fundamental order of the international system.[7] In response to Westerners' concerns, the Chinese government has quietly modified the term of "peaceful rise" or "peaceful ascension" into "peaceful development."[8] Theoretically, the global village is an international family. If every member of the family becomes strong, the international family would become stronger. Every nation has its own national interests, so real conflicts between different nations are inevitable. It is a natural process for a rising power to expand its business interests worldwide, as the nature of capital is to flow to wherever profits can be made. While China is rising, it is inevitable that the U.S. and other countries will face competition from China's growing economy. But in the era of globalization, no one should see economic competition as a threat. With its growing economic muscle, China naturally gains greater influence in international affairs, but this does not mean China seeks world dominance.

Practically, in order for the CPC to survive into the twenty-first century, China must make peace with the international society and develop a harmonious society at home. Without a doubt, the reform and opening up policy have boosted the Chinese economy and advanced sciences and technology, but it has also created thorny problems, such as corruption, widening wealth gaps and social injustice, which threaten social stability and the legitimacy of the rule of the CPC. Domestic problems remain the main headache of Chinese leadership. People's dissatisfaction could spark off social violence at anytime. The Chinese government feels very nervous with the people's discontent. This explains why Chinese internal security spending exceeded its defense budget in 2011.[9] To tackle domestic problems, China needs a peaceful global environment. There is no reason for China to upset the current world order by challenging U.S. dominance. The current order is Western-oriented, solid and not easy to overthrow. The Chinese government does not believe that challenging the U.S. serves China's best interests or that China's future rests on overturning the current international system.[10] The CPC passed the resolution, "On Major Issues Regarding the Building of a Harmonious Socialist Society" in October 2006, placing "building a harmonious society" at the top of its work agenda.

China has thrived to build a market economy that fits within the Western-orientated system. China has yet to improve its fledgling market economy by introducing more reforms in finance and services. China still needs to learn from the West—as it may be following the global financial crisis, and the U.S. and the European Union are China's largest export markets. For China, to challenge U.S. dominance may be economically self-destructive, and whenever possible, Beijing avoids public confrontation with Washington. In 2010, the Chinese government issued the White Paper on national defense which, once again, pledges that China will never seek hegemony or engage in military expansion.[11]

China and the United States share many common interests.[12] On the one hand, "there is no global issue that can be effectively tackled without Sino-American cooperation."[13] On the other hand, it is one of the greatest challenges for the United States to co-exist with China in the twenty-first century.[14] The Chinese economy heavily relies on Western expertise, Chinese foreign trade largely depends on foreign-invested companies, and about 30 percent of China's total exports are produced by foreign-funded enterprises. All of this makes China sensitive to the ups and downs of the international economy, in particular that of the American economy. If the U.S. economy has troubles, it hurts China's economic growth. In turn, China is the largest market for the U.S. Sara Bongiorni offers her true story that she and her family wanted to spend a year without buying anything made in China. She discovered it was not only difficult, but also not worthwhile to do so, because there are vast consumer areas that are nearly all Chinese-dominated. Thus, the United States cannot exclude China in globalization.[15]

A hostile relationship with China would damage both the interests of China and the U.S. As early as 60 years ago, an Australian ambassador warned the U.S. that it was very dangerous to be hostile toward China and suggested to keep China as a friend, because China might easily become a very powerful military nation in 50 years. John Ikenberry told Washington that the United States cannot stop China's rise.[16] If the U.S. tries to keep China weak, it would increase China's domestic instability which would negatively affect global peace and development. The most important thing for the U.S. to do is not to block China from becoming a powerful country, but to learn how to live with the rising China. In the meantime, the U.S. should urge the Chinese government to become a responsible and democratic stakeholder.[17]

According to the Chinese government, "China's relationship with the United States is a top priority."[18] Hu Jintao has promised that China would develop a friendly relationship with the U.S. When Hu Jintao visited the White House in 2006, Bush deliberately used the word "stakeholder" to describe the relationship between the two countries and pointed out that "as stakeholders in the international system, our two nations share many strategic interests."[19] Since China-U.S. relations were normalized in the 1970s, the two countries have gone through several crises, but the Chinese government has realized that the diplomatic approach is the best way to reduce the risk of international conflict that could lead to domestic disorder.

## A LONG TIME FOR CHINA TO CATCH UP

China is the fastest growing economy in the world with its gross domestic product (GDP) growing 10.3 percent annually in past three decades. According to a Pew Global Attitudes survey released in July 2011, most of these surveyed participants believe that China either will replace, or already has replaced the United States as the world's superpower. China's emergence as a great power has become inevitable.[20] However, the Asian Development Bank has predicted that China's growth rates in the next two decades will be only about half of what they were in the last 30 years.[21] In addition, several factors must be considered when discussing the development of the Chinese economy. First of all, there are many more statistics that come to the front of arguments questioning the size of the Chinese economy. In 2007, the World Bank shrunk China's economy by nearly 40 percent. The new data is widely believed to be more reliable and accurate than previous estimates.

The U.S. economy is currently about eight times the size of China's. China will take a long time to surpass the United States. In addition, China has a population of 1.34 billion. When China's GDP is divided by 1.34 billion, it decreases in value. China's per capita GDP surpassed $1,000 in 2003 and reached $1,714 in 2005, but China will not become moderately prosperous by 2020.[22] In 2007, its per capita GDP was only $2,000—compared to $42,000 in the United States. China's per capita income is only one-nineteenth that of the U.S.[23] At present, China does not rank among the 100 richest nations based on per-capita. Among 1.34 billion people, about 50 percent of Chinese people live in rural areas, 400 million people live on the less than $2 a day, and 200 million people live on less than a dollar per day.[24] China is still a developing country and it may take a long time, if not a century, to become an economic power, giving the United States sufficient time to comprehend the implications of China's rise before China reaches that point.

More importantly, China's rise is actually within the Western-orientated system. This Western-oriented system is the product of farsighted U.S. leadership and the best social and political system in the world. According to Robert Zoellick, "No major state can modernize without integrating into the globalized capitalist system."[25] Germany, Italy, and Japan merged into the democratic system after the two bloody world wars; the former Soviet Union and East European socialist campus collapsed in the 1990s after the Cold

War.[26] The Western-oriented system is valuable to China. China is working with this system instead of overthrowing it.[27] Since the reform movement began, the Chinese government has carried out a market economy. The Chinese market economy is very competitive. A new poll of 20 countries from around the world, conducted by the international polling firm, GlobeScan, finds the highest level of support for the free enterprise system was China, with 74 percent of respondents agreeing that a market economy is the best economic system.[28] This data suggests that China's market economy is rooted in the grassroots of Chinese society. John Ikenberry notes that the road to the East runs through the West; China's road to world power runs through the West. China can rise up only through this system. If the U.S. wants to preserve its leadership of the world, Washington has to strengthen the Western-oriented system and bring China into that system. If China continues to follow the existing global order and integrate itself into the Western-oriented system, the U.S. and other Western societies can live along with China, even though the U.S.'s global economic position may weaken.[29]

## MILITARY POWER IS STILL A MISMATCH

Washington today is very concerned about the development of China's military. The 2011 Report to Congress of the U.S.-China Economic and Security Review Commission pointed out that China has accelerated military modernization, including foreign purchases and indigenous production of high-technology equipment. China's military budget has rapidly grown. In 2010, China's defense budget was 532.115 billion *yuan* (USD $81.3 billion) and reached $106 billion from $95.6 billion in 2011. American officials have confirmed that China has deployed a long-range missile program which can carry 21 nuclear missiles to reach American cities. If one Chinese missile hit the U.S., many U.S. cities would be paralyzed. Bill Gertz, in his book *The China Threat: How the People's Republic Targets America*, revealed the so-called inside story that Communist China could attack the United States with nuclear weapons, if U.S. forces defended Taiwan in a regional conflict.[30] China has accelerated its military modernization, including foreign purchases and indigenous production of high-technology equipment.[31] Chinese J-20 fifth-generation stealth fighter has reached an initial operational capability and may contest U.S. air supremacy with the F-22.[32] China has developed an anti-ship ballistic missile—the DF-21D. American military experts point out that DF-21D is designed to sink American super-carriers and affect U.S. support for its Pacific allies.[33] China is developing "counter-space" weapons that could shoot down satellites. Gregory Schulte, Deputy Secretary of Defense for space policy, points out that "the investment China is putting into counter-space capabilities is a matter of concern to us."[34]

From an American viewpoint, since there is no obvious threat to China, why has China accelerated the process of military modernization?[35] Chinese military development lacks transparency, so U.S. officials remain largely in the dark about China's long term goals.[36] Many Americans think that China is seeking to become at least a regional superpower and seems ready to challenge the goal of Washington's foreign policy.[37] They believe that China is trying to drive the United States out of Asia by using a combination of military, diplomatic, and economic pressure.[38] According to Max Boot, the conventional wisdom that the war on terrorism had united the United States and China against a common enemy is only a rosy scenario, which is undermined almost daily by Beijing's actions.[39]

In fact, China spends one-eighth the amount of the U.S.'s military budget, and the U.S. has the largest defense budget in the world, accounting for 47 percent of the world's total military spending.[40] Although China has nuclear-weapon capability, the Chinese army is ill-equipped. Although China will most likely have more submarines than the United States by the end of this decade, they will still lag behind in overall ability.[41] China's military policy has largely revolved around defense. It is common sense that a nation's strength must be supported by military power. China needs a stronger military to protect its growing global interests. Dispatching naval warships to escort Chinese commercial ships to Somalia and help evacuate Chinese nationals in Libya is a good example. China could not have taken such actions 20 or 30 years ago when its military was weak. Another major reason for China to modernize its military force is to protect its territorial integrity, especially to prevent Taiwan from actually separating from China.

Some American scholars believe that China is departing from Deng Xiaoping's foreign policy of *tao guang yang hui* (hide brightness and nourish cherish obscurity, or bide our time and build up our capabilities) toward the U.S.[42] Elizabeth Economy, director for Asian Studies at the Council on Foreign Relations, notes that the consensus of the Deng era has begun to fray and that Beijing will expand its influence to the rest of the world.[43] Some Westerners are concerned about China's aggressive territorial claims and support for the governments of North Korea, Iran, Syria, and Sudan. There are also different views in China on why its relations with bordering countries are deteriorating. According to the 2011 Pacific Blue Book published by the Chinese Academy of Social Sciences, all problems with bordering countries are not the result of new Chinese foreign policy, but derived from the U.S. returning to Asia.

## WILL CHINA'S FOREIGN POLICY BECOME MORE ASSERTIVE?

Since the Eighteenth National Congress of the Communist Party of China last November, much of Western media has predicted that Xi Jinping will adopt a more assertive foreign policy in order to solve the territorial disputes between China, Japan and other neighboring countries. This has been worrisome for some of China's neighbors and their Western allies. Will Xi's foreign policy become more assertive? The answer is no. Xi does not intend to challenge the current global order. In fact, it will be very difficult for him to dramatically alter Hu Jintao's moderate foreign policy.

Although Xi holds three top posts—in the party, government and military—his fundamental objective is to maintain the one-party system. If he took a tougher stance, the party would face more challenges from the international community and internal opposition. This would do more harm than good to his primary goal. Xi is not an elected leader in the modern democratic sense, but a result of the negotiation among various elite groups in China. His foreign policy must represent the common interest of these factions. In addition, many Chinese officials have interests overseas and fear further deterioration of relations with other countries, particularly Japan and the West.

China is not ready to implement a more assertive foreign policy. And China will not be able to take a tougher stance without more internal coordination and support. The voice of China's foreign policy currently comes from different departments. They are not well coordinated and lack a strategy with a long-term vision. Thus China does not have a system for making consistent and workable foreign policy, and the top leader has not gained sufficient power to fully manage foreign relations. It will take Xi some time to reorganize the system and put any new policies in place.

At the same time, it is unclear if Chinese economic and military muscle are powerful enough to support a more assertive foreign policy. Japanese marine and air forces are strong. The United States claims that the 1960 U.S.-Japan Security Treaty covers the Senkaku/Diaoyu Islands, which makes Sino-Japanese relations more complicated. In addition, China is facing a mountain of domestic problems, including corruption in the military. It is not wise for China to adopt a tougher foreign policy in dealing with territorial disputes with various countries at the same time as it tries to maintain domestic social stability. The Chinese government has learned the lesson that a combination of internal violence and external conflict can contribute to the collapse of the regime.

Today nationalistic feelings remain strong. And a more assertive foreign policy could add fuel to the fire of Chinese nationalism. But this could also get out of control and possibly turn against the current government. It is possible that the current standoff between China and Japan is only a means for the government to strengthen the people's faith in the current regime. In the meantime, the stable growth of China's military expenditures has enhanced the government's bargaining power in the international system and preparedness for worst-case scenarios.

The new leader of the China might not have any other choice but to continue implementing Hu's moderate foreign policy of peaceful development—with some minor modifications. Ample evidence indicates that Xi is a pragmatic leader and will not put foreign policy at the top of the party's agenda. Instead, he is more likely to focus on China's domestic issues, improving living standards and quality of life, and lubricating potential conflicts between the government and the people.

In order for China to play a more prominent role in the international system and solve territorial disputes with its neighboring countries, new Chinese leaders will continue efforts to rebalance the relationship between China and the United States—while at the same time restoring the economic and military alliance with Russia. To do so, it is also necessary for the Chinese government to carefully balance the principles of Chinese territorial integrity with economic development, harmonize party legitimacy with Chinese nationalistic feeling, and weigh the interests of elite groups against Xi's ambitious goal of a great rejuvenation of the Chinese nation. Considering these challenges, it is unlikely that China's foreign policy will change significantly during the first five-year term of Xi's presidency.

## CHINA'S INTERESTS IN THE SOUTH CHINA SEA

The recent South China Sea sovereignty issue has intensified China's relations not only with some Asian countries, such as Vietnam and the Philippines, but also with the U.S. In June of 2011, China urged the U.S. to stay out of the South China Sea dispute, and warned that U.S. involvement may make the situation worse.[44] China and its neighboring countries have long been involved in various border disputes. The disputes between China and other countries over the South China Sea have become increasingly intensified in recent years.[45] Some countries suspect that China might actually use military force to facilitate desirable resolutions of disputed territorial claims.[46] In modern times, China has participated in over twenty territorial conflicts with other countries, but it has only used its military force a few times, such as the wars with India and Vietnam and the Soviet Union. However, the reason China used force to solve the conflicts was to protect its sovereignty. This means that China has compromised more frequently than it has used force.[47]

The central task of the Chinese government in the post-Mao era is to improve the living standard of the Chinese people and develop a harmonious society at home. The majority of Chinese people want peace, and only a small percentage of people advocate that China should use military force to solve the territory disputes. These people are usually young without the experience of wars. As early as the 1950s, the Chinese government began to implement the Five Principles of Peaceful Coexistence.[48] In the post-Mao era, Deng Xiaoping incorporated two basic principles into China's foreign policy: "*Tao guang yang hui, you suo zuo wei*"—keep a low profile and bide its time, while getting something accomplished.[49] In October 2007, Chinese president Hu Jintao introduced the concept of "harmonious world," the so-called "Good Neighbor Policy" ("*Mu lin you hao zheng ce*"), as the principle of foreign policy and tried to pursue better relations with neighboring countries.[50] This foreign policy strategy is likely to be maintained for years to come, if not until the nineteenth CPC Congress in late 2017.[51]

Strategically, it is in the best interest of all countries to pursue their common interests. For example, China and Vietnam are bordering countries. In a Chinese saying, close neighbors are better than distant relatives. Vietnam is an oil-poor country and China also needs natural resources. It will be good for both countries if they can work together and explore energy resources in the South China Sea in order to achieve their domestic economic success. If a war broke out between the two countries, both sides could not prevail, but damage both countries' national interests. However, China's good intention does not necessarily guarantee peace over the South China Sea. Although China claims Paracels and Spratlys, it actually has only occupied nine islands, Vietnam has occupied 28 islands, Philippines has occupied seven, Malaysia has occupied three, Indonesia has occupied two, and Brunei has occupied one. Vietnam is still not satisfied with their actual occupation. In the past decades, technically, the majority of disputed waters were beyond both nations to reach, but Vietnam relied on foreign countries' technologies to develop their deep sea drilling platforms over the disputed water, while China refused to accept technological help from the West.[52] In recent years, China has achieved a major breakthrough in deep-sea oil recovery technology, and has successfully developed operations in the deep sea drilling platform. China has claimed that the South China Sea is China's core interest and it has made great efforts in building up its marine force and aircraft carrier. In the past, the Chinese governments from the republican era to the communist regime have consistently claimed the nine-dashed lines, but they only kept their words, instead of displaying actions. Now, China's military power is capable of supporting its government to reclaim its territory. Obviously, there is great potential for a war if both nations do not take one step back. The United States is concerned about the disputes and is indirectly involved with the South China Sea conflicts, although the Chinese government insists that no matter what will happen over the South China Sea in the future, it is not an issue between the U.S. and China, but a regional issue.

# SINO-RUSSIA TIES DO NOT THREATEN AMERICA

Since the Cold War, the U.S. has been always concerned about the possibility of an alliance between Russia and China. Recently, Xi Jinping's first trip to Russia as the President of China has once again raised American concerns about the implications of Beijing-Moscow relations. American media more or less implies that China's motive of deepening its relations with Russia is anti-American. It is too simplistic to rush into any hasty conclusion. Moscow and Beijing are maybe on their honeymoon, but they do not necessarily take aim against the U.S.

In recent years, the U.S. has been strengthening its alliance with China's neighboring countries, including Japan, South Korea, Philippines, Afghanistan, and India. Other countries, such as Vietnam, Malaysia and Myanmar are drawing closer to the U.S. By contrast, China is losing its neighboring friends while its economic power is rising. The Chinese government views the regional tension as the outcome of Washington's "returning to Asia" strategy. Under this circumstance, on the one hand, China indeed needs help from Russia to avoid escalating confrontations with multiple neighboring countries; on the other hand, China's initial move reflects that Chinese leaders lack confidence in dealing with potential regional crises alone.

Beijing and Moscow have common interests. Beijing demands more oil and natural gas from Russia and needs more advanced military weapons supplies, including submarines, warships, and aircrafts. Russia wants more investments from China to speed up the development of the Russian economy. Arguably, China does not really need military technologies from Russia. For example, the Chinese J-20 fighter is more advanced than the Su-35, equivalent to Russia's T50 and the U.S. F-22. The purpose for China to purchase 24 Su-35 is not to bridge the gap between Chinese and U.S. military power, but to show its sincerity to consolidate the ties with Russia by offering economic incentives.

Will China and Russia be able to form a solid partnership? Superficially, the top leaders of the two countries can get along because their background is similar. However, their political ambition cannot be automatically translated into foreign policy. Chinese media gives much attention to the meetings between Vladimir Putin and Xi and highly praises the significance of current Sino-Russian relations. Yet, Russian media only views China as a junior partner because it believes Xi has not come into the role in global governance. This implies that meetings between the two top leaders are less than historic.

The Chinese foreign policy process is still guided by a small elite group, divorcing from public opinions to a certain extent. China's quick move closer to Russia has received a lukewarm response from public opinion in China. In a historical perspective, Chinese people have reasons to doubt Moscow's sincerity. Russia occupied China's territories totaling more than four million square kilometers from 1689 to 1898, forced China to sign the Yalta Agreement for recognizing Outer Mongolia as an independent country in the 1940s, and stopped all financial and technological aid during the Chinese economic crisis in the 1960s. Finally, the Zhen Bao Island military conflict in Helongjiang Province broke out in 1969. Although in 1991 Russia acknowledged the island belonged to China, the tension between the two countries along the 2,500-mile-long border remained high until the Chinese military troops retreated 500 kilometers in 2008. In comparison with China-U.S. relations, the U.S. never had a single territory dispute with China, so the Chinese people have not had a similar historical complex towards the U.S.

Russian public opinion also does not believe China is trustworthy in part because of the inconsistency of Chinese foreign policy. China aligned with Russia in the 1950s and with the United Sates in the 1970s, but implemented a non-aligned policy in the 1980s. The mutual distrust between the two countries partially explains why Chinese students do not enthusiastically choose to study in Russia. In 2012, about 350,000 Chinese students went abroad, but more than 50 percent of them chose to go to the U.S. The list of other favorite destinations for Chinese students does not include Russia, but Britain, Australia, Canada, Japan, France, Germany, Netherland, Singapore, and South Korea. As a result, Russian culture has had little impact on Chinese society and intellectual circles. However, American culture is very popular in China and positively affects public opinion. The future of Sino-Russia relations will be tested by public opinion in both China and Russia. It would be difficult for both countries to continue drawing closer without the support of public opinion.

The status of the current Sino-Russia relations is not a full-fledged alliance, but a quasi alliance. Nor is it designed to challenge the U.S. dominant power. At most, a close relationship between China and Russia could help China to get more leverage for bargaining with the U.S. to smoothly solve its territory disputes with neighboring countries. China has no need to seek an alliance with Russia. The main theme of world development is peace regardless of some regional military conflicts. The U.S. alliance is the by-product of the Second World War in response to Nazism. Nazi imperialism is over; the communist campus collapsed; and the non-aligned movement is dissolving. There is no evidence to suggest that World War Three is coming. In the nuclear age, the chance of conventional wars between big countries is rare. After September 11, terrorism has become the most dangerous threat, mainly targeting the West. There is no immediate threat to China. Under these circumstances, it is not necessary for China to align with Russia. According to the *Global Times*, the Russian ambassador also made it clear that Russia does not seek an alliance with China. If China unilaterally pursued the goal, the result would be negative.

The restoration of friendship between Beijing and Moscow is mainly driven by their domestic pressures and regional security issues. A stable relationship between the two countries will greatly relieve the financial burdens in support of the hostility along the sizeable border, allow China to put more investment in Western China while continuing to develop the economy in Eastern China, and deepen its relations with South Asia and Middle East countries, the so-called Xi Jin (China's West) strategy. It is groundless to predict that the two countries will become alliances in a decade. Even though Beijing and Moscow are on their honeymoon, in the long term, Beijing and Moscow might have more potential conflicts than cooperation and they could become main competitors and even rivals again.

Most likely, Chinese leaders will not move away from the U.S. through overplaying the "Russian card." In order to fulfill Xi's vision—restoring the order of post-World War II—the Chinese leader should carefully balance the triangle relations between China and the United States and Russia. The goal of restoring the order of post-World War II is fundamentally different from the goal of challenging the U.S. dominant power. The new Chinese leaders have promised that China will never seek hegemony. In fact, China does not have such a capability to support the pursuit. Ample evidence suggests that China-U.S. relations will continue to be at the top of China's foreign policy. When U.S. treasury secretary Jack Lew visited Beijing in March 2013, Xi assured him that ties with America were of great importance. Thus, the current Sino-Russia cooperation is largely symbolic and its impact is more psychological than of substance. It is not necessary for the U.S. to overestimate the significance of the cooperation of Beijing with Moscow.

## CHINA'S SOFT POWER DOES NOT HURT GLOBAL INTEREST

Soft power is becoming more important to a country's comprehensive power in international society, while hard power is becoming somewhat less important.[53] Many Western people see that China has expanded its soft power in the international society by spreading its culture to the West, providing scholarships for students to go to China to study, financially aiding many countries, and playing critical roles inside many international organizations. China joined the WTO in 2001, attended the Group of Seven major industrial nation meetings, and hosted the Olympic Games in 2008. Since the 1990s, China has achieved impressive gains in using soft power through implementing its "smiling" foreign policy, providing scholarships for foreign students in Chinese studies, financially aiding many countries, playing critical roles in many international organizations and meetings, and hosting the Summer Olympic Games in 2008. Joshua Kurlantzick believes one of the reasons for China's success is that China is using soft power to appeal to other countries and position itself as a model of social and economic success. Joshua Kurlantzick, in his book *Charm Offensive: How China's Soft Power Is Transforming the World*, has observed that China is emphasizing soft power strategies, because it sees this as the United States' weak point. America's weakness is its soft power, not its hard power. Since the Iraq war began in 2003, the United States has suffered a serious setback in terms of soft power. Driving China forward in its emphasis on employing soft power is not only a desire to advance its particular brand of political philosophy, but a deeper desire to rebuild national credibility greatly tarnished over the past 150 years.

The term soft power has a broad meaning. According to Joseph S. Nye, "soft power is the ability to get what you want through attraction rather than coercion or payments. It arises from the attractiveness of a country's culture, political ideals, and policies."[54] Soft power includes many aspects, but two things are very basic. The first basic aspect of soft power is education. China's educational system is far behind the level of developed countries' systems. The Chinese government spending for education is less than 4 percent of their GNP, while the world average is 5.1 percent of GNP.[55] Based on the total educational investment, each Chinese person spends only 32 *yuan* (about USD $4) per year for education. The CPC has recently attempted to revive Confucianism to help in developing harmonious society, but the result of this effort is uncertain.

Another basic aspect of soft power is cultural influence around the world. There is no doubt that the CPC is trying to expand Chinese cultural influence around the world by setting up Confucius Institutes that teach Western people about Confucianism and change the standard of value of Western people.[56] However, the overwhelming evidence suggests that Chinese traditional culture is waning on the mainland. Beijing Opera, a national treasure with a history of 200 years, was the most popular form of entertainment and was favored by the Chinese people from all ranks of Chinese society. Every city used to have at least one Beijing Opera troupe, but Beijing Opera is out of business in many cities today. Even in Beijing, the capital of China, Beijing Opera is performed only at two small theaters. Interestingly enough, the majority of people in the audience are foreigners, usually white people. Old people make up the majority among the Chinese audience. Chinese young people are much more interested in rock and popular music. Obviously, while the Chinese economy has become strong, Chinese traditional culture has become weak.

Contemporary society is in the era of globalization; and the world culture is transnational. Western culture is everywhere in China—McDonalds, Kentucky Fried Chicken, Wal-mart, Nike, Rebok, Holiday Inn, Ramada Inn, Hilton, and the Grand Hyatt. There are more than 200 five-star hotels in China, two-thirds of them are foreign investments. CNN and many other Western TV stations broadcast in China. Western print media, e.g., *Financial*

*Times*, are allowed to print in China. The Japanese Sony Company established the first joined-venture TV station in November 2004. The Chinese people, especially the youth, are increasingly becoming ensconced in Western culture, particularly American culture, including individual rights, material abundance, advanced technology, and popular culture. According to an investigation, the most popular key words on the Internet are closely associated with Western cultures, such as stock, the U.S., American music, NBA, chat room, game, dog, coffee, hair styles, makeup, and women's health. Many Chinese movie theaters only show American films. The Rolling Stones visited Shanghai in April 2006, filling the 8,500-seat Shanghai Grand Stage each day they performed, although the admission tickets were very expensive in terms of Chinese income, ranging from 300 *yuan* (USD $37.28) to 1800 *yuan* for each ticket.[57]

It will take a long time for the West to accept Chinese culture. While China's trade surplus exceeded USD $21 billion in 2010, its cultural trade deficit is growing. According to a *China Daily* report in 2006, the ratio of China's imports of cultural products to its exports was 10:1, and is believed to be much higher today. This reflects that the influence of Chinese culture in the West is very limited. More importantly, the CPC has not solved the puzzle of how to integrate its political system, one of the most important aspects of soft power, into the current mainstream global order.

The U.S. is worried about China's expansion into Africa and Latin America. In fact, China's policies toward Africa and Latin America obviously are more economically driven than cultural or political. China is acting similarly in Europe—the Chinese government has promised to help Spain and other European Union countries deal with their financial crisis and regain market confidence. Ideologically and politically, the world today is dominated by Western ideas and values. Most of the accepted "cosmopolitan values" originated in the West, such as human rights and democracy. According to Joseph Nye, despite China's efforts to enhance its soft power, the U.S. remains dominant in all soft power categories. In terms of soft power influence, China is still no match for the U.S. China is gaining soft power, but is still learning how to conduct itself on the world stage and will inevitably make its own mistakes.[58]

## CONCLUSION

Since a rising China poses no threat to the United States and the West, why is the "China threat" theory so popular in Western society? It is in part derived from the psychological impact of exaggerating China's rise. Thomas J Christensen, the Former Deputy Assistant Secretary of state for East Asian and Pacific Affairs, points out that the press has often exaggerated the influence of China's rise.[59] The reality is that the U.S. remains the dominant power in the world. Because the U.S. does not want to become the number two power in the world, the United States has tried to establish a strategic containment system targeting China. A conflict between China and the U.S. is imminent. The well-known People's Liberation Army strategist and General, Peng Guangqian, warns that "a future conflict with the United States is coming as a result of U.S. containment policies."[60] Whether or not China threatens the United States is not determined by China's economic strength, but by other factors, such as China's social instability. A strong China will not threaten the U.S. The collapse of China would inevitably disturb the global peace, especially for developed countries. A rising power will not necessarily threaten the U.S. and the West. The United States in the twentieth century is a good example of a state achieving eminence without conflict with dominant countries.[61] To stabilize and deepen U.S.-China relations, it is critical for both countries to understand each other and develop trust. The following chapter will objectively further discuss the two perspectives on China's rise.

## NOTES

1. Jeffrey A. Bader, John L. Thornton, and Richard C. Bush III, "Confronting the China Challenge," *The Baltimore Sun,* 20 April 2007.

2. Robert D. Kaplan, "How We Would Fight China," *The Atlantic Monthly,* 28 April 2005.

3. Quoted in Ikenberry, "The Rise of China & the Future of the West."

4. Fareed Zakaria, "The Rise of a Fierce Yet Fragile Superpower," *Newsweek,* December 31, 2007-January 7, 2008.

5. Susan L. Shirk, *China Fragile Superpower: How China's Internal Politics Could Derail Its Peaceful Rise* (Oxford: Oxford University Press, 2007), 9.

6. Zheng Bijian, "China's Peaceful Rise, to Great-Power Statues," *Foreign Affairs* (September/October 2005).

7. Robert Novak, "Is China a Threat?" *realclearpolitics.com ,* 27 October 2005.

8. Robert Harmann, "China Rising: Back to the Future," *Asia Times,* 16 March 2007.

9. "China Boosts Spending on Welfare – and on Internal Security, Too," *The Economist,* 10 March 2011 *http://www.economist.com/node/18335099* (30 March 2011).

10. Robert Novak, "Is China a Threat?," *Townhall,* Oct 27, 2005.

11. "China's National Defense in 2010," http://english.gov.cn/official/2011-03/31/content_ 1835499.htm (February 26, 2013)

12. Rober Zoellick, "Whiter China: From Membership to Responsibility?"

13. David M Lampton, "The United States and China: Competitors, Partners, or Both," http://www.comw.org/cmp/fulltext/uspolicy.html (10 February 2008).

14. John S. Gregory, *The West and China since 1500* (Hampshire: Palgrave Macmillan, 2003), 1.

15. See Sara Bongiorni, *A Year Without "Made in China": One Family's True Life Adventure in the Global Economy* (Medford, NJ: Wiley, 2007).

16. Ikenberry, "The Rise of China & the Future of the West."

17. Glenn Kessler, "U.S., China Stand Together but Are Not Equal," *Washington Post,* 20 April 2006.

18. Baker Peter and Gleen Kessler, "Bush, Hu Produce Summit of Symbols Protester Screams At Chinese President," *Washington Post ,* 21 April 2006.

19. John O'Neil, "China's President Ends U.S. Visit With Yale Speech," *New York Times,* 21 April 2006.

20. David M. Lampton, *Same Bed, Different Dreams: Managing U.S.-China Relations* (Berkeley: University of California Press, 2002), p. 59.

21. David Gordon, "Chinese Juggernaut?" *Foreign Policy,* Mar/Apr, 2011.

22. John O'Neil, "China's President Ends U.S. Visit With Yale Speech." *New York Times,* 21 April 2006.

23. C. Fred Bergsten, Bates Gill, Nicholas R. Lardy, and Derek Mitchell. *China, The Balance Sheet: What the World Needs to Know Now About the Emerging Superpower* (New York: Public Affairs, 2006), 4.

24. Robert Zoellick, "Whiter China: From Membership to Responsibility?" *U.S. Department of State,* http://www.state.gov/s/d/rem/53682.htm (3 February 2008).

25. Zoellick, "Whiter China: From Membership to Responsibility?"

26. Ikenberry, "The Rise of China & the Future of the West."

27. Ikenberry, "The Rise of China & the Future of the West."

28. "20-Nation Poll Finds Strong Global Consensus: Support for Free Market System," http://www.globescan.com/news_archives/pipa_market.html ( 2 Feb. 2008).

29. Ikenberry, "The Rise of China & the Future of the West."

30. See Bill Gertz, *The China Threat: How the People's Republic Targets America* (Regnery Publishing, Inc., 2000).

31. "Report To Congress of the U.S.-China Economic and Security Review Commission: One Hundred Eleventh Congress Second Session, November 2010" http://www.uscc.gov/annual_report/2010/annual_report_full_10.pdf (5 February 2011).

32. Adm. James Lyons, "China's Imperialism on Full Display," *Washington Times,* 11 January 2011.

33. Bill Gertz, "China Has Carrier-Killer Missile, U.S. Admiral Says," *Washington Times,* 27 December 2010.

34. Karin Zeitvogel and Agence France-Presse, "Chinese 'Counterspace' Weaponry Worries U.S.", *National Post,* 5 February 2011.

35. Michael Auslin, "Realism on China Is More Realistic," *Wall Street Journal Asia,* 17 January 2011.

36. "A Global Imperative: A Progressive Approach to U.S.-China Relations in the 21st Century," 2008, http://www.americanprogress.org/issues/2008/08/china_report.html (10 January 2010).

37. Michael Elliott, "The Chinese Century," *Time* 169, no. 4 (22 January 22, 2007): 1.

38. Max Boot, "Project for a New Chinese Century," *The Weekly Standard* 11, no. 4 (October 2005).

39. Boot, "Project for a New Chinese Century."

40. Trudy Kuehner, "Understanding China: A History Institute Report," *The Newsletter of RPRI's Marvin Wachman Fund for International Education* 12, no. 1 (March 2007).

41. David Lague, "Chinese Submarine Fleet Is Growing," *New York Times,* 25 February 2008.

42. Aaron Friedberg, "The New Era of U.S.-China Rivalry," *Wall Street Journal,* January 17, 2011.

43. Elizabeth Economy, "The End of the 'Peaceful Rise'?" *Foreign Policy,* Dec 2010.

44. "China Warns U.S. to Stay out of Sea Dispute," *Reuters,* 23 June 2011.

45. John Vasquez and Marie T. Henehan, "Territorial Disputes and the Probability of War, 1816-1992," *Journal of Peace Research* 38, No. 2 (2001): 123-138.

46. Taylor Travel, "Power Shifts and Escalation: Explaining China's Use of Force in Territorial Disputes," *International Security* 32, no. 3 (Winter 2007/08): 44.

47. Ibid.

48. Zhu Tingchang, "Lun Zhongguo mulin zhengce de lilun yu shijian" (On the Theory and Practice of China's Good Neighbour Policy), *Guoji zhengzhi yanjiu (Studies of International Politics),* no. 2 (2001): 45.

49. Chien-peng Chung, "The 'Good Neighbour Policy' in the Context of China's Foreign Relations," *China: An International Journal* 7, no. 1 (March 2009): 109-110.

50. Ibid., 107.

51. Ibid., 109-121

52. Zou Le, "South China Sea mapping underway," *People's Daily*, March 27, 2012.

53. Joseph Nye, Jr., "Think Again: Soft Power," *Foreign Policy,* Feb 23, 2006.

54. Joseph S. Nye, *Soft Power: The Means To Success In World Politics* (New York: Public Affairs, 2008), 12.

55. Stanley Rosen, "Education and Economic Reform," in *The China Handbook*, ed. Christopher Hudson (Chicago: Fitzroy Dearborn Publishers, 1997), 250.

56. Kuehner, "Understanding China: A History Institute Report."

57. Asia Pulse, "Rolling Stones to Rock Shanghai," *Asia Times,* 15 March 2006.

58. Joshua Kurlantzick, *Charm Offensive: How China's Soft Power Is Transforming the World* (Boston, Yale University Press, 2007), 23.

59. Thomas J. Christensen, *"The World Needs an Assertive China,"* *New York Times*, 21 February 2011.

60. Quoted in Miles Yu, "Inside China: PLA says war with U.S. imminent," *Washington Times*, June 27, 2012.

61. Henry A. Kissinger, "Avoiding a U.S.-China Cold War", *Washington Post*, 14 January 2011.

*Chapter Seventeen*

# Finding Common Ground for Chinese and Western Perspectives

China does not threaten the United States, but the conflict between China and the U.S. is real. The U.S. pessimistic view suggests that the relationship between the United States and China is the most tense, just second only to the period of time after the jet flights collision over Hainan Island in 2000. Aaron L Friedberg points out that "Hu Jintao's visit may mark the end of an era of relatively smooth relations between the U.S. and China."[1] The Chinese government insists that the responsibility for the difficulties in China-U.S. relations does not lie with China and it is up to the U.S. to improve relations between the two countries.[2] Ample evidence suggests that the U.S. is preparing for a long cold war with China.[3] Although both optimistic liberals and pessimistic realists in the U.S. have offered constructive opinions on the current status of U.S.-China relations, they have paid less attention to the issues of what caused such a difficult relationship in the first place, and how to improve it. This chapter will examine the main factors that affect U.S.-China relations, analyze the differences between Western and Chinese perspectives concerning China's rise, and explore remedies to improve U.S.-China relations. This chapter will also argue that the conflicts between the two nations are normal while China is rising, because the conflicts are derived from different perspectives on China's rise. The conflicts are real, but they might make the two nations more cautious in dealing with their relationship.

# ANXIETY IN THE UNITED STATES

While China is rising, the voice of American mainstream still does not believe that the U.S. is inevitably declining.[4] Thomas J Christensen, the former
Deputy Assistant Secretary of State for East Asian and Pacific Affairs, points
out that media has "often exaggerated China's rise in influence and the
declining power of the United States."[5] However, some argue that American
people have heard all these stories of American decline before, but this time
it is for real.[6] U.S. debts have reached another record high of $14 trillion and
reached 15 trillion in 2011. Every American shares almost $46,000 debt.[7]
About $4.4 trillion among $14 trillion debts was held by foreign governments that purchased U.S. securities. This reasonably raises a question: who
owns the U.S.?[8]

American people increasingly feel that China is catching up to the U.S.
According to a survey conducted by the Washington-based Pew Research
Center for the People and the Press in 2011, about 47 percent of participants
say China, not the U.S., is the world's top economic power, while 31 percent
of participants continue to name the U.S.. The result of the survey obviously
contradicts the reality, but it reflects that the American people feel anxious
with China's growing power and influence. U.S. officials have admitted that
China's rise is a source of anxiety, as they worry that the U.S. is at risk of
falling behind China in a global battle for influence.[9] Secretary of State
Hillary Clinton has warned that the U.S. is struggling to hold its role as
global leader.[10]

The majority of Americans are not happy that China will become the
largest economy, superseding the United States.[11] Both optimists and pessi-
mists hold mixed feelings about China's rise, viewing China as an economic
competitor and political rival.[12] Thomas Friedman points out that "China is a
threat, China is a customer, and China is an opportunity."[13] Generally, realists believe that the relationship will basically be stable and peaceful,[14] but
pessimistic realists always suggest that "rising states usually want to translate
their power into greater authority in the global system in order to reshape the
existing global order in accordance."[15] They believe that since the start of the
world financial crisis in 2008, China has begun to stand up by taking an
assertive strategy toward to the U.S.[16]

Elizabeth Economy, director for the Asian Studies at Council on Foreign
Relations, notes that the consensus of the Deng era has begun to fray and
Beijing has begun to expand its influence to the rest of the world.[17] In an
ASEAN meeting in 2010, Chinese foreign minister Yang Jiechi told South-
east Asian counterparts that "China is a big country and other countries are
small countries, and that is just a fact."[18] China claims that the South China
Sea is a core interest of the nation and it opposes to any attempt to interna-
tionalize the South China Sea issues. China's assertive approach has stirred

anxiety across Asia.[19] As a result, some of China's neighboring countries, such as India, Indonesia, Japan, and Vietnam, are working more closely with the U.S. as a balance to the expansion of China's influence. John Lee, a foreign policy specialist, warns that China is losing friends worldwide and it may be the loneliest rising power in recent history.[20] The U.S. claims that the U.S. still has a vital role in helping to manage this changing balance of power in Asia.[21] The majority of Asian countries welcome the presence of the U.S. Seventh Fleet in Asia.[22] The U.S. remains the most powerful country in the world, and China does not have the political, military and economic power to challenge the U.S. regardless of its intentions. The U.S. must be confident of its leading position in the international society in order to appropriately manage China's rise in the twenty-first century.

## TWO PERSPECTIVES ON CHINA'S RISE

Conflicts between the U.S. and China are real, but they will not necessarily turn into a war. Instead, the conflicts will remind both sides that they should carefully examine the direct source of the conflicts—different perspectives— in order to find a common ground to peacefully co-exist. Most scholars agree that the conflict between the two countries mainly includes their economic competition, army race, and political incompatibility.

First, the intensive economic competition may constitute one of the biggest barriers to the bilateral relations. China is the fastest growing economy in the world with an average growth rate of 9 percent a year over the past three decades, about five times faster than the U.S. While some American analysts believe that a healthy Chinese economy is vital to the U.S., others argue that China's growing economic power will threaten U.S. hegemony due to various reasons. They are concerned about the U.S. trade deficit with China continues. China holds almost $1 trillion in U.S. government bonds, but it lags far behind other Asian and European countries in direct investment in the U.S. While Chinese companies invested only $791 million in U.S. companies in 2009, South Korean companies invested $12 billion, Japanese firms $264.2 billion, German firms $218 billion, and British companies $453 billion.[23]

China's GDP is still less than (or around) the half of the U.S. economy, but "China surpassed the U.S. to become the world's biggest trading nation last year as measured by the sum of exports and imports of goods, official figures from both countries show. U.S. exports and imports of goods last year totaled $3.82 trillion. China's customs administration reported last month that the country's trade in goods in 2012 amounted to $3.87 trillion."[24] Some American experts suggest that the trade imbalance stems in part from under-valued Chinese currency. The U.S. accuses China of artificially lowering the cost of the goods it exports to attract foreign companies to locate their production in China. The U.S. believes that it hurts American exports and damages the financial recovery around the world. Although the U.S. Treasury refrained in February 2011 from labeling China a currency manipulator, it warned that the *yuan* is still substantially undervalued, and thus, "more rapid progress is needed."[25] The Chinese government holds a different point of view that it is the U.S., not China, that aims to manipulate currency policy. The U.S. allowed the dollar to fall 23 percent from its early 2002 peak against all of trading partners. By contrast, in 2010 China's central bank issued a statement pledging to increase currency flexibility. China already let its currency rise against the U.S. dollar from 8.27 *yuan* for every dollar to 6.23 *yuan* by February 2013.

Second, while China is rising, the military dimension becomes more important to U.S.-China relations. There is a growing debate in the United States on the future of Chinese military development, concerned with China's military capabilities and intentions.[26] China's military development has drawn concerns from the U.S. and also alarmed many of its Asia-Pacific neighbors, who fear the consequences of a strong Chinese military. In December 2010, U.S Defense Secretary Robert Gates visited China and concluded that China's military development will challenge U.S. military power in Asia and may challenge the capability of the U.S. military operations worldwide. An American military officer suggests that Chinese military ambition shows that "China's imperialism is on full display."[27]

From a Chinese perspective, as major powers rise economically, military modernization usually follows. It is necessary for China to modernize its military force, because Chinese military lags far behind the U.S. and the European countries. It is not China, but the U.S., that has the largest defense budget in the world, accounting for 47 percent of the world's total military spending. There are about 154 countries with U.S. troops and 63 countries with U.S. military bases and troops.[28] The Chinese Defense Minister Liang Guanglie told Robert Gates that China is not an advanced military country. Moreover, neither the U.S. nor China is able to dominate each other. A military clash between them would exhaust both countries.[29] Chinese Vice-Foreign Minister, Cui Tiankai, has made similar comments: "I don't think anyone in the Asia-Pacific region has the ability of encircling China, and I do not think that many countries in the Asian-Pacific would become part of that circle. China and the U.S. don't have any other choice but to work together."

Third, a country's foreign policy is the extension of its internal political system; and political differences between the two countries fundamentally affect U.S.-China relations. The nature of China's foreign policy toward the West is not rooted in the growing economic power of China, but is fundamentally driven by the nature of the Chinese political system. As discussed in previous chapters, China's rapid economic growth has generated changes in all social aspects, but it continues to carry out the communist political system. Although China is no longer a typical Leninist state, it remains unchanged in its political nature.[30] Gabriella Montinola observes that "nearly all of the formal aspects of democracy are absent, notably, individual rights of free speech and political participation, a viable system of competition for political office, and a set of constitutional limits on the state."[31]

Americans view the Chinese political system as directly countering the core values of the West, and they see no fundamental way for the two countries to co-exist because Americans do not trust a communist system that denies basic freedoms to its own people.[32] For example, many Westerners do not agree that in 2010 the Chinese government negatively responded to Nobel Peace Prize Committee's decision to honor Chinese political dissident Liu Xiaobo. Liu was put in jail after the crackdown of Tiananmen Square Incident and was released in early 1991, but the Chinese government arrested him again after Liu wrote the *Charter 08*, which called for modern democracy and an end to the Communist Party's political dominance.[33] The Chinese government believes that the Nobel Peace Prize Committee's decision was an attempt to deny the legitimate Chinese judicial judgment and undermine the Chinese political system.[34] The Chinese government defied the Nobel Peace Prize decision by continuing to jail Liu and forbidding any members of his family to attend the Nobel ceremonies in Oslo. During the ceremony, the president of the Nobel Committee placed Liu's Nobel diploma and medal on an empty chair where Liu was supposed to be sitting. One commentator notes that "there could be no clearer evidence of the fundamental differences between China's political system and America's than the empty chair that represented Liu on the Nobel stage."[35]

However, the Chinese government has insisted that China's development must come with "socialism with Chinese characteristics," the so-called "China model" or "Beijing Consensus." Chinese official media has persistently argued that it is wrong for the West to impose its ways on other cultures. It means that China may reform its political system within the current political system, but China's road toward democratization might be different from the normal pattern of Western societies. John and Doris Naisbitts believe China has a different type of democracy than Western nations, which deters an overly quick rush to judgment of China using Western values.[36] Gordon White notes that "many of the current proposals for rapid and radical democratization are fraught with wishful thinking, and many of the assertions about the punitive complementarities between democracy and socio-economic progress are simplistic and misleading."[37] Most likely, the CPC will continue to postpone fundamental political reform, and the political and ideological conflicts between the two nations will be inevitable.

Practically, Western political leaders often take realistic approaches and push aside political disagreements in favor of maintaining the crucial economic relationship, because many Westerners see the economic ties between the two nations as a means of binding them together. Idealists define Chinese president Hu Jintao's state visit to the United States as a "trade mission."[38] The agenda of the 2010 summit indicates that China's political issue is not Washington's top concern. During the joint press conference, President Obama emphasized the different historical tradition and cultural system, which sounds to defend Chinese political system. The Obama administration took a soft attitude toward China's political issue instead of angering the Chinese government.

As a matter of fact, non-democratic China can peacefully co-exist with the U.S. A democratic government does not necessarily make peace with other democratic ones. For example, there are many conflicts between the U.S. and other democracies. On the other hand, a democracy could cooperate with a non-democracy, like relationship between the U.S. and Saudi Arabia. There is no reason why the U.S. could not co-exist with China, even though for the time being it is non-democratic country. To be sure, different nations have different national interests; and every nation puts its national interests as a top priority. Conflicts of interest between different nations are very normal. Benign economic and cultural competition between different nations is healthy.

China and Western societies need to work closely together in order to maintain global peace. China has worked with Western governments and hosted the six party talks.[39] China took tough actions against Iran's nuclear program, showing the seriousness of its commitment to non-proliferation. The U.S. and China share many common interests of a broad range, including the fields of energy, environment, nuclear proliferation, human rights, anti-corruption, social welfare, the role of nongovernmental organizations, AIDS, avian flu epidemics, global warming, UN reform, and the fields of counterterrorism. In the past three decades, the U.S. and China have achieved progress in cooperation in economic, trade, and other fields, including military cooperation in three areas: exchange of antiterrorism information, prevention of nuclear proliferation, and the hosting of six-party talks on the North Korea nuclear program. At present, the Afghanistan war is not yet over, al-Qaida terrorism remains active, and the issue of nuclear proliferation is still in the air. China and the United States have recently signed an agreement to open a military hot line between their defense departments. This is a good sign, indicating the cooperation of the two countries in a broad range.

## BUILDING MUTUAL TRUST AND UNDERSTANDING

Although the U.S. and China hold different perspectives on China's rise, the two nations are interdependent during the age of globalization. Neither side wants to be dependent on the other, but neither side can afford a split.[40] If the two governments do not compromise their different perspectives, a cold war between the two nations is possible, but it would inevitably damage the interests of the both countries. When Henry Kissinger was interviewed by Fareed Zakaria from CNN in June 2011, he made it clear that another Cold War is not the answer.[41] Henry Kissinger in his book *On China* suggests that the best outcome in the American debate would be to combine the two approaches: for the idealists to recognize that principles need to be implemented over time and hence must be occasionally adjusted to circumstance; and for the realists to accept that values have their own reality and must be built into operational policies. This recommendation can also be applied to China.

The U.S. and China should find a realistic way to prevent bilateral relations from getting worse. Both sides should accept the other's differences. The Chinese government does not want to see the West apply universal values to China, nor Western support of Tibetan and Taiwanese independent movement, nor the sale of weapons to Taiwan. By contrast, the U.S. demands some change in China, including reforming the Chinese political system, increasing Chinese individual and religious freedoms, improving market economy to ensure equal competition, expanding citizen participation, and making military development transparent. Obviously, there is an "increasing unwillingness of Washington and Beijing to understand each other's viewpoints."[42] This suggests that both sides need to patiently and gradually narrow the gap between the two perspectives. In the political area, China's political reform is necessary, but it cannot completely change the system overnight. Although it is proper to criticize China for its human rights violations, the U.S. should not ignore the substantial progress China has made since 1978.[43] In the economic area, protectionism would harm both nations, but active engagement is the best way to minimize the conflicts. In the military area, although the U.S. has reasons to take China's recent military development cautiously, Chinese military force remains a decade behind the United States.[44] China is not an existential challenge to the United States.[45] If the U.S. keeps its confidence, it will be able to manage all challenges from China's rise.

It should be noted that the mistrustful feelings and negative images continue to grow in both countries. The U.S. viewed the Soviet Union and China as their chief enemies during the Cold War. The anti-China strategy of the United States was aimed at strangling China's socialism.[46] Even today, Americans always ask: Do the Chinese like us? Are we friends? Can we be friends with them?[47] Quite a few American scholars believe that a war between China and the United States is likely.[48] The negative image of Chinese people and China come from various sources, such as cultural differences and miscommunication. Old perceptions also contribute to the negative image of the Chinese people. For example, poor, uneducated Chinese workers who came to work in gold mines and build railroads in the western United States offered another source of biased thinking. Hollywood films, of course, produced a great deal of fantasy about China, in which Chinese women are depicted as seductive courtesans or fearsome dragon ladies, while Chinese men are depicted as always smoking opium. The images of old China town and Chinese orphans created a stereotype image of China.

China used to portray the U.S. as a kind of enemy, because the U.S. was giving open support to hostile forces inside China before the reform movement. At present, China has two basic viewpoints toward the United Sates: one sees the United States not just as a strategic partner, but an economic and technological helpmate, while the other sees the United States as both a moral and cultural danger to China and as the ultimate obstacle to its national ambitions.[49] America's image in China has changed from time to time. The image of the U.S became worse during the first term of the George Bush administration, with favorability ratings dropping as low as 39.6 percent in 2003. In the beginning of the Obama administration between 2008 and 2009, Chinese youth began to show a higher favorability rating of the United States with the figure peaking in 2008 at 75.6 percent, because during this period there were no political incidents that could strain that bilateral relationship. Also during this time, the U.S. did not exert further political pressure on China concerning human rights issues resulting from the Tibet and Xinjiang incidents, so Chinese youth viewed President Obama positively. According to the most recent survey on U.S.-China relations, the basic Chinese public perception is that American and Chinese people stand somewhere between friendship and enmity. They believe the United State has become more diversified and viewed global political power, but arrogant, performing as the world police. The current Chinese impression of the U.S. has become more related to politics. For example, the two new categories of arrogance and world police in the 2009 survey may reflect the Chinese public's view of itself as a rising power.

China's public media sometimes still shows its discomfort with the U.S. global predominance and hopes that the government will show its strong side and stand up to the United States. It is not easy for the Chinese government to balance national interests and the public opinion. In order to avoid a disastrous war between China and the U.S., it is a very important task to build up a relationship of trust between the two countries. According to the survey, conducted by the Chicago Council on Global Affairs and the Asia Society in 2006, the Chinese people understand the U.S. more than American people understand the Chinese. Chinese people trust the U.S. more than American people trust China.[50] In the U.S., "Congressional staffers hold a much lower opinion of China than the other samples. The general public with a higher income are more likely to hold a negative opinion of China than those in the lower income bracket. Caucasian Americans are also more likely to hold an unfavorable opinion than Hispanic and African Americans."[51] Thus, the U.S. should make efforts to understand China's historical social and political transformation and its significant consequences.

Mutual understanding is critical to narrowing the gap between the two perspectives. At the present time, the "mistrust of Beijing throughout Asia and in Washington is palpable."[52] It is widely believed that most Americans not only distrust, but also despise China.[53] During the U.S.'s mid-term election in 2010, many candidates played the China card, running advisements on U.S. televisions against China. Similarly, Beijing does not share many of the same interests as the United States and its allies.[54] A significant number of Chinese people believe that the U.S. has been trying to block China's rise.

Mutual understanding is at least partially based on a common value system. The U.S. remains the leader of the existing global order and the value of democracy continues to be the mainstream of the existing global order. The core values of modern democracy, which includes individual rights, justice, equality and common good, are the cornerstone of Western societies that guide their governments in making foreign policy. Thus, Chinese political liberalization is essential to building mutual trust. China is well positioned to keep growing for years to come. The question is where China is going. Is China departing away from the West? Or, is China heading toward the West? Although nobody knows where China is headed,[55] it is evident that China's growing economic power does not automatically translate into political power and international authority. It is hard to believe that China could become an internationally recognized world leader without accepting universal values. In order to make peace with the existing global order, China needs to make well-balanced development between economic growth and political liberalization through domestic political reform. If China becomes democratic, its relationship with U.S. will stabilize and, ultimately, "it will enter into the democratic zone of peace."[56]

The Chinese cultural and historical tradition will affect the process of China's democratization, so it is important to begin with an appreciation of China's long history in order to understand China's future world role.[57] China was humiliated by the West for a century, so nationalism in China is very strong. Chinese State Councilor, Dai Bingguo, at the Joint Press Conference of the Second Round of the China-U.S. Strategic and Economic Dialogues in 2010 explained that "China's number one core interest is to maintain its fundamental system and state security; next is state sovereignty and territorial integrity; and third is the continued stable development of the economy and society."[58] Theoretically, it is most important for the CPC to maintain its communist political system; practically, territorial integrity is the essential issue among China's core interests, especially the territorial integrity of Taiwan with China. If the U.S. makes a wrong policy on the Taiwan issue, it could hurt the feelings of the majority of the Chinese people and trigger anti-American nationalism. Charles Glaser, director of the Institute for Security and Conflict Studies at George Washington University, recently suggested that the U.S. should modify its foreign policy and make concessions to Beijing, including the possibility of backing away from its commitment to Taiwan in order to avoid a war between the U.S. and China.[59]

For the long term, cultural exchange is the key to building mutual trust and understanding between the two countries. Nevertheless, China's three decades of economic development represent a single-minded pursuit of economic growth. To reduce the distrust between China and the U.S., China should renovate its culture by introducing universal values and advanced world cultures into China, but it is uncertain if the CPC is willing to open up its political domains to facilitate the emergence of a modernized culture.[60] The CPC's recent attempt at reviving Confucianism does not only indicate that the CPC has exhausted its cultural resources, but also implies that the reinvention of Chinese cultural tradition has become desperately urgent.

International relations are directed by countries' governments; the top leaders of both countries are significantly important in making U.S.-China foreign policy. The American president's decision is determined, not only by its domestic economic situation, but also by influences from Congress and public opinion. In this sense, the American president plays a lesser role in making foreign policy. Since the charismatic leader Chairman Mao died in 1976, the power of the CPC has been decentralized. Although China's policymaking process has become pluralized, the top leader of the CPC still plays a critical role in making foreign policy due to the nature of communist political system. The political orientation of other top Chinese leaders and the leaders of the Foreign Ministry also contribute to foreign policy making. In order to avoid unnecessary mistakes in the foreign policy making process, both countries' leaders need to be open-minded and carefully listen to the voices coming from think tanks and common citizens.

## CONCLUSION

China's economic and military power is growing, but China's international influence is still constrained by the stagnation of its political system, cultural deficit, and the low level of comprehensive economic and military power. The United States remains the dominant power in the world. The exaggeration of China's power is in part derived from psychological impact and media exaggeration. The United States should remain confident and accept challenges from the rising power. Different perspectives could generate healthy competition, in which people can learn how to live with others during the age of globalization. The disagreements between the two giants will continue. The CPC will maintain the basic attributes of a communist political system. Market economic competition continues to be driven by making profits. Both sides will keep defending their national interests through developing their military muscles. Nobody can stop all these disagreements, but there is no reason to fear different perspectives, if both sides treat each other carefully. Overestimating China's economic and military power will create anxiety; overacting to China's rise would worsen bilateral relations. The most important thing for both sides to do is to understand that political isolation, economic protectionism and military confrontation are not the solution. Realistically, building mutual trust and understanding through cultural exchange programs and positive engagement is the best way to reduce the risk of a great power war.

## NOTES

1. Aaron Friedberg, "The New Era of U.S.-China Rivalry," *Wall Street Journal*, 17 January 2011.

2. "Quotes of the Day," *Time*, 8 March 2011.

3. Stephen Glain, "Washington Is Preparing a Long War with China," *U.S. News*, 31 March 2011.

4. Bret Stephens, "China and the Next American Century: Beijing's Politburo Has Nothing on Mark Zuckerberg," *Wall Street Journal*, 21 December 2010.

5. Thomas J Christensen, "The World Needs an Assertive China," *Foreign Affairs*, 21 February 2011.

6. Gideon Rachman, "Think Again, American Decline: This Time Is for Real," *Foreign Policy*, 18, January 2011.

7. "International Focus on the United States Break the 'Debt Ceiling' Difficult," Finance Online.   http://www.finance-ol.com/2011/06/international-focus-on-the-united-states-break-the-debt-ceiling-difficult/ (25 June 2011).

8. Greg Bocquet, "Who Owns the U.S.?" http://finance.yahoo.com/banking-budgeting/article/112189/who-owns-the-us?mod=bb-debtmanagement (28 February 2011).

9. Elaine Shannon, "China Rising: Small World, Big Stakes," *Time*, 20 June 2005.

10. Daniel Dombey, "US Struggling to Hold Role as Global Leader," *Politics and Foreign Policy*, 6 March 2011.

11. Benjamin I. Page and Tao Xie, *Living with the Dragon: How the American Public Views the Rise of China* (New York: Columbia University Press, 2010).

12. James Mann, *The China Fantasy: How Our Leaders Explain Away Chinese Repression* (New York: Viking Penguin, 2007), xii.

13. Thomas L Friedman, *The World is Flat: A Brief History of the Twenty-first Century* (New York: Picador/Farrar, Straus and Girousx, 2007), 82.

14. Aaron Friedberg, "The Future of U.S.-China Relations Is Conflict Inevitable?," *International Security*, Vol. 30, Number 2 (Fall, 2005), 10.

15. Fareed Zakaria, "The Rise of a Fierce Yet Fragile Superpower," *Newsweek*, 7 January 2008.

16. Aaron Friedberg, "The New Era of U.S.-China Rivalry," *Wall Street Journal*, 17 January 2011.

17. Elizabeth Economy, "The End of the 'Peaceful Rise," *Foreign Policy*, December 2010.

18. John Lee, "China's National Insecurity," *Wall Street Journal Asia*, 21 December 2010.

19. Friedberg, "The New Era of U.S.-China Rivalry," 17 January 2011.

20. John Lee, "The End of the Charm Offensive," *Foreign Policy*, 26 October 2010.

21. Fareed Zakaria, "The Dangerous Chip on China's Shoulder," *Time*, 12 January 2011.

22. John Lee, "The End of the Charm Offensive," *Foreign Policy*, 26 October 2010.

23. Kevin Hall, "Think China Has Big Stake in U.S. Business? Not Yet," *Miami Herald*, 18 January 2011.

24. "China Eclipses U.S. as Biggest Trading Nation," Bloomberg, February 10, 2013. http://www.bloomberg.com/news/2013-02-09/china-passes-u-s-to-become-the-world-s-biggest-trading-nation.html ( February 14, 2013)

25. Ian Talley and Tom Barkley, "Treasury Slightly Steps Up Criticism on Yuan's Level," *Wall Street Journal*, 5 February 2011.

26. James R. Lilley and David Shambaugh (eds), *China's Military Faces the Future* (New York: M.E. Sharpe, 1999), 3.

27. Adm. James Lyons, "China's Imperialism On Full Display," *Washington Times*, 11 January 2011.

28. "U.S. Military Troops and Bases around the World," Department of Defense, "Base Structure Report, FY 2002" and "Active Duty Military Personnel Strengths by Regional Area and by Country, December 31, 2001," Zoltan Crossman, "New U.S. Military Bases," 2 February 2002, *Monthly Review*, 2002.

29. Henry A. Kissinger, "Avoiding a U.S.-China Cold War," *Washington Post*, 14 January 2011.

30. Richard Bernstein and Ross Munro, *The Coming Conflict with China* (New York: Alfred A. Knopf, 1997), 15.

31. Gabriella Montinola, "Federalism, Chinese Style: The Political Basis for Economic Success in China," *World Politics*, 48 (1995), 52.

32. Warren Cohen, *America's Response to China: A History of Sino-American Relations* (New York: Columbia University Press, 2010), 287.

33. Cara Anna, "Contender for Nobel Prize in Chinese Prison," *The IRRawddy*, 7 October 2010.

34. John Lee, "China's National Insecurity," *Wall Street Journal Asia*, 21 December 2010.

35. Michael Auslin, "Realism on China Is More Realistic," *Wall Street Journal Asia* , 17 January 2011.

36. John and Doris Naisbitt, *China's Megatrends: The 8 Pillars of a New Society* (Harper Business, 2010).

37. Gordon White, "Democratization and Economic Reform in China," *Australian Journal of Chinese Affairs* , 31 (1994), 82.

38. Ian Johnson, "For China, Relief after a Successful Trip," *New York Times*, 21 January 2011.

39. Laura MacInnis, "N. Korea agrees to disable Nuclear Program in 2007," *Reuters*, 2 September 2007.

40. Zachary Karabell, "U.S.-China Friction: Why Neither Side Can Afford a Split," *Time*, 8 February 2010.

41. CNN Wire Staff, "Kissinger: China Poses 'Big Challenge' for U.S.," *CNN.com*, 12 June 2011. http://edition.cnn.com/2011/POLITICS/06/12/kissinger.china/

42. Rana Mitter, "Henry Kissinger Offers an Erudite and Elegant Insight into the New World Superpower," *Guardian*, 5 May 2011.

43. James A. Dorn, "How to Improve U.S.-China Relations in the Wake of CNOOC," *The Korean Journal of Defense Analysis*, Vol. 17, No. 3 (Winter 2005), 63.

44. Stefan Halper, "The China Threat, Can the United States Really Make a Peaceful Hand-off of Power to Authoritarian China?" (letter), *Foreign Policy*, March/April 2011.

45. Joseph S. Nye, Jr., reply to Stefan Halper's letter "The China Threat: Can the United States Really Make a Peaceful Hand-off of Power to Authoritarian China?" (letter), *Foreign Policy*, March/April 2011.

46. Richard Bernstein and Ross H. Munro, *The Coming Conflict with China* (New York: Vintage, 1998).

47. James Kynce, "Can We Be Friends," in *China Shakes the World* (New York: Houghton Mifflin Company, 2006), 236.

48. Richard Bernstein and Ross H. Munro, *The Coming Conflict with China* (New York: Vintage, 1998).

49. Ibid.

50. Jim Lobe, "Greater China: Two Countries, One Survey," *Asia Times,* 12 December 2007.

51. Committee of 100, "2007 Survey: Hope & Fear: American and Chinese Attitudes toward Each Other, Parallel Survey on Issues Concerning U.S.-China Relations." http://www.survey.committee100.org/2007/files/C100SurveyFullReport.pdf (Accessed in 4 August 2008).

52. Thomas J Christensen, "The World Needs an Assertive China," *Foreign Affairs*, 21 February 2011.

53. Benjamin I. Page and Tao Xie, *Living with the Dragon: How the American Public Views the Rise of China* (New York: Columbia University Press, 2010), 74.

54. Michael Auslin, "Realism on China Is More Realistic," *Wall Street Journal Asia* , 17 January 2011.

55. Elizabeth Economy, "The End of the 'Peaceful Rise.'"

56. Aaron L Friedberg, "The Future of U.S.-China Relations: Is Conflict Inevitable?," International Security, 30.2 (2005), 16.

57. Henry Kissinger, *On China* (The Penguin Press, 2011).

58. "Remarks by State Councilor Dai Bingguo at Joint Press Conference of the Second Round of The China-U.S. Strategic and Economic Dialogues," Ministry of Foreign Affairs of the People's Republic of China http://www.fmprc.gov.cn/eng/wjdt/zyjh/t705280.htm (10 January 2011).

59. Charles Glaser, "Will China's Rise Lead to War? Why Realism Does Not Mean Pessimism," *Foreign Affairs*, March/April 2011.

60. Zhao Litao and Tan Soon Heng, "China's Cultural Rise: Visions and Challenges," 103.

## Chapter Eighteen

# The Future of China: Undemocratic China Can't Rule the World

Since the CPC launched the reform movement in 1978, China has shifted from Mao Zedong's revolutionary model of development to an economy centered strategy. The China model worked in the past three decades and achieved remarkable economic success. As a result, the concepts of G2 (or Chimerica) have emerged, although the Chinese government made it clear during President Obama's state visit to China in 2009 that it disagreed with the G2 concept. The Chinese government has firmly upheld and will continue to follow the China model and believed that the model will continue to work for China and other countries as well. In contrast, while acknowledging China's economic success in the past, the mainstream of Western academia views the China model as "the Beijing consensus," as opposed to "the Washington consensus," which emphasizes free markets and private enterprise. [1] They also wonder if the China model will sustain the development of the Chinese economy and help China to become a superpower. Not so long ago, Yan Xuetong addressed the issue of "how China can defeat America" in the *New York Times*, pointing out that China must share global responsibilities and develop more high-quality diplomatic relationships. According to Yan, "the key to international influence was political power." [2] This chapter will examine the model of Chinese development in the past three decades, discuss the advantages and shortcomings of the Chinese development model, explore various possibilities for China's future, and conclude that China will not be able to become a superpower without democratization.

# RE-GAINING LEGITIMACY THROUGH ECONOMIC GROWTH

China used to be the most developed country in the world, but it gradually lost its leading position after the seventeenth century and was humiliated by Western powers for a century. The Revolution of 1911 overthrew the Qing Dynasty, but the Republic of China seldom exercised its sovereign rights to develop its domestic economy. The Chinese economy neither grew in size nor altered in structure to any significant degree under the nationalist government.[3] Mao Zedong profoundly transformed the ownership system, the class structure, and the political culture, but his revolutionary policy brought China to the verge of economic bankruptcy.[4] After Mao died in 1976, the top priority of the CPC was to improve the living standard of the Chinese people during the transition. If the CPC failed this historical task, it could not justify its legitimacy of governance. Deng Xiaoping took this historical opportunity and introduced the China model.[5] As a result, in the past three decades, China has been the fastest growing economy in the world and has become the world's second largest economy.[6]

How has China achieved such remarkable economic success in the past three decades? While leading American scholars believe that five key factors underlie China's stunning growth performance over the past three decades,[7] the Chinese government has been developing its own theory of economic growth to influence non-democratic states,[8] so-called "socialism with Chinese characteristics," categorized by scholars around the world as "China Model" or "Beijing Consensus" to describe the development of China over the past 30 years, which is a mix of authoritarianism and socialist market economy with the unique qualities of China's culture, geography and governing philosophies.[9] Weiwei Zhang, former Deng Xiaoping's interpreter and senior fellow in the Centre for Asian Studies at University of Geneva, in his book *China Shock: A Civilized Nation to Rise*, claims that the China model shocked the world in three ways: the shock of the rise of peaceful development, the shock of the rise of the development model and the shock of the rise of political values. In April 2011, *China Daily*, CPC's mouthpiece, published three articles that highly praised Zhang's book, reflecting the positive attitude of the CPC toward the theory of the China model.

Wei Pan, director of Peking University's Center for Chinese & Global Affairs, puts it in this way: "The China model consists of four sub-systems: a unique way of social organization, a unique way of developing its economy, a unique way of government, and a unique outlook on the world."[10] However, in present-day China, all Chinese social organizations are controlled by the CPC, the Chinese market economy is managed by the Chinese government, all Chinese governments are ruled by the CPC, and the official Chinese outlook of the world is Marxism, represented by the thoughts of Deng Xiaoping, Jiang Zemin and Hu Jintao. In this sense, the China model is the path of

China's development guided by the CPC. Yang Jisheng points out that the China model includes five elements: praising the current Chinese political system, affirming China's achievements in the past 30 years, advocating centralized authoritarian government, rejecting modern democracy and denying universal values, and finally, promoting neo-Confucianism through defending the CPC.[11] Apparently, the spirit of the China model is that the CPC continues to carry out socialism with Chinese characteristics, control the market system, implement limited privatization, and exclude the separation of three powers.

Rowan Callick characterizes the China model as economic freedom, plus political repression.[12] This implies that the Chinese government has developed its economy without the coordination of a democratic system for thirty years. Yet, the core of "socialism with Chinese characteristics" is the "Four Cardinal Principles" set by Deng Xiaoping — adhering to the socialist road, the dictatorship of the proletariat, Marxism-Leninism and Mao Zedong Thought, and CPC leadership, which enabled Deng to launch the reform and go through the social and economic transition. Although in the post-Deng era, the CPC has emphasized the theories of the Jiang Zemin's "three represents" and Hu Jintao's "harmonious society," practically, it continues to uphold the Four Principles. Thus, it can be said that the core of the China model is fundamentally the current Chinese political system; the China model is a theorization of the path of China's development directed by the CPC. Chen Jinhua, former vice chairman of the national committee of the Chinese People's Political Consultative Conference (CPPCC), in her article "China Model and China's System" published by the *People's Daily* on July 5, 2011, criticizes that the media ignores the key issue of the China model in their discussions and points out that the key of the China model is China's current fundamental system.

The China model emerged in a specific historical context from the transition of the Mao regime to the post-Mao era. According to the Chinese official media, the development models of Latin America and Asia have obvious shortcomings, and the Washington Consensus does not show its effectiveness, but produces some problems. That is why China has to take its own path to develop its economy and political system. The China model has demonstrated its great strengths, especially during the Asia financial crisis in 1998 and the recent world financial crisis. As a result, the theory of the collapse of China, represented by Gordon Chang, who predicted ten years ago that China would collapse (*The Coming Collapse of China*), has collapsed itself no matter how Gordon Chang has attempted to defend his major argument recently. Because the China model produces some positive impact on the global economy, some American scholars suggest that Chinese development takes a different path from the Western societies, so the China model will eventually reverse the one-way flow of Westernization.

Has China created a better development model than the West? In comparison with other political systems, modern democracy is the best social and political system in the world; it may constitute the "final form of human government" and the "end of history."[13] Although Chinese official ideology views Fukuyama's model of social development as a Western model, there is not any other social and political system available in human history that is better than modern democracy. The China model has worked because it embraces both universal norms and unique Chinese characteristics. Chinese economic growth has basically benefited from the "reform and opening up" policy, which essentially grants the Chinese people the individual rights to develop economy. The success of China's economic development has demonstrated that universal norms, including globalization, marketization and privatization, are the right direction for China. Thus, other countries may learn from the China model but they can never copy it, simply because "Chinese characteristics" are not universal.

## WILL THE CHINA MODEL SUSTAIN CHINA'S FUTURE?

The China model might work for China temporarily, but will not work for the world.[14] It is uncertain if the China model sustains China's future and helps China to become a superpower. By definition, a world superpower is a country with a dominant position in the international system and is able to have influence anywhere in the world. In addition to population size and a strategic geographic location, a world superpower should possess four attributes, a large diversified national economy, major conventional military force, sophisticated nuclear weapon capability, and advanced political influence.[15] These characteristics are inseparable. The Chinese economy will most likely continue to grow in the years to come. If the Chinese economy continues to develop at such large growth rates, China will emerge as an economic power and challenge America's leading position.[16] *The Economist* recently predicted that China will overtake the United States as the world's largest economy within the next ten years.[17] However, this prediction is a mathematical formula and does not take social factors into consideration. The most critical question here is how long Chinese economic freedom and political repression can continue to coexist in China.[18] The CPC "has remained surprisingly resilient,"[19] but, since the reform opened up, the development of the Chinese economy has heavily relied on trade, foreign investment, domestic savings, and now the property market. To be sure, the resilience of the authoritarian regime without political and cultural support will be out of source.

Although the national economy is the basic criterion among all characteristics of a world superpower, soft power is a more important aspect for being a superpower in contemporary society. An economic giant would not automatically become a world leader without the coordination of enhanced soft power. Most existing literatures adopt a micro-analytical approach by emphasizing China's domestic problems, which hinder China's further development. As early as 1997, economist Penelope B. Prime wrote an article *"China's Economic progress: Is It Sustainable?"* in which she discussed the issue of how China's problems hindered the development of Chinese economy.[20] A decade after Prime's predication, China's domestic problems have become more severe, so many scholars continue to address China's economic and social problems which might affect the path of China's development.[21] James Mann, in his book *The China Fantasy,* systematically discusses eight of China's internal problems.[22] James Kynge also observes many problems, such as a shortage of arable land, serious environmental devastation and pollution, systemic corruption and of resources, and points out that China will have to manage all these problems with partners on the economic and geopolitical playing fields.[23] The micro-analytical approach suggests that China will not be able to sustain its dynamic economic growth, if the government could not appropriately handle all the problems. However, this approach gives little attention to the deficiency of the official philosophy behind the China model.

First, the center of the China model is the slogan of four modernizations—modernization of industry, agriculture, national defense, and science and technology. In 1964, Premier Zhou Enlai formally proposed to the whole nation a magnificent program for modernizing these four, but under Mao's regime the economy-centered model of socialist construction was viewed as a rightist line. In 1978, the Four Modernizations were officially re-proclaimed. However, each of the four modernizations relates to economics, not politics. Economic wealth does not automatically bring a society to democratization. Without the coordination of political reform, the Four Modernizations alone cannot sustain Chinese economy and maintain social stability.

Second, the principle of the China model is Deng Xiaoping's pragmatic theory. Chinese economy was guided by Marxist economics during the Mao era. When Deng came to power, China's economic situation was at its worst period of time during the communist regime. In order to keep the socialist system running, the important aspect of a theory was not whether it conformed to Marxism, but whether it worked. That is why Deng sets forth his pragmatic theory, such as "let some people get rich first," "cross the river by groping the stones on the riverbed," and "a cat that catches mice is a good one whether it is black or white." Deng's pragmatism generated Chinese people's enthusiasm devoted to economic activity in the beginning of the reform movement, but China could not maintain its economic growth by relying on his pragmatic ideas alone. Deng died ten years ago, but his theory has remained at the center of the China model.

Third, the theory of gradual reform could be an excuse for the CPC to reject political reform. China has taken a gradual reform approach, which is a less-than-radical departure from the socialist system. One of the reasons for the reform's success is that China allows only a partial reform and leaves the most difficult reform task—political reform—for an uncertain future. However, the government exaggerates the extent to which its gradual approach achieved the positive effects of the big bang approach, but avoided its costs.[24] If the gradual approach continues, it must be understood that a reform movement develops step by step, from economic reform to political reform and democratization. Otherwise, gradual reform will become an obstacle to Chinese democratization, in order for China to develop its economy smoothly.

Fourth, the China model only implements partial open-door policy. Under the Mao regime, the government carried out a closed-door policy. Since 1978, China has reopened its doors to the rest of the world. The practice of an open-door policy has significantly contributed to Chinese economic growth. As Western technology, sciences, and capitals flow into China, Western cultural and political values have increasingly influenced Chinese society. The government clearly sees the potential threat to the regime, so it tightly monitors the influences of Western culture and politics, and blocks some politically sensitive information. Thus, China's door, in fact, is not fully opened. This partial open-door policy is an invisible force postponing the process of China's democratization.

In sum, the official Chinese philosophy of the China model is an economy-centered approach. It is time for the CPC to think of how to maintain the China model as the main driving force for China's development toward an internationally recognized world leader. To accomplish this more important transition, the CPC is required to reshape the foundation of the China model to make it as a four-wheel drive: a real combination of industrialization, urbanization, marketization and globalization, so that China's development will become well-balanced between economy, politics, culture, society and environment.

The development of the Chinese economy without the coordination of social and political reform will run out of steam sooner or later. Even the development of economy in democratic countries, such as Japan and South Korea, has also slowed after a 30 year high of economic growth. It is predicted that the Chinese economy will sharply slow after 2013.[25] The Asian Development Bank recently has foreseen that China's growth rates in the next two decades "will be only a little more than half of what they were in the last 30 years."[26] Albert Edwards has recently warned that because of lack of a democratic policy process, the Chinese economy is out of control and the bubble of Chinese economy is bursting. If the bubble bursts, it will be the greatest danger to the world economy.[27]

## NEGATIVE CONSEQUENCES OF THE CHINA MODEL

All regimes seek to legitimize themselves in order to efficiently govern their countries. The legitimacy of governance is especially important for the CPC to become a real insider of the international society. The Chinese government had a long history of struggling to achieve legitimacy. Pre-modern Chinese governments tried to legitimize its governance by using the will of Tian/God; the Republic regime tried to use military force to justify its rule; the Mao regime tried to legitimize its governance by orthodox ideology—Marxism; and the post-Mao government has tried to enhance the legitimacy level of governance through improving the living standard of the Chinese people and justifying the official ideology.

Legitimacy and economic performance are closely linked, but not identical. If a regime heavily relies on its performance, it can easily deteriorate when the economy falls. In other words, if legitimacy is only maintained by the economic growth, the nation would be in danger, because the authority is away from the roots of society. Legitimacy is the popular acceptance of governance, which rests on its representation of the interests of the majority people . Thus, a legitimate government is a government of the people, by the people, and for the people. Gaining legitimacy means gaining the people; and gaining people means gaining the hearts of the people. Obviously, legitimate government must be built upon the trust between government and its citizens.[28]

If the people support the government, it means it is probably high in legitimacy. Modern democratic government has legitimized its rule by voters, the majority of people, in which the major form of expressing the will of the people is the general election. If the majority of the people are not satisfied with their governance, they can replace the rulers. The electoral democracy is the key to a legitimate government. A government can deprive the people's right for election, but the invisible of judgment in their heart remains valid. The government cannot win the will of the people by coercive force.

Government transparency is critical to legitimacy and government capability.[29] If the government knows what the people want and respond accordingly, it greatly improves the people's support. Democratic governments represent the people, thus, they are not afraid of their own people, but allow the people to know the truth. All modern democracies have large policies of transparency, but authoritarian governments often have much less. When the government keeps the public in the dark, it is impossible for the people to believe in the government and follow it.

However, the legitimacy of CPC's governance lacks all of these characteristics. At the present time, a low percentage of Chinese citizens have strong faith in the government's ability to tell the truth.[30] China's official

value system has lost touch with the Chinese people, and government credibility has dropped to below the minimum level. China's social instability
reflects that the Chinese government does not meet the needs of the Chinese
people and the Chinese people do not trust their own government. Because
the CPC endorses the China model, the legitimacy of the CPC has been
mainly maintained by the performance of economy.[31] The communist political system still dominates every aspect of society.[32] It is important for the
Chinese government to share ideas and values with its people to enhance its
legitimacy and to build the trust between the government and the people
through developing a civil society.

Internationally, determined by the Chinese political system, China has
distanced itself from the current global order. When China makes foreign
policy, the Chinese government views the CPC's interest as the top priority.
Chinese State Councilor Dai Bingguos pointed out that China's number one
core interest is to "maintain its fundamental system and state security."[33]
What is the basic system of China? It is the one-party system. It means that
the CPC's interest is superior to all. While American people view the Chinese political system directly countering the core values of the West,[34] the
Chinese government strongly opposes applying Western values in China. It
will continue to be difficult for the CPC to communicate with Western societies in cultural and political spheres.

Domestically, the China model has contributed to social instability. First
of all, the China model allows the CPC to exercise a monopoly of power on
political decision making. Nobody knows what goes on with government
policies until they are announced. When a bad government policy merges,
the damage is already done. Second, the China model creates conflicts between the government and society. Because the China model is economy-
centered, the Chinese government has become the largest corporation and
major player as well as decision-maker, regulator and price-setter on market.
Under this system, whoever has political power can sell their power for
money. Consequently, China's corruption has become systematic and the gap
between the rich and the poor is increasingly widening. After the financial
crisis, the rich people in China are even richer, while the poor are poorer. The
widening gap will continue to contribute to social instability.[35] Third, the
reform movement produces a large number of disadvantaged people. The
first group of disadvantaged people is farmers who have lost their land. Since
the reform movement, "more than 50 million farmers have lost all their land
and nearly half of them have no jobs or social insurance. This caused social
conflict."[36] New statistics suggests that "about 65 percent of mass incidents
in rural areas are triggered by land disputes."[37] Another group of disadvantaged people is domestic migrants. The total of China's floating population
could be around between 250 million and 300 million and they endure hardship in many ways and are treated unfairly. The laid-off workers consist of

the third group of disadvantaged people. By July 2009, China's registered unemployment rate was only about 4.3 percent, but the actual unemployment rate was about nine percent. These three groups are the major source of social protests in China.

Chinese society is full of people's dissatisfactions and social conflict. A recent survey shows that only 6 percent of Chinese people see themselves as happy.[38] In the next several years, China may face even more conflicts that will seriously challenge the governing abilities of the CPC.[39] The escalation of mass protests has caused the CPC to worry. The Chinese government feels the pressure of people's discontent and has a deep sense of domestic insecurity. Susan Shirk suggests that "the worst nightmare of China's leaders is a national protest movement of discontented groups against the regime."[40] According to a Chinese official report, China's internal security spending hit new heights and exceeded defense budget in 2011.[41] This indicates that the Chinese political system remains vulnerable, although the Jasmine revolution is unlikely to take place in China in the near future. In order to guarantee economic growth, the CPC should seriously re-make its legitimate ground to fit in the new era in the global context.

## ROAD TOWARD A SUPERPOWER

It is difficult to precisely predict China's future because "the future of China is in the eyes of the beholder."[42] Any glowing prediction of China's future easily becomes a form of utopianism because economic growth could come from both economic mechanisms and political institutions. However, it is safe to describe the possibilities of China's future. According to Jae Ho Chung, there are at least six possible scenarios for China's future. The first scenario is the Yugoslavian model—the worst of all possibilities, non-democratic, poor, and weak government and the fragmentation of the state. The second scenario is the Indonesian scenario—a weak China that fails to accomplish the task of dual transition, economic development and democratic transition. The third scenario is the Latin American model—the non-democratic and corrupt, but brutal regime may effectively rein in ethnic conflicts, but fail to bridge the widening income and social disparities. The fourth scenario is an Indian scenario—China could manage to attain democratic transition, but fail to sustain high level of economic growth. The fifth scenario is an open-ended scenario—this model could go in two opposite directions. The sixth scenario is more successful in both advancing economically and democratizing politically. The remaining two contingencies refer to the most successful scenarios that project China as one of the most powerful nations in the system—that is, the hegemony or a hegemonic competitor.[43] Because the term "China's future" here refers to what roles China will play in the global governance in the future, what we can say about China's future is how to avoid the worst and to achieve the best scenario.

China's future depends not only on further economic reform in industrial structure, fiscal policy, state owner of enterprises, the financial system, the social security system, and market mechanisms, but, more importantly, depends on China's full reform movement and fostering a democratic system; ultimately, it depends on willingness to remake the ground of the China model to fit in the globalized world. The relationship between China and globalization is twofold. First, China's rise has a profound impact on the international community. Historically, China has its glorious history and advanced culture. The U.S. has only been dominant in the last 50 years, but China was dominant in 1,800 of the last 2,000 years. It is very important to begin with an appreciation of China's long history in order to understand China's future world role.[44] The further understanding of China, including the China model, would bring the world closer to China. Nowadays, "From Vietnam to Syria, from Burma to Venezuela, and all across Africa, leaders of developing countries are admiring and emulating what might be called the China Model."[45] It is at least one of assumptions that the China model will possibly dominate the 21st century.[46] Secondly, China's development is inevitably affected by globalization. Chinese economic development relies heavily on trade, foreign investment and science and technology, so China's future development needs international support. China could not become an internationally recognized world leader without accepting universal norms and values. However, the current global order is Western oriented. Unavoidably, the interaction between China's development and globalization will make the China model change. As time goes by, the China model will gradually lose the unique Chinese characteristics, while it gains universal values.

It is worth noting that neither neo-Maoism nor neo-Confucianism can guarantee to turn an economically strong China into an internationally recognized world leader. In the first 30 years of CPC governance in China, Maoism had created an equally poor socialist society and inhumane relationship between the government and society. The attempt to revive Confucianism will not narrow the gap between China and the mainstream of the global order. Confucius tried to justify absolute rule and advocated unlimited authority for the monarchal government by man instead of by law. Essentially, Confucianism is an obstacle to the adoption of individual rights and a democratic system.[47] If China only relies on Confucianism, it will never rule the world.[48]

A new China model must include modern democracy, because modern democracy guarantees individual rights, moderates conflicts, regulates political competition, makes government more legitimate, improves the quality of government, provides the best means for supervising the bureaucracies of the modern state, and prevents government leaders from abusing their powers.[49]

Theoretically, the process of truly globalizing China should be the same process of China's democratization. In practice, if China continues to reject remaking the foundation of the China model, the China model will increasingly conflict with globalization. As time goes by, globalization will inevitably force the China model to respond to this challenge. Consequently, China will have to choose between the two: resisting globalization or introducing democracy. If China fails to take a crucial step toward democratization, it may remain a self-confined and self-centered country despite its strong economic muscle. In order for the China model to become an integrated part of globalization, there is only one way out: injecting modern democracy into the China model.

The CPC remains powerful and influential. It is realistic for China to "reform the Chinese political system within the current political system."[50] Historically, the CPC has been able to renew itself. This is why the party has survived into the twenty-first century and still has a strong impetus to develop in the years to come. Nevertheless, the reality has given the CPC a wake-up call. It's time for the party to respond to the wake-up call. Remaking the foundation of the China model is the best way to justify and boost the CPC's legitimacy and enhance its governance capability.

Political reform is the most difficult task for the CPC to implement. The Chinese people have been fighting for democracy since 1898, but they have made a little progress.[51] Maoist China totally rejected modern democracy and the current top leaders have just begun talking about democracy.[52] In China, there is still no other opposition party to challenge the CPC's ruling position.[53] Conventional wisdom suggests that capitalism will inevitably lead to democracy, but it so far is not the case in the post-Mao era. The Chinese people are becoming wealthier and the number of people in the middle class is expected to increase to 40 percent of total population by 2020. The reality is that China's middle class wants to see the current political system last longer instead of supporting political reform, because they have greatly benefited from the political system.

China is a massive country that has a lot of land and the largest population, and a high percentage of the Chinese people are less educated and lack democratic experience. It is, thus, feared that any mistake during political reform could result in domestic chaos and international crisis. China suffered from bloody wars and social chaos in modern history. The country simply can no longer afford another chaotic revolution. Moreover, some Chinese scholars and politicians still believe that Western democracy does not apply adequately to China.[54] Many inside and outside China remain skeptical about modern democracy.[55] China's democratization will face resistance from various directions and the Chinese political reform will be a slow process.

Shaohua Hu, in his recent book, expresses a different opinion. He predicts that China "will become democratic by 2011," and that the one-party system will be history by that time.[56] Hu's overly optimistic telescoping is probably a utopian dream and is misleading to both the Chinese people and readers in Western countries. Richard Bernstein and Ross H. Munro have explained why China's political reform is a slow process. First, the Chinese political culture restricts the development of democracy and for 3,000 years "has developed no concept of limited government, protections of individual rights, or independence of the judiciary and the media."[57] Second, the CPC gives no sign of surrendering its powers at present. Third, if China were to carry out a democratic system, it would have to give up the right to control Taiwan: "Democracy in China would force China's leaders to acknowledge the right of the people of Taiwan."[58] Obviously, it is naïve to expect that China will become a democratic society anytime soon.[59] Thus, the demand for radical democratization might turn to chaos if the CPC is dissolved before reforming the Chinese political system.

Chinese leaders may be at the crossroads: retaining the CPC's monopoly of power or moving forward to go through another great transformation from an authoritarian regime to a democratic one. It is a misconception that the two goals are incompatible: maintaining one party rule while introducing democracy. If the CPC could properly manage the process of democratization, it is possible for the CPC to reach to two goals at the same time. But, if the CPC rejects political reform, it could possibly lose both. As a result, revolution-styled transformation will make a comeback to dash the hopes for China to become an internationally recognized world leader.

## CONCLUSION

The CPC has regained its legitimacy through improving the living standard of the Chinese people in the post-Mao era. However, the legitimacy of the CPC has been largely built upon economic growth and ideological control. The rapid growth of Chinese economy has not resulted in democratization, i.e., modern democracy is still absent from the model of China's development. While some scholars totally deny the China model—the Beijing Consensus—others insist that China should continue its paradigm with Chinese socialist characteristics. The China model—legitimacy without democracy—was a workable strategy during the historical transition, but, in the long run, the CPC must share common cultural and political values with Chinese citizens and the mainstream of the international community in order to become a superpower. China will not be able to become a superpower without democratization during globalization. The legitimacy of governance must include democratic values. The absence of democracy might be an important factor for the declining legitimacy of the CPC. If the CPC could not fundamentally change its political system, it would undermine its legitimacy of governance and postpone the transformation from an economic giant to a world leader recognized by the international society. China's democratization is a crucial step not only to China's economic success, but also to its relations with the international society.[60] Western societies expect to have a strong partnership with China, not just economically, but politically and culturally.[61] If the CPC continues to reject modern democracy, China's domestic conflict could not only trigger serious social chaos at home, but also could escalate conflicts with the mainstream of the international society. As a result, China's ambitious goal of becoming a world superpower will be postponed to an uncertain future.

## NOTES

1. See *Economist* at http://www.economist.com/debate/overview/179.

2. Yan Xuetong, "How China Can Defeat America," *New York Times*, November 20, 2011.

3. Albert Ferwerker, *The Chinese Economy: 1912-1949* (Ann Arbor, Michigan: Michigan Papers in Chinese Studies, 1968), 1.

4. Mark Selden, *The Political Economy of Chinese Development* (Armonk, N.Y.: M.E. Sharpe, 1993), 17.

5. Michel Chossudovsky, *Towards Capitalist Restoration? Chinese Socialism after Mao.* (New York: St. Martin's Press, 1986), 1.

6. Nicholas R. Lardy, "China's Economy: Problems and Prospects," *China Digital Times*, February 2007.

7. Bergsten, C. Fred, Bates Gill, Nicholas R. Lardy, and Derek Mitchell. *China: The Balance Sheet: What the World Needs to Know About the Emerging Superpower* (New York: PublicAffairs, 2007). According to these scholars, "five key factors underlie China's stunning growth performance over the past three decades: the embrace of market forces, the opening of the economy to trade and inward direct investment, high levels of savings and investment, the structural transformation of the labor force, and investments in primary school education."

8. Shogo Suzuki, "Chinese Soft Power, Insecurity Studies, Myopia and Fantasy," *Third World Quarterly* 30, no. 4 (2009): 780.

9. Stefan Halper, "The Proposer's Opening Remarks," *The Economist*, 21 March 2011.

10. Wei Pan, "The Chinese Model of Development," Conference Paper, http://fpc.org.uk/fsblob/888.pdf (10 May 2011)

11. Yang Jisheng, "My View on China Model," *People's Forum,* 16 January 2011.

12. Rowan Callick, "The China Model," *Journal of American Enterprise Institute*, November/December Issue, 2007. http://www.american.com/archive/2007/november-december-magazine-contents/the-china-model (1 May 2011)

13. Francis Fukuyama, *The End of History and the Last Man* (New York: Maxwell Macmillan International, 1992), 34.

14. John Ikenberry, "The Future of the Liberal World Order," *Foreign Affairs,* May/June, 2011.

15. Francis A. Lees, *China Superpower: Requisites for High Growth* (New York: St. Martin's Press, 1997), 40.

16. Benjamin Schwarz, "Contending effectively with China's ambitions requires a better understanding of our own: Managing China's Rise," *The Atlantic.com*, http://www.theatlantic.com/doc/prem/200506/schwarz (10 Feb. 2008).

17. "How to Gracefully Step Aside," *Economist,* 10 January 2011.

18. Rowan Callick, "The China Model," *Journal of American Enterprise Institute*, November/December Issue, 2007. http://www.american.com/archive/2007/november-december-magazine-contents/the-china-model.

19. Andrew Nathan, "China's Authoritarianism: Still Resilient?" Public Lecture given at the University Of Hong Kong, on 4 June 2011.

20. Penelope B. Prime, "China's Economic Progress: Is It Sustainable?" in *China Briefing: The Contradictions of Change,* William A. Joseph, ed. (Armonk, N.Y.: M.E. Sharpe, 1997), 77.

21. Penelope B. Prime, "China's Economic progress: Is It Sustainable? In *China Briefing: The Contradictions of Change,* ed. William Joseph (New York: M.E. Sharpe, 1997). Charles Wolf, Jr., K.C. Yeh, Benjamin Zycher, Nicholas Eberstadt, Sung-Ho Lee. *Fault Lines in China's Economic Terrain.* (Santa Monica: Rand, 2003). Peter Navarro, *The Coming China Wars: Where They Will Be Fought, How They Can Be Won* (FT Press, 2006). Social Science Academy of China: *Blue Book of China,* http://news.xinhuanet.com/politics/2006-12/26/content_5531627.htm (5 March 2010).

22. See James Mann, *The China Fantasy: How Our Leaders Explain Away Chinese Repression* (Viking Adult, 2007).

23. James Kynge, *China Shakes the World: A Titan's Rise and Troubled Future and the Challenge for America* (Geneva, IL: Houghton Mifflin Harcourt, 2006).

24. Justin Yifu Lin, *Fang Cai, and Zhou Li* , "The Lessons of China's Transition to a Market Economy," *Cato Journal* 16, no. 2. http://www.cato.org/pubs/journal/cj16n2-3.html (18 May 2011)

25. Quoted in Alan Wheatley, "Calculating the Coming Slowdown in China," *New York Times*, 23 May 2011.

26. Quoted in David Gordon, "Chinese Juggernaut? China's Rapid Growth is a Legitimate Worry for Leaders in Washington—and Beijing," *Foreign Policy,* March/April, 2011.

27. "China's Economy Has Been Out of Control," *Bern Daily,* 1 June 2011.

28. Bruce Gilley. "The Determinants of State Legitimacy: Results for 72 Countries," *International Political Science Review*, 27. (2006): 50.

29. Stirton, Lindsay, and Martin Lodge. "Transparency Mechanisms: Building Publicness into Public Services." *Journal of Law and Society* 28, no. 4 (December 2001): 471.

30. Will Clem and Lilian Zhang, "Shanghai Vows Transparency," *South China Morning Post* (March 20, 2009).

31. The People's Republic of China at 50: National Political Reform, John P. Burns, *The China Quarterly*, No. 594 (Sep., 1999), 582.

32. Michael Wines and Edward Wong, "An Unsure China Steps Onto the Global Stage," *New York Times*, 1 April 2009.

33. Dai Bingguo, "The Core Interests of the People's Republic of China," *China Digital Time*, 16 August 2009.

34. Warren Cohen. *America's Response to China: A History of Sino-American Relations* (New York: Columbia University Press, 2010), 287.

35. Xie Yu, "Poll: Corruption, Public discontent Most Worrisome," *China Daily,* 9 July 2010.

36. Quoted in "China: More than 50 Million Farmers Have Lost Land since the 1980s," Frontlines Revolutionary, http://revolutionaryfrontlines.wordpress.com/2010/11/13/china-more-than-50-million-farmers-have-lost-land-since-the-1980s/ (12 August 2011)

37. Ibid.

38. "Only 6 Percent Happy, Survey Finds," *China Daily,* 3 March 2011. http://www.china.org.cn/china/2011-03/03/content_22041375.htm (30 March 2011)

39. Jane Macartney, "China Fears Year Of Conflict As Millions Struggle To Find Jobs," *Times,* 7 January 2009.

40. Susan L. Shirk. *China Fragile Superpower* (Oxford: Oxford University Press, 2007), 7.

41. "China boosts spending on welfare—and on internal security, too," *The Economist*, 10 March 2011. http://www.economist.com/node/18335099 (30 March 2011).

42. Jae Ho Chung, "Charting China's Future: Scenarios, Uncertainties, and Determinants," in *Charting China's Future: Political, Social, and International Dimensions,* edited by Jae Ho Chung (New York: Rowman & Littlefield Publishers, Inc, 2006), 3.

43. Ibid.

44. CNN Wire Staff, "Kissinger: China poses 'big challenge' for U.S," CNN, Jun 12, 2011.

45. Rowan Callick, "The China Model," *Journal of American Enterprise Institute*, November/December Issue, 2007.

46. Stefan Halper, *The Beijing Consensus: How China's Authoritarian Model Will Dominate the Twenty-First Century* (Basic Books, 2010).

47. William Theodore De Bary, *Confucianism and Human Rights* (New York: Columbia University Press, 1988).

48. Troy Parfitt, *Why China Will Never Rule the* World (New York: Western Hemisphere Press, 2011).

49. Andrew J. Nathan, *Chinese Democracy* (New York: Knopf, 1985), 225.

50. Jinghao Zhou, "Undemocratic China Can't Rule the World," *Asia Times,* 16, July 2011.

51. Trudy Kuehner, "Understanding China: A History Institute Report," *The Newsletter of RPRI's Marvin Watchman Fund for International Education 12*, no. 1 (March 2007).

52. John O'Neil, "China's President Ends U.S. Visit with Yale Speech," *The New York Times*, 21 April 2006; "China Maps Slow Path to Democracy," *Los Angeles Times*, 17 March 2007.

53. Richard McGregor, *The Party: The Secret World of China's Communist Rulers*, Harper Press, 2010.

54. An Chen, "Capitalist Development, Entrepreneurial Class, and Democratization in China," *Political Science Quarterly* 3 (2001): 412.

55. John L. Thornton, "Long Time Coming: The Prospects for Democracy in China," *Foreign Affairs*, January/February 2008.

56. Shaohua Hu, *Explaining Chinese Democratization* (Westport, Conn.: Praeger Publishers, 2000), 160.

57. Richard Bernstein and Ross H. Munro, *The Coming Conflict with China* (New York: Alfred A. Knopf, 1997), 15-17.

58. Ibid.

59. Robert Lawrence Kuhn, *How China's Leaders Think: The Inside Story of China's Reform and What This Means for the Future,* Wiley, 2009.

60. Quoted in Quansheng Zhao, "American's Response to the Rise of China and Sino-U.S. Relations," *AsiaJournal of Political Science* 13 (2005): 14.

61. Tony Blair, "We Can Help China Embrace the Future," *Wall Street Journal*, 26 August 2008.

# Bibliography

## BOOKS

Afshar, Haleh, ed. *Women, State, and Ideology: Studies from Africa and Asia.* New York: State University of New York Press, 1987.

Aikman, David. *Jesus in Beijing: How Christianity Is Transforming China and Changing the Global Balance of Power.* Washington, D.C.: Regnery Publishing, Inc. 2003.

Andors, Phyllis. *The Unfinished Liberation of Chinese Women, 1949-1980.* Bloomington: Indiana University Press, 1984.

Aslanbeigu, Nahid, Steven Pressman and Gale Summerfield, eds. *Women in the Age of Economic Transformation: Gender Impact of Reforms in Post-Socialist and Developing Countries.* London: Routledge, 1994.

Bai, Shouyi, ed. *An Outline History of China.* Beijing: Foreign Languages Press, 1976.

Barrett, David B. ed. *World Christian Encyclopedia.* New York: Oxford University Press, 1982.

Barrett, Michele. *Women's Oppression Today: Problems in Marxist Feminist Analysis.* London: Verso Editions and NLB, 1980.

Barry, Kathleen. *Female Sexual Slavery.* New York: New York University Press, 1979.

Bennet, Garry and Roberta Perkins. *Being a Prostitute: Prostitute Women and Men.* Boston: Allen and Unwin, 1985.

Bergsten, Fred, Bates Gill, Nicholas R. Lardy, and Derek Mitchell. *China: The Balance Sheet: What the World Needs to Know Now About the Emerging Superpower.* New York: Public Affairs, 2006.

Bernhard, Kathryn and Philip C. Huang. *Civil Law in Qing and Republican China.* Stanford: Stanford University Press, 1999.

Bernstein, Richard and Ross H. Munro. *The Coming Conflict with China.* New York: Alfred A. Knopf, 1997.

Bertz, Bill. *The China Threat: How the People's Republic Targets America.* Washington, D.C.: Regnery Publishing, Inc., 2000.

Bianco, Lucien. *Origins of the Chinese Revolution, 1914-1949.* Stanford: Stanford University Press, 1971.

Birke, Lynda. *Women, Feminism and Biology: The Feminist Challenge.* New York: Methuen, 1986.

Bishirjian, Richard J. *A Public Philosophy Reader.* New Rochelle, NY: Arlington House, 1978.

Bodde, Derk. *Chinese Thought, Society, and Science: The Intellectual and Social Background of Science and Technology in Pre-Modern China*. Honolulu: University of Hawaii Press, 1991.

Bongiorni, Sara. *A Year Without "Made in China": One Family's True Life Adventure in the Global Economy*. Medford, NJ: Wiley, 2007.

Boyle, Kevin and Juliet Sheen. *Freedom of Religion and Belief*. New York: Routledge, 1997.

Bozan, Jian, Shao Xunzheng, and Hu Hua. *A Concise History of China*. Beijing: Foreign Languages Press, 1981.

Bray, Francesca. *Technology and Gender: Fabrics of Power in Late Imperial China*. Berkeley: University of California Press, 1997.

Brook, Timothy and Hy V. Luong, eds. *Culture and Economy: The Shaping of Capitalism in Eastern Asia*. Ann Arbor, MI: University of Michigan Press, 1999.

Bulbeck, Chilla. *Re-Orienting Western Feminisms: Women's Diversity in a Postcolonial World*. Cambridge: University Press, 2003.

Chan, Adrian. *Chinese Marxism*. New York: Continuum, 2003.

Chang, Chun-shu, ed. *The Making of China: Main Themes in Premodern Chinese History*. Englewood Cliffs, New Jersey: Prentice-Hall, Inc., 1975.

Chang, Gordon. *The Coming Collapse of China*. New York: Random House, 2001.

Chen, Jingpan. *Confucius as a Teacher: Philosophy of Confucius with Special Reference to Its Educational Implications*. Beijing: Foreign Languages Press, 1990.

Cheng, Tun-jen and Deborah A. Brown, eds. *Religious Organizations and Democratization*. New York: M.E. Sharpe, 2006.

Cheung, Frederick Hok-ming, ed. *Politics and Religion in Ancient and Medieval Europe and China*. Hong Kong: The Chinese University Press, 1999.

Ching, Julia. *Chinese Religions*. Maryknoll, N.Y.: Orbis Books, 1993.

———. *Confucianism and Christianity: A Comparative Study*. New York: Kodansha International, 1977.

Chossudovsky, Michel. *Towards Capitalist Restoration? Chinese Socialism after Mao*. New York: St. Martin's Press, 1986.

Chow, Tse-tsung. *The May Fourth Movement: Intellectual Revolution in Modern China*. Stanford, Calif.: Stanford University Press, 1967.

Chu, Godwin and Yanan Ju. *The Great Wall in Ruins: Communication and Cultural Change in China*. Albany: State University of New York Press, 1993.

Chung, Jae Ho, ed. *Charting China's Future: Political, Social, and International Dimensions*. New York: Rowman & Littlefield Publishers, Inc, 2006.

Clark, Paul. *Chinese Cinema*. Cambridge: Cambridge University Press, 1987.

Clarke, Richard and Robert K. Knake. *Cyber War: The Next Threat to National Security and What to Do About it*. New York: An Imprint of Harper Collins Publishers, 2010.

Cohen, Warren. *America's Response to China: A History of Sino-American Relations*. New York: Columbia University Press, 2010.

Covell, Ralph R. *Confucius, the Buddha, and Christ: A History of the Gospel in Chinese*. New York: Orbis Books, 1986.

Croll, Elisabeth. *Changing Identities of Chinese Women*. London: Zed Book, 1995.

———. *Feminism and Socialism in China*. Schocken Books: New York City, 1980.

Cui, Shuqin. *Women Through the Lens: Gender and Nation in a Century of Chinese Cinema*. Honolulu: University of Hawai'i Press, 2003.

Dalpino, Catharin E. *Deferring Democracy: Promoting Openness in Authoritarian Regimes*. Washington, D.C.: Brookings Institution Press, 2000.

Dardess, John W. *Confucianism and Autocracy: Professional Elites in the Founding of the Ming Dynasty*. Berkeley: University of California Press, 1983.

Davin, Delia, *Woman-Work: Women and the Party in Revolutionary China*. New York: Oxford University Press, 1980.

Davis, Nanette J. *Prostitution: An International Handbook on Trends, Problems, and Policies*. Westport, CT: Greenwood Press, 1993.

De Bary, William Theodore. *The Liberal Tradition in China*. New York: Columbia University Press, 1983.

————. *The Trouble with Confucianism*. Cambridge: Harvard University Press, 1991.

————. *Confucianism and Human Rights*. New York: Columbia University Press, 1988.

Ding, X.L. *The Decline of Communism in China: Legitimacy Crisis, 1977-1989*. New York: Cambridge University Press, 1994.

Dobson, W.A.C. H. *Mencius: A New Translation Arranged and Annotated for the General Reader*. Toronto: University of Toronto Press, 1979.

Dorn, James, ed. *China in the New Millennium*. Washington, D.C.: CATO Institute, 1998.

Doyle, Michael. *Ways of War and Peace: Realism, Liberalism, and Socialism*. New York: W.W. Norton, 1997.

Drachkovitch, Milorad, ed. *Marxist Ideology in the Contemporary World: Its Appeals and Paradoxes*. New York: Pall Mall Press, 1966.

Eber, Irene. *Confucianism: the Dynamics of Tradition*. New York: MacMillan Publishing Company, 1986.

Ebrey, Patricia Buckley. *The Inner Quarters: Marriage and the Lives of Chinese Women in the Sung Period*. Berkeley: University of California Press, 1993.

————. *The Cambridge Illustrated History of China*. New York: Cambridge University Press, 1996.

————. *Women and the Family in Chinese History*. New York: Routledge Curzon, 2002.

Eide, Asbjorn, ed. *The Universal Declaration of Human Rights: A Commentary*. New York: Scandinavian University Press, 1993.

Elvin, Mark. *The Pattern of the Chinese Past*. Stanford, Calif.: Stanford University Press, 1973.

Evans, Harriet. *Women and Sexuality in China: Female Sexuality and Gender Since 1949*. New York: The Continuum Publishing Company, 1997.

Falkernheim, Victor, ed. *Chinese Politics from Mao to Deng*. New York: Paragon House, 1989.

Ferguson, K.E. *The Feminist Case against Bureaucracy*. Philadelphia: Temple University Press, 1984.

Ferweker, Albert. *The Chinese Economy: 1912-1949*. Ann Arbor, Michigan: Michigan Papers in Chinese Studies, 1968.

Finnane, Antonia and Anne McLaren, eds. *Dress, Sex, and Text in Chinese Culture*. Australia: Monash Asia Institute, 1999.

Fishman, Ted. *China, Inc.: How the Rise of the Next Superpower Challenges America and the World*. New York: Scribner, 2005.

Frederic, Wakeman, Jr., and Wen-hsin Yeh, eds. *Shanghai Sojourners*. Berkeley: Center for Chinese Studies, 1992.

Friedman, Thomas L. *The World is Flat: A Brief History of the Twenty-first Century*. New York: Picador Farrar, Straus and Girousx, 2007.

Fukuyama, Francis. *The Great Disruption: Human Nature and the Reconstitution of Social Order*. New York: Free Press, 1999.

————. *The End of History and the Last Man*. New York: Maxwell Macmillan International, 1992.

Gamer, Robert E. ed. *Understanding Contemporary China*. Boulder: Lynne Rienner Publishers, 2008.

Gardner, H. Stephen. *Comparative Economic Systems*. New York: the Dryden Press, 1998.

Gasster, Michael. *Chinese Intellectuals and the Revolution of 1911*. Seattle: University of Washington Press, 1969.

Gernet, Jacques. *A History of Chinese Civilization*. New York: Cambridge University Press, 1982.

————. *China and the Christian Impact: A Conflict of Cultures*. Cambridge, England: Cambridge University Press, 1985.

Gilmartin, Christina K. ed. *Engendering China: Women, Culture, and the State*. Cambridge: Harvard University Press, 1994.

Girling, John. *Corruption, Capitalism and Democracy*. New York: Routledge, 1998.

Gottlieb, Roger. *Marxism, 1844-1990: Origins, Betrayal, Rebirth*. New York: Routledge, 1992.

Gregor, A James. *Marxism, China & Development: Reflections on Theory and Reality*. New Brunswick: Transaction Publishers, 1995.

Gregory, John S. *The West and China since 1500*. Hampshire: Palgrave Macmillan, 2003.

Gross, Susan Hill & Marjorie Wall Bingham. *Women in Traditional China: Ancient Times to Modern Reform.* Hudson, Wisconsin: G.E.McCuen Publications, 1973.

Hagan, John. *Structural Criminology.* New Brunswick: Rutgers University Press, 1989.

Halper, Stefan. *The Beijing Consensus: How China's Authoritarian Model Will Dominate the Twenty-First Century.* Basic Books, 2010.

Harvey, Thomas Alan. *Acquainted with Grief: Wang Mingdao's Stand for the Persecuted Church in China.* Grand Rapids, Mich.: Brazos Press, 2002.

Hawkesworth, M.E. *Beyond Oppression: Feminist Theory and Political Strategy.* New York: The Continuum Publishing Company, 1990.

Heidenheimer, Arnold and Michael Johnston, eds. *Political Corruption: Concepts & Contexts.* Transaction Publishers, 2002.

Heidenheimer, A. J., Michael Johnston, and Victor T. LeVine, eds. *Political Corruption: A Handbook.* New Brunswick: Transaction, 1989.

Henley, B. Thorne, ed. *Language and Sex: Difference and Dominance.* Rowley, Mass: Newbury House, 1975.

Henriques, Fernando. *Prostitution and Society.* New York: The Citadel Press, 1962.

Hershatter, Gail. *Women in China's Long Twentieth Century .* University of California Press: Berkeley, 2007.

Ho, John. *East Asian Philosophy: With Historical Background and Present Influence.* New York: Peter Lang, 1992.

Hsiung, Ping-Chun, Maria Jaschok and Cecilia with Red Chang, eds. *Chinese Women Organizing: Cadres, Feminists, Muslims, Queers.* London: Berg, 2001.

Hsü, Immanuel C. Y. *The Rise of Modern China.* Oxford: Oxford University Press, 2000.

Hu, Shaohua. *Explaining Chinese Democratization.* Westport, Conn.: Praeger Publishers, 2000.

Hudson, Christopher, ed. *The China Handbook.* Chicago: Fitzroy Dearborn Publishers, 1997.

Huntington, Samuel. *Clash of Civilizations and the Remaking of World Order.* New York: Simon & Schuster, 1996.

———. *Political Order in Changing Societies.* New Haven: Yale University Press, 1968.

———. *The Third Wave: Democratization in the Late Twentieth Century.* Norman, Oklahoma: University of Oklahoma Press, 1991.

Jaschok, Maria and Shui Jingjun. *The History of Women's Mosques in Chinese Islam: A Mosque of Their Own.* Richmond, England: Curzon Press, 2000.

Jeffreys, Elaine. *China, Sex and Prostitution: Telling Tale.* New York: Routledge, 2004.

Jie, Tao and Zheng Bijun, and Shirley L. eds. Mow. *Holding Up Half the Sky.* New York: The Feminist Press, 2004.

Jochim, Christian. *Chinese Religions: A Cultural Perspective.* Englewood Cliffs, N.J.: Prentice- Hall, Inc., 1986.

Johnson, Kay Ann. *Women, the Family and Peasant Revolution in China.* Chicago: The University of Chicago Press, 1983.

Jone, Francis, ed. *Documents of the Three-Self Movement: Source Materials for the Study of the Protestant Church in Communist China.* New York: National Council of the Churches of Christ in the U.S.A., 1963.

Jonsson, John, ed. *Contemporary Religious Trends within the Socio-Political Climate of East Asia.* Waco, Texas: mimeographed, Baylor University, 1996.

Joseph, William, ed. *China Briefing: The Contradictions of Change.* Armonk, N.Y.: M.E. Sharpe, 1997.

Joshua, Mingchien. *Modern Democracy in China.* Shanghai, China: Commercial Press, 1923.

Judd, Ellen. *The Chinese Women's Movement Between State and Market.* Stanford: Stanford University Press, 2002.

Kassiola, Joel Jay and Sujian Guo, eds. *China's Environmental Crisis.* New York: Palgrave Macmillan, 2010.

Kazuko, Ono. *Chinese Woman in a Century of Revolution, 1850—1950.* Stanford University Press: Stanford, 1989.

Kindopp, Jason and Carol Lee Hamrin, eds. *God and Caesar in China: Policy Implications of Church-State Tensions.* Washington, D.C.: Brookings Institution Press, 2004.

Kissinger, Henry. *On China*. New York: The Penguin Press, 2011.

Ko, Dorothy. *Teachers of the Inner Chambers: Women and Culture in Seventeenth-Century China*. Stanford, Calif.: Stanford University Press, 1994.

Kuhn, Robert Lawrence. *How China's Leaders Think: The Inside Story of China's Reform and What This Means for the Future*. Wiley, 2009.

Kung, Hans and Julia Ching. *Christianity and Chinese Religions*. New York: Doubleday, 1989.

Kuo, Tai-Chun and Ramon H. Myers. *Understanding Communist China: Communist China Studies in the United States and the Republic of China, 1949-1978*. Stanford, Calif.: Hoover Institution Press, 1986.

Kurlantzick, Joshua. *Charm Offensive: How China's Soft Power Is Transforming the World*. New Haven, Conn.: Yale University Press, 2007.

Kwong, Chunwah. *Hong Kong's Religions in Transition*. Waco, Texas: Tao Foundation, 2000.

Kwong, Julia. *The Political Economy of Corruption in China*. New York: M.E. Sharpe, Inc., 1997.

Kynge, James. *China Shakes the World: A Titan's Rise and Troubled Future and the Challenge for America*. Geneva, IL: Houghton Mifflin Harcourt, 2006.

Lakoff, Robin Tolmach. *Language and Woman's Place: Text and Commentaries*. Oxford: Oxford University Press, 2004.

Lampton, David. *Same Bed, Different Dreams: Managing U.S.-China Relations*. Berkeley: University of California Press, 2002.

Larner, John. *Marco Polo and the discovery of the world*. New Haven: Yale University Press, 2001.

Lees, Francis. *China Superpower: Requisites for High Growth*. New York: St. Martin's Press, 1997.

Leng, Shao-chuan. *Changes in China: Party, State, and Society*. New York: University Press of America, 1989.

Li, Cheng. *Rediscovering China: Dynamics and Dilemmas of Reform*. New York: Rowman & Littlefield Publishers, 1997.

Li, Chengyang, ed. *The Sage and the Second Sex: Confucianism, Ethics, and Gender*. Chicago: Open Court, 2000.

Li, Yi, *Structure and Evolution of Chinese Social Stratification*. Lanham MD: University Pres of America, 2005.

Li, Yu-ning, ed. *Chinese Women: Through Chinese Eyes*. Armonk, New York: M.E. Sharpe, 1992.

Li, Zhisui. *The Private Life of Chairman Mao*. Random House: New York, 1994.

Lieberthal, Kenneth. *Governing China: from Revolution through Reform*. New York: W.W. Norton & Company, 1995.

Lilley, James R. and David Shambaugh, eds. *China's Military Faces the Future*. New York: M.E. Sharpe, 2010.

Lin, Lean Lim, *The Sex Sector: The Economic and Social Bases of Prostitution in Southeast Asia*. Washington, D.C.: International Labor Office, 1998.

Lin , Mousheng. *Men and Ideas: An Informal History of Chinese Political Thought*. New York: Hohn Day, 1942.

Lin, Yu-tang, ed. *Chinese Women Through Chinese Eyes*. Armonk: M. E. Sharpe, 1992.

Liu, Alan P.L. *Mass Politics in the People's Republic: State and Society in Contemporary China*. Boulder, Colo.: Westview Press, 1996.

Liu, Shia-ling. *U.S. Foreign Policy toward Communist China in the 1970's: The Misadventures of Presidents Nixon, Ford and Carter*. Taibei: Kuang Lu Publishing Company, 1988.

Lopez, Donald. ed. *Religions of China in Practice*. Princeton, N.J.: Princeton University Press, 1996.

Lu, Sheldon Hsiao, ed. *Transnational Chinese Cinemas: Identity, Nationhood, Gender*. Honolulu: University of Hawai'i Press, 1997.

Lu, Tonglin, ed. *Gender and Sexuality in Twentieth-Century Chinese Literature and Society*. New York: State University of New York Press, 1993.

Mann, James. *The China Fantasy: How Our Leaders Explain Away Chinese Repression*. Viking Adult, 2007.

Marsh, Christopher. *Making Russian Democracy Work: Social Capital, Economic Development, and Democratization.* Lewiston, N.Y.: Edwin Mellen Press, 2000.

Massonnet, Philippe. *The New China: Money, Sex, and Power.* Boston: Tuttle Publishing, 2000.

McCormick, Barrett L. *Political Reform in Post-Mao China: Democracy and Bureaucracy in a Leninist State.* Berkeley: University of California Press, 1990.

McGregor, Richard. *The Party: The Secret World of China's Communist Rulers.* Harper Press, 2010.

McLellan, David. *Marxism after Marx: An Introduction.* New York: Harper & Row, 1980.

Meisner, Maurice. *Marxism, Maoism, and Utopianism: Eight Essays.* Madison University of Wisconsin Press, 1982.

Melden, A. I. ed. *Human Rights.* Belmont, California: Wadsworth Publishing Company, Inc. 1970.

Meskill, John. *The Pattern of Chinese History: Cycles, Development, or Stagnation?* Westport, Conn.: Greenwood Press, 1965.

Misra, Kalpana. *From Post-Maoism to Post-Marxism: The Erosion of Official Ideology in Deng's China.* Taylor & Francis,1998.

Moody, Peter R. *Political Opposition in Post-Confucian Society.* New York: Praeger, 1988.

Moreno, Pedro, ed. *Handbook on Religious Liberty around the World.* Charlottesville, Va.: the Rutherford Institute, 1996.

Mote, F. W. *A History of Chinese Political Thought.* Princeton, N.J.: Princeton University Press, 1979.

Mueller, J. Theodore. *Great Missionaries to China.* Grand Rapids, Mich.: Zondervan Publishing House, 1947.

Myron, Paul Myron and Anthony Linebarger. *The Political Doctrines of Sun Yat-sen: An Exposition of the San Min Chu.* Westport, Connecticut: Hyperion Press, 1936.

Naisbitt, John and Doris Naisbitt. *China's Megatrends: The 8 Pillars of a New Society.* Harper Business, 2010.

Nair, Chandran. *Consumptionomics: Asia's Role in Reshaping Capitalism and Saving the Planet.* New York: Wiley, 2011.

Naughton, Barry. *Growing Out of Plan: Chinese Economic Reform, 1978-1993.* Cambridge University Press, 1995.

Nathan, Andrew J. *Chinese Democracy.* New York: Knopf. 1985.

Navarro, Peter. *The Coming China Wars: Where They Will Be Fought: How They Can Be Won.* FT Press, 2006.

Ngai, Pun. *Made in China: Women Factory Workers in a Global Workplace.* Durham and London: Duke University, 2005.

Nye, Joseph. *Soft Power: The Means To Success In World Politics.* New York: Public Affairs, 2008.

Nylan, Michael. *The Five Confucian Classics.* New Haven: Yale University Press, 2001.

O'Brien, Kevin J. *Reform without Liberalization: China's National People's Congress and the Politics of Institutional Change.* New York: Cambridge University Press, 1990.

Ogden, Suzanne. *China's Unresolved Issues: Politics, Development, and Culture.* Englewood Cliffs, N.J.: Prentice Hall, 1995.

Overholt, William. *The Rise of China: How Economic Reform Is Creating a New Superpower.* New York: W.W. Norton & Company, 1994.

Page, Benjamin and Tao Xie. *Living with the Dragon: How the American Public Views the Rise of China.* New York: Columbia University Press, 2010.

Pan, Suiming. *Three Red Light Districts in China.* Beijing: Qunyan Publishing House, 1999.

Parfitt, Troy. *Why China Will Never Rule the World.* New York: Western Hemisphere Press, 2011.

Pearce, Diana and Harriette McAdoo. *Women and Children: Alone and In Poverty.* Washington D.C.: National Advisory Council on Economic Opportunity, 1981.

Pei, Minxin. *From Reform to Revolution: The Demise of Communism in China and the Soviet Union.* Cambridge, Mass.. Harvard University Press, 1994.

Perry, Elizabeth J. and Mark Selden, eds. *Chinese Society: Change, Conflict and Resistance*. New York: Routledge, 2002.

Pohl, Karl-Heinz. *Chinese Thought in a Global Context*. Boston: Brill, 1999.

Pye, Lucian. *The Mandarin and the Cadre: China's Political Cultures*. Ann Arbor, Michigan: The University of Michigan, 1986.

Raphals, Lisa. *Sharing the Light: Representations of Women and Virtue in Early China*. Albany, New York: State University of New York Press, 1998.

Ren, Xin. *Prostitution and Employment Opportunities for Women under China's Economic Reform*. Johannesburg, South Africa: Lola Press, 2004.

Ropp, Paul S. ed. *Heritage of China: Contemporary Perspectives on Chinese Civilization*. Berkeley: University of California Press, 1990.

Rosebaum, Arthur Lewis. *State and Society in China: The Consequences of Reform*. Boulder, Colo.: Westview Press, 1992.

Rozman, Gilbert, ed. *China's Modernization*. Jiangsu Province: China: People's Publishing House, 1998.

Rubin, Vitaly A. *Individual and State in Ancient China: Essays on Four Chinese Philosophers*. New York: Columbia University Press, 1976.

Ryan, Mary Meghan. *Handbook of U.S. Labor Statistics: Employment, Earnings, Prices, Productivity, and Other Labor Data*. Lanham, MD: Bernan Press, 2009.

Sargent, Lydia, ed. *Women and Revolution: A Discussion of the Unhappy Marriage of Marxism and Feminism*. Boston: South End Press, 1981.

Schwartz, Benjiamin Isadore. *China's Cultural Values*. Arizona: Lionheart Press, 1993.

———. *Reflections on the May Fourth Movement: A Symposium*. Cambridge, Mass.: Harvard University Press, 1972.

Selden, Mark. *The Political Economy of Chinese Development*. Armonk, N.Y.: M.E. Sharpe, 1993.

Shi, Tianjian. *Political Participation in Beijing*. Cambridge, Mass: Harvard University Press, 1997.

Shiffrin, Harold. *Sun Yat-sen, Reluctant Revolutionary*. Boston: Little, Brown and Company, 1980.

Shirk, Susan L. *China: Fragile Superpower: How China's Internal Politics Could Derail Its Peaceful Rise*, Oxford: Oxford University Press, 2007.

———. *The Political Logic of Economic Reform in China*. Berkeley: University of California Press, 1993.

Singer, Peter. *Marx: A Very Short Introduction*. Oxford University Press, 2000.

Slote, Walter H. and George A. De Vos. *Confucianism and the Family*. New York: State University of New York Press, 1998.

Spence, Jonathan. *The Memory Palace of Matteo Ricci*. New York: Penguin Books, 1985.

———. *Chinese Roundabout: Essays in History and Culture*. New York: W.W. Norton, & Company, 1993.

Stacey, Judith. *Patriarchy and Socialist Revolution in China*. Berkeley: University of California Press, 1983.

Starr, John Bryan. *Ideology and Culture: An Introduction to the Dialectic of Contemporary Chinese Politics*. New York: Harper & Row, 1973.

Stetson, Dorothy McBridge and Amy Mazur, eds. *Comparative State Feminism*. London: SAGE Publications, 1995.

Su, Shaozhi. *Marxism and Reform in China*. Spokesman Books, 1993.

Thomas, James. *Chinese Politics*. Jiangsu, China: People's Publishing House of Jiangsu, 1992.

Tong, Yanqi. *Transition from State Socialism: Economic and Political Change in Hungary and China*. New York: Rowman & Littlefield Publishers, 1997.

Tu, Wei Ming. *Centrality and Commonality: An Essay on Confucian Religiousness*. Albany, NY: State University of New York Press, 1989.

Uhalley, Stephen and Xiaoxin Wu, eds. *China and Christianity: Burdened Past, Hopeful Future*. New York: M.E. Sharpe, 2001.

Veer, Peter Van der and Hartmut Lehmann, eds. *Nation and Religion: Perspectives on Europe and Asia*. Princeton, N.J.: Princeton University Press, 1999.

Wang, Gung-hsing. *The Chinese Mind*. New York: John Day Company, 1946.
Wang, Zheng. Women in the Enlightenment. Berkeley, Calif.: University of California Press, 1999.
Watson, Rubie and Patricia Buckley Ebrey, eds. *Marriage and Inequality in Chinese Society*. Berkeley: University of California Press, 1991.
West, Jackie, Zhao Minghua, Chang Xiangqun, and Cheng Yuan, eds. *Women of China: Economic and Social Transformation*. New York: St. Martin's Press, 1999.
White, Gordon. *Riding the Tiger: The Politics of Economic Reform in Post-Mao China* Stanford, Calif.: Stanford University Press, 1993.
Wilson, Richard. *Value Change in Chinese Society*. New York: Praeger, 1979.
Wilson, Richard W. Sidney L. Greenblatt, and Amy Auerbacher Wilson, eds. *Moral Behavior in Chinese Society*. New York: Praeger, 1981.
Winkler, Edwin A. ed. *Transition from Communism in China*. Boulder, Colo.: Lynne Rienner Publishers, 1999.
Wolf, Charles, K.C. Yeh, Benjamin Zycher, Nicholas Eberstadt, Sung-Ho Lee. *Fault Lines in China's Economic Terrain*. Santa Monica: Rand, 2003.
Wolf, Margery and Roxane Witke, eds. *Women in Chinese Society*. Stanford, Calif.: Stanford University Press, 1975.
Womack, Brantly, ed. *Contemporary Chinese Politics in Historical Perspective*. Cambridge: Cambridge University Press, 1991.
Yang, Fenggang and Joseph Tamney, eds. *Confucianism and Spiritual Traditions in Modern China and Beyond*. Leiden, the Netherlands: Koninklike Brill, 2012.
Yim, Kwan Ha, ed. *China and the U.S. 1964-72*. New York: Facts on File, 1975.
Young, Marilyn B. *Women in China: Studies in Social Change and Feminism*. Michigan: Center for Chinese Studies, the University of Michigan, 1973.
Zhang, Yingjin. *Screening China*. Ann Arbor, Michigan: Center for Chinese Studies, the University of Michigan, 2002.
_____. *Chinese National Cinema*. New York: Routledge, 2004.
Zheng, Shiping. *Party vs. State in Post-1949 China: The Institutional Dilemma*. New York: Cambridge University Press, 1998.
Zhou, Jinghao. *China's Peaceful Rise in a Global Context: A Domestic Aspect of China's Road Map to Democratization*. Lexington Book, 2010.
_____. *Remaking China's Public Philosophy and Chinese Women's Liberation: The Volatile Mixing of Confucianism, Marxism, and Feminism*. New York: Mellen Press, 2006.
_____. *Remaking China's Public Philosophy for the Twenty-first Century*. Westport, CT: Praeger Publishers, 2003.

# ARTICLES

Andors, Phillis. "Women and Work in Shenzhen." *Bulletin of Concerned Asian Scholars* 20, no. 3 (1988): 22-24.
Bates, Searle. "Churches and Christians in China, 1950-1967: Fragments of Understanding." *Pacific Affairs* 41, No. 2 (Summer, 1968): 211.
Bauer, John. "Gender Inequality in Urban China." *Modern China* 18, no. 3 (1992): 333- 48.
Belger, Christine M. "The Changing Role and Status of Women in China." *The Third World Law Journal* 20 (2000): 26-42.
Boot, Max. "Project for a New Chinese Century." *The Weekly Standard* 11, no. 4, 10 October 2005.
Brook, Timothy. "Rethinking Syncretism: The Unity of the Three Teachings and Their Joint Worship in Late-Imperial China." *Journal of Chinese Religions* 21 (Fall 1993): 13-14.
Callick, Rowan. "The China Model." *Journal of American Enterprise Institute*, November/ December Issue, 2007.
Cao, Shixiong, and Xinqing Wang "Unsustainably Low Birth Rates: A Potential Crisis Leading to Loss of Racial and Cultural Diversity in China." *Journal of Policy Modeling* 32, no. 1 (January/ February, 2010): 159-75.

Chakrabarty, Dipesh. "Postcoloniality and the Artifice of History." *Representations* 37 (1992): 1-26.

———. "The World Needs an Assertive China." *Foreign Affairs*, 21 February 2011.

Chen, An. "Capitalist Development, Entrepreneurial Class, and Democratization in China." *Political Science Quarterly* 3 (2001): 412.

Chen, Cunfu and Huang Tianhai. "The Emergence of A New Type of Christians in China Today." *Review of Religious Research* 46, No. 2 (Dec., 2004): 184.

Chen, Kathy. "Workplace: A nervous China Awaits Women of the World: China's Women Face Obstacles in the Workplace." *Wall Street Journal* (1995): 1.

Chen, Stephen. "Thought Control Called for at Universities." *South China Morning Post*, 5 January 2012.

Chen, Yong and Wang Yiqian. "Qionghai Lake, Sichuan, China: Environmental Degradation and the Need for Multidimensional Management." *Mountain Research and Development* 23, no.1 (2003): 65-72.

Cheng, Hefa. "Municipal Solid Waste (MSW) as a renewable source of energy: Current and Future Practices in China." *Bioresource technology* 101 (2010): 3816-3824.

Chey, J. "Chinese 'Soft Power', Cultural Diplomacy and the Confucius Institutes." *The Sydney Paper Summer* 2008: 40.

Chow, Esther Ngan-ling and S Michael Zhao. "The One-Child Policy and Parent-Child Relationships: A Comparison of One-Child with Multiple-Child Families in China." *The International Journal of Sociology and Social Policy* 16, no. 12 (1996): 55.

Christensen, Thomas J. "Fostering Stability or Creating a Monster? The Rise of China and U.S. Policy toward East Asia." *International Security* 31. No.1 (2006): 81-126.

Chung, Chien-peng. "The "Good Neighbour Policy" in the Context of China's Foreign Relations," *China: An International Journal* 7, no. 1 (March 2009): 107-123.

Clinton, Hillary. "America's Pacific Century." *Foreign Policy*, November 2011.

Cull, N.J. "Public Diplomacy: Taxonomies and Histories." *The ANNALS of the American Academy of Political and Social Science*, 616 (2008:1): 55.

Davin, Delia. "The Impact of Export-Oriented Manufacturing on Chinese Women Workers." *United Nations Research Institute for Social Development* 8 (2001): 15.

Dickson, Bruce J. "China's Democratization and the Taiwan Experience." *Asian Survey* 38 (April 1998): 350.

Dittmer, Lowell. "Leadership Change and Chinese Political Development." *China Quarterly*, 146 (2003): 903.

Dombey, Daniel. "US Struggling to Hold Role as Global Leader." *Politics and Foreign Policy*, 6 March, 2011.

Dong, Qi, Yanping Wang, and Thomas H Ollendick. "Consequences of Divorce on the adjustment of Children in China." *Journal of Clinical Child and Adolescent Psychology* 31, No. 1 (2002) 101-110.

Dorn, James A. "How to Improve U.S.-China Relations in the Wake of CNOOC." *The Korean Journal of Defense Analysis* 17, No. 3 (Winter 2005).

Eberstadt, Nicholas. "China's Family Planning Goes Awry." *Far Eastern Economic Review*, 4 December 2009.

Economy, Elizabeth. "The Great Leap Backward? The Costs of China's Environmental Crisis." *Foreign Affairs* 86, No. 5 (September, 2007): 38-59.

———. "The End of the 'Peaceful Rise.'" *Foreign Policy*, December, 2010.

Elliott, Michael. "The Chinese Century." *Time* 169, no. 4, 22 January 2007.

Erbaugh, Mary. "Chinese Women Face Increased Discrimination." *Off Our Backs: A Women's News Journal* 20, no. 33 (March 1990): 9-27.

Fan, Chengze Simon and Herschel I. Crossman. "Entrepreneurial Graft in China." *Providence Journal*, 3 May 2001.

Fan, Cindy C. "The State, the Migrant Labor Regime and Maiden Workers in China." *Political Geography.* 23 (2004): 288-316.

Ferdinand, Peter. "Social Change and the Chinese Communist Party: Domestic Problems of Rule." *Journal of International Affairs* 49 (Winter 1996): 478-92.

Filfoyle, Tim J. "Prostitute in History: From parables of Pornography to Metaphors of Modernity." *The American Historical Review* 104, no. 1 (February 1999): 118.

Florig, H. Keith. "China's Air Pollution Risks." Environmental Science & Technology 31, No. 6 (1997): 274-279.

Fong, Vanessa L. "China's One-Child Policy and the Empowerment of Urban Daughters." *American Anthropologist* 104, no. 4 (December, 2002): 1098-1112.

Friedberg, Aaron L. "The Future of U.S.-China Relations: Is Conflict Inevitable?" *International Security* 30, no. 2 (Fall 205): 8.

Geng, Yong. "Developing the circular economy in China: Challenges and opportunities for Achieving 'Leapfrog Development.'" *International Journal of sustainable Development & World Ecology* 15 (2008): 231-239.

Gillespie, Kate and Gwenn Okruhlik, "The Political Dimensions of Corruption Cleanups: A Framework for Analysis." *Comparative Politics* 24, no. 1 (Oct., 1991): 77.

Gilley, Bruce. "The Determinants of State Legitimacy: Results for 72 Countries." *International Political Science Review*, 27. (2006): 50.

Gilmartin, Christina. "Gender in the Formation of a Communist Politic." *Modern China* 19, no. 3 (July 1993): 299-329.

Glain, Stephen. "Washington Is Preparing a Long War with China." *U.S. News*, 31 March 2010.

Glaser, Charles. "Will China's Rise Lead to War? Why Realism Does Not Mean Pessimism." *Foreign Affairs*, March/April, 2011.

Goldstone, Jack A. "The Coming Chinese Collapse." *Foreign Policy* 99 (Summer 1995): 43.

Goodkind, Daniel M. "China's Missing Children: The 2000 Census Underreporting Surprise." *Population Studies* 58, No. 3 (November, 2004): 281-295.

Gordon, David. "Chinese Juggernaut? China's Rapid Growth Is a Legitimate Worry for Leaders in Washington and Beijing." *Foreign Policy*, March/April, 2011.

Gu, Edward X. "Cultural Intellectuals and the Politics of the Cultural Public Space in Communist China 1979-1989: A Case Study of Three Intellectual Groups." *Journal of Asian Studies* 58, No. 2 (May 1999): 392.

Halper, Stefan. "The Proposer's Opening Remarks." *The Economist*, 21 March 2011.

———. "The China Threat: Can the United States Really Make a Peaceful Hand-off of Power to Authoritarian China?" *Foreign Policy*, March/April, 2011.

Hartig, Falk. "Confucius Institutes and the Rise of China," *Journal of Chinese Political Science* 17, no. 1 (2012): 52-74.

He, Zhengke. "Corruption and Anti-corruption in Reform China." *Communist and Post- Communist Studies* 33 (2000): 250.

Henriot, Christian. "From a Throne of Glory to a Seat of Ignominy: Shanghai Prostitution Revisited (1849-1949)." *Modern China* 22, no. 2 (April 1996): 155.

———. "La Femeture: The Abolition of Prostitution in Shanghai, 1949-58." *The China Quarterly* 142 (June 1995): 467-86.

Hershatter, Gail. "The Hierarchy of shanghai Prostitution, 1870-1949." *Modern China* 15, no. 4 (October 1989): 463.

Hesketh, Therese, Li Lu, and Wei Xing Zhu. "The Effect of China's One-Child Family Policy After 25 Years." *The New England Journal of Medicine* 353, no. 11 (September 2005): 1171-76.

Hirschman, Charles and Ronald Rindfuss. "The Sequence and Timing of Family Formation Events in Asia." *American Sociological Review* 47, No 5 (October 1982): 660-680.

Hong, Yan and Li, Xiaoming. "Too Costly to Be Ill: Health Care Access and Health Seeking Behaviors among Rural-Urban Migrants in China." *World Health Popul.*(2006): 22-41.

Honing, Emily. "Socialist Revolution and Women's Liberation in China—A Review Article." *Journal of Asian Studies* 44, no. 2 (February 1985): 329-336.

Huang, Jiku and Scott Rozelle. "Environmental Stress and Grain Yields in China." *American Journal of Agricultural Economics* 77, No. 4 (Nov., 1995): 853-864.

Huang, Lucy Jen. "The Role of Religion in Communist Chinese Society." *Asian Survey* 11, No. 7 (July 1971): 694.

Huang, Qifei. "The Current Situation of solid Waste Management in China." *Journal of Material Cycles and Waste Management* 8 (2006): 63-69.

Husted, Bryan. "Wealth, Culture, and Corruption." *Journal of International Business Studies* 30, no. 2 (2cd Qtr., 1999): 342.

Hyde, Sandra Teresa. "Selling Sex and Sidestepping the State: Prostitutes, Condoms, and HIV/ AIDS Prevention in Southwest China." *International Quarterly* 18 (Winter 2000): 112.

Ikenberry, John. "The Rise of China & the Future of the West." *Foreign Affairs*, January/ February, 2008.

———. "The Future of the Liberal World Order." *Foreign Affairs,* May/June, 2011.

Jahiel, Abigail R. "The Contradictory Impact of Reform on Environmental Protection in China." *The China Quarterly* 149 (1997): 81-103.

Johnson, Ian. "For China, Relief after a Successful Trip." *New York Times*, 21 January 2011.

Johnsson, Sten, and Ola Nygren. "The Missing Girls of China: A New Demographic Account." *Population and Development Review* 17, no. 1 (March, 1991): 25-51.

Johnston, Michael & Yufan Hao. "China's Surge of Corruption." *Journal of Democracy* 6, no. 4 (1995): 80.

Kane, Penny, and Ching Choi. "China's One Child Family Policy." *British Medical Journal* 319 (October 1999): 992-94..

Karabell, Zachary. "U.S.-China Friction: Why Neither Side Can Afford a Split." *Time*, 8 February 2010.

Kaufmann, Daniel. "Corruption: The Facts." *Foreign Policy* 107 (Summer,1997):120.

Keidel, Albert. "China's Social Unrest: The Story Behind the Stories." *Policy Brief* 48, September 2006.

Kent, Ann. "Waiting for Rights; China's Human Rights and China's Constitutions, 1949-1989." *Human Rights Quarterly* 13 (1991): 170-201.

Kissinger, Henry. "Avoiding a U.S.-China Cold War." *Washington Post*, 14 January 2010.

Kramer, John M. "Political Corruption in the U.S.S. R." *The Western Political Quarterly* 30, no. 2 (June, 1977): 213.

Kueher, Trudy. "Understanding China: A History Institute Report." *The Newsletter of RPRI's Marvin Watchman Fund for International Education 12*, no. 1 (March 2007).

Lai, Gina. "Work and Family Roles and Psychological Well-Being in Urban China." *Journal of health and Social Behavior* 36, no. 1 (March 1995), 15.

Lai, H.H. "Religious Polices in Post-Totalitarian China: Maintaining Political Monopoly over a Reviving Society." *Journal of Chinese Political Science* 11, no. 1 (Spring 2006): 55.

Lambert, Tony. "Counting Christians in China: A Cautionary Report." *International Bulletin of Missionary Research* 7, no. 1 (January 2003): 6.

Larson, Wendy. "Never This Wild: Sexing the Cultural Revolution." *Modern China* 25, no. 4 (October 1999): 423.

Leader, Shelah Gilbert. "The Emancipation of Chinese Women." *World Politics* 26, no. 1(October 1973): 55-79.

Lee, John. "The End of the Charm Offensive." *Foreign Policy*, 26 October, 2010.

Levy, Richard. "Corruption, Economic Crime and Social Transformation since the Reforms: The Debate in China." *The Australian Journal of Chinese Affairs* 33 (Jan., 1995): 4.

Li, Shaomin, Mingfang Li, and J. Justin Tan. "Understanding Diversification in a Transition Economy: A Theoretical Exploration." *Journal of Applied Management Studies* 7 (June 1998): 77-95.

Li, Shichao. "Recycling behavior Under China's Social and Economic Transition: The Case of metropolitan Wuhan." *Environment and Behavior* 35 (2003): 784-801.

Li, Shuzhuo, Marcus W. Feldman, and Xiaoyi Jin. "Marriage Form and Family Division in Three Villages in Rural China." *Population Studies* 57, No. 1 (March, 2003): 98-102.

Li, Weil. "The Impact of Economic Reform of the Performance of Chinese State Enterprises, 1980-1989." *Journal of Political Economy* 105 (October 1997), 1082.

Lin, Justin Yifu. "The Needham Puzzle: Why the Industrial Revolution Did Not Originate in China." *Economic Development and Cultural Change* 43 (January 1995): 269-92.

———. *Fang Cai, and Zhou Li.* "The Lessons of China's Transition to a Market Economy." *Cato Journal* 16, no. 2 (2011).

Ling, L.H.M. "Sex Machine: Global Hypermasculinity and Images of the Asian Woman in Modernity." *Positions: East Asia Cultures Critique* 7.2 (1999): 279-96.

Lubman, Stanley. "Introduction: The Future of Chinese Law." *China Quarterly* 138 (March 1995): 16.

Lum, Thomas. "Social Unrest in China." *Congressional Research Service, The Library of Congress,* CRS Report for Congress, 8 May 2006.

Macartney, Jane. "China Fears Year Of Conflict As Millions Struggle To Find Jobs." *Times Online,* 7 January 2009.

Magee, Darrin. "China Is My Backyard: China's Environmental Degradation in Global Context." *Georgetown journal of International Affairs 12, no.* 2 (Summer/fall 2011): 120-127.

Maume, David J. and Marcia L. Bellas. "Chinese Husbands' Participation in Household Labor." *Journal of Comparative Family Studies* 31 No. 2 (Spring 2000): 191-215.

McGee, Robert and Danny Kin-Kong Lam. "Hong Kong's Option to Secede." *Harvard International Law Journal* 33, no. 3 (Spring 1992): 438.

Mei, Chengrui & Harold E. Dregne. "Silt and the Future Development of China's Yellow River." *The Geographical Journal* 167, No. 1 (Mar., 2001): 7-22.

Meier, Kenneth and Thomas M. Holbrook. "I Seen My opportunities and I took 'Em:' Political Corruption in the American States." *Journal of Politics* 54, no. 1 (Feb., 1992): 138.

Merli, M Giovanna, and Herbert L Smith. "Has the Chinese Family Planning Policy Been Successful in Changing Fertility Preferences?" *Demography* 39, no. 3 (August, 2002): 557-72.

Montinola, Gabriella. "Federalism, Chinese Style: The Political Basis for Economic Success in China." *World Politics* 48 (1995): 52.

Ness, Peter Van. "China's Response to the Bush Doctrine." *World Policy Journal* (Winter 2004/2005): 44.

Nie, Yilin and Robert J. Wyman. "The One-Child Policy in Shanghai: Acceptance and Internalization." *Population and Development Review* 31, no. 2 (June, 2005): 313-36.

Nolan, Peter and Robert F. Ash. "China's Economy on the Eve of Reform." *China Quarterly* 144 (December 1995): 997-98.

Nye, Joseph S., Jr. "The China Threat: Can the United States Really Make a Peaceful Hand-off of Power to Authoritarian China?" *Foreign Policy*, March/April, 2011.

———. "Think Again: Soft Power." *Foreign Policy,* 23 February 2006.

Peng, Peiyun. "Accomplishments of China's Family Planning Program: A Statement by a Chinese Official." *Population and Development Review* 19, No. 2 (June 1993): 399-403.

Pimentel, Ellen Efron. "Just How Do I Love Thee? Marital Relations in Urban China." *Journal of Marriage and Family* 62, No. 1 (February 2000): 34-56.

Pimentel, Ellen Efron and Jinyun Liu. "Exploring Nonnormative Coresidence in Urban China: Living with Wives' Parents." *Journal of Marriage and Family* 66, No. 3 (Aug., 2004): 821-836.

Platate, Erika. "Divorce Trends and Patterns in China: Past and Present." *Pacific Affairs* 61, No. 3 (Autumn 1988): 428-45.

Putterman, Louis. "The Role of Ownership and Property Rights in China's Economic Transition." *China Quarterly* 144 (December 1995), 1049.

Qi, Jean. "The Role of the Local State in China's Transitional Economy." *China Quarterly* 144 (December 1995), 1148.

Rachman, Gideon."Think Again: American Decline: This Time Is for Real." *Foreign Policy*, 18 January 2011.

Rauhala, Emily. "A Powerhouse Province Wants to Relax China's One-Child Policy-But Don't Bet On a Baby Boom." *Time*, July 12, 2011.

Retherford, Robert D. Minja Kim Choe, Jiajian Chen, Li Xiru, and Cui Hongyan. "How Far Has Fertility in China Really Declined?" *Population and Development Review* 31, no. 1 (March, 2005): 54-72.

Rhys, J. Howard W. "Religion and National Identity." *Faculty of Religious Studies* 19 (Spring 1991): 47.

Rocca, Jean-Louis. "Corruption and Its Shadow: An Anthropological View of Corruption." *China Quarterly* 130 (June 1992), 402.

Root, Hilton. "Corruption in China: Has it Become Systemic?" *Asian Survey* 36, no. 8 (August 1996): 742- 65.

———. "Corruption in China: Has it Become Systemic?" *Asian Survey* 36, no. 8 (August 1996): 749.

Rosen, Stanley. "Women and Political Participation in China." *Pacific Affairs* 68, no. 3 (Autumn 1995): 315.

Ruskola, Teemu. "Law, Sexual Morality, and Gender Equality in the Qing and Communist China." *Yale Journal of Law & Feminism* 103, no. 8 (June 1994): 2531

Sachs, Jeffrey D. and Wing Woo. "Structural Factors in the Economic Reforms of China, Eastern Europe, and the Former Soviet Union." *Economic Policy* 18. no. 1 (1994): 102-45.

Schafer, Sarah. "Not Just Another Pretty Face." *Newsweek*, 13 October 2003.

Shambaugh, David. "Introduction: The Emergence of "Greater China." *The China Quarterly* 136 (Dec., 1993), 653.

Shannon, Elaine. "China Rising: Small World, Big Stakes." *Time*, June 20 2005.

Shao, Min, Xiaoyan Tang, Yuanhang Zhang and Wenjun Li. "City Clusters in China: Air and Surface Water Pollution." *Frontiers in Ecology and the Environment* 4, No. 7 (Sep., 2006): 353-361.

Shen, Jianfa. "China's Future Population and Development Challenges." *The Geographical Journal* 164, no. 1 (March 1998): 32-48.

Sicuar, Terry. "Redefining State, Plan and Market: China's Reforms in Agricultural Commerce." *China Quarterly* 144 (December 1995): 1020.

Stephens, Bret. "China and the Next American Century: Beijing's Politburo Has Nothing on Mark Zuckerberg." *Wall Street Journal*, 21 December, 2010.

Stirton, Lindsay, and Martin Lodge. "Transparency Mechanisms: Building Publicness into Public Services." *Journal of Law and Society* 28, no. 4 (December 2001): 471.

Sun, Laixiang and Liang Zou. "State-Owned versus Township and Village Enterprises in China." *Comparative Economic Studies* (Summer/Fall 1999), 151-75.

Sutton, Donald. "Sex, law, and Society in Late Imperial China." *Journal of Social History* 35 (September 2002): 712-29.

Suzuki, Shogo. "Chinese Soft Power, Insecurity Studies, Myopia and Fantasy." *Third World Quarterly* 30, no. 4 (2009): 780.

Tang, Taryn and Oatley, Keith. "Impact of Life Events and Difficulties on the Mental Health of Chinese Immigrant Women." *Immigrant Minority Health* 9 (2007): 287-302.

Tang, Zhongjun. "Determining Socio-Psychological Drivers for Rural Household Recycling Behavior in Developing Countries: A case Study From Wugan, Hunan, China." *Environment and Behavior* 43, no. 6 (2011): 848-877.

Tannor, Murray Scott. "China Rethinks Unrest." *The Washington Quarterly* 27, no.3 (2004): 138.

Thornton, John L. "Long Time Coming: The Prospects for Democracy in China." *Foreign Affairs*, January/February 2008.

Ting, Kwok-fai and Stephen W. K. Chiu. "Leaving the Parental Home: Chinese Culture in an Urban Context." *Journal of Marriage and Family* 64, no. 3 (August, 2002): 620-641.

Travel, Taylor. "Power Shifts and Escalation: Explaining China's Use of Force in Territorial Disputes," *International Security* 32, no. 3 (Winter 2007/08): 44-83.

Vaclav, Smil. "Environmental Problems in China: Estimates of Economic Costs." *East-West Center Special Reports* no. 5 (April, 1996): 3.

Vasquez, John and Marie T. Henehan. "Territorial Disputes and the Probability of War, 1816-1992." *Journal of Peace Research* 38, No. 2 (2001): 123-138.

Walder, Andrew G. "China's Transitional Economy: Interpreting Its Significance." *China Quarterly* 144 (*December* 1995), 967.

Wang, Lu L. and Xue-jun Ye. "Mental health status of Chinese rural-urban migrant workers: Comparison with permanent urban and rural dwellers." *Social Psychiatry Epidemiol* 42 (2007): 716- 32.

Wang, Wei. "The Current Situation of Solid Waste Generation and its Environmental Contamination in China."*Journal of Material Cycles and Waste Management* 8 (2006): 63-69.

Warren, Mark E. "What Does Corruption Mean in a Democracy?" *American Journal of Political Science* 48, no. 2 (April 2004): 329.

Wei, Shang-jie. "Local Corruption and Global Capital Flows." *Brookings Papers on Economic Activity 2* (2000): 303.

Welch, Holmes. "Buddhism under the Communists." *The China Quarterly* 6 (April-June, 1961): 1.

Wenger, Jacqueline E. "Official vs. Underground Protestant Churches in China: Challenges for Reconciliation and Social Influence." *Review of Religious Research,* 46, No. 2 (Dec., 2004):169.

White, Gordon. "Democratization and Economic Reform in China." *Australian Journal of Chinese Affairs* 31 (1994).

Whyte, Martin King. *"Continuity and Change in Urban Chinese Family Life."* *The China Journal* 53 (January, 2005): 9-30.

Whyte, Bob. "The Future of Religion in China." *Religion in the Communist Lands* 8 (1980): 7.

Wiest, Jean-Paul. "Religious Studies and Research in Chinese Academia: Prospects, Challenges and Hindrances." *International Bulletin of Missionary Research* 29, no.1 (January 2005): 21.

Wong, Daniel, Fu Keung and Grace Leung. "Mental health of migrant workers in China: Prevalence and correlates." *Social Psychiatry Epidemiol* 43 (2088): 483-501.

Wood, James E. "Religion and the State in China: Winter Is Past." *Journal of Church and State* 28 (Autumn 1986): 394.

Woon, Yuen-fong. "From Mao to Deng: Life Satisfaction Among Rural Women in an Emigrant Community in South China." *The Australian Journal of Chinese Affairs* 25 (January 1991): 139-169.

Wu, Bangguo. "Chinese Economy in the Twenty-first Century." *Presidents and Prime Ministers* 9 (Jan. 2000): 16-20.

Wu, Renhong. "Which Way for the Chinese Economy?" *World and I* 13 (October 1998): 46-52.

Xu, Xiaoqun. "The Dilemma of Accommodation: Reconciling Christianity and Chinese Culture in the 1920s." *Historian* 60 (Fall 1997): 22.

Yan, Xuetong. "The Instability of China-US Relations." *The Chinese Journal of International Politics* 3 (2010): 263-292.

Yang, Xiaoliu and Jinwu Pang. "Implementing China's Water Agenda 21." *Frontiers in Ecology and the Environment* 4. No. 7 (2006): 362-68.

Yi, Zeng & Wu Deqing. "Regional Analysis of Divorce in China since 1980." *Demography* 37, No. 2 (May 2000): 215-219.

Yu, Guangqian, Dianjun Sun, and Yan Zheng. "Health Effects of Exposure to Natural Arsenic in Groundwater and Coal in China: An Overview of Occurrence." *Environmental Health Prospectives* 115, no 4 (2007): 636-42.

Zackey, Justin. "Peasant Perspectives on Deforestation in Southwest China: Social Discontent and Environmental Mismanagement." Mountain Research and Development 27, No. 2 (May 2007): 153-165.

Zakaria, Fareed. "The Rise of a Fierce Yet Fragile Superpower." *Newsweek.* December 31, 2007-January 7, 2008.

———. "The Dangerous Chip on China's Shoulder." *Time*, 12 January 2011.

Zhai, Fuhua and Qin Gao. "Center-Based Care in the Context of One-Child Policy in China: Do Child Gender and Siblings Matter?" *Population Research and Policy Review* 29, no. 5 (October, 2010): 745-74.

Zhang, Dong Qing. "Municipal solid waste management in China: Status, problems and challenges." *Journals of Environmental Management* 91 (2010): 1623-1633.

Zhang, Hong. "From Resisting to 'Embracing?' the One-Child Rule: Understanding New Fertility Trends in a Central China Village." *The China Quarterly* 192 (December, 2007): 855-75.

Zhang, Jim and Kirk R. Smth. "Household Air Pollution from Coal and Biomass Fuels in China: Measurements, Health Impacts, and Interventions." *Environmental Health Perspectives* 115, No. 6 (Jun., 2007): 848-859.

Zhang, Weijiong. "Can China Be a Clean Tiger? Growth Strategies and Environmental Realities." *Public Affairs* 72, no. 1 (Spring 1999): 23-37.

Zhang, Zhiping. "Does China Need a Red-Light District?" *Beijing Review,* 12 June 2000, 31.

Zhao, Litao and Tan Soon Heng. "China's Cultural Rise: Visions and Challenges." *China: An International Journal* 5, No. 1 (March 2007).

Zhao, Quansheng. "American's Response to the Rise of China and Sino-US Relations." *Asia-Journal of Political Science* 13 (2005): 14.

Zheng, Bijian. "China's Peaceful Rise, to Great-Power Statues." *Foreign Affairs* September-October 2005.

Zhou, Scott. "China's reverse population bomb." *Asia Times,* 1 November 2006.

Zhu, Tingchang. "Lun Zhongguo mulin zhengce de lilun yu shijian" (On the Theory and Practice of China's Good Neighbour Policy), *Guoji zhengzhi yanjiu* (*Studies of International Politics*), no. 2 (2001): 45.

Zhuo, Xinping. "The Significance of Christianity for the Modernization of Chinese Society." *Crux* 33 (March 1997), 31.

# Index

aging society, 39
agriculture, 5, 8, 9, 38, 74, 75, 76, 89, 93, 98, 259
Alopen, Nestorian, 148
All-China Women's Federation, 50, 67, 108
American, 2, 3, 80, 90, 182, 196, 209, 210, 211, 212, 213, 214, 215, 216, 217, 218, 223, 225, 227–228, 229, 232, 235, 242, 243, 244, 245, 246, 247, 248–249, 249, 250, 256, 257, 262, 263; anti-American nationalism, 249; boat/ship, 210, 212; culture, 233, 235; economy, 225, 242; educational system, 210; Environmental Protection Agency. *See* EPA; era, 80; films, 196, 235; history, 2, 213; interests, 214; Latin American, 3, 263; liberalism, 182; military, 213, 216, 218, 227–228, 244; national interests, 217; people, 90, 215, 223, 228, 242, 245, 248–249, 262; president, 250; program, 80; scholars, 114, 211, 215, 217, 218, 228, 243, 247, 256, 257. *See also* Sino-American relations, United States
Analects, 17, 135, 164, 172
arable land, 31, 32, 37, 89, 94, 258
Australia, 27, 120, 216, 225, 233
Asia/Asian, 9, 13, 27, 90, 93, 95, 120, 134, 169–170, 171–172, 211, 212, 213, 216, 218, 220, 223, 226, 228, 230, 232, 234, 236, 242, 243, 244, 248–249, 256, 257, 260
authoritarianism, 12, 95, 109, 112, 256
authoritarian regime, 93, 95, 154, 159, 258, 266

belief. *See* Chinese belief
Beijing, ix, 7, 9, 32, 34, 51, 55, 64, 88, 94, 122, 143, 170, 181, 183, 196, 203, 211, 214, 218, 220, 223, 225, 227, 228, 232, 234, 235, 242, 245, 247, 249, 255, 256, 266; consensus (*see* China Model)
Bible, 48, 143–144, 157, 172; schools, 144
*Blush*, 202, 204
boss Christians, 153
Boxer Rebellion, 212
bribery, 120, 122, 124, 125–126
Britain, ix, 75, 106, 184, 202, 233
brothels, 202, 203
Buddhism, 7, 134, 135–136, 137, 142, 143, 149, 167
Bush, George H. W., 158, 211, 214, 219
Bush, George W., 225, 248

campaign, 6, 54, 75, 76, 97, 107, 112, 115, 123, 183, 185, 204, 212; against communist movement, 212; climate change, 97; The Cultural Revolution, 54, 75; ideological, 76, 183; political, 76, 107, 112, 115, 123, 185, 204

# About the Author

**Jinghao Zhou** is associate professor at Hobart and William Smith Colleges in Geneva, New York. He is the author of three books: *China's Peaceful Rise in a Global Context: A Domestic Aspect of China's Road Map to Democratization* (Lexington Books, 2010; paperback edition, 2012), *Remaking China's Public Philosophy and Chinese Women's Liberation: The Volatile Mixing of Confucianism, Marxism, and Feminism* (Edwin Mellen Press, 2006), and *Remaking China's Public Philosophy for the Twenty-first Century* (Praeger Publishers, 2003). His thirty-plus articles in English appear in various journals and newspapers, such as *The Journal of Comparative Asian Development, American Journal of Chinese Studies, Journal of China: An International Journal, Asian Mission, Asian Perspective, Journal of International Women's Studies, Journal of Religion and Society, In the National Interests, Journal of Church and State, International Journal of China Studies, China Review International,* and *Asia Times*. He has also published more than forty articles in Chinese journals and newspapers.

CPSIA information can be obtained
at www.ICGtesting.com
Printed in the USA
LVHW080304090522
718238LV00013B/324